Growing Independent Learners

Debbie Diller

Growing Independent Learners
From Literacy Standards to Stations, K-3

Stenhouse Publishers
www.stenhouse.com

Credits
page 13: *Ralph Fletcher: Author at Work* used by permission of Richard C. Owen Publishers, Inc. www.RCOwen.com.

page 60: "April Rain Song" from THE COLLECTED POEMS OF LANGSTON HUGHES by Langston Hughes, edited by Arnold Rampersad with David Roessel, Associate Editor, copyright © 1994 by the Estate of Langston Hughes. Used by permission of Alfred A. Knopf, an imprint of the Knopf Doubleday Publishing Group, a division of Penguin Random House LLC. All rights reserved.

page 75: *The Little Engine That Could* by Watty Piper, illustrated by Mateu. Used by permission of Penguin Random House LLC. All rights reserved.

page 80: *A Kiss Goodbye* and *The Kissing Hand* by Audrey Penn used by permission of Tanglewood Press.

page 96: Cover illustration from *NO, DAVID!* By David Shannon. Scholastic Inc./Blue Sky Press. Copyright © 1998 by David Shannon. Used by permission.

page 125: Frayer Model Graphic Organizer from *A Schema for Testing the Level of Cognitive Mastery* by D. Frayer, W. C. Frederick, and H. J. Klausmeier, copyright © 1969 by Wisconsin Center for Education Research. Used by permission.

page 137: Cover illustration copyright © 2006 by Lambert Davis from *THE JOURNEY: STORIES OF MIGRATION* by Cynthia Ryland. Scholastic Inc./Blue Sky Press. Used by permission.

page 173: From HOORAY FOR FLY GUY! By Tedd Arnold. Scholastic Inc./Cartwheel Books. Copyright © 2008 by Tedd Arnold. Used by permission.

page 198: NORTH: THE AMAZING STORY OF ARCTIC MIGRATION. Text copyright © 2011 by Nick Dowson. Illustrations copyright © 2011 by Patrick Benson. Reproduced by permission of the publisher, Candlewick Press, Somerville, MA on behalf of Walker Books, London.

Library of Congress Cataloging-in-Publication Data
Diller, Debbie, 1954–
 Growing independent learners : from literacy stations to standards, K-3 / Debbie Diller.
  pages cm
 Includes bibliographical references.
 ISBN 978-1-57110-912-5 (pbk. : alk. paper) -- ISBN 978-1-62531-068-2 (ebook) 1. Reading (Primary) I. Title.
 LB1525.D55 2015
 372.4--dc23
                                                    2015015917

Cover and interior design by Martha Drury
Typesetting by Victory Productions, Inc.

Manufactured in the United States of America

 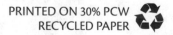
22 21 20 19 18 17 16   9 8 7 6 5 4 3

To my new little sprout, Chloe

Contents

Introduction: Growing Independence

I am a gardener. My father and my paternal grandmother were gardeners, too. Planting seeds and watching them grow makes me smile. I live for the promise of spring, curious to see what will return from last year. My gardens have taught me many lessons: patience and the value of paying attention; the need to weed and prune; and that there is no substitute for good planning and preparation.

I've learned that plants have individual needs and require specialized attention. Some like sunny conditions, whereas others prefer shade. All plants need water and food, but they don't all need the same amounts. It is my responsibility as a gardener to tend my plants, and their health and vigor is usually a direct result of the work I've invested in their care, especially during their early stages of growth. Of course, there are some things beyond my control, and I've learned to accept each season and the changes it brings. What I've learned in the garden parallels what I've learned about teaching. In fact, my gardening experiences have helped shape my views about the role of teachers as seed sowers who nurture growth of understanding and help young children grow to independence. All of these experiences have shaped my beliefs about life and about growing independent learners.

As a teacher, I've been planting seeds of learning for almost four decades. Sometimes those seeds take deep roots and become beautiful blooming plants. At other times, they can be slow to germinate and require extra attention. But I am patient and keep learning and teaching! I constantly strive to accept and work with whatever the winds of change bring to the world of education: new technology, new legislation, updated standards, and more. Over the years, I've had to reinvent myself as a teacher many times. There will always be something new coming our way, and it will undoubtedly affect our students' ability to work on their own, especially as more and more is expected of them and of us. But in many ways isn't that what teaching is really all about—learning how to adapt and change to meet the needs of our children and the world in which we live? To survive and thrive, we need a code to teach by, a set of beliefs to guide our instructional decision making and to keep those seeds of learning healthy, regardless of the education climate or season.

My Beliefs About Teaching for Independence

I have always had a set of beliefs about teaching and learning that guide my instruction. These beliefs have strengthened across time as I've gained experience as an educator. They are part of my foundation—the place from which I make decisions as a teacher. They shape every instructional decision I make and form the basis from which I have written this book. This is what I believe about helping children become independent learners:

1. All children *can* learn to work independently of the teacher.
2. It is the teacher's responsibility to create a setting in which children can work independently.
3. To help children become independent, teachers must release responsibility and control to them over time.

My thinking about independent learning has been shaped by my experiences as a classroom teacher, literacy coach, and national consultant. By visiting thousands of classrooms in diverse settings, I have observed situations in which children ages four through fourteen have worked very well independently. And I've seen places and times where students have been disruptive and unable to work on their own. Underlying it all, I've noticed that the accountability for independent learning lies first with the teacher, the adult in charge of what happens day to day in that classroom community. From there, children are accountable to one another and to themselves for learning.

All children can learn to work independently of the teacher.

My earliest years in teaching were spent with three- and four-year-olds. During this time, I learned that some of the children's favorite words were "Me do it myself!" Young children have an inherent desire to become independent. They experience a strong sense of accomplishment when they can do things on their own. The trick is to set them up for tasks that they will be able to accomplish independently with success.

It is a bit like planting seeds in conditions in which they will thrive. I plant succulents in pots on my patio, because I can leave them for a week or two at a time without water. I've learned to plant zinnias in full sun in well-draining soil, because they'll rot if their roots stay too wet. Azaleas are tricky—they have special food and light requirements, but are worth it for their spectacular blooms.

When children are asked to work by themselves on tasks that are too difficult (or too easy), they often are frustrated, which can lead to off-task behavior. Students do not intentionally play around during independent reading time. When they stare into space or flip through books without reading, it is often because they haven't found the right book. I believe it is crucial to set up a classroom library in every room where children learn how to choose books they can read. Teaching children how to select "just-right" books is one of the first routines to establish. We can then connect this learning to the wider arena of choosing books at school, in the public library, or in a bookstore. Helping students choose "just-right" books can help them work independently of the teacher.

Early in the year, kindergartners learn to sort read-aloud books into fiction on the left and nonfiction on the right of this open-faced bookshelf. The top of the shelf holds three baskets with leveled books. Children's names are listed below their independent reading basket to help them choose "just-right" books.

Sometimes during literacy work stations time, well-meaning teachers pair a student who *can* do the work with a child for whom the work will be too difficult. This dynamic often puts both students in an unsuccessful situation; one student does the work for the other, and neither finish with a feeling that they've learned very much. I've found that it is often beneficial to pair students who need to work on a task at the same level, because they will work together to figure it out or explore even further without being superior to the other. Of course, there are many ways to pair children. Sometimes, one child will be able to support another so both learn together. Use what you know about your students to make these decisions, and be flexible on a daily basis.

As Marie Clay (1994) wisely said, "Don't do for the child what the child can do for himself." I have watched special education students work independently of the teacher when the work is at a level they *can* do. One day I visited a kindergarten where the teacher told me she had a child who constantly left the ABC station and wandered to the puzzles shelf in her room. When I asked her what the child could do with the alphabet, she said, "Oh, he really doesn't know any of his letters." That was why this child was walking over to the puzzles—it was something he *could* do. I asked the teacher to find some magnetic letters while I typed the alphabet the same size as those letters, and in a few minutes, there was a task this child could do at the ABC station. He worked on matching the magnetic letters to the printed version in a puzzle-like fashion. It was a first step in helping this child move toward letter recognition; a next step would be to provide opportunities for him to work with the letters in his name to provide a meaning base for this learning. He could match magnetic letters to a card with his name, practice writing and naming the letters used, or sort letters that have the same feature, such as those with sticks, or letters with dots. If a few other students need similar instruction, this work could be done in a small group and then moved to a literacy station so the children could practice again and again.

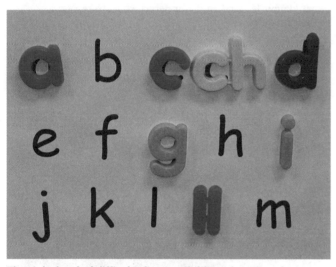

The right level of difficulty for one child just learning about print in Spanish was to match magnetic letters to typed letters on a piece of paper attached to a magnetic board.

It is the teacher's responsibility to create a setting in which children can work independently.

In the garden, I must prepare the site so my plants will develop strong root systems. Before I sow seeds or plant seedlings, I choose the location and prepare the soil by digging and weeding it, loosening and smoothing it, and digging an appropriate-sized hole. I make sure that I have pulled any weeds that might impede the plant's growth. If I'm container gardening, I choose a pot and use special potting soil. Sometimes I label what I've planted so I can remember its location and pay attention to its particular needs.

Likewise, students need to work in a safe, accepting environment to take risks on their own to grow independently. In today's world, many children live in transient circumstances and may feel unsettled or insecure. In addition, they come to us from homes with widely varying parenting styles. Some children have had few opportunities to practice independence, because their parents may be hesitant to let go of their babies. At the other extreme are children whose parents have given them too much independence, often with few or inconsistent boundaries. There are varying levels of support for schoolwork at home, too, because of parents' work schedules, kids' after-school commitments, or even parents' personal anxieties.

No matter what our children's circumstances outside of school, it is our responsibility to support students as they grow toward independence. It is our job to build a classroom community where they can learn to work independently. This huge task takes much love, commitment, and time. Input equals output is what I've found to be true: time invested in teaching kids what we expect is time well spent, and in return, over time, our students will be able to take on new learning and work independently. A second-year, second-grade teacher I worked with showed me just that in one of the lowest-income public schools in Houston, where I live.

After visiting several classrooms where students sat at their desks and did worksheets, I walked into this amazing second-grade classroom during students' time at literacy work stations. While the teacher met with a guided reading group at her small-group table, kids were working in pairs at desks, on the floor, by a bulletin board, and on the computer. They were having conversations with one another about what they were learning, their voices were quiet and calm, and they were successful with mostly on-grade-level tasks related to English language arts standards. Students were reading and writing important facts about lizards at one station; they were searching for words with specific phonics patterns and jotting them on sticky notes in familiar books at another station; and they were interviewing each other and taking notes about each other's lives at yet another station, where they also read and discussed biographies. I asked the teacher how she was able to orchestrate this kind of independent learning in her room, and she explained:

"At first, we tried using stations, and kids got out of hand. We began with just one literacy station (buddy reading) that I introduced for all students to do in pairs. I was clear and explicit about what I expected, but after just a few minutes there were kids goofing around and making way too much noise. So I called them to our whole-group meeting area, and we talked about why I'd stopped stations. Instead of lecturing them, I had them tell me what they needed to do differently tomorrow. The next day we tried again. It took about three weeks of being consistent with my expectations, reiterating and showing my class what they were supposed to be doing, and providing appropriate materials and feedback. My kids love going to stations, so I didn't have to offer any rewards. Stations were reward enough."

This teacher was patient, consistent, and persistent. She never gave up on her students or on her expectations for her classroom. She invested time and belief in her class and helped them experience success—over time. The following year, she looped with them, and they were easily able to begin literacy work stations the first week of school because they knew what the expectations were. Other teachers from her building can visit her classroom and learn from what she is doing with her students.

As I garden, I consider the needs of each plant variety and adjust my care based on what I know about that plant. Then I keep watch over my new plants, looking for new growth and signs of good health. I weed and prune, as needed. This is exactly what this teacher did. Each day, she adjusted instruction based on what she saw her students needed. When behaviors didn't match her expectations, she stopped stations and brought the class together to reteach. She looked for signs of growth and celebrated by having children share with one another what they were learning and doing at stations.

To help children become independent, teachers must release responsibility to them over time.

As in the above scenario, the teacher had her students take responsibility for their actions and didn't expect overnight results. She knew it would take time. In the world of high-stakes testing and changing standards, it is often difficult to invest time in this way. However, I have learned that most things that are worth doing take time, and lots of it!

Second graders work together at an expository-text station where they read informational text and create a KLW (what I know, learned, and wondered) chart to respond to their reading.

These two girls are interviewing each other at the biography station, as well as reading biographies.

Sometimes it is hard to release control, especially in the classroom. We fear that if we don't watch kids every step of the way, they might make mistakes, even if we've taught well. But isn't that part of practice and learning, too? When I was in elementary school, I took piano lessons by choice. I begged my parents for a piano and promised to practice daily. My mom didn't sit beside me on the bench and watch my every move. (She was usually busy cooking dinner but could hear that I was practicing—mistakes and all.) My mom didn't run in and try to fix my errors. Every Wednesday I walked to Mrs. Mummert's home for my weekly piano lesson.

At that time, she could gauge my practice by how well I played the pieces I'd practiced during the week.

A similar dynamic is possible in our classrooms. It is not necessary to hover over students at work stations to be sure they are doing everything right. It is important to teach well in whole group with a standards-based focus made explicit to the class by posting and referring to it throughout a mini-lesson and to observe students as they read and write along with us. Share high-quality children's literature—stories, informational text, poetry, dramatic readings—that match this focus while modeling how to read like an author and write like a reader. Give students opportunities to do this same kind of work, over time, as you spend time with them during reading workshop to allow the ideas you've planted to germinate. Pay attention to your students and give them all the support they need. Then move those same materials and activities to practice with partners at work stations, over time, as you see students showing that they can do this same kind of reading, writing, speaking, listening, and working with words without you sitting right beside them.

Take time to work with some children in small group, too. There you can give children just what they need, adjusting what you've taught previously in whole-class lessons and ensuring a strong foundation for them as they work independently. In small group, be sure you can see the rest of the class at work stations so you can quickly observe how they are doing, too. And be sure to bring reading workshop to a close with a brief "sharing time." Have the class gather in the whole-group meeting area to reflect on what they've learned that day. This gives them responsibility for their learning, which leads to further independence.

A student shares her work from the writing station with the rest of the class during "sharing time" at the end of reading workshop.

If you're wondering how to know it's time to move the work to a station, consider what a gardener does. Watch for signs that students understand well enough to work independently. Ask yourself: "What level of reading and writing can these students do without my being beside them? What activities have we done together in whole group (or small group) that students can now manage on their own? What kinds of support (in the way of familiar materials) can we place at a station to help students be successful?"

Remember that stations are where students develop independence, especially by working with tasks and texts that have been modeled previously. Familiarity breeds independence. For example, teach and then post anchor charts and references at stations for support, and remind children to use these tools.

Moving the writing rubric and student samples that had been used extensively during whole-group instruction to the writing station helps students write more effectively on their own.

It is quite possible to help children work independently, even if you are the only adult in the classroom. In many schools, there is just one teacher for every twenty to thirty students. If there are two adults in the classroom, arrange schedules so that both can teach in small groups during station times. I've seen excellent results when the classroom teacher and another adult (a special education or Title I teacher, or an assistant) meet with small groups; there are still plenty of children working independent of the teacher, and teachers can easily meet with every group each day between the two of them.

Surprisingly, there can be situations in which too many adults are available and it hinders student independence. I've been in classrooms where there were three or four adults working simultaneously with young children in small groups and/or monitoring their independent work. It was detrimental to students' independence because there was always someone there to help them, and they didn't have to figure out anything on their own. If you have several adults available, you might plan for them to work with specific students rather than circulate and monitor the room. Also, it is wise to be consistent and have everyone follow the same expectations about interruptions. If children learn that a particular person will always help them, they won't try to do things by themselves.

Growing Independent Learners Model

As I've worked with teachers across North America, I've developed a visual model (see Figure 1) that demonstrates how to grow independence. This model is the basis for this book. Use the model to help you think about the connections you're making throughout the day and across lessons with your students to help them "grow" into independent learners. Prepare the soil by setting up a well-designed learning environment. Then "plant the seeds" of your standards, curriculum, and what you know about your students as you teach whole-group mini-lessons. From there, watch for "sprouts of understanding" and then move what you've been teaching in whole group (or small group) to literacy work stations (and independent reading) over time.

A Quick Look at What's Ahead

As you read this book, the Growing Independent Learners model can help you think about "growing" student independence as you "reseed" what you're teaching in whole group (or small group) into literacy work stations over time. The first four chapters of this book will help you "prepare the soil" in which you'll be planting instructional routines for learning and "observe for root development" before moving the work to stations. Chapter 1 is about how to teach and plant the seeds of standards in whole-group instruction with focused standards-based mini-lessons to establish a strong foundation for later work at stations. Chapter 2 moves beyond my book *Spaces & Places* to give you ideas for how to make your classroom learning environment support independence, including my latest thinking about storage and wall spaces. Chapter 3 is centered on how to plan for instruction and related literacy work stations using standards. I examined standards from every state and created tools and processes for you to use that will strengthen instruction as well as save you time. And Chapter 4 takes a look at anchor charts, a subject I've been studying for the past few years as teachers have become more aware of this powerful teaching tool. You'll learn how to plan, design, create, and manage anchor charts, as well as how to use them at literacy work stations as a tool to increase students' independent learning.

Chapters 5–9 focus on how to nurture the seeds and watch sprouts of understanding grow into meaningful practice at specific standards-based stations. Each of these chapters is centered on an English language arts

Figure 1 **Growing Independent Learners Model**

strand, such as reading literature; reading information-al text; foundational skills; writing; and speaking, lis-tening, and language. Within these chapters you'll find many ideas for how to plan for and teach the skills nec-essary to meet the standards, as well as how to connect these to meaningful stations practice where students work independently.

In Chapters 5–9, I've provided a comprehensive picture of what instruction can look like when you fol-low the Growing Independent Learners model. These chapters provide a structure that's predictable and easy to follow and takes you through every phase of the planning and instructional process. Each chapter con-tains helpful tools for you to use in teaching specific concepts within the standards. These tools are repeated throughout the chapters and have the following titles:

- "Sifting Through the Standard" breaks down the standard to help you understand its meaning, in-structional implications, and real-world importance.
- "Team Planning Tool" shows ideas for planning to teach that standard, including important academic vocabulary to use, plans for whole-group instruction, and suggestions for literacy work stations.
- "Lessons That Last" contains detailed whole-group lesson plan templates.
- "Connections to Whole-Group Lessons" can help you extend the concepts from the lesson into oth-er areas of your daily instruction, including ideas for independent reading, small-group instruction, writing, and evaluation.
- "Mentor Texts" gives lists of exemplary children's books to use while teaching the standard.
- "Teaching Tips Across the Grade Levels" provides suggestions for building the skills necessary to reach the standard in pre-K through fifth grade.

Each of the "Lessons That Last" is focused on a particular standard. Each lesson is meant to be taught in whole group with engaging texts (see the "Mentor Texts" section for ideas). These lessons can be (and of-ten should be) repeated multiple times using different books—that's what makes them lessons that last! The lessons don't have to be taught in one sitting. Please observe your students, and stop when their interest wanes; you can pick up the lesson where you left off the next day.

A Note About Standards

In writing this book, I searched the standards found across the United States, including the Com-mon Core State Standards (CCSS), the Texas Essential Knowledge and Skills (TEKS), the Standards of Learning (SOL), from Virginia, and the Indiana Academic Stan-dards. Instead of trying to include every single stan-dard from every state, I zeroed in on these four sets and found many similarities. These I came to think of as "big ideas"—standards I would continue to teach even if every standards movement disappeared. In the online appendix, available at www.stenhouse.com/gilappendix, I have included charts that show the stan-dards highlighted in this book compared across CCSS, TEKS, SOL, and Indiana Academic Standards. I think you'll find it interesting—as I did—to see the many commonalities.

I've included an exact standard in each section to show how to use standards as starting points, but I've varied the reference to a particular standard from les-son to lesson to make the teaching ideas in this book inclusive. In other words, some lessons start with standards defined by the CCSS, and others are based on a TEKS or SOL or Indiana standards. You can con-sult the appendix to reference your state's specific standards. Please use the resources in this book flex-ibly. Read the material, examine the standards from your state that correspond to it, and adapt as neces-sary, even if the grade level on the lesson is different from the one you teach. You should be able to apply the information in any lesson or related idea to those connected to the specific state in which you teach and use tools provided to think about how to adapt it for your grade level.

How to Get the Most from This Book

Think about how you'd read a gardening book if you were getting ready to plant. You would want to read some pages very carefully and from beginning to end—those that talk about preparing soil, fertilizing, planning the layout of the garden, drainage, and so on.

Then, you'd choose specific pages pertaining to the particular plants that you were working with, based on the time of year or geographical location in which you were gardening. You might read about specific herbs if you wanted to plant an herb garden. Or you'd read the parts about preparing your garden for winter just before that season.

I recommend you approach this book in exactly the same way. Read the first three chapters in their entirety to get started. Planning an engaging classroom, getting organized to support student independence, and thoughtful lesson planning can't be skipped. The plants will suffer! You might read Chapter 4 on its own to think about how to integrate anchor charts into your instruction most powerfully. But after that, the chapters do not have to be read in order or read all at once. You can take them slowly according to the standard you are teaching. Then come back to the book in several weeks when you are ready for the next standard.

It is my hope that this is a book you will return to again and again. It is meant to be a guidebook, a faithful companion to help you as you approach teaching the standards with depth and complexity and help your students grow into independent learners. Thank you for joining me on this quest to "grow" independence as we teach thoughtfully and with purpose at every turn.

Digging Deeper

This book could serve as the foundation for powerful ongoing professional study with colleagues, too, with a study group reading the first four chapters together, then practicing with the materials in Chapters 5–9 over time, sharing successes and generating new instructional ideas together based on your learning and experience. To facilitate that type of group study, each chapter in this book ends with questions and/or exercises to help your learning go deeper. It is my hope that you will reflect on these questions as you read and study with your colleagues. Additionally, I am often on Facebook on Sunday evenings and post weekly questions for teachers to respond to. I hope you'll visit my page at www.facebook.com/dillerdebbie.

Think and discuss with colleagues the following questions now that you've read this introductory chapter:

1. What are your beliefs about independence? What has shaped these beliefs?
2. How have you released control to your students over time? Are there any areas in which you are still struggling to release control? Or are there areas where you might have released control too quickly?
3. At which literacy stations are your students working most independently? Discuss what conditions enabled this to happen.
4. Make a plan for reading this book with your colleagues. Begin with Chapters 1–3. Then choose which standard you will be teaching next and plan to read the accompanying chapter.
5. Consider reading Chapter 4 as a stand-alone chapter in conjunction with looking at anchor charts and how you're using them in your classroom.
6. Find one of the "Lessons That Last" in Chapters 5–9 to match a standard you're teaching. Discuss with a colleague how you might break this lesson into several sessions, as needed by your students. Look at the accompanying "Mentor Texts" and talk about how you could repeat this lesson with a different text. What would be the advantages of teaching this lesson more than once with a different book?

1

Teaching in Whole Group
with Standards-focused Mini-Lessons

It is midmorning as I enter one of my favorite second-grade classrooms to observe during reading workshop. Immediately, my attention is drawn to the twenty-five young children gathered on the rug with their teacher for a whole-group mini-lesson. They are engaged in a conversation about *The Wall*, a picture book by Eve Bunting (1992). They've been studying this author, comparing and contrasting many of her titles. Today, the teacher is reading aloud a new book and modeling how to ask and answer questions before, during, and after reading. She points to an anchor chart the class has recently started making, titled "Readers Ask Questions," and they read it together to review what they've learned so far: "Readers ask questions to help them comprehend and to find new information."

The teacher tells students that today they will practice asking questions *before, during,* and *after* their reading and then search for answers to their questions. She adds these words to the chart, and then they take a few seconds to act out how they will search for answers as they listen to this story. The teacher has set the purpose for listening by explicitly teaching that readers ask and answer questions.

The teacher and students made this anchor chart over several days and used it as the students learned to ask and answer questions about new books.

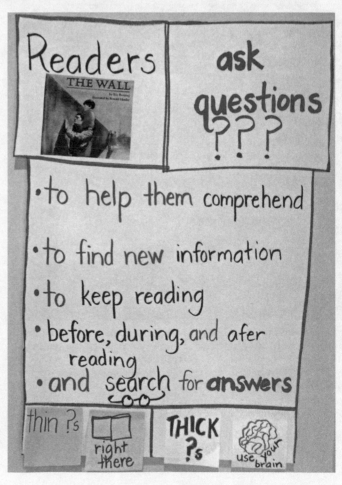

9

Second graders act out how they will search for answers to questions before listening to a book read aloud.

Before reading the new book, *The Wall*, students turn and talk about questions they have based on the cover. Then the teacher jots these on sticky notes and places them on another chart. The class will listen and search for text evidence to answer these questions during the read-aloud over several days.

After they look at the book cover and read the title together, students turn and talk to each other for a minute or two, sharing questions they have about the story. The teacher charts several of their questions on a different chart titled "The Wall," posting them on sticky notes under the word *Before*, to remind the students that they are expected to think and ask questions before they read this (and any) book. Their questions include "Where is the wall?" "What is that writing on the wall?" "Why are they touching and looking at the wall?" and "I wonder what is behind the wall."

The teacher reads the beginning of the book aloud while students listen for answers to their questions and formulate new ones. New questions are added on a different-colored sticky note to a section on the chart labeled *During*. As questions are answered, they are removed from the chart and placed in the book to show where they were answered. To keep students engaged, the teacher doesn't read aloud the entire book but finds a good stopping point from which she can continue reading and modeling how to ask and answer questions the following morning. She keeps her eye on the clock and limits the lesson to about twenty minutes, because she wants to give students plenty of time to practice what she has been modeling.

During the next fifteen minutes or so, they will read independently with sticky notes and jot down questions they have before, during, and after reading on their own. Then they will talk briefly with a partner to share what they learned. As they read, the teacher will circulate among them, conferring with individuals and taking notes about what she's noticing.

The mini-lessons I have observed in reading (and writing) will be taught multiple times throughout the year, not just once or twice during this week. The teacher will model and help kids ask and answer questions often as they read a wide variety of fiction, poetry, and informational text. They will use the anchor chart constructed during this lesson and others until they no longer need this scaffold.

Planting Seeds of Independence

When I walk into a classroom, I ask myself three questions:

1. Are the students and teacher engaged in learning during whole-group (or small-group) instruction—and throughout the day?

2. Is this a student-centered classroom with ample room for kids to think and learn in an organized, clutter-free, and inviting environment?

3. What "tracks of student learning" give visitors and the students evidence of what the students have been studying?

The smiles on these students' faces, their enthusiastic head-nodding, and the intense conversations between the students and teacher tell me this is a community of learners. What I have seen here answers my first question: yes, everyone is engaged in the learning. Evidence of thoughtful planning abounds. There are clearly stated standards-based learning objectives, the instruction is focused, and students are thinking together. This teacher has integrated several standards throughout her fifteen- to twenty-minute mini-lesson, including asking and answering questions (reading: literature) and participating in collaborative conversations with partners about texts (speaking and listening).

After the whole-group mini-lesson and independent reading, children will go to two literacy work stations with a partner for about twenty minutes each while the teacher meets with two different small groups. Pairs of children will practice previously taught standards as they read, write, listen, speak, and study words together. Some, but not all, of the stations will include work that has kids asking and answering questions.

Later in the day the class will extend their learning about asking and answering questions into writing workshop. Their teacher has already planned to help them make connections between what readers and writers do—they will access the "Readers Ask Questions" anchor chart as they write together, thinking about how writers consider questions readers may have about their writing and be sure they answer them. They examine a piece of student writing and ask questions, such as "What questions do you have as you read this?" "What are you wondering?" and "What details can the author add to answer those questions?" The teacher will direct students' attention to the anchor chart as she teaches, pointing to the part about asking questions *during* and *after* reading, and remind children to read their writing and think about what questions their audience might have.

Over the next few days, they'll make a small anchor chart (on 12-by-18-inch paper) about how writers ask and answer questions, too. This chart, shown in the photo, will be moved to the wall by the writing station for student reference after the teacher has taught with it for a week or two. She plans to move the "Readers

Ask Questions" anchor chart for reading near her small-group teaching area soon, so she can refer to it during lessons there. In a few days, she'll send home the chart with the sticky notes on it that the class co-created about *The Wall* with a student who needs to remember to ask questions as he or she reads. That way her walls won't become too cluttered.

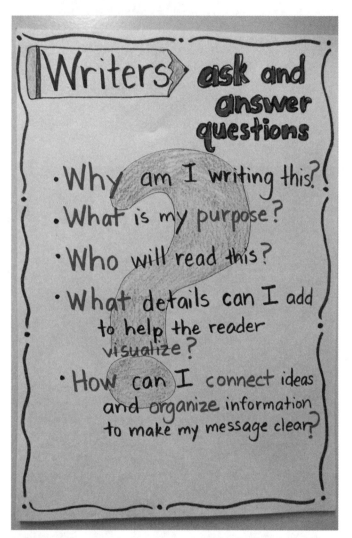

Second graders and their teacher made this anchor chart on "Writers Ask and Answer Questions."

Next, my eyes move around the classroom to survey the learning environment, and I ask my second question: "Is this a student-centered classroom with ample room for kids to think and learn in an organized, clutter-free, and inviting environment?" Thoughtful furniture arrangement leads to more space for students and ultimately, for thinking.

In this classroom, a large rug defines the whole-group meeting area where students gather to learn and think together; small groups of students meet with the teacher at appointed times throughout the day at a kidney-shaped table; and there are other organized spaces around the room, including a well-stocked classroom library with separate shelves for fiction and nonfiction, filled with baskets labeled by topics and genres to help students make thoughtful book choices for independent reading. There is also an area with leveled books. Nearby are individual book boxes, each with a student's name and photo on the front. On the floor beside the teacher, I note a basket of books labeled "Eve Bunting" with the author's photo on it. This connects to the whole-group instruction about this author and will eventually be added to the fiction section of the classroom library along with a chart with a photo and information about Eve Bunting.

An organized small-group area allows a teacher to work with groups efficiently by having all materials at her fingertips in labeled baskets.

Classroom library baskets with labels and pictures help students with book choice in another room.

Finally, I study the walls and ask one last question: "What 'tracks of student learning' show visitors and the students evidence of what the students have been studying?" As I look around, I notice that the day's objectives are posted near the whole-class area and that what is being taught matches these goals. Each morning before the children arrive, the teacher uses her lesson plans to record what The Learner Will (TLW) do in each subject area; she also refers to these standards-based goals during whole-class lessons to set the purpose for what children are learning about that day.

A first-grade teacher from this same school uses her lesson plans to record what The Learner Will (TLW) do in each subject area before kids enter the classroom for the day, which helps focus the learning. Posting and referring to what children will learn to do each day is a schoolwide expectation that clarifies learning goals for everyone involved.

There are anchor charts that document previously taught concepts, vocabulary, and strategies on labeled walls. All the reading-related charts are in one spot labeled "Reading" (one on visualizing, another on story elements, and one that includes a list of illustrated vocabulary from a read-aloud with a picture of the book cover on it). Writing anchor charts are on another wall and include "Where to Get Ideas for Stories," "How Authors Choose Words," and "Read My Writing" (with a kid-friendly rubric). There's also a wall devoted to math learning, and cabinet doors are covered with social studies and science information.

An author study station includes information about and photos of familiar authors along with a basket of their books. To help them focus, students refer to an "I Can" list, which was brainstormed by the class.

Social studies and science charts and related vocabulary are posted on labeled cabinet doors, because wall space is limited in this first-grade classroom.

Beside the classroom library on another cabinet door, there is information posted about authors this class has studied, along with an anchor chart on author's purpose that is being added to throughout the year. Student work is displayed on wall space titled "Gallery," and writing samples spill over onto the hallway walls where the learning these children are doing can be celebrated with the whole school. Again, thoughtful planning—of wall space, this time—yields strong evidence of what students have been studying and shows that this is a student-centered classroom where children are expected to work and think deeply and independently.

I want you to think of the three questions from the start of this section periodically throughout the school year, especially as you plan instruction:

1. Are my students and I engaged in learning during whole-class instruction—and throughout the day?
2. Is our classroom student centered, with ample room for kids to think and learn in an organized, clutter-free, and inviting environment?
3. What "tracks of our learning" show visitors and the students evidence of what the students have been studying?

Germination in Stations

When I arrive in this same classroom the next week, I see that some of the seeds planted in the previous week's lessons have germinated, and students are working with some of the same ideas and materials at a few of their literacy work stations, including the listening station. Many, but not all, of the stations involve asking and answering questions, the focus of last week's lessons. Two children are seated on the floor listening to a recorded book while jotting down questions on sticky notes. After listening, they share their questions with each other and then stick them in a community journal, a spiral notebook with the name of the recorded book on the top of each page. The community journal stays at this station for other children to use, too.

This space is labeled "Listening Station" and has an "I Can" list posted that includes "Ask and answer questions" as an option to help students stay focused here. The "I Can" lists have been generated with the class over time and offer kids several choices at each station, which keeps the work long lasting, like perennial plants. They don't have to be replanted constantly! On the wall is a small version of the "Readers Ask Questions" anchor chart for reading that I saw the teacher refer to in last week's whole-class mini-lessons. I love the way this teacher is "recycling" what she's taught and having kids practice independently of her. She won't need to change this station very often. Periodically, she'll place new recorded books (both literature and informational texts) here for kids to listen to.

Next I spy the "Author Study Station," where two children are reading and discussing several books by Eve Bunting. The station sign is posted low on the wall and an "I Can" list hangs beside it, reminding kids to

- read with a buddy,
- compare and contrast books, and
- ask and answer questions about books.

The partners have chosen to compare and contrast Eve Bunting's books *Ducky* and *Night Tree*, and they are talking and jotting down their ideas about how the two stories are alike and different on a laminated Venn diagram poster that is kept there. "In *Ducky*, the plastic duck is all alone on the ocean, but in *Night Tree* there is a family celebrating together," says one child.

"Yeah, but they're the same in a way, too," replies the other. "Both stories take place outdoors in nature."

Their teacher has read these books aloud to the class, so the stories are familiar, which allows students to think more deeply about them as they compare and contrast. Several other Eve Bunting books, including *The Wall*, are available for kids to read at this station, too. Children have choices when they come to this station. Some read and practice fluency while asking and answering questions about the stories; others choose to compare and contrast characters, settings, adventures, and themes. But they are always practicing standards-based strategies that have been previously taught.

I note that the "Writers Ask and Answer Questions" anchor chart for writing is now posted in the writing station, and two children are seated there talking about narratives they are writing. "I have a question," says one student. "Why did you have to get rid of the hamster? That detail would help me understand your story better." They refer to the anchor chart and "I Can" list that reads, "Write narratives" and "Ask and answer questions" posted above the table where they work. Other pairs of students are working together around the classroom in all sorts of spaces. At a station labeled "Word Study 1," two children stand beside a pocket chart stapled to a wall and sort words representing a spelling pattern they've been studying in their small group. Their words and a long-*i* miniature anchor chart hang in a zip-top bag with a green dot on it, signaling that children who are in the green guided-reading group should work with them first. An "I Can" list beside the station sign reads

- sort long and short vowels.
- highlight letters that represent the vowel sound.
- hunt for words in my books with this vowel sound.

They take turns sorting word cards with short- and long-*i* patterns, including *light, fire, sipped,* and *frightening*. They use highlighter tape to highlight letters that represent the sound of *i* in each word. Then they

choose books from their book boxes and reread old favorites, hunting for other long-*i* words and jotting them down on individual index cards to add to the sort. Working with familiar concepts and books gives them independent practice and a feeling of success. This word work connects to authentic reading, moving it beyond isolated skill and drill practice.

This long-*i* mini-anchor chart is in a zip-top bag with a green dot and has been used with students in small-group instruction.

Partners highlight long-*i* patterns in familiar books with highlighter tape and copy these words on cards.

Another pair of kids sits beside a filing cabinet labeled "Word Study 2." (There are two word-study stations, because student data have shown the teacher that many children in this class need practice decoding at this time of year.) The "I Can" list here includes *sort syllables, buddy-read familiar books from book boxes,* and *find and build two-syllable words with long-vowel patterns.* They use magnetic letters (blue for consonants and red for vowels) to build each syllable inside two-box frames made of colored tape on the side of the metal filing cabinet; one child builds the first syllable in the first box, and the other builds the second syllable in the second box. They also record the two-syllable words they built in a community journal that stays at this station for others to use. They write each vowel in red and the consonants in blue, so it is easy to see the patterns formed in the two-syllable words. They will share some of the words they found with the class during Sharing Time, a five-minute reflection time at the end of reading workshop.

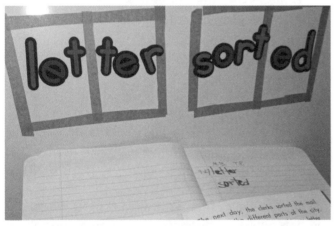

Students have used magnetic letters to write two-syllable words found in familiar books. Then they copy these words into a community journal at Word Study Station 2.

If you have an uneven number of students, three might work together at the newspaper station, as shown in this photo. They read sections together and jot down key details and interesting facts on sticky notes. They also discuss what they've read.

A quick glance around the rest of the room shows pairs of children at a variety of other stations that have been carried to students' desks, such as a newspaper station where they read and discuss current events using a kid-friendly newspaper the class subscribes to, a science station where kids do short science experiments related to science concepts previously taught and write simple lab reports, and a poetry station where partners read familiar poems chorally to build oral reading fluency and ask and answer questions about the poems to deepen comprehension. There is also a drama station with reader's theater scripts, retelling pieces, and familiar books from whole-group instruction. Students work together, reading and retelling dramatic texts to build comprehension, vocabulary, and fluency related to previously taught standards that are posted at each station.

Three children work independently on technology at their desks. This teacher has two laptops and an iPad. She has bookmarked sites that provide individual programs for these students to work on during this round of literacy work stations. On other days, kids listen to stories on iPads, record themselves reading, or work on a variety of apps. They use the laptops to search for information to answer questions posed in social studies or science; sometimes partners watch short video clips and take notes or read texts and share what they learned with the class.

A pair of students works together at a second-grade science station set up on some low shelves. They've been studying sound and are doing simple experiments, which are posted in this area.

Partners in a kindergarten class read poems together. They practice reading fluently and looking for high-frequency words from the word wall.

The teacher is meeting with four children at a table in her small-group area. They are reading a short story from *Highlights* magazine. I note that she has a small desktop dry erase magnetic easel on her table and has written "FOCUS: ask and answer questions" at the top of it. Students are using sticky notes to jot down questions as they read. The teacher circulates around the table, conferring with each child as they read this text with just a little bit of support. There is conversation throughout the small-group lesson, between the teacher and individuals and among the children themselves as they share their thinking about what they read.

The teacher has set her cell phone timer for twenty minutes to signal when to switch groups and stations. When the timer buzzes, she finishes the small-group lesson and dings a music wand, telling children to finish up and get ready to move to the next station. This structure allows all students to participate in a variety of literacy activities with a partner and keeps engagement high. It also gives the teacher a chance to meet with two different small groups to provide exactly what they need during this time.

After kids have gone to two rotations (either at a station or in a small group with the teacher), they clean up and meet back on the carpet for Sharing Time to reflect on what they did as readers and writers today. The teacher leads a discussion as children share what they learned and what didn't go so well. She learns that the students are asking and answering questions before, during, and after reading, and she is pleased with the depth of their questioning. The students who were at the writing station share the questions they asked one another and how it improved their writing. Those at word study read some of the words they found using the community journal from that station and show how understanding long vowels and syllabication helped them decode.

At the Start of the Season

Just as a garden doesn't magically appear, neither did the literacy stations in this second-grade classroom. The teacher carefully planted the seeds by teaching well. She set expectations, modeled how to work in each station, and gave kids time to practice in pairs while she circulated around the classroom observing during the first few weeks of school. She got stations going before she started working with small groups.

The first three stations (listening, buddy reading, and writing) were introduced, one at a time, during the first couple of weeks of school. The teacher modeled expectations for each station, introducing one a day, and had the whole class practice. For example, the first week she taught everyone how to buddy-read with a partner, and that was the only station that was "open" until kids knew how to do it.

Meanwhile, during writing workshop she taught the class how to write short personal narratives about their experiences. Once kids were familiar with writing routines, she had everyone work with a partner to share their writing and give feedback during stations time. Soon she had half the class buddy-read and the other half share their writing. Once they could do those things, she introduced how to operate several listening devices, including a portable audio player with a splitter so two kids could listen at once, an iPad, and an old-fashioned tape recorder. At that point, several students listened to recorded texts while others were assigned to buddy-read and the rest of the class wrote together in pairs. Now she had three stations rolling. At this point, she introduced a management board (described on the next page and shown in the photos on page 18) and assigned kids to work with partners in specified spaces around the classroom.

The teacher continued introducing new stations, one at a time and never more than one a day, throughout the first four to six weeks of school. As she taught something new related to her state standards in reading or writing workshop and kids began to show signs of understanding, she transferred those tasks to a station. For example, using reader's theater scripts together in whole group, she modeled how to read with intonation and expression. The teacher wrote the names of characters (and the narrator) on individual index cards and handed them out to small groups of two to three kids in the class so that everyone had a part. She even color-coded the parts by highlighting the characters' names in the script and the matching index cards to make it easier for kids to find and read their parts. She then created and introduced a puppet theater made with a piece of colored foam board, scored to divide the board into three parts so it would sit on a desktop. If you want to do this yourself, just cut a large rectangle from the middle and fasten fabric scraps to the inside with duct tape to create curtains, as pictured below.

After kids had practiced reading several scripts, these same materials (scripts and index cards with character names and the puppet theater) were moved to a portable drama station for partners to read together during stations time. This became a favorite station that lasted all year long. She simply changed the scripts and added retelling pieces over time.

Kids use scripts and retelling pieces at the drama station to read with intonation and expression all year long.

The second-grade teacher in this classroom started the year by duplicating stations. Even now she has duplicates of two stations—technology and word study. You don't have to have twelve different stations. Start slowly, and layer on new stations as you teach new standards and see the need for students to practice in new ways.

In another second-grade classroom, children learned how to work in pairs at several different stations early in the year. The teacher circulates, checking in with students to be sure they know what to do.

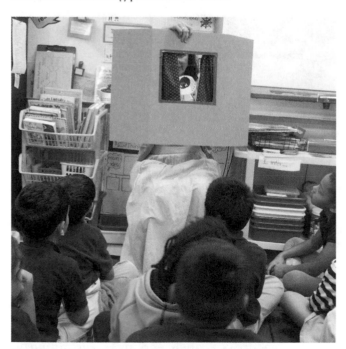

I introduce a homemade puppet stage in whole-group instruction in a first-grade classroom.

Eventually, you'll want to add a management board. I recommend doing this when you have enough stations introduced and are ready to assign students to particular stations. You'll soon be ready to work with small groups, too, and will want to show that on your board. In the photos on the next page, you'll see several management boards that use a pocket chart or an interactive whiteboard. Each day, the teacher moves the icons to show kids where they'll work for those two or three station rotations. Likewise, she puts her name or photo on the board to show which groups she'll work with. Most teachers don't try to work with every reading group every day during this time, unless they have an assistant who also works with small groups.

Young children check the management board to see which station they're going to first and then second in this classroom. The goal is for kids to read the board independently.

A first-grade teacher places her "Meet with Me" cards over icons to show which groups she'll meet with before kids arrive in the morning.

This kindergarten management board is from early in the year. Partners work at a variety of stations, including Names, ABC, Buddy Reading, Let's Talk, Read to Self, and Computers. There are multiples of several stations.

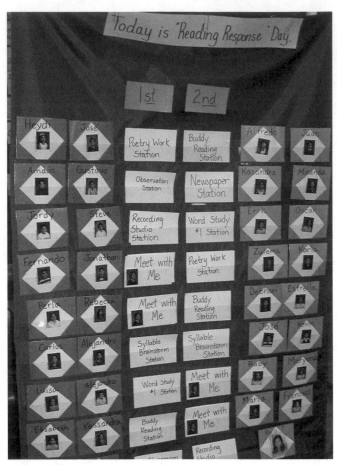

This third-grade teacher sees two classes a day. Her morning ELA classroom has names of kids listed on blue cards on the left side of her chart. Her afternoon class's photos and names are on the right, on green cards. She moves the icons down the middle to show which stations students will go to each day.

Some teachers create a template on their interactive whiteboard to use as a management board. They use it much like a pocket chart, but it takes less wall space.

You'll notice that these management boards and the ideas in the rest of this book reflect my belief that children practice best when working *in pairs* during literacy work stations. I've been studying this dynamic since 1995 and find that student engagement increases when kids work with a partner. Having kids work in twos (rather than in groups of three, four, or five) cuts down on many behavior problems, including children arguing about materials, just a few kids doing the work, and too much noise.

As I've observed in hundreds of classrooms, I've noticed that students working at a similar level often make the best matches. Of course, it's important that they also get along well! Oftentimes, pairing children who read at advanced levels with kids who are struggling readers causes frustration for both of them. The biggest thing to remember is that there needs to be something at each station that every child in your classroom *can* do, as I said in the Introduction. Of course, there are exceptions to every rule, so use your judgment and wisdom to make the best decisions for what works with your students *this year*.

Ensuring Seedlings' Growth: Making Stations Meaningful

Once teachers have begun literacy work stations, I am frequently asked, "How do we make our stations meaningful and keep kids engaged?" I have found that the answer begins in whole-group instruction. If students aren't engaged during whole-group lessons, their practice at stations won't be strong either. If we want to improve what students do at stations, we should begin by planning and teaching meaningful whole-group lessons that plant the seeds for what they will do at engaging literacy stations.

For example, if we teach well with repeated readings of Big Books in kindergarten during shared reading, modeling how to read the title and make predictions, pointing to each word, and linking known words to the word wall, we will expect children to do these same tasks at the Big Book station using the materials we have used during instruction. Likewise, in third grade, if we model how to determine the main idea of a text using informational texts related to science or social studies content in multiple lessons and show our thinking about key details and how they support the main idea on a related graphic organizer, partners can use these and other informational texts about the same topics, and the same graphic organizer,

at a buddy-reading station. The key is to model, model, model and include students in the interaction during whole-group instruction. Then move those same tasks and materials to stations for independent practice over time.

Ask yourself this: "Am I modeling how to read and write, or am I giving instructions?" Modeling and thinking together are very different from giving directions during whole-group instruction. I've visited rooms where the teacher is spending much of the time giving directions: *"Class, please turn to page sixty-four in your books. We are going to read this story and answer questions. Listen to the recording and follow along. Then we'll read it with a partner. After that, you'll answer questions on page seventy. Be sure to listen carefully so you can answer the questions."* In this scenario, the children might behave and do what the teacher directed. But there is no strong focus or modeling taking place. Students might be compliant, but that doesn't mean they are engaged.

Compare the scenario above with the lesson that opened this chapter where the teacher was modeling explicitly with interesting text and children were interacting. Whole-group lessons should be clear and focused on standards, not just giving students directions. This requires thoughtful planning—of how you set up your classroom and teach kids to work together, as well as the teaching you'll do before students ever set foot in a station. Read on to Chapters 2–4 to learn about planning for instruction and classroom space. Then go through your school's standards, using the resources you've been given (curriculum documents, core programs, and so on) combined with what you know about your kids *and* your own instincts and training to make your classroom the best it's ever been!

Digging Deeper

Now that you have a clear picture of what literacy work stations look like and how they can run smoothly in a classroom, use the following questions to think about your next (or first) steps:

1. "Are my students and I engaged in learning during whole-group instruction—and throughout the day)? What enabled that to happen (or kept it from happening)?" Reflect on lessons you've been

teaching, and compare them with the scenarios in this chapter. Also use information from Chapter 3 to help you with planning and teaching whole-group lessons.

2. "Is our classroom student centered, with ample room for kids to think and learn in an organized, clutter-free, and inviting environment? What areas are crowded or need to be purged? Which parts of our classroom feel inviting? Which areas don't feel comfortable?" Chapter 2 will give you further information on classroom setup.

3. "What 'tracks of our learning' show visitors and the students evidence of what the students have been studying?" Visit colleagues' classrooms together and ask each other what it looks like you've been teaching. Put yourself in the place of the children you teach as you do this. Read Chapter 4 for ideas on creating and using anchor charts with your class.

4. What did you learn about literacy work stations in this chapter? What will you try as a result? Chapters 5–9 are filled with ideas for teaching and moving standards to literacy stations for practice.

5. If you haven't yet started literacy work stations, create a plan for how you'll get started. Work with others from your grade-level team, if possible. Plan for a management board, too. Talk about the power of pairs, and commit to giving that a try if you've not yet done so.

2
Organizing for Independence

"This was the best year I've ever had," said my friend Sage, a kindergarten teacher, in June. "Having you come to my room before school started and planning for my space—the teaching areas and kid-friendly spaces, walls, and storage—was the key. Every place in my classroom had a purpose."

In the spring, I make a plan for which flowers and herbs I'll plant in my garden. I check to see what's survived the winter and where I need taller plants as a backdrop as well as low, creeping ones for borders, and where I'll place them. I also think about soil amendments needed for the new season. When I go to my favorite garden center, I have a plan for what to purchase and plant.

Just like preparing a garden for each new season, setting up a classroom thoughtfully lays a foundation for the work we will do with our students there. When every space in the room is oriented toward instruction, we find ourselves being more intentional about our teaching. We are able to focus on kids rather than searching for our stuff.

Preparing the Soil: Setting Up Your Classroom

Many teachers find themselves headed to their classrooms a few weeks before school begins to "do the furniture shuffle." We push tables and desks all around, trying to find that perfect fit for everything that is in the room. As I've worked with teachers across the country, I've learned valuable lessons about classroom setup. Here are a few of them, adapted from my book *Spaces & Places* (2008):

- If you plan your space on paper first, you can save about eight hours of backbreaking labor.
- Work *with* someone to plan and to move furniture. Don't try to do it alone!
- Setting up classrooms as a team builds camaraderie and helps create shared vision.
- Uncluttered, well-organized classrooms can positively affect student behavior.
- Cluttered, junk-filled classrooms can exacerbate behavior problems.
- To make the most of your (often limited) classroom space, plan for literacy teaching places in this order:

1. Whole-group teaching area
2. Small-group teaching area
3. Classroom library

- Consider technology as you're setting up your room, but be flexible. Wireless options help.
- Plan for and set up desks, including the teacher desk if you have one and those for students, *last* instead of first.
- Keep your entry open to invite children in.
- Use furniture so that each piece has a purpose and sometimes does double duty.
- Remove excess furniture to make space for students.
- If furniture is tall, place it against a wall. Just think, *Tall against the wall!*
- Make your classroom library a focal point in the room to encourage reading.
- Use just two to three colors in the room to visually enlarge the space and help students focus.
- Cover all bulletin boards in one of those colors and use one simple complementary border to help students pay maximum attention to what you post on the walls.

When I worked with Sage, we first drew a map of his classroom on a piece of 9-by-12-inch white construction paper, noting the location of all the nonmovable features that we'd have to maneuver around—cabinets, doors, windows, cubbies, a sink, and a bathroom.

First, we drew a map of all the built-in features of the classroom. Simply use white paper and a marker.

Next, we thought together about his most important teaching spaces and what was needed for each. We began with the whole-group teaching area, since it was where he would teach standards-based mini-lessons daily for reading, writing, word study, math, science, and social studies. This space needed to be large enough for his twenty-plus students to sit comfortably, and it made sense to have it near a large whiteboard and screen, which he'd use for modeling. We also liked the location we had chosen because there were no distractions from windows or doors nearby. There was a data jack, which was needed when he used technology in whole-group instruction. And it was near a large dry erase board we could convert to a word wall, which I find very important in pre-K through grade one. We wrote "WG area" (for whole-group area) on a sticky note and placed it on the classroom map.

Next, we thought about a small-group teaching space. Sage had a kidney-shaped table in his room that he planned to use for small groups for literacy (during reading and writing workshops) and for math (during math workshop). We decided to place it in front of some built-in cabinets where he could store materials for small group. These cabinets would be a great place to post some of the anchor charts he'd made during whole-group instruction and to help students connect to them during small group. But most important, he would be able to sit at this table and view every inch of space in the room as he taught in small group and kids worked at stations. Nobody would be hidden from his sight. We found a three-foot-tall shelf that would be perfect for this area, too, and decided to place it at a ninety-degree angle from the wall, separating the small-group area from the computers that would have to be placed beside it (since that was where the computer connections were). We added sticky notes for the small-group area and the computers on the map.

The third very important place we planned for was the classroom library. This was where students would both choose books for independent reading time and have additional reading time on their own during literacy work stations. We wanted the classroom library to be a focal point, a space that children would automatically spot upon entering the room and gravitate toward. We chose a corner that was directly across from the entrance and marked it with a sticky note on our map. Sage had three shelves and a small table and chairs that would fit nicely in the spot. We planned to angle one shelf in the corner to invite kids into that special area.

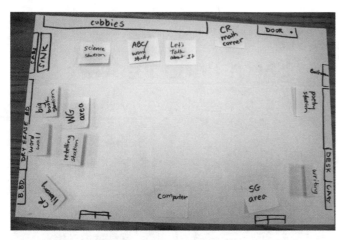

Sticky notes on Sage's completed classroom map show the placement of important teaching spaces as well as station areas for independent practice time.

Because Sage teaches all subjects, we also planned for a classroom math corner as suggested in *Math Work Stations* (Diller 2011), a space for his math stations and materials related to the math concepts he'd be teaching at that time. Since the children would work with counting and beginning number concepts at the beginning of the year, we planned for a space to display counting materials. Sage owned inexpensive white plastic shelves that would fit in that space by his door.

Planning the Garden: Designing Student Spaces

Now it was time to think about the kinds of stations Sage's kids would use independently and plan for spaces for each of them, even though he wouldn't introduce stations until he had established basic routines for working together and for independent reading, in-

dependent writing, and buddy reading during the first few weeks of school. It's helpful to plan for possible stations and corresponding spaces in the room *before* school begins so that you won't be looking around the room trying to decide where to put them later. Of course, you might be reading this book at a time other than the start of the school year, but you can use this planning-for-space-on-paper protocol at any time.

Sage and I worked together to make a list of the stations he'd have his students use this year and put the name of each one on a separate sticky note. Then we thought about a logical spot for each one on the map. Some stations would be portable and others would be stationary. That would help us maximize every inch of space in his classroom. Sage's list, including notes on why we put each one where we did, is shown in Figure 2.1.

We'd already planned where to put a few of the stations while we looked at big instructional spaces. For example, the Big Book station would go in the whole-group instruction area, because that's where Sage's Big Book easel was. We planned to convert the large dry erase board in the whole-group area into a word wall by using colored tape to make a grid, because that would help him connect his teaching to word study for reading and writing during whole-group instruction. I always recommend placing a high-frequency word wall in or near the whole-group area in pre-K through grade one, since those are the ages when children are learning the most about print and how it works. Having the word wall in his whole-group meeting area allowed Sage to make constant connections to high-frequency words during shared reading and writing.

Figure 2.1 **Sage's plans for possible stations**

Stationary Stations

- classroom library (corner that invites kids in and is easily seen upon entering)
- writing (near cabinet doors where we can display anchor charts and student work; built-in countertop provides a writing surface and saves space)
- computers (near data jack)
- Big Book (in whole-group area, using the Big Book easel there)
- word wall (in whole-group area to make it easy to connect word study to reading and writing; there's a large magnetic dry erase board here for making the word wall interactive and accessible to children)
- retelling (on a large, low, dry erase board on wheels that separates the whole-group area from the classroom library)
- science (on a small, low, square table placed near the sink area)

Portable Stations

- poetry (a garment rack with wheels that has poems written on charts attached to wire hangers with clear packing tape)
- "let's talk" for oral language development (flip chart of large photos of common objects that could be moved flexibly around the room)
- ABC/word study (in baskets that can be taken to student tables)
- math work stations to be used during math workshop (lidded, clear plastic containers stacked on a shelf by a wall)

Sage's word wall is on a large dry-erase board, divided with tape to create a space for each letter, and has vowels backed in a different color to make them stand out.

Content-area words with illustrations are listed on a small chart for the topic being studied.

In grades two and three, I often place the word wall near the writing station and am sure students can clearly see the words from their desks, too, so they can use word wall words as they write. I also recommend making and posting vocabulary charts with words related to the content-area topics you are teaching. For example, with your class write the title "Earth Land Features" on a piece of 12-by-18-inch white construction paper, if that's what you're studying, and then make a list of related words with matching illustrations and display them with other social studies information.

A second-grade word wall is near the small-group area and easily visible from the writing station.

Finally, we planned for the kids' desks/tables and a teacher desk. I recommend setting up desks last, not first. You'll find that they somehow fit, and you'll use the space in the entire room more efficiently this way. If you have a large number of students, especially in grade two and above, you might think about having fewer desks than students to save space. Some teachers have three to five kids sit at the small-group table instead of at desks during times when all students need to have a hard-surfaced work space. Or they have a few students sit on floor spaces with clipboards during these times. It's your classroom and your call. Be creative to make space for your students!

Also, instead of putting your desk in the "prime piece of real estate," you might make that area a student space. Sometimes teachers put their desk in the best part of the room—the sunniest space, the first place you see when you enter the room, or the coziest spot. Often, that same space makes a wonderful classroom library or writing area.

Sage decided not to have a separate teacher desk. Instead, he used his small-group teaching table, which was placed near a large cabinet, as his desk when he wasn't teaching (during planning times or after school). "I never used my big teacher desk, except for stacking things," Sage told me. "After I got rid of my desk last year, I never missed it, and I found that my kids had more space. I just used a cabinet and some stacking drawers for storing things I normally would have put in my desk." Sage put his students first as he designed his classroom spaces. He still planned for a space for his things, but he did that *after* he thought about spaces for his students.

If you have a traditional teacher desk, consider making it a flexible, multipurpose space. Some teachers turn the front of their desks into a magnetic station for word work or poetry (using materials from www.magneticpoetry.com). Others convert their teacher desk into a writing station.

The teacher desk is used for word study during stations time (*top*). Or it might be turned into a writing station (*bottom*).

After planning Sage's classroom spaces on paper, we worked together to move his furniture to the designated spots. We completed the mapping and moving work in about an hour and a half! Now it was time to think about a plan for storage areas and walls.

Sage's small-group area is ready to go.

Sage's classroom library just needs books and kids.

Sage's finished room as seen from the entry

The Garden Shed: Planning for and Organizing Materials in Storage Spaces

Every gardener has gardening supplies. I have a small place on my patio for potting soil, gardening tools, my favorite gloves, and extra pots. It makes it easier for me to grab what I need when I get a few minutes to work in my flower beds.

Likewise, every teacher has teaching supplies—usually lots of them! It can be tricky figuring out where to put everything so that it doesn't spill out into spaces that could be used by our students. Also, if we want students to work independently of us, it's helpful for them to be able to easily access materials by themselves. Thus, I've found it crucial to plan for storage places just as I do for teaching spaces. If you've been teaching for several years in the same classroom, it's really important. The longer we've taught in a room, the greater the likelihood that we have lots of "stuff" hidden behind closed doors or in drawers. Again, working with a partner can make this task easier. Start with a plan like Sage and I did, even if you think everything is pretty well organized. If you're not good at organizing, ask a friend to help you.

Begin by looking at any storage spaces you have (built-in or portable)—shelves, cabinets, file cabinets, desk drawers, stacking drawers, and the like—and plan on paper how to use each one. Sage was blessed with built-in cabinets in his new classroom, so we planned on paper how to maximize them, rather than just putting things on shelves behind closed doors. This new plan would help him get and stay organized, and we could see what materials had been left by the teacher who had used the classroom the previous year.

As we thought about all the materials that needed to be stored, we began by making sticky notes for each subject area Sage would be teaching: reading, writing, math, science, and social studies. This enabled us to think about putting all the reading materials together, organizing all his math manipulatives in another cabinet, and so on. We also made sticky notes for other stuff we knew he'd be storing: art supplies, such as paper, pencils, scissors, and glue; healthy-kid supplies such as Kleenex and hand sanitizer; and textbooks. Then we placed each sticky note on his storage map, thinking about which place would be most logical to store each group of items for easy access for both him and his students.

Because Sage decided not to have a teacher desk, we also planned for where he'd keep things traditionally kept in a desk. He had stacking drawers that he'd labeled the year before to house items such as his stapler, staples, tape, scissors, paper clips, and rubber bands, so we placed them by his small-group table. We strategically placed the table near a cabinet, too, so he could use a shelf inside the cabinet for larger items he would have otherwise kept in his desk.

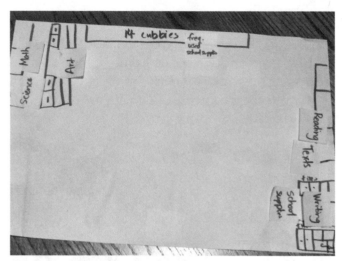

Sage's storage spaces map

After creating a paper plan, we took all the items out of Sage's cabinets and sorted them. It can be intimidating to do that alone, so set aside a chunk of time and *work with someone* to tackle this all-important task! It's important to realize that if you don't take things out of storage areas, you'll never know what you have, what's not necessary, or what you need. Again, if you have taught in the same classroom for many years, it's important to do this. Sometimes teachers have inherited somebody else's stuff. If you're not sure if you need to keep certain items, ask your administrator. Out-of-date materials, including reading programs not currently being used in your school system, should be removed from your classroom (or sent home with students to use there if cleared with the administration). Be prepared to toss anything (and recycle paper) that's no longer needed!

Sage and I wrote the name of each storage category on a large sheet of paper and placed the sheets around the room on the floor and tables, so we could sort his materials into piles of similar items. Then, as we took things from the cabinets, we moved each one to the category it matched. For example, all reading-related supplies such as magnetic letters, high-frequency word games, and phonics went on a pile marked "Reading" on the floor. Writing materials went on a table labeled "Writing." Math materials were placed in another part of the room near the cabinet where we'd later organize all his math manipulatives and so on. We purged broken items and old papers as we sorted.

Language arts materials are now stored in labeled containers on labeled shelves in this cabinet to help the teacher stay organized.

Materials are sorted by category after being removed from cabinets.

Next, we tackled one pile at a time, sorting it into smaller parts and making a label for it. For example, his reading materials were divided into phonics CVC, blends, high-frequency words, sentences, letter ID, vowels, consonants, and so on. He had lots of books that we placed either in the classroom library or his small-group area. Because Sage's classroom was in a fairly new building, and he wasn't a big "collector," there wasn't much extra stuff to get rid of. In fact, we found quite a few materials that he needed to implement instruction as we took everything out of his cabinets. Once we knew what he had, his principal told him to make a list of things to be ordered and offered to purchase materials as he found funds to do so.

Finally, we moved the sorted materials onto a shelf where they fit and were easy to access, taking care to place items in containers in which they fit well and didn't leave any "dead space." Then we labeled each space. Surprisingly, it took us only about half a day to finish organizing his storage spaces. It was worth every minute we invested, because it saved Sage time all year long. He knew what he had and where to find it.

Storage Spaces: Doors, Drawers, and Shelves

If you are fortunate enough to have closets, cabinets, and drawers in your classroom, use them wisely. It's easy to get in the habit of stashing stuff behind closed doors! I've found it helpful to organize and label everything in designated spaces, especially in closets and drawers. It's wise to plan for one storage area for all language arts materials and a separate space for math, science, and social studies.

Organizing materials can also help you when planning for instruction. When you know *what* you have to teach with, it makes it easier to think about *how* you will teach. In Sage's room, we even printed out the state standards matching each curriculum area and posted them inside the cabinet doors with those teaching materials. Every time he looked at his instructional supplies, he was reminded of what he should focus on in his teaching. Simple and effective.

Posting state standards inside cabinet doors near matching curriculum materials makes planning easier and teaching more focused.

Think about organizing materials for students to access easily, too. One teacher who had drawers placed often-used supplies, such as sticky notes, index cards, crayons, and paper clips, in the drawers and added labels with pictures. She even had a drawer for zip-top bags—just like in her kitchen at home. Students could easily help her retrieve those items, since they were in labeled drawers.

Plan for spaces for community supplies that all children can access, using low shelves in noncrowded areas of the room. For example, have a place for paper that students can go to on their own, so that you don't always have to hand it out. To make it manageable, don't put out all the paper you own, and negotiate how much and when children can help themselves to paper. Do the same for pencils, crayons, scissors, and so on. Some teachers plan for community supplies to be kept in the middle of each set of desks or table group. The key is to have a plan that makes materials management easy for your students. The more independent the children are, the freer you are to teach and facilitate their learning. Labels, especially those with pictures, and clear expectations can help develop student independence with classroom supplies.

Shelves can be great for storing organized teaching supplies. And it's a plus to have built-in or stand-alone shelves in a classroom. They are necessary for classroom library setup. Shelves are also great for storing teaching supplies. However, without a plan, shelves can look messy and distract students from learning. Some teachers choose to cover part of their shelves with fabric curtains to "hide" materials and keep kids from being distracted.

Help! I Don't Have Any Storage Spaces

Some teachers I've worked with, particularly in temporary buildings, have limited or no storage areas. In these cases, we've had to get creative. I recommend using portable shelving from home supply stores. You might use wire cubes, plastic modular shelving (which usually comes in black or white), stacking drawers, or whatever you can find.

Another possibility is to attach a fabric skirt to a table with Velcro. No sewing required! Just measure the length of the table and cut a piece of fabric that size. Make it long enough to barely touch the floor. Secure the fabric to the edge of the table with Velcro dots. Then "hide" materials under the table. This technique can keep your classroom from looking cluttered and provides storage when you have no other options.

Shelves: before and after

These shelves were converted to a kindergarten classroom library.

One alternative to built-in storage is stacking wire baskets.

Student supplies are well organized, labeled, and easy to access.

Skirted tables provide "hidden" places to keep materials in classrooms with limited storage.

Trellises, Arbors, and Pergolas: Using Wall Space

When designing a garden, you think about the vertical spaces for growing as well as the ground. You might use trellises, arbors, or pergolas to support vines or other plants that grow tall. Likewise, classroom walls are important vertical learning spaces to consider. I often think of the walls as a "second teacher" in the classroom, since students definitely spend time looking at them. Our walls tell a lot about what we value; they reflect what we've been teaching and give messages to our students, their parents, and administrators who enter our classrooms. Recently, I began paying as much attention to walls as I do to furniture placement. We'll go into more detailed discussion in Chapter 4, but here are some of the ways we can plan for effective use of wall spaces:

- Planning ahead for space and labeling walls helps teachers find room for important things to put on the walls.
- When walls are labeled, they are usually better used both by teachers and children.
- Clustering anchor charts according to subject helps students easily locate information for reference.
- Using simple borders and solid bulletin board backgrounds (rather than lots of patterned designs) helps children focus on the boards' displays.
- Black or dark blue backgrounds really help material "pop" on visual displays.
- Minimizing clutter on walls allows students to focus on instruction.
- It's important to put some "white space" between charts and displays to help students read and use them more easily.
- Displaying anchor charts made with the class and student work (rather than lots of commercial wall-display stuff) shows that children are valued in a classroom.
- Placing items closer to kids' eye level helps them pay more attention to the displays and use them as resources.
- Cabinet doors, closet doors, and even windows can be used to extend wall space.

Planning for Wall Displays

As Sage and I worked together to design his kindergarten classroom, we made a simple map of his walls and determined how to label each space he would need for instructional displays, such as anchor charts. We used sticky notes that said "Reading," "Writing," "Word Wall," "Math," "Science," "Social Studies," and "Gallery" (for student work) and placed them on the map in areas where they made the most sense instructionally.

For example, we placed the "Word Wall" sticky note in the whole-group area. He would use this wall for teaching high-frequency words as he modeled and made connections between these words found in Big Books and poems during shared reading. He'd also refer to words on the word wall as he wrote with his class in modeled writing and during morning message as the class read and wrote together about their day. Students could easily access the words as they read and wrote independently, too.

We put the "Math" sticky note by the space designated for math work stations. There was a long space above his nearby built-in cubbies where we could display anchor charts and math vocabulary cards made with the class during math workshop.

Likewise, we stuck the "Writing" sticky note near the cabinet doors where his writing work station would be. The 12-by-18-inch white construction paper he'd use for anchor charts made during writing workshop would fit perfectly on the cabinet doors and turn them into usable "wall space."

The "Reading" label went on the long wall near his small-group teaching area and classroom library. As the class created anchor charts and used graphic organizers in whole group during reading workshop, they would be posted on the reading wall, where students could easily access them while they were reading.

We chose a space to display student work on a wall by the classroom door and labeled it "Gallery." Overflow student work would be posted in the hallway outside Sage's room for others to view. We decided to post the "Science" wall label near the sink where kids would be working independently at a science work station and "Social Studies" between the US and Texas flags hanging in the front of his classroom.

After we planned for wall spaces, we made simple signs to label the walls. We used the die-cut machine and yellow construction paper to create large capital letters, which we glued onto blue construction paper backgrounds to make the signs. We stapled the wall labels to the appropriate walls so they were ready to display materials as they were created *by* and *with* the children. Before school began, there wasn't much on the walls, but there was space for children's work and the work that would be created with them.

Some teachers are concerned about what parents will think about having such bare walls at the start of the year. Explain that you are making room for children and waiting for them to come to school to add to the walls. One friend hung signs saying, "Under Construction . . . Kids' Work Coming Soon" on her blank labeled walls to ease the transition.

Sage's labeled walls help him plan ahead for where he will display anchor charts and student work.

A Word About Word Walls

Since the early 1990s, word walls have been a big part of primary classroom literacy instruction. In her classic book *Phonics They Use* (2012), Patricia Cunningham, the inventor of the word wall, defines this as "an area in the classroom where words are displayed—but not just any words—truly important ones. They are systematically organized and a tool designed to promote group learning."

In kindergarten and first grade, I recommend placing a high-frequency word wall in or near your whole-group teaching area where you and your students can access it easily during and beyond instruction. In Sage's room, we used the dry erase board at the front of the room for his word wall. Making a grid with removable blue painter's tape for each letter of the alphabet organized the space for this important teaching tool. We then used alphabet teaching cards (with upper- and lowercase letters and a picture cue) that came with his reading series and that he was required to post in his room to label each space in alphabetical order on the word wall. We placed the letters *A–M* across the top and *N–Z* across the bottom, leaving space in each grid for words (with magnetic tape on back) to be displayed as he taught with them. We mounted the vowels on yellow paper, so they could be easily distinguished from the consonants.

No words were on the wall at the start of the year! Three to five words were added each week as he taught with them. In kindergarten, Sage began with the children's names as he introduced them in whole-group lessons and used them to anchor letter learning to these familiar pieces of print. High-frequency words were added as he taught with them in shared reading and writing.

In second and third grade, it isn't as critical for the words to be front and center in the whole-group area. But you should be sure students can easily see the words and that you make constant reference to them as you teach students how to use them. I often place the word wall in these grades near the writing station, so kids can quickly refer to them as they write. The expectation should be for children to spell these words correctly as they write stories, poems, and information pieces. Again, make a grid on the word wall using tape or drawing lines and put the words in alphabetical order so kids can easily find the word they need. A word wall that is used for teaching can be used as a literacy station, too, in kindergarten–first grade. Kids can read the words together, play high-frequency word games with words on the wall, and locate these words in familiar books.

Digging Deeper

I hope that your mind is now abuzz with ideas about your classroom environment. Take a deep breath and think about where to begin. Don't try to tackle everything at once, or you may get overwhelmed and get nothing accomplished. Here are some possibilities to help you think about your classroom setup:

1. Work with a partner to make a plan for your teaching spaces on paper, as modeled in this chapter. Use paper and sticky notes, and then move furniture. Look at your whole-group teaching area. Is it large enough for your class to sit comfortably? Can you see every inch of space from your small-group area, and do you have everything organized and at your fingertips here to maximize instruction?

2. Examine your classroom library. Is it a focal point for your students? Can they easily choose books for independent reading here? How can you make this space inviting and connected to reading instruction?

3. Make a list of stationary and portable stations, as Sage and I did in Figure 2.1. Plan for space to engage students using every part of the room. Consider countertops, shelves, and even the teacher desk.

4. Make time to look at what you have stored. This will probably require several blocks of time. Again, work with a partner to organize your materials that may be behind closed doors. You may find a new lease on teaching when you know what you've got and can find things quickly and easily. Take before-and-after pictures and inspire each other!

5. Where and how are you storing community supplies for students? Talk with your children about their materials and what they need to access easily. Create a system with kids in mind. Visit one another's rooms to get ideas.

6. Last, but not least, take photos of your walls. Look at each wall with a critical eye, again keeping your students in mind. You might want to label each wall with a subject area and organize anchor charts and teaching resources accordingly for easy student access. Look at your word wall. Is it kid-friendly? Are your students using it effectively? Remove things that may be distracting your students from what you'd like them to pay attention to.

3

Planning for Literacy Work Stations

Organizing your classroom will yield you and your students extra time, because you won't have to search for materials or help kids do things they can take care of themselves. Invest the time you gained in planning, and you'll reap even further benefits. Here are some of the reflections teachers have shared with me about planning:

"Now that my classroom is better organized, I can easily find what I need to teach and it's easier to plan."

"If I planned better, my mini-lessons would stay mini."

"I realize that when I really understand what I'm teaching, my kids understand it better, too. That comes from thoughtful planning."

Reaping the Best Crops: Planning with Standards Before School Begins

A friend who teaches third grade recently reflected with me about the way planning instruction in a simple, focused way has had the biggest effect on her students' work in stations. She continued, "That day we sat together and planned for stations, starting with several of our standards (not the whole year's worth), made all the difference. I prepared for powerful whole-group reading and writing instruction and then charted how I was going to move that same work into literacy stations. The plan we created also helped me know how to keep adding to them gradually. It really gave me a jump start compared with previous years."

We'd met for lunch at my house one day in August before school began, taking along Michelle's state standards and district curriculum documents, conveniently found online. Over a three-hour lunch and lots of iced tea, we used a *six-week standards process* (as described later in this chapter) and mapped out the big ideas for the first six weeks of reading instruction, paying careful attention to comprehension, vocabulary, fluency, and phonics applied to reading and writing of literary and informational texts. Likewise, we thought about the big ideas in writing instruction, including craft, conventions, and procedures. We didn't try to include every standard we could find, but instead focused on several important ones that fit the beginning of the year.

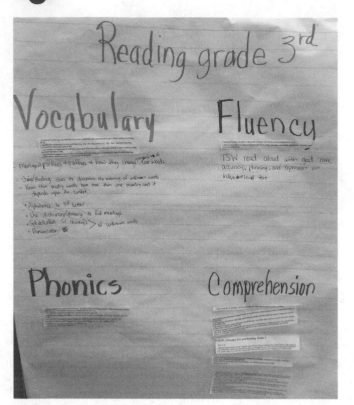

To plan for the first six weeks of school, we printed and then cut apart the Texas Essential Knowledge and Skills (TEKS) standards. Then we pasted them into categories and summarized the big ideas Michelle needed to teach in each area. This gave us a clear picture of where we were headed.

Then we jotted down tried-and-true teaching ideas, best practices, and related literacy work stations connected to these standards using a *team planning tool* (described later in this chapter). As we planned together, we scanned Michelle's district curriculum documents and chose a few basic teaching ideas instead of trying to figure out how to fit them all in. By the time we had finished, this teacher had a clear picture of where she was headed, right from the start, and it made a solid impact on her students and the work they did during independent time all year long. The critical piece was to focus on a few important standards to start the year and think clearly about their relationship and how to best teach them so they made sense to the kids.

A few weeks after our meeting, we began a *literacy work stations journal* to record ideas. We also saved our plans in an online folder to streamline preparation for the following school year and beyond. We included photos of the stations in action, our team planning notes, and work samples, such as "I Can" lists to create a valuable resource that we could reference and tweak for years to come.

Starting with a Few Standards

When I design my garden, I often begin with just a few plants—standard varieties that I can rely on. I don't try to plant every flower I love or my garden will become overwhelming. The same principle applies to planning with your teaching standards. Approach planning calmly and focus on your literacy standards, one chunk at a time. In an age when we are flooded with information, it can be overwhelming to know what to teach, no matter how many years we've been teaching. I find it helpful to have standards at my fingertips *every time* I plan for instruction with teachers, no matter where I go.

According to *Merriam-Webster Learner's Dictionary*, a standard is a level of quality and achievement that is considered desirable or acceptable. There are standards in every industry, for which I am thankful. We welcome standards for vehicles, medicine, food products, building, and even clothing. Imagine a world without them—yikes!

In education, we have entered a new era where standards have become the rule. Today's children live in a world where transiency is common; many of our students move from place to place throughout their school career—from one city to another or from one state to a different one. I've worked with children who have even moved several times within one school year! Standards help students have a more consistent education in environments that sometimes lack constancy. Standards also help teachers know what to focus on while teaching. Standards name what children should be able to do as readers and writers as a result of instruction. They give us goals to strive toward. I welcome standards in education as well as in other areas of life.

In fact, as I wrote this book, I examined standards across the United States and found my own teaching to be changed as a result. As I looked at the Common Core State Standards (CCSS), Texas's TEKS, Virginia's Standards of Learning (SOL), and the Indiana Academic Standards, I dug deeply, searched for patterns, and established what I considered to be "big ideas" for teaching and often "stuff that's really hard to teach." In doing so, my instruction was transformed. I found myself thinking more deeply than I ever have about what I was teaching and what it would look like for students to do those particular tasks.

Producing the Best Fruit: Using Standards to Plan for Depth at Stations

Recently, as I worked with a group of kindergarten and first-grade educators, one teacher said she was having trouble knowing how to make her writing station more engaging for her students. Another teacher replied, "Remember what Debbie showed us at our training last week: look at your standards first. They will help you know what you should be teaching, and then you can have your kids practice exactly what you've been doing in instruction." Bingo! That is the process, as illustrated below, that I've discovered works every time.

At this campus, we looked closely at state standards for K–1 and focused on the three types of writing their students were expected to do—opinions, informative/explanatory texts, and narratives. Next, we noted specific expectations for kindergarten for the type of writing they were teaching (opinions), such as tell a reader the topic or the name of the book they are writing about and state an opinion or preference about the topic or book. Moving to first grade, we saw that we'd also need to teach students to supply a reason for their opinion and provide some sense of closure to their writing.

From there, we planned what we'd need to model in writing opinions, starting with simple book reviews connected to read-alouds. We created a sample book review and discussed a few good read-alouds we might use to teach this. Over time, we'd move this task to the writing station, complete with labeled writing samples that noted what to include when writing an opinion piece and a few familiar books kids might use. (See photos below for samples displayed at this new and improved writing station over time.)

Knowing What to Plant: Using Standards to Plan in a New Grade Level

At another school, I met Dylan, a teacher who had just moved from fourth grade to second grade. He was feeling overwhelmed as the year began. His kids were quite a bit younger than what he was accustomed to, and he wasn't sure where to start. Again, we began with his current grade-level standards and compared them with what he'd done in fourth grade. This gave Dylan something to hold on to as he learned more about second graders throughout the year. The good news is that once he knew what to focus on, he could also think about how to stretch his children's learning to higher levels, since he knew what would be expected of them over time.

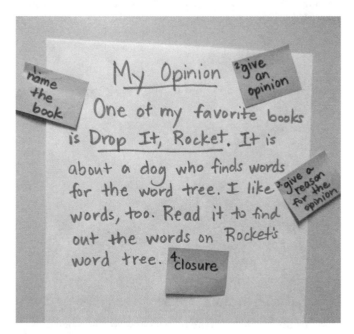

Samples of writing opinions in a kindergarten (*left*) and first grade (*right*) are labeled and posted at the writing station to provide support for young writers there. The connection between standards and the writing children do is clear to the kids and anyone who visits this classroom.

We examined the second-grade reading standard for vocabulary, which was worded as follows: "Use context to determine the relevant meaning of unfamiliar words or multiple meaning words." As we read this together, Dylan said, "That is exactly what my fourth graders needed! Not stopping to figure out what words meant really affected their reading comprehension. I had to teach them to slow down when they came to an unfamiliar word and use clues in the text to figure it out. This especially affected their reading of informational text."

His eyes lighted up as he realized that it was exactly what he needed to teach his second graders, too. The major difference was that Dylan's kids would use second-grade reading materials instead of fourth-grade materials to practice and own the skill. "If my second graders learn how to figure out what new words mean as they read, it will help them a lot by the time they get to fourth grade! I'm actually excited about teaching this now."

We used the same team planning tool that Michelle and I used to plan from there. Figure 3.1 shows the example for Dylan's second grade.

Figure 3.1 Dylan's Team Planning Tool: Vocabulary—Second Grade

Standards We're Teaching	**Second grade:** Use context to determine the relevant meaning of unfamiliar words or multiple meaning words
Academic Vocabulary We'll Use and Expect to Hear	• *unfamiliar word* • *determine the meaning* • *multiple-meaning word* • *clues from the text*
Whole-Group Ideas	• Model how to stop and figure out what a new word means by reading the sentences before and after it, search the picture for clues, try another word that might make sense in the word's place; make an anchor chart with these strategies. • Identify informational text related to science and social studies topics. • Use highlighter tape for marking the new word. • Apply different-colored highlighter tape to mark multiple-meaning words; model how to stop and figure out what the word means; make an anchor chart for multiple-meaning words.
Partner Practice at Literacy Work Stations	**Informational text station:** Kids buddy-read nonfiction and use highlighter tape to mark unfamiliar words as they read here; they record new words, what they think they mean, and clues from the text in a community journal. **Word-study station:** Partners work together to make a page for a multiple-meaning word book using the Frayer model; provide word list from words encountered in class reading from which kids can choose.

Students use highlighter tape to mark new words in books they read together at the informational text station. Then they record the words and their meanings in a community journal used by other members of the class.

This page was made by second graders to represent a word with multiple meanings at a word study station.

Finding Time for Planning

The vignettes that opened this chapter show a variety of ways teachers used to plan for instruction and stations in simple, focused ways rather than looking at stations as "just one more thing." The teachers' planning ahead, one bite at a time, led to high-quality stations that met the needs of their students and promoted the use of academic vocabulary as well as deeper thinking (for both the teachers and ultimately, their students).

By now you may be wondering, *I'd like to do this, but how do you find time to use these planning ideas in an already crowded school day?* Follow the lead of the teachers you've met in this book. Don't try to use every idea immediately. Choose the ones that you feel are doable right now and work with a grade-level team, or plan on your own if you're alone.

I've found that we make time for what we value the most. If I want to have a beautiful, vigorous garden, I need to care for it. I have to plan for time to water, pull weeds, inspect for bugs, and deadhead flowers to generate new blooms. If I don't, my garden will become overgrown, or worse yet, wither and die.

The same thing holds true for stations. If we want students to thrive and grow during partner work at literacy work stations, it's our responsibility to make time to plan for what they will practice in advance. Just putting books, writing supplies, and word study games in stations around the room isn't enough. I recommend that you first think about *what* you want students to practice and *why*, rather than to just set up stations and then think about the activities students might do there.

A teacher with whom I worked recently told me that she and her teammates did just that. They looked at their existing stations and recognized the need to plan better for what students were doing in them. They wanted to add more meat to their stations and knew that thinking about what they were teaching and then moving their ideas to stations would do the trick. So they went to their principal with a specific written plan, noting *what* they wanted to accomplish (adding depth to their stations), *when* (during an extended planning period of two hours with some possible dates/times), and *why* (to increase student achievement and connect to their standards). Ask and it shall be given!

Because they were proactive, organized, and goal oriented (and their principal valued their time and their plan), these teachers accomplished a tremendous amount of planning in a short amount of time. After their planning meeting, they took the time to write their principal a thank-you e-mail and included what they'd accomplished. Then they invited her to visit their classrooms to see evidence of that specific work several weeks later.

Perhaps you've sat through more than one uninspiring early release day or one too many faculty meetings. Be a part of the solution rather than lamenting the lack of time for high-quality planning. Help make a plan to get the most out of professional learning community (PLC) time if your school has this set aside. If you're one of the fortunate few who is given a half day for planning every month, try some of the ideas from this chapter to maximize your time. Or schedule time after school to apply some of these planning ideas every few weeks.

Whatever you do, include clear goals in each planning session. What specifically do you plan to accomplish? Realistically, how long can you focus and get things done? (Work expands to the amount of time you give it!) It's also a good idea to have someone appointed "taskmaster" to keep everyone on track and be sure that your goals are met. Gather all the materials you think you'll need ahead of time and bring your standards to your planning meeting.

Start by looking at just a few important standards, breaking them down, and then deciding how to best teach them. Work together, if possible, and use your standards and the best resources you've got to work smarter, not harder. The rest of this chapter contains tools that you can use to plan for stations to use throughout the school year.

The Gardening Crew: Divide and Conquer to Save Time

When I have a big gardening job to do, I sometimes enlist the help of a gardening crew (or friends and family)! If you have others to plan with, you might want to divide and conquer to save time, like a team of second- and third-grade teachers with whom I worked in Tennessee did. They were feeling overwhelmed by the task of planning, so I asked them to think about their own and others' strengths as planners. From there, we created jobs for each member of the team, which they wrote on sticky notes to wear during our planning meetings:

- Idea generator (collect teaching ideas related to the standard)
- Kiddie lit (gather related children's books for read-aloud)
- Tech expert (find apps and programs related to this standard)
- Graphic organizer guru (locate graphic organizers that will help students think)

- Materials manager (bring things needed for making teaching materials at the next team meeting)
- Data gal (examine data for patterns of what to include in instruction and at stations)
- Poetry lover (bring related poetry to teach with and use at literacy stations)

Tennessee teachers wear sticky notes with their planning job titles, such as *data gal, kiddie lit,* or *tech expert* to divide and conquer the work during team planning for instruction and literacy stations.

Delineating roles made the task of planning seem less daunting and helped focus team members. We tried a similar strategy in an elementary school in Texas. There we worked together to create nameplates to use at a team planning event. Teachers helped one another identify strengths, and each person designed a table sign to remind them of a specific contribution they could make as they planned together. This activity involved everyone and created a spirit of playfulness as well. Their nameplates read as follows:

- Creative/Resources
- Organized/Quality Control
- Reflective/Writer
- Mathematician/Connector to Community and World
- Reading/Visualizer
- Data/Sifter

The principal and teachers have fun as they create nameplates identifying their strengths to use during team planning sessions.

No matter how you approach this task, sharing the workload helps to reduce stress. Some teams do their six-week planning and then meet every two to three weeks to use the *team planning tool*, working from standards to stations to reflect on students' progress and to plan further. In preparation for these meetings, teachers look at the big ideas for six weeks and then bring materials and ideas to the biweekly meetings, focusing on their particular job. This can dramatically reduce the time needed for planning in the group.

For example, one team knew they would be teaching long-vowel patterns. The *kiddie lit* person brought related children's literature that included word play with long vowels. The *text expert* brought several apps to share on her iPad, and the *poetry lover* shared several poems that highlighted vowel teams. The *data gal* examined student data to see which long-vowel patterns children already knew and which they needed more practice with across the grade level to help focus whole-group instruction. The *materials manager* made a list of materials they'd need to make or gather for instruction as they met and planned. Working together made the task of planning more efficient and even enjoyable! There was a spirit of camaraderie and collaboration that was ultimately infused into their classrooms as well.

Using Tools: Six-Week Standards Process

In some school systems, teachers are given a road map of which standards to teach over a block of time, such as a month or six weeks or even nine weeks at a time. In others, teachers are told to cover the standards throughout the year and have to figure out for themselves how to divide and organize the work. And in some, a core reading program adopted by the school system is to be taught week by week.

No matter which of these scenarios you may relate to, I've found that it's wise to look at a chunk of time to plan for the big ideas you want to teach your students, just as Michelle and I did in the opening of this chapter. I like using a *six-week standards process* to do so. Before school starts is a great time to begin using this, too. How many times have you wished you'd leave back-to-school training with an actual plan for instruction to rely on during that first month or so? Here's your ticket!

Although I love using technology in my work and personal life, my favorite way to approach this task is to use old-fashioned chart paper and markers with a team of teachers from a grade level, if possible. There is something powerful about having everyone look at the ideas on one big page and see connections among them. Sometimes as I've worked with a grade-level team, we've used sticky notes; at times we've written out the standards on the chart; other times we've printed out the standards and cut them apart to manipulate

them on the large chart. Whichever way you approach this task, it is wise to do so as a team if you have others at your school who teach the same grade level you do. Two or three or four heads are better than one! Your teaching will be stronger and more consistent across the grade level if you plan together in this way, rather than everyone planning in isolation. (Even if you don't have colleagues who teach the same grade level, you can use these ideas on your own.)

First-grade teachers sorted their reading standards into categories for the first six weeks at a back-to-school campus training in Texas.

You might make one chart for reading instruction, dividing the paper into boxes labeled "comprehension," "phonics," "fluency," and "vocabulary" (and "phonemic awareness" if you teach kindergarten or first grade). Then look at your state standards and sort them into those categories for the six weeks you are approaching. Be sure to write out the words; don't just list the number for the standard. Writing the standard in words will familiarize you with it and may even prompt questions about exactly what it means, which will help to clarify it, too. I've found that rich discussions often occur around the standards (and how to teach them most effectively) when approached this way.

In a summer meeting with kindergarten teachers, we did something similar but with a slight twist. First, we jotted down each literacy state standard for the beginning of the school year on a sticky note and arranged them into the big categories of reading, writing, and word study on a large dry erase board, as pictured in the photos below. Then we moved the sticky notes to a chart for reading with boxes labeled "print awareness," "phonological awareness," "phonics," "comprehension," "fluency," and "vocabulary." The word study–related sticky notes were placed in the "phonics" and "vocabulary" boxes. We also made another chart titled "Writing Standards for the First Six Weeks" and sorted the writing standards into boxes labeled "craft," "conventions," and "procedures."

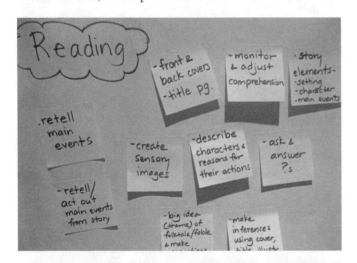

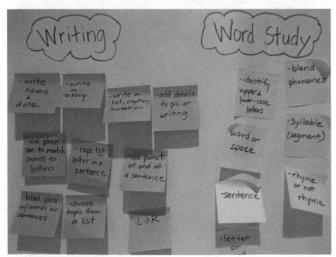

ELA standards are jotted onto sticky notes and then sorted into categories for reading, writing, and word study in kindergarten.

As teachers reflected on the process of working with the six-week standards process, they said things like, "Doing this together made the standards clearer and less overwhelming," "I now know where I'm headed in my teaching for several weeks at a time, not just this Monday through Friday," and "It will be easier to focus my teaching and plan for appropriate literacy work stations."

Looking at the standards for a six-week (or four- or nine-week) period in this manner helped teachers visualize in their minds the short- and long-term instructional path. Instead of just reading through curriculum road maps or pacing guides a week at a time, this exercise of "beginning with the end in mind" created a clear picture of the instructional goals for the month or semester. This then allowed teachers to make connections among standards and better plan for independent learning over time. At this point, they were better able to use curriculum guides and other resources from their school system.

To return to the gardening analogy, this planning is much like glancing through gardening magazines to get a picture of what you want your garden to look like in summertime bloom. You plan ahead, ordering seeds from catalogs or searching plant nurseries to get the annuals or perennials you need to create that look. Your resulting garden is much more pleasing than if you'd just grabbed random plants at the local hardware store and stuck them into the ground.

Using Tools: Team Planning Tool from Standards to Stations

You've already seen an example of this planning tool earlier in this chapter and it will be repeated many times in Chapters 5–9. Let's take a step-by-step look at how to work with it. Even if you don't have a team to plan with, you can use this by yourself. (See Figure 3.2.)

Figure 3.2 Sample Team Planning Tool for Reading: Informational Text—First Grade

Standards We're Teaching	**First grade:** Describe the connections between two individuals, events, ideas, or pieces of information in a text.
Academic Vocabulary We'll Use and Expect to Hear	• *connections* • *connected* • *linked* • *individuals* • *events* • *ideas* • *information*
Whole-Group Ideas	• Read and think aloud from *The Life Cycle of a Frog,* modeling how to find connections between two people, events, ideas, or pieces of information in a variety of informational texts. • Show graphic organizer for charting connections between two individuals, events, ideas, or pieces of information. • Use paper strips with events, people, or information on them linked to show connections.
Partner Practice at Literacy Work Stations	**Classroom library station:** Read informational text and then discuss connections between people, events, ideas, or pieces of information using examples from the text and a graphic organizer. **Buddy-reading station:** Read together and place a sticky note where you see ideas, people, or information connect. **Listening station:** Listen and follow along in the book; use a graphic organizer to explain how ideas, people, or information are connected. **Science or social studies station:** Read and discuss ideas, events, and information that is connected in the book. Jot each idea on a paper link and connect them; then use them to explain the connections.

Step One: Begin by copying the grade-level standard you'll be teaching in the first section of the team planning tool, and launch your instructional plans from there. Write out the entire standard to become familiar with it over time. It's important to pay close attention to the wording of the standards, especially if you have changed grade levels or taught one grade for any length of time, or your standards have recently changed. We are often inclined to teach what we've always taught, because we are creatures of habit. For example, in the past we may have been satisfied if first graders could make a text-to-self connection between something they read and an experience they've had. This is certainly a place to begin, but today's standards go way beyond that. For example, in the Common Core State Standards, first graders are expected to describe the connections between two individuals, events, ideas, or pieces of information in a single text.

Step Two: Next, think about academic vocabulary you'd like to hear students use over time. When we write down these specific words and phrases in the second section of the team planning tool, there is a greater likelihood that we'll include them in our teaching and that children will use them independently over time. These words may be included on anchor charts (as described in Chapter 4) and/or conversation cards created for use in whole group first, and then eventually moved to specific literacy stations. You may want to make conversation cards on 4-by-6-inch index cards with speech bubbles drawn on them, being flexible to adjust the language slightly to match your students' natural language patterns once they are using them. See the photo on the next page for sample conversation cards to use at a first-grade station related to making connections while reading informational text. Use a different-colored ink to write academic vocabulary on the cards to help students pay close attention to these special words. Remind kids to use them for talking about what they are learning. The goal is to have children use the cards while speaking, not to write on the cards.

Conversation cards remind kids to think about connections authors make in informational text. Use the cards in whole group and move them to stations, over time, for independent use by pairs of students.

Step Three: From here, move to the third section of the team planning tool, where you'll jot down specific ideas for whole-group instruction, including materials and texts to be used as you think about them. Use ideas from district curriculum documents and/or core program resources (if you have them) that match your standards, keeping in mind that whole-group instruction should be based on your grade-level standards but with more complex texts than those your students can read independently. Exposing all children to rich examples of literary and informational text in whole-group lessons gives them opportunities to deepen their thinking and learn more advanced vocabulary than they may on their own. (Suggestions for children's literature or *mentor texts* to use in whole-group mini-lessons are included in Chapters 5–9.) Plan for strong modeling during whole-group instruction to build a foundation for what you ultimately want students to practice at literacy work stations with partners.

Think about what your expectations are for students as they work with this standard. Ask yourself, for example, "How will a first grader make connections among ideas while reading informational text?" If we want students to read science texts thoughtfully, to be on the lookout for connections the author makes, it will be important to choose texts that contain several examples of that and to use those texts in shared reading with the class. Model ways of thinking about how an author connects ideas through pictures, diagrams, boldface words, and other nonfiction text features, as well as the words of the text. After much modeling in whole-class instruction, our expectation will be for first graders to have conversations with a partner about connections among ideas in informational text. Using the conversation card you've modeled with during whole group can provide support.

Over time, you might hear something like this snippet using conversation cards, which took place at the science station while two children partner-read a section of the book *The Life Cycle of a Frog*, an informational book the teacher modeled with during whole group:

> *"The author connected the frog eggs in this picture with the penguin eggs in this picture. These animals start as eggs before they grow up."*

> *"This picture is the same as the one on this page. The author connected them. Oh, the egg is going to turn into a tadpole. It's the same here and here."*

> *"I see a connection. The eggs are in the water. And the tadpole hatches in the water. This makes me think that the frog needs water to live."*

In section three of the planning tool, you can also write names of texts you might use for modeling as well as any graphic organizers you might have students use related to the standard. Because we were working with informational text in this example, we decided to use books related to the science and social studies topics students were studying in first grade. Teachers would also teach with a simple graphic organizer that had boxes with arrows connecting ideas, events, or people for kids to jot notes and help them remember connections an author made. List any activities that might help students develop conceptual understanding of this standard, too.

This graphic organizer, which helped students connect ideas, events, and people, was used in whole group and eventually at a listening station.

Step Four: Now it's time to list work stations where students can eventually practice using this standard with a partner while they read, write, listen, speak, or work with letters and/or words. Remember that students might practice with this standard at several stations. I often find it easiest to name a particular station and then draw arrows from section three to section four to show how materials and activities can be moved directly to a station for practice over time.

Alternatively, you could simply jot down what students will do at each station where this standard might be applied. For example, for the science station, it could say, "Read about owls and use conversation cards to describe connections between two events or ideas; use graphic organizer to record their thinking about these connections." For the buddy-reading station, it might say, "Read informational text from small group with a partner and highlight connections between ideas, events, and individuals, using a graphic organizer." The listening station could say, "Listen to informational text about topics being studied in science (life cycle of frogs) or social studies (types of homes) and discuss connections using conversation cards." You might hear students saying things such as, "The author connected huts and igloos. They're both kinds of homes, and that's what this book is about." Or "I see a connection between the frog's legs on this page and this one. This makes me think that the frog's legs are really important. The frog eats with its legs. Ooh!"

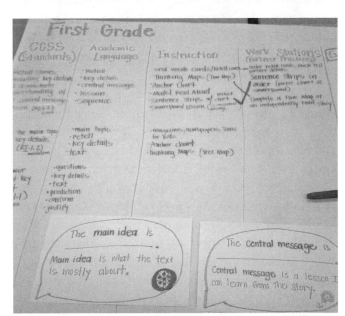

Two examples of first-grade planning using the team planning tool from standards to stations

Additional completed samples of the team planning tool can be found throughout this book, especially in Chapters 5-9. I hope they will provide you with inspiration for planning instruction that connects standards to stations.

Using Tools: Daily Lesson Plan Template

Planning for big ideas as a team (if you have one) makes sense and can streamline what we do as a grade level. But what about daily lesson plans? I've found that they are best designed by you, the individual teacher, for your own classroom.

Often teams try to divide and conquer by having one teacher write all the reading plans, another teacher write the math plans, and so on. However, I've observed in many, many classrooms at schools where the task of planning has been parceled out, and I can readily spot the teacher who wrote the original plans. Although I understand that this type of planning is done to save time, it sometimes results in fuzzy lessons that actually take longer to teach and may not meet the needs of your students.

If you plan as a team for how you will teach in a general way using the team planning tool, moving from standards to stations, you can then take those ideas and translate them into your own plans, using a daily lesson plan template to save time. I think it's important to plan as a team to ensure that *what* you teach is the same, although *how* you teach it can vary from classroom to classroom.

I recommend writing your own plans for whole group for one week at a time, paying particular attention to the *focus*, which should be tied to the standards you are teaching. In contrast, I write plans for small group one day at a time and keep them in a small-group planning notebook at the guided-reading table, as described in my book *Making the Most of Small Groups* (2007). I find it is helpful to plan for small group on an as-needed basis, because differentiation is most easily accomplished by planning for what just a few students need at a time, and those needs can change readily.

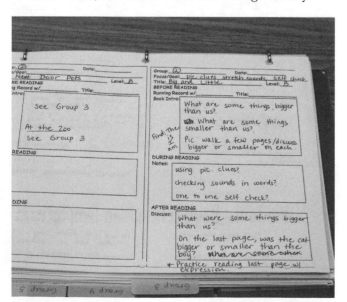

An example of Kindergarten guided-reading plans kept in a notebook at the small-group teaching table for easy reference. The teacher writes plans daily for the new groups she'll work with the following day.

Using Tools: Literacy Work Stations Observation Notes

Throughout the year, it's a good idea to observe students at work at literacy stations every few weeks to be sure that what they're doing is vigorous and is helping them grow as readers, writers, and thinkers. It's tempting to always work with small groups during stations time, but I've found that it's important to also tend those stations to be sure they're yielding the growth you desire.

I like to record observations at stations to help me remember what I've seen, so that I can use the information to continue to plan high-quality instruction and practice. You might do this alone, but if you can arrange with your administrator for coverage, try what we did as a team in the following scenario:

In the fall, I worked with a group of first-grade teachers who told me, "We're ready to add more power to our stations. We want more ideas of what our kids can do on their own there." I wanted to help teachers build on what they were already doing and the resources they had in their rooms, so the principal provided coverage in each classroom for about an hour so all four first-grade teachers could walk together as a grade-level team to observe the children at stations. We allotted about ten to fifteen minutes per classroom while students were at stations for these observations.

Each teacher went to her room a few minutes before we entered to be sure kids were settled at stations, and then we observed in that room. We visited each class together, watched students working at their literacy stations, and took notes in sections labeled *reading, writing, listening, speaking,* and *working with words* to guide our thinking.

That morning as we walked together from room to room, we watched pairs of children stamping spelling words, playing computer games, and sorting words by short-vowel patterns on an interactive whiteboard. There were students writing about a pumpkin at a writing station, listening to recorded books at a listening station, and making words with magnetic letters on the side of a file cabinet at a word-study station.

"I know this station needs help," Amber told us as she pointed to a basket in her room filled with copies of a cut-and-color worksheet. "I put it here to go with the season, but I know there's something better for my kids to do," she continued with raised brows and a wrinkled nose. "As I look at the observation form, there's nowhere for me to jot this one down because it has nothing to do with literacy!"

"My kids like reading the Big Books I've taught with, but what else can they do here?" Robyn asked as we watched two first graders read a familiar Big Book together in her room. She noted that the children were reading the text successfully but that she wanted them to go deeper with their work.

After returning to our meeting room to debrief, we contemplated what we'd seen and used our notes and questions to probe more deeply. Routines were in place in these classrooms. Children were behaving and knew what was expected of them. There was a strong structure for stations, but we knew kids could do more. They were working on the surface, and we wanted to see them go deeper. We wanted the work that partners were doing at stations to provide genuine practice of what was being taught in whole group and not just busywork. Our next step was to plan for the work that children could do at stations, using the structure that was already in place and the standards teachers were teaching.

We began with Robyn's notes on the Big Book station. Her question led us to look at what she'd been teaching the children to do as readers and writers in whole group. As we reflected on whole-group instruction for phonics, Robyn realized that her children could search for words with patterns they'd been studying, such as long vowels or consonant blends. Pairs could also work together to examine authors' word choices in the Big Books, since word choice was a focus during writing workshop.

As a result of our thinking about instruction, we planned for teaching tools Robyn would use in whole group and then move to the Big Book station. She'd make two magnifying glasses from a die cut, with one labeled "spelling patterns" and the other "word choice." Children could choose a lens for closer examination of the Big Book after reading it, and highlight and discuss words. They would also use a conversation card made from a 4-by-6-inch index card with a sentence frame saying, "I spy the spelling pattern _____ in the word _____. If I can spell _____, I can spell _____." Another conversation card would say, "I think the author chose the word _____ here because _____." This thinking would

take the reading that children did at the Big Book station to a much deeper level that could then be applied to their writing as well.

New tools used in whole group and then at the Big Book station

Next, we looked at Amber's dilemma of the cut-and-paste activity that was truly not a meaningful literacy activity. Again, we focused on what she'd been teaching her students to do in whole-group reading and writing instruction, and we looked at the needs of her class. "I realize that as I look at my data, I have a lot of students who need to work on fluency," said Amber. "Many of my kids read word by word, and they need to move to fluent, phrased reading." Her teammates chimed in that they recognized a similar need.

I'd noticed that only one of the teachers had a listening station in her room. Listening stations can be used for models of fluent reading; they can also be used as recording studios where children record themselves and then listen to their reading and self-evaluate their fluency using a rubric.

The teachers told me that they didn't have listening stations because they had no recorded books or even a CD player or tape recorder. So we looked at what they *did* have—a few computers, an interactive whiteboard, and a document camera in each classroom. Both the school and their local public library had some recorded books they could borrow. They decided to keep their eyes open for CD players at garage sales; one teacher realized she had two old ones in her kids' closet at home that she could bring to school.

I told them about the question I'd sent out on my Facebook for Educators page asking how folks used technology to record books. I looked up the post dated October 6, 2013, and shared those recording ideas. As a result, the first-grade teachers I was meeting with decided to investigate recording options using GarageBand, Evernote, or Audacity on their classroom computers. They would also look for Franklin pens, which have a recording feature, or iPod Shuffles that could easily be used by young students. In addition, the teachers would be sure to model how to read fluently in phrases during shared reading of Big Books and poems in whole-group instruction.

Listening stations take a variety of forms in primary classrooms. They can be used for listening and responding to develop reading comprehension (*top*) or for recording and playing back for fluency practice (*bottom*).

Using Tools: Literacy Work Stations Journal and Online Files

Use what you've got! is a reminder I often give teachers (and myself) when we work together. Sometimes we have so much stuff that we forget what we already have and end up reinventing the wheel. To prevent this from happening, I recommend using tools to help you think about what's worked well at literacy stations. Just like some gardeners keep a special journal of what they've planted and when, you might also want to create a literacy stations journal—a place for jotting down things you noticed that worked well, ideas and brainstorms, and lists of what you want to add or change. Choose a little notebook or journal with a cover you love, and you might be more likely to use it! (See a sample of mine in the photo below.)

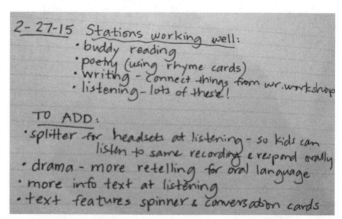

I keep a literacy stations journal to reflect upon what's working well during partner practice in a classroom I'm working in regularly. I found an attractive notebook that I want to write in (*top*). See my sample notes from a recent visit to this classroom (*bottom*). I keep photo files on my computer with the month, the year, and the station name.

You might also keep literacy work stations folders on your computer or tablet. Periodically, take photos of kids at stations that are working really well. You might organize your photos by station name or keep monthly files. You could also take photos of any team planning charts you make. If you keep track of your planning and what you actually used at literacy work stations this year, you can use that information as a starting point for next year (and save time in the process). Some teachers even film their kids at stations and show it to the next year's parents (and kids) to inform them about what to expect during independent time.

Regardless of the tools you use for keeping track of things that work well with stations this year, it's a good idea to have some kind of system to help you remember what's been successful to help you in the coming months. Find something that's easy to keep up with and works for you!

Digging Deeper

Now that you've read about many options and tools for planning for literacy work stations, try putting some of the ideas into practice. Start with just one or two. If you're using this book as part of a book study, here are some questions to use for discussion:

1. Examine how you've been planning for literacy work stations. Where do you get your ideas? What might you use from this chapter to help you plan for instruction and/or literacy work stations? Remember to start small.

2. What is your biggest challenge in planning? How can you overcome this obstacle?

3. Which of the planning tools from this chapter will you try first? Choose one and work with a colleague or two to put it to work. Plan to meet as a grade-level team (if you have one) and share what you've tried and how it's worked for you. Bring samples to share. Reflect on how more depth has been added to selected stations.

4. What can you try if there's no one else on your grade level to plan with? Share with a colleague on another grade level.

5. Download the free standards app for your state from www.masteryconnect.com and use it on your smartphone or tablet in all planning meetings. Or print your state standards to have at your fingertips. How will you use standards for planning for literacy stations?

6. What are your strengths in teaching? What are your interests? Use these to help your team with planning. You might use the divide-and-conquer ideas from this chapter to make planning for stations easier.

4

Teaching with Anchor Charts from Whole Group to Stations

"Last year I fell in love with anchor charts," a second-grade teacher told me. "I'd always wanted to teach with them but was a bit overwhelmed figuring out how to make them and where to put them. In the past, I'd bought charts from teacher supply stores and dabbled in making a few of my own, but they often ended up being kind of messy, and I was embarrassed to hang them up."

She continued, "I never admitted this to you, but when we first met and you kept talking about anchor charts, I wasn't quite sure what they were. But when you demonstrated how to plan for them and then make them with my class, it gave me the tools and confidence I needed to use them successfully. Also, at the beginning of the year, when we started with blank walls and labeled them by content area, it created the space I needed to display the charts our class made together during mini-lessons." When we set up her classroom, we made large labels—for reading, writing, math, science, and social studies—and hung them on specific areas on her walls and cabinets to designate the places she'd hang anchor charts throughout the year.

Listening to this teacher reflect, I became freshly aware of the angst that can accompany anchor charts.

So many questions surround the use of these amazing visual teaching tools: "How do I make them?" "Where do I put them all?" "Should I make them ahead of time or in front of my class?" "How do I get my students to use the anchor charts?" "How do anchor charts connect to literacy work stations?" In this chapter, you'll find the answers you've been looking for and the encouragement you need to create charts that you and your students will love.

What Is an Anchor Chart?

Teachers have been making and using charts with students for many years. In fact, a vintage teaching poster used in a German university to teach biology in the early 1900s hangs above my fireplace! Guess what's on it? A plant, of course—the pictorial life cycle of a horsetail fern. More recently, anchor charts were made popular by Debbie Miller in *Reading with Meaning* (2012). In the first edition of this book, published in 2002, we viewed colorful, meaningful charts made with students in a first-grade class. Miller explains that anchor charts do the following:

- Make thinking permanent and visible
- Allow connections from one strategy to another
- Clarify a point
- Build on earlier learning
- Help students remember a specific lesson simply

In a subsequent book, *Teaching with Intention* (2008), Miller adds that an anchor chart

- focuses on one key idea,
- is co-constructed with students, and
- is readable and clearly organized; that is, kids can read the words and understand the ideas.

In my own work since 1995, I've seen charts of all sizes, shapes, and configurations hanging across classrooms in North America. As I've thought deeply about anchor charts and consulted multiple dictionaries about the meanings of the words *anchor* and *chart*, I've created the following definition:

> An *anchor chart* is a visual display (using wise design) that shows information in a way that is easy for children to understand and reference. It is created with and used by students as a support for learning things that are difficult to remember, incorporating academic vocabulary. To be most effective, an anchor chart is planned ahead and connected to learning goals, standards, and big ideas. It is made during whole-group mini-lessons that anchor the students' learning to help them remember concepts, procedures, and strategies.

Figure 4.1 shows at a glance some of the most important features of high-quality anchor charts. Some interesting questions I've been asked by educators are "Are all charts anchor charts? What about graphic organizers? How about commercially produced charts? Are those anchor charts?" I think that some graphic organizers can function as anchor charts if they're focused on one big idea, contain academic vocabulary, and have strong visuals to help students remember the concept being taught. Sometimes, I integrate a graphic organizer into the anchor chart, as in the top right photo.

Commercially produced charts are often too busy, have too much information on them, and frankly, just become wallpaper. But even anchor charts you make

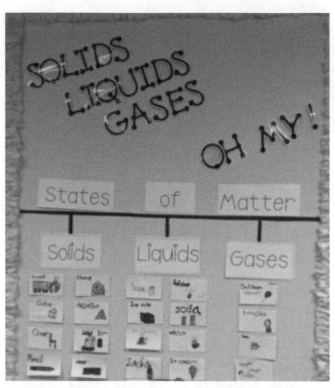

Note the use of a graphic organizer, the tree map, integrated into this science anchor chart on states of matter made with third graders.

with your class can end up being too busy or wordy. If you find that an anchor chart you've made didn't turn out the best, you can always cut it apart and create a better chart, as shown in the photos below.

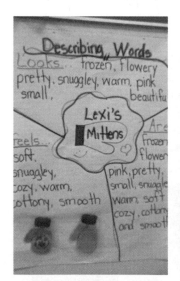

BEFORE (*left*): This kindergarten anchor chart about describing words had a category that didn't belong (the "Are" category). The chart was hanging in a place where kids couldn't easily access it.

AFTER (*right*): Now the describing-words chart focuses on how things *look* and *feel* with visuals added and clearer examples. We moved the chart to kids' eye level near a countertop and created an observation station. Students can look at and touch objects (such as the pineapple) and write describing words.

Figure 4.1 **What Makes a High-Quality Anchor Chart?**

Anchor Chart Elements	Purpose of This Element	Teaching Tips
Title	• Helps students think about the big idea • Makes it easy to find when you need this reference	• Keep it simple. Use bold print and underline or frame the title.
Focus on one big idea	• Helps students remember key points related to one important concept or standard	• Consult your standards and be clear on what is most important before making the chart with your class.
Made *with* your class	• To create ownership of the ideas and the anchor chart (which will become a visual reference tool)	• Plan ahead to save time and focus on the most important points and academic vocabulary.
Language is concise, mirrors the standard, and kid-friendly	• To help kids access information quickly and easily • Student ownership encourages kids to apply the information	• Include academic vocabulary on the chart (see Chapters 5–9 for suggestions). • Ask the class, "Is this how you want to say it?" (but integrate academic vocabulary, too). • If a child uses nonstandard English, restate the idea using standard grammatical structures as a model but keep the meaning of the child's words intact.
Uses color	• Is visually appealing • Makes key ideas stand out	• Repetition of colors can unify the big ideas on the chart. • Use just a few colors that coordinate. • Limit use of red, orange, pink, yellow, and green print, which are hard to read from a distance.
Has visuals/pictures for support	• The brain remembers in pictures more than in words. • Visuals should support specific words and/or the big idea represented on the chart, and be memorable for your kids.	• Simple pictures help English learners and students with special needs access information. • You might have students help sketch supporting visuals, especially in second grade and up.
Moves kids to independence and is used by them as a resource	• This chart is for kids to use on their own over time. • Our goal is for students to access and use the chart to solve problems independently.	• Display and store anchor charts and mini–anchor charts where they are easily accessible to kids. • Refer to these charts (point to them) as you teach, and encourage students to do the same.
Has a border	• The brain loves borders. • Borders "hold in" the information and help the brain pay attention to the ideas within.	• Use a color that coordinates with those used on the chart. • Keep the border simple, so it doesn't interfere with the information.

Remember that anchor charts are made *with* students to help them remember concepts, procedures, and strategies you're teaching. Ownership by your students leads to increased engagement and independence, as demonstrated in the following classroom example.

Planning for and Making Anchor Charts in Whole Group

As you read this section, please refer to Figure 4.2, "Making the Most of Anchor Charts," to maximize every

Figure 4.2 **Making the Most of Anchor Charts**

BEFORE the lesson:

1. **PRIME:** Prime your students by exposing them to the topic for which you will be making an anchor chart. (Include real-world examples and relevant experiences. You might use picture or digital books, online articles, video clips, or hands-on activities.)
2. **PLAN ON PAPER:** Think about the important elements, including academic vocabulary, you want to include on this chart ahead of time. (Making a sketch of the chart on plain white 8½-by-11-inch paper may be helpful, especially if you've never made an anchor chart on this topic before.)
3. **PREMAKE PARTS:** Consider making parts of the chart (such as the border, a title, or part of a picture) beforehand to save time during the mini-lesson, but be sure to include your students in the creation of the anchor chart itself.
4. **PREP MATERIALS:** Have all your materials handy before the lesson, so you don't waste time looking for a marker that works or a glue stick to affix something to your chart.

DURING the lesson:

1. **TAP INTO BACKGROUND KNOWLEDGE:** Have your students participate by sharing what they know related to the topic of the anchor chart. Relate to prior experiences with this concept by using a familiar picture book, online article, a photo, or something that will help them remember. In doing this, you tap into prior knowledge and help kids connect what they already know to the new concept represented on the anchor chart.
2. **TITLE:** Have the class read the title of the anchor chart together, or ask them to help you think of a good title. Incorporate academic vocabulary that you want students to use and remember. Underline the title or put a bubble around it, so it stands out.
3. **BIG IDEAS:** Use different-colored markers as you talk with your class and jot down the important ideas you'd planned to include. Solicit student ideas. (Be flexible, because kids might come up with something you hadn't thought of ahead of time.) Limit the number of words on the chart, so that it is easy to read. And be sure to add visual supports, such as simple pictures, photos, or diagrams to make the big ideas as clear as possible to your students.
4. **TOUCH THE CHART:** As you make the chart, touch the visual elements you want kids to remember; point to important parts repeatedly as you speak about those ideas. Involve kids in helping to make the chart by gluing on a picture, underlining a special word, or adding a simple illustration. The more involved they are, the more memorable the chart will be to them.
5. **REREAD:** As you make the chart together, continually reread the title and academic vocabulary on the chart to reinforce it. Invite children to use these words, too.
6. **MONITOR AND ADJUST:** Be sensitive to time. Watch your children carefully as you create the anchor chart together. Keep the lesson moving, and don't get hung up on making everything picture-perfect. Having a plan will help the finished chart be visually appealing. You'll get more fluent as you create charts with your kids. Remember that you don't have to finish every anchor chart in one sitting. You can add to the anchor chart across multiple mini-lessons.

AFTER the lesson:

1. **DISPLAY:** Display the chart in or near the whole-group teaching area in a prominent place close to eye level, so you and your class can easily access it for several days after creating it. Then move the anchor chart to a wall labeled with its corresponding content area, such as *reading, writing,* or *science.* This will help you plan thoughtfully for space and help your students easily locate the chart they are looking for.
2. **REFER:** Be sure to refer to the chart multiple times across lessons about the concept visually represented by the anchor chart. Touch the chart as you talk about it, and include opportunities for your kids to do so, too.
3. **RECYCLE:** Incorporate opportunities for students to use the anchor chart in varied ways. Make related conversation cards using the same language and examples that are represented on the anchor chart. Over time, move some charts to your small-group teaching area, so kids can reference them there. You might take a photo of an anchor chart, print it on 8½-by-11-inch paper, and place it in a clear plastic sleeve in a three-ring binder for use in small group. Also consider placing an anchor chart (or a smaller version that I call a mini–anchor chart) at selected literacy work stations. To make a mini–anchor chart, simply take a digital photo of a chart and then reduce its size (4 by 6 inches or 5 by 8 inches), and print it on a card to place at a station for reference. You could place it in a photo sleeve for protection. The more available you make the charts, the more students will use them.

step of the way while creating and teaching with anchor charts in your classroom. This figure is divided into sections for what to do *before*, *during*, and *after* your lessons that incorporate anchor charts; those sections correspond with the sample poetry anchor chart lessons below.

Before the Lesson

It's January, and I'm working in Tracy's first-grade classroom in Houston, Texas. She has twenty-seven students who speak a total of five languages and whose reading levels range from kindergarten to third grade. Using the process described in Chapter 3, Tracy and I began with her standards, as well as the needs of her children, to plan for today's mini-lesson in reading workshop. According to Tracy's district curriculum map, she is slated to be teaching poetry. Specifically, students are expected to respond to rhythm, rhyme, and alliteration in poems in first grade. They are also expected to write short poems that convey sensory details.

Using the team planning tool as described in the previous chapter and pictured in Figure 4.3, Tracy and

I have mapped out what we will teach in whole group and eventually move to stations. As part of our discussion, we've examined the academic vocabulary her first graders will need to learn. *Rhythm*, *regular beats*, *alliteration*, *rhymes*, *repetition*, and *sensory details* are words that we have highlighted.

Because this vocabulary doesn't typically occur naturally in young children's conversations about poems, we plan to teach these words and use them often. We'll strive to have the *kids* use the words as well! Creating anchor charts as a visual reference will help cement children's learning of these terms and contribute to students' better understanding poetry and how it works. Furthermore, we plan for conversation cards, as described in Chapter 3, to support children in using academic vocabulary during whole group and eventually in literacy work stations.

Once again, we discover that as we plan together, focusing on anchor charts this time, it clarifies our thinking and gives us a deeper understanding of what we're teaching and how to teach it. In fact, as we discuss the standards and discover how much there is to teach, we realize we'll have to focus on poetry beyond the two weeks prescribed by the district; we'll

Figure 4.3 **Team Planning Tool for Poetry Standards for Tracy's First Grade**

Standards We're Teaching	Students are expected to respond to and use rhythm, rhyme, and alliteration in poetry; and to write short poems that convey sensory details.
Academic Vocabulary We'll Use and Expect to Hear	• *rhythm* • *rhyme* • *repetition* • *alliteration* • *poem/poetry* • *sensory details* • *visual image*
Whole-Group Ideas	• Make three anchor charts for poetry: one on what a poem looks like; one for what a poem sounds like, including elements of rhythm, rhyme, repetition, and alliteration; and another for sensory details. • Conduct shared reading of poems on charts that include these poetry elements. • Use highlighter tape and a variety of different-colored tape flags to mark poetry elements. • Use conversation cards for poetry. • Use short poems as mentor texts in writing. • Model how to write short poems using sensory details.
Partner Practice at Literacy Work Stations	**Poetry station:** Read and respond to poetry elements using mini-anchor chart and conversation cards and a variety of colored tape flags **Pocket-chart station:** Put poems in order line by line, and use highlighter tape to respond to poetry elements. **Writing station:** Write short poems that convey sensory details (include mini-anchor charts for poetry). **Buddy-reading station:** Choose between poems or stories; recognize which texts are poems and then work with poetry elements (find rhyming words, tap the rhythm, and so on) on those texts.

definitely plan to continue this work throughout the school year. The subsequent practice children will get at literacy work stations will provide review over time with poetry and deepen students' roots of understanding about this genre.

We decide to make three different poetry anchor charts because poetry is fairly new for Tracy's first graders. We'll build from what a poem looks like in the first anchor chart (its structure) to how a poem sounds (the language of poetry) in the second one. On the third chart, we'll focus on sensory details in poetry, since Tracy's students need to include those when they eventually write their own poems.

Yesterday, we created the first poetry anchor chart with the children. They enjoyed helping us think about how poetry looks as we wrote the lyrics to "I'm a Little Teapot" on the chart in front of them and had them tell what made it look like a poem.

Anchor chart 1 for poetry in Tracy's room shows "What Poetry Looks Like."

Today's lesson will focus on what a poem sounds like, and we'll introduce the academic vocabulary word *rhyme*. In the morning before the children arrive, I help Tracy plan a sample anchor chart with a simple pencil sketch on plain white 8½-by-11-inch paper. Doing this ahead of time will save time later while teaching the lesson and keep students' attention focused. It also gives us a chance to play with design elements and

then add color. If we can make the information on the anchor chart pop with color, it is more likely that kids will pay attention to these elements and thus, learn the concept more expediently. Also, by having a plan in front of us, we can create the anchor chart with the students quickly and keep them engaged in the lesson. We decide to use the poem "Fuzzy Wuzzy, Creepy Crawly" by Lilian Schulz Vanada (1986) and place a copy of it in the middle of the new anchor chart. This poem contains the elements of rhythm, rhyme, repetition, and alliteration, and the children will love it.

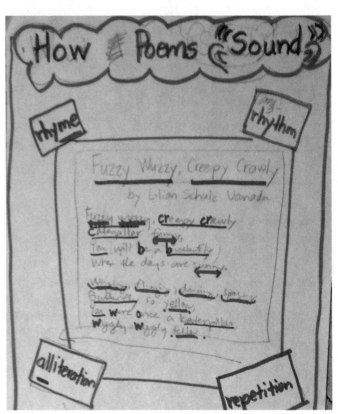

Our plan for the anchor chart on how a poem sounds is done in pencil first on 8½-by-11-inch white paper and then traced in color to play with visual design. This will save time when making the chart with students.

Also before teaching the lesson, I place some plain white index cards, a glue stick, and a box of colored markers in the whole-group area. We write the academic vocabulary words *rhyme, rhythm, repetition,* and *alliteration* using different colors on individual cards to be used during the next couple of lessons. We'll have kids help glue these to the chart as we teach about each element. I print a small picture of clapping hands found on Google Images to use on the chart to represent *rhythm* when we get to that (because that would be hard for me to draw).

During the Lesson

I begin the fifteen- to twenty-minute poetry mini-lesson by gathering the students on the carpet in front of a large easel. Yesterday's poetry anchor chart is displayed beside me, and we read it to quickly review what we learned about how poems *look*. Then I direct the children's attention to the new, partially made anchor chart displayed on the easel, and tell them that today we'll learn how poems *sound*. Together, we create a title for the new chart: "How Poems Sound."

The children's interest is piqued as I show them the new poem we'll work with today. One child says, "It looks like a poem!" Another adds, "It has lots of spaces like 'I'm a Little Teapot.'" Tracy and I are delighted that the children are already noticing what makes this a poem. I refer to yesterday's chart and today's, pointing out the spaces in both poems. We read the new poem together just to enjoy it and hear its sounds. Then I ask the class what they notice about how the new poem sounds.

Immediately, some children notice that a few of the words rhyme. I tell them that some words in this poem do rhyme but that not all poems have rhyming words. On an index card, I write the word *rhyme* in thick red marker and draw a red bubble around it. We talk about how rhyming words sound the same at the end of the word, and we repeat the words *fuzzy* and *wuzzy* from the rhyme on the chart.

Then I ask them for two rhyming words that I can draw a picture of on the index card that says *rhyme*. They choose *pan* and *man* (probably because the *-an* chunk is one they know well and because they've recently fallen in love with "The Gingerbread Man" story), and I write both words below *rhyme*, using black marker for the *p* and the *m* and red for the *-an* chunk, so they'll focus on the ending part being the rhyming chunk. I sketch a picture of a pan and a man, too, to help those students who read below the first-grade level and/or need help with rhyming. These drawings and the use of color will help all children in the class use this chart successfully. Attention to small details matters when making teaching tools children will ultimately use on their own. I ask a child to place this index card on the left-hand side of the anchor chart with a bit of glue (that I've applied to the back of the card).

Then I have another student come up to the chart and point to the rhyming words in the poem while the others say the words in their heads. As the class reads the rhyming words one more time, we underline the words *fuzzy* and *wuzzy*, and then *funny* and *sunny*, and so on, in red since the word *rhyme* is also in red on the anchor chart. We talk about how poets sometimes use rhyming words to create a visual image. We decide that in this rhyme, it's kind of *funny* that the caterpillar hasn't become a butterfly yet. It will be at a later time when the days are *sunny*. We discuss what we see in our minds with the rhyming words chosen by the poet, and one child remarks, "*Yellow* and *fellow* rhyme, too. I think the poet wants us to see a yellow butterfly." Then we talk about the word *fellow*. I tell them that a *fellow* is usually a man or a boy but can also be someone you have something in common with. In this poem, the caterpillar and butterfly have something in common—the caterpillar became a butterfly. "The *yellow* butterfly used to be a caterpillar, a wiggly *fellow*," I say with emphasis on the rhyming words as I point to them on the chart.

Then we read the poem one more time and listen for additional rhyming words. They hear *winging*, *springing*, and *flinging*. The *-ing* chunk is another familiar one, and I connect this to a phonics anchor chart with this phonics pattern that hangs on the classroom wall labeled "Reading." A child underlines these rhyming words in red, too. Once more, I point to the word *rhyme* on our chart and remind the class that poets often use rhyme in poems, but not always. I'll be sure to share nonrhyming poems with them in upcoming lessons, too.

To wrap up today's poetry lesson, we review that we read a poem and learned about *rhyme*, which we'll often hear in a poem. Over the next few days, we'll add the academic vocabulary words *rhythm*, *repetition*, and *alliteration*, one at a time, to the anchor chart and listen and look for examples of them in "Fuzzy Wuzzy, Creepy Crawly" and other poems. We'll continue to read all sorts of poetry as we study these structural elements. It's important that we teach children that poets use the elements on the chart to create sounds in their poems, but poets don't always use all these elements in every poem.

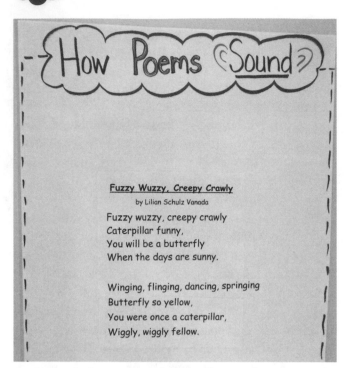

To prepare for lesson two on how a poem sounds, we've typed and glued a poem to the chart to save time and provide a clear model.

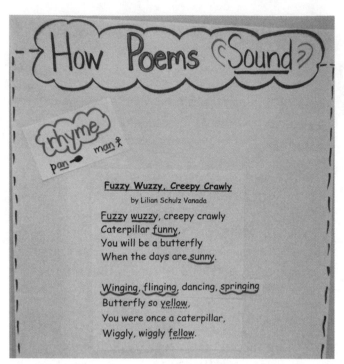

Here the same anchor chart has been marked and written on during the lesson. Other cards will be added to the chart as we explore other poetry terms.

Connecting the Anchor Chart to Literacy Work Stations with Conversation Cards

To end the lesson, I connect to our anchor charts before kids go to literacy stations. I want children to begin using the poetry terms from the charts while working at literacy work stations today, especially at the pocket-chart station where kids place sentence strips with lines from familiar poems in order. I quickly make a conversation card by writing "_____ and _____ rhyme" in a speech bubble on a 3-by-5-inch plain white index card to remind students that this is the language we expect them to use at the station. I write the word *rhyme* in red to match the word on the anchor chart. I tell the students that I want them to use this "conversation card" at the pocket-chart station to help them better understand poetry. Remember, the purpose of this card is to support students' academic vocabulary and connect it to the work done with the anchor chart that day. By providing this language again in print on the conversation card at a station, children will be encouraged to use these academic words over and over again until they have a strong grasp of them and can use them independently.

We try out the conversation card with a poem from the pocket-chart work station. It's called "Rules Rap" and is familiar to the class. As we read the poem together, we listen for the rhyming words. I show the class the conversation card, and ask two students to use the sentence frame on it: "*Good* and *should* rhyme. *Wrong* and *along* rhyme." Then we place the conversation card at the pocket-chart station for kids to use there today, along with red Wikki Stix, wax-coated pieces of yarn that they can use to circle printed rhyming words.

I remind them one last time that although many of the poems they read will rhyme, some won't have any rhyming words. I also tell them that I've placed some books with poems at the buddy-reading station. While there, they can be reading and talking about which pieces are poems by how those look.

After the Lesson

The kids are ready to go to their stations. They read the management board independently and move to their partner work at literacy stations while Tracy teaches a small guided-reading group. (Photos of sample management boards can be found in Chapter 1.) I give the children a few minutes to get started and then stop by the pocket-chart station. Two boys are there assembling poems, line by line, and using the conversation card to name the rhyming words. "Do *out* and *hat* rhyme?" they ask. I notice that finding rhyming words isn't as easy for them as I thought while teaching the whole-group lesson.

They have easily put the poems in order, line by line, but there is support for doing this: a copy of the poem is glued to the front of the large brown envelope that contains the matching poetry sentence strips. As I watch these kids struggle with finding rhyming words, I realize that support for rhyming may be necessary at this station as well. I bring the anchor chart to them, and we read the part about rhyming together. We point to the pictures of the pan and the man on the chart to read the rhyming words. Then, using the conversation card, we say, "*Pan* and *man* rhyme." I point out that the ending chunk of these words, the part in red, sounds the same and that's why they rhyme.

I ask the boys at this station if it will help to add the picture example from the anchor chart to the back of their conversation card. It does! I have them use the Wikki Stix to underline the parts of the words that rhyme. I help them for a few minutes as they read a new poem, circle words they think rhyme, and listen for the ending sounds, periodically consulting the pictures on the conversation card. As I walk away, they are saying, "*Fat* and *hat* rhyme." I'll ask them to share what they learned with the class at the end of stations time.

I observe students at several other stations, including the classroom library where several children have chosen poetry books to read. I'm pleased to see them already applying the reading mini-lesson to their independent book choice. Also at the buddy-reading station, today's book choice has been influenced by this powerful mini-lesson. A pair of students are reading a book of nursery rhymes and talking about rhyming words—without prompting!

At the word-study station, a girl who speaks Arabic is working on a rhyming-words puzzle task. Leyla has a choice of several word-study tasks but has chosen rhyming today. As I observe, I note that she is matching up cards with rhyming pictures and words by using the puzzle piece patterns. She is not reading the words and listening for the rhyme.

I make another copy of the conversation card for rhyming to use at this station, too. It takes only a minute, and Leyla watches while I create the card and point back to the anchor chart from today's lesson. Then I invite her to use the card as she names the rhyming pictures and words each time she makes a match. "*Horn* and *corn* rhyme. *Floor* and *door* rhyme. *Pie* and *eye* rhyme. . . ." I realize that it would help her to have a partner to work with; it will give her a chance to talk and use the conversation card. Each time she does so, the concept of rhyming is reinforced as she reads and hears the rhyming word pairs along with the academic vocabulary. I also note that it would be helpful to have a mini-version of the rhyming anchor chart at this station, and plan to tell Tracy about that later.

A student works at the pocket-chart station using a conversation card for rhyming.

A conversation card is used for rhyming at a word-study station, too.

Of course, rhyming and reading poetry is not being practiced at every station. Children are listening to recorded books at several tech-related stations; another pair of kids read fiction books at a second buddy-reading station; several students write letters to friends and family members at the writing station; and two girls are jotting down information from informational text they're reading on sticky notes at the inquiry station.

After the children have worked at their first literacy station for twenty minutes, Tracy signals them with her music wand to clean up and return to their seats. They clean up quickly and are eager to share what they did and learned during stations and small group. Providing five to seven minutes for kids to share what they did keeps them focused on what they should be doing during stations.

Tracy and I call on several students to share, including the pair from the pocket-chart station. They walk to this station, eager to show the class how they marked rhyming words with the new highlighter tape strips and used the new conversation card with the picture clues for *pan* and *man* on the back just like on the anchor chart. This reinforces expectations for stations for the rest of the class and saves the teacher time in having to show how to use these new materials.

We ask Leyla to share how she used the conversation card for rhyming at the word-study station. I hand her the materials she used there, and quietly, she stands beside me and shows the rest of the class how she matched two cards and said the rhyming words, such as "*Star* and *car* rhyme." She smiles shyly as I thank her for sharing.

Tracy thanks them for their reflections and reminds the class that they will have another chance to share after going to their second station. When I later ask this teacher how she made time for sharing after stations, she replies, "I can't imagine not giving them time to share what they learned. It helps them reflect upon their learning and gives me an idea of what they did and learned today. Many of my students are learning English, and it gives them a chance to speak to the class. It's a very valuable time of day for all of us."

Children share what they learned at literacy stations during Sharing Time after independent work and small-group time. These girls show how they found misspelled words in their writing and fixed them together by looking carefully at vowel patterns in words and clapping syllables for longer words at the word-study station today.

Reflecting on the Lesson and Planning for Tomorrow

The poetry mini-lesson and creation of an anchor chart has gone well. Students have good beginning exposure and a strong anchor to the term *rhyme*. We will continue to reinforce this concept by referring to the anchor chart as we teach with poetry. In addition, we will add new academic vocabulary to the chart over several lessons.

Tomorrow, we'll introduce *rhythm* using today's anchor chart and clap on each syllable of the poem on the chart. I'll invite children to clap the rhythm of other poems they can read, too. Tracy will make a second conversation card that reads, "We can clap the *rhythm* of a poem," writing the word *rhythm* in green to match the anchor chart with a small picture of a clapping hand (just like on the chart), and she'll place that card at the pocket-chart station, too. She'll also add a third index card to the anchor chart and write the word *repetition* on it in purple marker. Then students will find words that repeat in the poem on the anchor chart and underline them in purple. As a class, they'll reread a poem or two and look for repetition, underlining the repeated parts in purple with a dry erase marker.

Conversation cards for talking about poetry are at the poetry station. Small pieces of highlighter tape are placed on a card for kids to use to mark rhyming words. Kids clap the rhythm as they read a poem.

On the day after that, Tracy will add a fourth index card to the anchor chart that says "alliteration" in blue marker. She'll follow the same steps we've used in previous poetry mini-lessons and have children find examples of alliteration on the chart and in poems, underlining examples of alliteration in blue. Another conversation card will be created that says, "_____ and _____ use *alliteration*." She'll put this card at buddy reading with some first-grade poetry books.

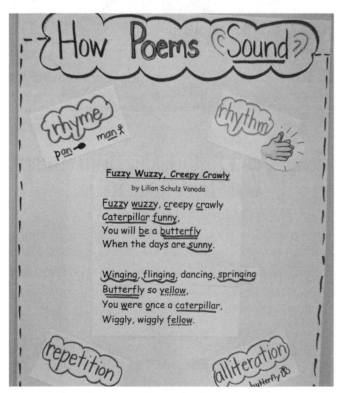

Poetry anchor chart 2 as it has evolved over several lessons

Follow-Up Lessons on Poetry That Include Anchor Charts and Literacy Work Stations

As originally planned, we created a third poetry anchor chart about a week or so later; this one focused on sensory details. See photos for the sketch we made before teaching the lesson and for the anchor chart we created during reading workshop and also used in writing workshop. In the middle of this chart about sensory details, I copied the poem "April Rain Song" by Langston Hughes ahead of time. In the introductory lesson on identifying sensory details, we talked about how poets use words to help readers create movies in our minds by using sensory details, and we use our five senses to do so. As the children named their five senses, I wrote a sentence frame, such as *I see* or *I hear* on a sticky note and added these above the poem. Next, we watched a forty-three-second YouTube video by the New York Botanical Garden about "April Rain Song," and I had kids think about their senses as they watched this movie: What did they see, hear, feel, smell, taste? I reminded them that Langston Hughes used sensory details by choosing his words carefully as he wrote this poem.

Finally, together we read "April Rain Song" several times and listened for words and phrases that created sensory images. Then kids took turns placing sticky notes or colored tape flags beside the sensory language it matched. For example, a student put the *I feel* sticky note beside the word *kiss;* another put the *I hear* sticky note by the words *plays a little sleep song on our roof.*

This kind of work germinated quickly and was easily transferred to the poetry station; students loved manipulating the sticky notes as they found sensory details in this and other poems. It's so important to include tactile experiences like this during whole group and at stations for kinesthetic learners, especially those that struggle with reading or writing. This type of work benefits children reading above grade level as well as those who read below or on level.

This work really encouraged students to read closely and pay attention to the words poets chose as they crafted their poems. Over time, as we also modeled how to write poems, students used this chart and other poems we worked with in whole group as supports to help them write their own poems that communicated sensory details both during writing workshop and again at the writing station.

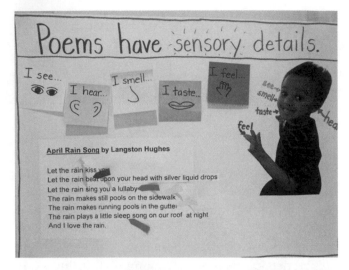

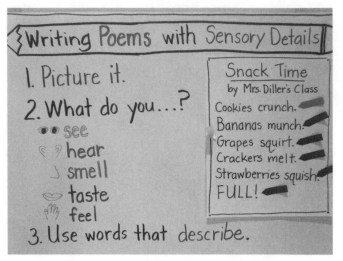

An anchor chart on writing with sensory details is made with the class to help them write their own poems.

An anchor chart is titled "Poems have sensory details" (*top*), and children use a mini version of this chart along with sticky notes at a poetry station (*bottom*). They position the sticky notes beside words that give sensory details.

This chart is then moved to the writing station over time to help first graders write their own poems conveying sensory details.

Teaching with Poetry Anchor Charts in Other Grade Levels Across States

The same process that Tracy and I used for planning and teaching with anchor charts for poetry is easily transferred to other grade levels, no matter which state you live in. Start with your poetry-related standards. I think you'll find it helpful to look across the grade levels to see how each standard grows from kindergarten to grade three in the online appendix. I also found it interesting to examine the same standard across multiple states; it helped me establish commonalities and often see what was most important about that standard.

First graders add sticky notes to the anchor chart on sensory images in the poetry station. They jot down examples of word choice from poems they are reading here.

Plan and sketch out sample anchor charts as you confer with colleagues about the big ideas and academic vocabulary you expect your students to learn and apply. Then make anchor charts with your students. Teach with the charts; refer to them regularly as you read and explore poetry together. Include academic vocabulary as listed in your standards. The photos below show some anchor charts we created to teach poetry standards for upper grade levels.

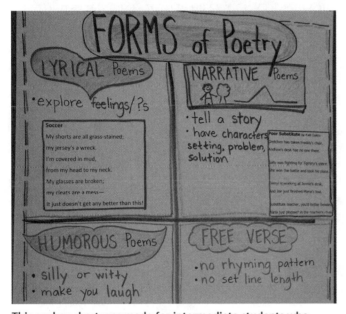

This anchor chart was made for intermediate students who needed to learn different forms of poetry, according to their state standards. Check your standards to create charts that match what you are supposed to teach.

Another anchor chart for intermediate students helps them remember structural elements of poetry used in both reading and, eventually, writing their own poems.

Designing Anchor Charts

Now that you've read lots about teaching with anchor charts, you're probably thinking about making some with your students. But do you ever get overwhelmed or intimidated when you look at "perfect" anchor charts online or in a colleague's classroom? I know I do. This is probably because many of us do not have a background in design. You might check out sites such as www.pinterest.com or teacher websites for ideas, but don't feel like you just have to copy or even buy those premade charts. The best anchor charts are designed with your students and your standards in mind. Use any inspiration you can find, and then roll up your sleeves and give it a try! Include help from technology, such as Google Images or photos from your own classroom. Work with your colleagues to plan and design anchor charts. We usually improve as we work with ideas over time.

My background is not in design, but it's an area in which I've always been interested. I love fashion, and there's nothing I like better than browsing through gardening and home décor magazines. Recently, I read in Daniel Pink's *A Whole New Mind* (2006) that in today's world we must all be designers. The author says that "companies traditionally have competed on price or quality, or some combination of the two" (2006, 77). But in today's world, according to Norio Ohga—former chairman of Sony—"design is [often] the only thing that differentiates one product from another in the marketplace" (Pink 2006, 78). Think about it. Why did you choose the phone or tablet you have? It probably had a lot to do with design.

I believe that in our classrooms, design matters, too. It will help students know what to pay attention to, what to focus on. Design brings a sense of order to our environments (and our anchor charts). Some studies, such as those as listed in the Commission for Architecture and the Built Environment (2002) report, have found that improving a school's physical environment increased student achievement by as much as 11 percent. I believe that anchor charts are an important part of that environment.

Robin Williams, author of *The Non-Designer's Design Book* (2008), outlines an acronym representing four principles of design: contrast, repetition, alignment, and proximity. Having been a staff developer for

several decades, I just couldn't imagine presenting this acronym to a group of teachers! I believe we teachers need to understand simple design principles in order to create meaningful anchor charts, so I've adapted the acronym to spell CROPS, explained in Figure 4.4.

Take a look around your room at anchor charts you've already made with your students. Ask a partner to join you! Which of these design elements do you feel you've used well? Browse anchor charts online and do the same. Developing an eye for design takes practice.

As I've worked with teachers around the country, they've asked many questions about how to design high-quality anchor charts. I hope the ideas that follow will answer your questions about good design, too.

Figure 4.4 **CROPS: Five Design Principles for Creating Anchor Charts**

Contrast (and Color)	Visual elements (fonts, color, size, line thickness, space, and so on) should draw the eye to the most important parts of the chart.
Repetition	Repeating visual elements directs attention to the most important ideas on the anchor chart. This can be done with fonts, colors, or shapes.
One Idea	Stick with one big idea on the chart.
Purpose	Every visual element should have a purpose.
Spacing	Items relating to one another should be grouped close together on the chart. Allow white space.

Design Tips for Making Anchor Charts with Your Class

What materials do I need for *planning* anchor charts?	• plain 8½-by-11-inch paper • pencil and eraser • state standards • colored markers (for playing with color)
What materials do you recommend for *making* anchor charts with my class?	• colored markers, such as Crayola Washable Markers (that work and have good tips—throw away old, dried-up markers when you come across them!) • large unlined white paper (I often use 12-by-18-inch white construction paper or 18-by-24-inch drawing paper from craft stores to save wall space.) • crayons (for adding a bit of color that doesn't interfere with the words on the chart) • 6-by-8-inch sticky notes in bright colors • plain white index cards in a variety of sizes • repositionable glue sticks
What materials do I need for making *mini–anchor charts* for kids to use as reference in small group and at stations?	• clear plastic photo sleeves for refill pages, size 4 by 6 inches, to use at literacy work stations • colored copies of anchor charts printed on 4-by-6-inch cards to use at literacy work stations • clear plastic sleeves and colored copies of anchor charts printed on 8½-by-11-inch paper to use in small group in a labeled binder
What *size* print should we use on our anchor charts?	• Every 1 inch of letter height provides 10 feet of readability with the greatest effect (a credit or ID card is about 2 by 3½ inches). • Play around with print size on a scrap chart; then post it and check if you and your kids can easily read it where you have it posted.

(continued on next page)

Design Tips for Making Anchor Charts with Your Class

My *handwriting* is sloppy. What do I do?	• You might prepare the title and academic vocabulary ahead of time by typing the words onto paper and having them ready to glue onto the anchor chart. • Make a "rough draft" of the chart with your class, and then type the words, print them, and have kids help you glue them onto the chart the next day as you read the chart together. • Have a student with good handwriting help you write words on the chart. • Create some of your charts on an interactive whiteboard.
Should I make all my anchor charts on an *interactive whiteboard*?	• Technology can certainly enhance our teaching, but it must be used wisely. • You might use your interactive whiteboard to make charts sometimes, but not all the time. • Be sure to print out the charts you make, hang them, and teach with them. • Don't store your anchor charts on the Smartboard—they will be stored in the computer's memory, not your students'.
What are the best *colors* to use when writing text on an anchor chart?	• Dark colors are most easily read from afar. • Blue, purple, black, dark green, and brown are easy to read. • Use red and green sparingly, since they are hard to read from far away. • Avoid light colors, such as pink, yellow, lavender, and pastels. • Bright, fluorescent colors can grab attention (but don't overdo it).
What else should I consider when using *color* on the charts?	• Use several colors, but be thoughtful about how you use them. • Use color to grab students' attention (contrasting colors work well). • Think about what you want kids to pay the most attention to, and use color on those parts.
Design-wise what else *grabs attention* on anchor charts?	• bold • variety of easy-to-read fonts • size of print and visuals • Be thoughtful about what you want kids to pay the most attention to.
Do you have tips on *titles*?	• Titles should grab kids' attention and relate to the big idea you are trying to help them remember (use the design ideas above). • Ask kids for their ideas for titles for your charts (but have a plan of your own ahead of time). • Underline or put the title in a bubble or in large print so it stands out and is the first thing the reader sees.
You've addressed print. What about *visuals*?	• An anchor chart is a *visual display* that shows information in a way that is easy for children to understand. • Pictures on the chart are as important as the words. • Visuals should support specific words and/or the big idea represented on the chart and be memorable for your kids. • Visuals should be simple and strong.
What if I *can't draw*?	• Planning ahead can help with this dilemma. • Use Google Images or clip art. • Use drawing books such as those by Ed Emberley for help. • Use student work or drawings. • Boardmaker Software offers picture communication symbols and is owned by most special education departments.

Chapter 4

Using Anchor Charts as Supports at Literacy Work Stations

Originally, this book was going to be devoted solely to anchor charts. But as I worked with and wrote about the charts over several years, I realized that it could be much more. We'd created anchor charts with children so they would use them independently. What better place to use them than at literacy work stations!

The key was to teach well with the anchor charts (and make them with the children) first. As we created an anchor chart, it was also important to think about how it could support students as they worked independently with a partner at literacy stations. In some cases, the full-sized anchor chart could be moved directly to that station if it was near a wall and in a permanent place. For example, anchor charts about reading strategies could be hung in the classroom library area. Likewise, anchor charts about writing would be moved to the writing-station space.

But some of our stations were portable, and kids couldn't carry a big chart along. Necessity is the mother of invention! We simply took a digital photo of an anchor chart that could support students at a particular station, printed the chart in color onto white cardstock (4 by 6 inches or 8½ by 11 inches, depending on the chart and age of the students), and stuck it into a clear plastic photo sleeve or sheet protector. For example, a portable word-study station housed in a clear plastic, lidded container held magnetic letters, word lists, and little books from guided reading. We taped a related phonics mini-anchor chart to the inside lid of this word-study station for students to access easily.

During whole-group instruction, we were sure to model how to use the mini-anchor chart at a station for support as we moved it there. This worked really well with some of the poetry-related anchor charts we created that are pictured earlier in this chapter. In one third-grade room, the poetry station was portable. The teacher had borrowed several poetry books from the school library and placed them in a clear plastic container. The poetry anchor chart she'd made with her students focused on structural elements of poetry, including the academic vocabulary *line breaks*, *rhyme*, *rhythm*, *repetition*, and *alliteration*. Showing kids how to access the mini-anchor chart as they read and talked about poems at this station was a huge support. The visuals on the chart really scaffolded kids' learning of this new vocabulary and helped them understand the meaning of the poems as well as their construction. Previously, this teacher had assumed her students would look on the wall to access the terms and information they needed as they worked at stations. Adding the mini–anchor chart to the poetry station made all the difference. Proximity breeds engagement.

Third graders work at a portable poetry station with mini–anchor charts and conversation cards added. These tools help kids think more deeply about the poems they read as they work together here.

Making Space for All Those Charts on the Walls

A final problem many teachers often ask for help with is that they run out of room for all the anchor charts they make with their kids. Also, sometimes it's hard for students to read charts hanging high up on the walls (if you even have walls and are allowed to use this space). Here are several wall space and storage solutions:

- *Use every space available as a "wall," and size charts accordingly.* Look at the space around your classroom, such as cabinet doors (if you have them) and use these as "walls." Make your anchor charts fit the spaces you have. Consider making smaller charts, such as 18 by 24 inches, rather than always using large easel chart paper, which often measures 25 by 30 inches.
- *Label your walls to create zones for current anchor charts.* Adding simple, bold labels to your walls for each subject area, as described in Chapter 2, can help you plan for where to put class-made anchor charts. It will also help your students know where to look to access a chart.
- *Place today's new anchor chart in a special place by the door.* Students can "tap" the poem on their way out the door like a sports team and remember it by looking at it one more time.

"Retire" some of your anchor charts. When a wall space gets full, reflect on which charts you're currently teaching with and that your children are referencing. You might ask your class to help decide what stays and what can come down. In a third-grade classroom, for instance, the teacher had her students meet *outside* of the classroom and list every chart they regularly used. That meant they had to recall from memory what they found helpful, which made it easier for them to discern which ones they were actually using. Take a digital photo of the chart before you "retire" it. Recycle it into a small-group anchor chart notebook and/or into stations where some children may still use it as a support.

Use "retired" anchor charts as school-home connections. Send home old anchor charts with your students, especially those kids who need the extra support. If they hang a chart in their bedroom, perhaps they'll look at it before they go to sleep and make the learning on it stick. This is also a good way to communicate with parents what you've been teaching at school.

Hang anchor charts on a garment rack. In several classrooms I worked in, we resolved the issue of limited wall space by fastening finished anchor charts onto colored plastic clothing hangers with clear packing tape. Then we hung them on an adjustable garment rack. I used a different-color hanger for each subject area. For example, all of our reading charts were hung from red hangers, writing charts from blue hangers, and math charts from green hangers. This helped the kids (and the teacher) quickly find what was needed.

We also placed a Command-brand hook (which adheres quickly and easily and won't damage wall surfaces when removed) in the whole-group area, so the teacher could hang up a chart for reference during a mini-lesson and then return it to the rack afterward. In those rooms, the kids asked if they could have an anchor chart station. They reread and used old anchor charts with a partner there.

Don't keep old anchor charts. It will save space to keep a digital photo of the anchor charts that worked best rather than to keep the whole chart. Also, I recommend keeping no more than one chart-size storage box in your room for maps, charts, and large calendars. Limiting the amount of space you dedicate to large items will make more space for your students!

Smaller anchor charts are made to fit on cabinet doors.

Chapter 4

Label walls with names of subjects you teach to make space for anchor charts displayed in an organized way. This teacher is short on wall space, so we're using cabinet doors as walls. She'll plan for anchor charts to fit this space as she makes them with her class.

This teacher stores old anchor charts on hangers on a teaching easel. She also sends retired charts home with students who need them.

Anchor charts can be stored on a garment rack (*center*) by taping each chart to a colored hanger. Use a different color for each subject. Then move the chart to a Command hook stuck to a board in the whole-group teaching area (*bottom*) to teach with it.

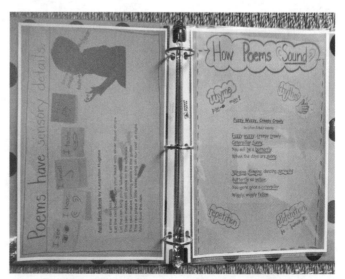

Take photos of anchor charts and print them onto 8½-by-11-inch paper. Store each one in a clear plastic sleeve in a notebook at your guided-reading table for easy reference during small-group instruction.

Digging Deeper

Your mind is probably filled with visions of anchor charts and all their possibilities as you finish reading this chapter. Breathe deeply, and take it one step at a time. If you're studying this book with others, you can use the following questions to help you plan the smartest use of anchor charts in your classroom and at stations:

1. Look at the charts hanging in your classroom. Which are anchor charts? What other kinds of charts are displayed? Which do your kids use? Why do you think this is so? How are you using space for displaying anchor charts? Are your walls too crowded? How can you create space for what's most important? Use ideas from this chapter to help.

2. Refer to Figure 4.1, "What Makes a High-Quality Anchor Chart?," and reflect with colleagues on the anchor charts you've made. Which elements do you think are your strongest suit? What will you work on as you continue to make anchor charts with your students?

3. As a team, use your state standards for poetry and plan an anchor chart (or two or three) integrating academic vocabulary your students need to learn. Use the ideas in this chapter to help you plan. Which did you find most helpful?

4. Make an anchor chart with your students, using the suggestions from Figure 4.2, "Making the Most of Anchor Charts," and share how it went with your colleagues.

5. Plan for ways to move anchor charts into literacy work stations in your classroom. Share examples and discuss how it supported students' independence and use of academic vocabulary.

6. What did you learn about designing anchor charts from reading this chapter? Which principles of design will you be more intentional about as you create anchor charts with your students?

7. What tips will you use to "recycle" some of your anchor charts?

Chapter 4

5

Literacy Work Stations for Reading: Literature

Standards Covered in This Chapter	Lessons Described in This Chapter
Retelling Literature and Determining a Story's Central Theme, Moral, or Lesson	B-M-E Sticky-Note Retelling Myths and Morals
Describing Characters, Settings, and Major Events in a Story	Characters We Love
Acknowledging Differences in Characters' Points of View	Character Cards and Point of View

It is a joy to watch young readers engaging in reading literature at stations time. In the classroom library, I spy two children reading the adventures of *Skippyjon Jones* by Judy Schachner (2003). At a listening station, another pair of students is reading along with a recording of *The Three Billy Goats Gruff* as they hold the book and join in with the familiar refrain, "Trip-trap, trip-trap, trip-trap. Who's that crossing over my bridge?" Over in the corner, two kids read a favorite poem, "Snowball" by Shel Silverstein (1996), written on a chart attached to a hanger on a garment rack. They laugh together at its silliness and talk about what they read. I hear them using academic vocabulary as they discuss the words the poet chose. "I made it some *pajamas* and a *pillow* for its head.' That's alliteration.

Pajamas and *pillow* start the same way. My mom would be mad if I had a snowball in my bed!"

We read literature for enjoyment and entertainment. It enriches our lives. Stories can transport us to other times and places and broaden our horizons. Poems express simple longings and deep desires; they can make us laugh or cry, and touch our souls. Literature encompasses stories, dramas, and poetry. Our classroom libraries should overflow with tales of lands near and far and include poems that move us to laughter and tears. Our students should have opportunities to dramatically read and enact short plays and reader's theater scripts. The chart in Figure 5.1 includes a sampling of the types of literature our children should be exposed to at school.

Figure 5.1 Types of Literature for Children to Read

Stories	Dramas	Poetry
• adventure stories • folktales • legends • fables • mysteries • fantasy • realistic fiction • historical fiction • myths	• plays • reader's theater scripts	• nursery rhymes • narrative poetry • humorous poetry • free-verse poetry • limericks

As we read aloud literature in whole-class mini-lessons, these texts will anchor the learning children do. With exposure to the right books, the youngest children can begin to analyze characters and make predictions about what these people and animals will do in further adventures. Our students will keep poems in their pockets and learn lessons from fables and folktales that they can apply to their lives over the years. With our support, they will learn to retell favorite stories to one another at school and to their families at home; perhaps one day they will tell those same stories to their own children.

As our students compare and contrast literature, they'll learn about authors and how these artists craft stories, dramas, and poetry. They'll discover the power of words to create visual images and make scenes jump off the page. You never know—you may have a future screenwriter, poet laureate, or Academy Award–winning actor in your classroom this year.

In this chapter (and in Chapters 6–9), you will find examples of the kinds of work your students may do with you in whole-class lessons and later, independently, at literacy work stations. You'll find a structure that repeats from section to section and chapter to chapter that consists of the following in this order: a particular standard explained; examples of team planning tools; *long-lasting* lesson plans that you can teach as often as needed; connections to independent reading, small group, and writing; suggested mentor texts; and tips to teach this standard from pre-K through grade five. These are followed by sections with photos of sample anchor charts and literacy stations to inspire you to focus your teaching on what matters most, using your state standards to

guide you. To help you navigate, a chart at the beginning of each chapter lists that chapter's standards and lessons.

Because there is not enough room in any book to include every single mini-lesson or literacy work station you might have during the year, I've chosen to focus on several important standards that echo across grade levels and state lines. If you don't find the exact standard you need, please be flexible and use what you do find to plan interesting, engaging work for your children. Just as when a gardener visits the nursery and discovers that a favorite plant isn't in stock, be willing to substitute something similar in its place. By doing so, you will create an amazing, memorable year for your children. They will leave with a rich understanding of literature and be affected by the work you've done together.

Retelling Literature and Determining a Story's Central Theme, Moral, or Lesson

People love to tell stories. We tell stories for fun; we tell stories to connect with others; we tell stories to teach life lessons or morals. Our beloved folktales and fairy tales were passed from generation to generation across cultures in the oral tradition long ago and continue to be important today for all these reasons.

Stories are often centered on themes such as family relationships, adventures with friends, or overcoming difficulties. When children learn how to retell stories and determine themes, morals, and lessons, they can comprehend deeply and apply what they've learned to their lives. Young children enjoy using props, like retelling pieces and stick puppets, to tell stories they've heard or read. They'll learn about story structure, including beginning, middle, and end, as they play with stories. You'll hear them mimic the voices and language of literature you've shared. Eventually, it will influence the narrative writing they do as well.

Sifting Through the Standard: Retelling Literature and Determining a Story's Central Theme, Moral, or Lesson	
What It Is	• Telling key details from the beginning, middle, and end of a story in order • Including a description of characters and setting and their importance to the story • Including the problem and solution (plot) • The ability to discuss what a piece of literature teaches us (its central message, lesson, or moral)
Why It's Important	• Retelling is a skill we use daily to recapture our life experiences. Learning to retell in the early grades lays the foundation for being able to summarize by grades four and five. • Research studies (Dunst, Simkus, and Hamby 2012) show that children's story retelling positively influences comprehension of fiction and improves expressive vocabulary. • Understanding a story's central message, lesson, or moral will often help us take away life lessons that can enrich our lives.
Prerequisites Needed	• Ability to identify the beginning, middle, and end of a story, comprehend, and paraphrase • Knowing how to determine what is important in a certain part of a story (in the beginning or the middle or the end) • Ability to identify characters, setting, problem, and solution in a story
Academic Vocabulary	Kindergarten: • *retell a story* • *beginning/middle/end* • *key details* First grade: • *central message* • *lesson* Second grade (and above): • *moral/theme*
Real-World Connections	• Help kids see real-life examples of when retelling is used in the world (for example, some cultures tell stories to pass them along). • Folktales and fairy tales are retellings. Point out the words *Retold by . . .* on the front cover of those books. • Familiarity with legends and Greek myths builds background necessary for interpreting and understanding some modern-day texts.
Example Test Questions	• "What is the central message or lesson (or theme) of this story?" • "Which sentence best describes the moral of this fable?"

Chapter 5

Team Planning Tool:
Retelling Literature—Kindergarten

Standard We're Teaching	**Kindergarten:** With prompting and support, retell familiar stories, including key details.
Academic Vocabulary We'll Use and Expect to Hear	• *retell* • *story* • *fiction* • *key details* • *in the beginning* • *characters* • *setting* • *in the middle* • *problem* • *at the end* • *solution*
Whole-Group Ideas	• Read aloud books (multiple times) with simple, clear beginnings, middles, and endings. • Label the beginning, middle, and end of a book with colored sticky notes labeled "B" (green), "M" (yellow), and "E" (red). • Model how to read the beginning of a story and then stop and retell the key details (then do the same for the middle and ending, too). • Use laminated large paper with three columns (each part labeled with colored letters for B, M, E) to jot down key details from each part of the story. • Use retelling pieces or retelling cards (sometimes provided by core reading programs) to retell stories. • As a class, write key details in order from a familiar story with each detail on a separate sentence strip with a picture for support. Then hand out the strips to kids and have them put the story in order on a pocket chart to retell it. • Make an anchor chart for retelling stories. • Make conversation cards for retelling.
Partner Practice at Literacy Work Stations	**Buddy-reading station:** Partners work together to read, retell using conversation cards, and then write the key events of a familiar story (used in whole group) on paper folded into thirds and labeled "B," "M," "E." **Drama station:** Use retelling pieces and conversation cards to retell key ideas from the beginning, middle, and end of familiar stories. Kids may use simple stick puppets that match the characters. **Retelling station:** Partners work together and put retelling cards from your reading series in order as they tell key details from the beginning, middle, and end. They use the book and picture cards for support. **Pocket-chart station:** Kids put sentence strips in order to retell a story. (Picture support can help.)

**Lessons That Last:
Whole-Group Mini-Lesson Plan for Retelling Literature—Kindergarten**

B-M-E Sticky-Note Retelling

Focus: retelling a story in order with key details from the beginning, middle, and end

Method to Maximize Student Engagement: a favorite story kids will love; showing my thinking and jotting it down in pictures on an anchor chart; buddy talk (kids retell a part to someone sitting beside them)

Materials: favorite story with a clear beginning, middle, and end (such as *The Three Little Pigs, Goldilocks and the Three Bears,* or *The Little Engine That Could*) and a thumbnail book cover to match; green, yellow, and red sticky notes placed in the book to mark the beginning, middle, and end; 12-by-18-inch white construction paper and colored markers for an anchor chart on retelling with three boxes drawn for *B, M,* and *E*; die-cut letters, and a glue stick (*B* in green; *M* in yellow; *E* in red) for the anchor chart.

Model: how to think about and then jot down key details or what's most important (in the beginning, middle, and end of a story)

Prompting for Independence:

- "If you wanted to tell a friend about what you just read, what would you say? Tell just the key details, the most important things."

- "Most stories consist of a beginning, a middle, and an end. Read a part, and then stop and think about what happened."

- "What were the key details or most important parts in the beginning? In the middle? At the end?"

Mini-Lesson Procedure:

1. Choose a *short*, interesting story that kids will enjoy retelling. Mark the beginning of the book with a green sticky note, the middle with a yellow sticky note, and the end with a red one. Label them "B," "M," and "E." Prepare your anchor chart before the lesson by leaving space for the title and then dividing the chart into thirds. Have the other anchor chart materials at your fingertips for the mini-lesson, since your kids will be helping you to construct it.

2. To begin the mini-lesson, tell students that retelling can help them better understand what they read. Explain that we don't tell every single thing that happened, because it takes too long. We just tell the key details or most important parts to help us remember what the story was about. On the top of your anchor chart, write, "I can retell _____." Read this with the class and orally fill in the blank with the title of the book you'll retell.

3. Show students the read-aloud book. They'll probably notice the colored sticky notes in the book. Explain that a story has a beginning (*B*), a middle (*M*), and an end (*E*) as you point to the sticky notes. Have a student glue the thumbnail picture of the book cover you use for retelling at the top of the chart to help them remember where they learned about retelling.

4. Read aloud the text, one part at a time, pausing to think with students about the key details or what was most important at the end of that section. Also cue them into how you know you're reading the beginning or moving to the middle or are at the end. For example, read the first page or two and then stop and tell students, "We just read the beginning of the book. In the beginning of a story, the author tells us about the main character or *who* it's about, and the setting, the *where* and *when* it takes place." (Point out the *B* on the sticky note and have a student glue the green *B* to the anchor chart in the far left column.) "Which details are key or important in the beginning of the story? We should tell about the characters and setting, since this is fiction." (With student input, draw something to represent the character and setting at the top of the *B* section of the anchor chart, such as a person and a house and sun.) Think aloud about what the key details are from the beginning. Ask students for their input.

5. Continue this procedure throughout the text, reading the middle next and thinking about the key details or most important parts with the class. Tell the children how you know it's no longer the beginning of the book: "Now we're moving into the middle of the book. I can tell because things are starting to change. The train's engine just broke down. A problem is starting to emerge." Have a student glue the *M* to the middle section of the anchor chart. Talk about the problem the characters have in the middle of the story. Again, use a picture suggested by kids to represent a problem. Finally, read the end of the story and retell the key details.

(continued on next page)

Again, cue kids into how you know it's the end of the story: "I can tell we're at the end of the story. We're almost on the last page, and the action has changed again. The problem is getting fixed. The little engine is saying, 'I think I can' and is going down the mountain. Yes. That's how the story ends." Add the *E* to the right side of the anchor chart with an illustration that represents a solution or how the problem is fixed.

6. When finished, have kids reflect on what they learned about retelling.

7. Use the same anchor chart on another day with a new story that has sticky notes marking the beginning, middle, and end. Again, read the book aloud, one part at a time, pointing to the anchor chart and stopping to reflect on key details from each section. This time invite kids to talk to a buddy about key details, and call on several of them to share about each part. Add the words *In the beginning* to the "B" section on the anchor chart. Add *In the middle* to the "M" section and *At the end* in the "E" section. Repeat this lesson with new books until students appear to understand how to retell with a partner.

8. Also make a conversation card for retelling and project it with a document camera, so kids can see it while you use it for retelling. *In the beginning, _____. In the middle, _____. At the end, _____.*

9. Then put kids in pairs, and give each pair a familiar book from guided reading to share, plus one green, one yellow, and one red sticky note (labeled "B," "M," and "E"). Have them work together to mark the beginning, middle, and end of their books. After this, they read a section together, and then stop and retell, using words from the anchor chart, until they have read and retold the book together.

10. Laminate the anchor chart so it can be reused multiple times in whole group as well as at a literacy work station. Over time, write and/or draw about what happened in the beginning, middle, and end on the chart as you retell.

On-the-Spot Assessment: Have partners share their retellings from the beginning, middle, and/or end of the books you are reading together. Do the same with books they read and retell together.

Connections to Whole-Group Mini-Lesson

Independent Reading Connection: Have students work with a partner to read and retell. Give each pair of children a green, a yellow, and a red sticky note to mark the beginning, middle, and end of a self-selected book they can read on their own. Encourage students to read a part, stop and think about what it was about, retell it together, and then do the same for the next part. When they are finished, have students practice retelling the whole story, including the beginning, middle, and end.

Small-Group Connection: You might have students place a sticky note on preselected pages at the end of the beginning, middle, and end of a short book. Have them jot down what they think was most important in each segment. Then work together after reading to retell the story. Use retelling pieces if needed to help children retell.

Writing Connection: Teach students how to fold a paper into thirds and label the sections "B," "M," and "E" to match the anchor chart you've been using in reading. Model how to draw pictures and write words to show the key details from each section read. Have students practice doing this with books you've read aloud and/or their guided-reading or self-selected books, too.

Evaluation: After ample instruction and practice, read aloud a story and have students draw and/or write their own retellings using BME-labeled paper. Use a rubric to evaluate.

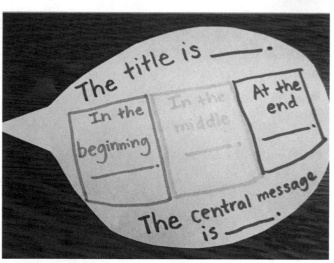

Before reading aloud, I marked the book with colored sticky notes labeled "B," "M," and "E" to show where the beginning, middle, and end were. Then we stopped after each segment for kids to retell what they'd heard thus far.

Project a conversation card to support retelling during whole-group instruction. Students can use this same card independently at literacy stations for retelling, too.

Kids work in pairs around the whole-group area with little books they can read. Together, they mark the beginning, middle, and end with sticky notes labeled "B," "M," and "E" and practice retelling.

Team Planning Tool: Determining a Story's Central Theme, Moral, or Lesson—Third Grade	
Standard We're Teaching	**Third grade:** Recount stories, including fables, folktales, and myths from diverse cultures, determine the central message, lesson, or moral, and explain how it is conveyed through key details in the text.
Academic Vocabulary We'll Use and Expect to Hear	• *fable* • *folktale* • *myth* • *central message* • *lesson* • *moral* • *key details in the text*
Whole-Group Ideas	• Read aloud stories, including fables, folktales, and myths. • Use retelling ideas (from previous section) and help kids think about beginning, middle, and end. • Create anchor chart on central message, lesson, or moral. • Make a chart of ongoing lessons learned from various stories, fables, folktales, and myths (include thumbnail photo of the book). • Use conversation cards to guide talk about central message, lesson, or moral.
Partner Practice at Literacy Work Stations	**Classroom library:** Students can choose to read books from book baskets labeled "Fables," "Folktales," and "Myths." They can put fiction books in this category as they find books that belong in that genre. **Buddy-reading station:** Partners read together stories, fables, folktales, or myths, and use conversation cards to discuss message, lesson, or moral. **Listening station:** Pairs listen to stories and discuss message, lesson, or moral.

**Lessons That Last: Whole-Group Mini-Lesson Plan
for Determining a Story's Central Theme, Moral, or Lesson—Third Grade**

Myths and Morals

Focus: recounting a myth, telling the central lesson

(Note: Similar lessons should be taught using fables and folktales, as well as other stories.)

Method to Maximize Student Engagement: short video on King Midas; turn and talk; conversation cards

Materials: video on King Midas; *Greek Myths* by Deborah Lock; *The Chocolate Touch* by Patrick Skene Catling; conversation card; anchor chart on morals, lessons, or central theme of stories; chart paper and markers; thumbnail photo of King Midas; glue stick

Model: how to read and think about the lesson or moral in a myth

Prompting for Independence:

- "A *myth* is an *ancient,* or very old, story that has been told for a very long time to teach a lesson."

- "Many myths we learn about in school *originated,* or began, in ancient cultures, such as Greece, Rome, and Egypt."

- "The *moral* or *lesson learned* from this myth is . . ." (You might make a conversation card, too.)

Mini-Lesson Procedure:

1. Tell students they will be reading stories called *myths* that are ancient, or very old, tales told and passed down through generations to teach morals or lessons.

2. Show a brief video clip about King Midas to pique their interest. Tell students to pay attention to the main character and what he does. We will learn the lesson from him. Have kids turn and talk to each other about what they learned about King Midas.

3. After discussing the video and what kids learned about King Midas, read aloud the title "The Foolishness of Midas" from the book *Greek Myths.* Have kids turn and talk about what they learn from the title.

4. Then read the story aloud. Ask kids to pay attention to Midas being foolish in the book. You might ask them to put their hands on their heads when they hear a part where Midas is foolish. Stop at those points and chart the events. (See the photos on page 69 for a sample chart.)

5. When finished reading, look at the events listed and help students come up with the lesson learned from this story. Use a conversation card that says, "The moral or lesson learned from this story is _____." Help kids fill in the blank orally with "Be careful what you wish for." Then add this moral or lesson to an ongoing three-column chart that lists "Themes, Lessons, and Morals Learned from Stories." Glue a photo of King Midas on the left column with the book title recorded in the middle column and the lesson learned in the third column. Place this chart near the classroom library. Continue to add to the chart throughout your study of themes, morals, and lessons. Invite students to do the same when they are at the classroom library. Ask them to write their ideas on sticky notes affixed to the chart.

6. As a follow-up, you might read aloud *The Chocolate Touch* by Patrick Skene Catling, a story with connections to King Midas. Again, help students determine the central message, lesson, or moral from this new piece of literature.

On-the-Spot Assessment: Were students able to identify parts in the story where King Midas was foolish? Did they identify the lesson or moral in the myth? Could they connect what they learned to the new book?

This sample chart about the foolishness of King Midas was made with a third-grade class.

A three-column chart made with the class includes thumbnail photos of book covers with corresponding titles and lessons learned. It can be added to over time.

Chapter 5

Mentor Texts for Modeling:
Retelling Literature and Determining a Story's Central Theme, Moral, or Lesson

For retelling:
- Short folktales, such as *Goldilocks and the Three Bears* or *The Three Little Pigs*
- *Bear's Shadow* by Frank Asch
- *Caps for Sale* by Esphyr Slobodkina
- *Last One in Is a Rotten Egg* by Leonard Kessler
- *Flower Garden* by Eve Bunting
- *Knuffle Bunny* by Mo Willems
- *Hattie and the Fox* by Mem Fox
- *My Friend Rabbit* by Eric Rohmann
- *The Gigantic Turnip* by Aleksei Tolstoy
- *Clever Jack Takes the Cake* by Candace Fleming

- *The Princess and the Pig* by Jonathan Emmett
- *A Piece of Cake* by LeUyen Pham

For determining a story's central theme, moral, or lesson:
- *Fables* by Arnold Lobel
- *Greek Myths* by Deborah Lock
- *The Chocolate Touch* by Patrick Skene Catling
- *The Can Man* by Laura Williams
- *The Teddy Bear* by David McPhail
- *The Recess Queen* by Alexis O'Neill
- *Peanut Butter and Jellyfish* by Jarrett Krosoczka
- *Sparrow Girl* by Sarah Pennypacker
- *Templeton Gets His Wish* by Greg Pizzoli
- *City Dog, Country Frog* by Mo Willems

Teaching Tips for Retelling Literature and Determining a Story's Central Theme, Moral, or Lesson Across the Grades	
In Pre-K and Kindergarten	• Choose simple stories for retelling with clear beginnings, middles, and endings. • Familiar folktales work well for retelling. • Use retelling pieces and a BME (beginning-middle-end) map. Have kids move the retelling pieces to the appropriate box as they retell.
In Grades One–Two	• Be sure to use fables by second grade (as well as folktales). They will help students find lessons or morals that may not be as evident in other stories. • These same folktales can be used for comparing and contrasting, too.
In Grades Three and Up	• If students have a good foundation of retelling in K–3, summarizing will be much easier for them by fourth grade. Students will need to recognize summaries on tests. Help them select from multiple choices, telling *why* some are not the best summary (for example, *doesn't include the most important information; too many details; inaccurate*). • Familiarize older students with Greek myths. Do this only after they can identify morals or lessons from folktales and fables, since myths are more sophisticated.

Sample Anchor Charts for Retelling Literature and Determining a Story's Central Theme, Moral, or Lesson

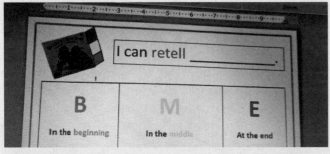

This simple BME anchor chart made with kindergartners uses color and picture support to help young children retell. The photo of the Goldilocks and the Three Bears book with colored sticky notes marking the book's beginning, middle, and end serves as a reminder for when and how they learned about retelling key details from the story. If the chart is laminated, it can be written on and used over and over again.

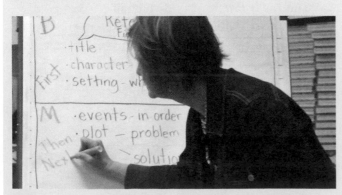

We focused on words that show time order on this retelling anchor chart made with a first-grade class.

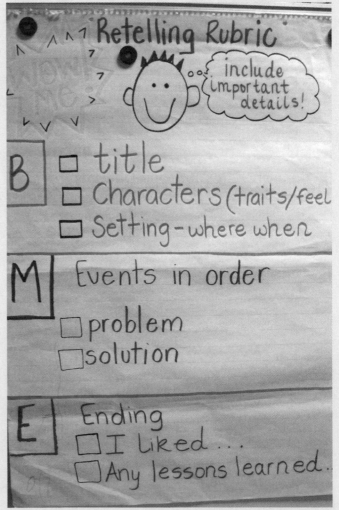

This retelling anchor chart made with a second-grade class can also be used for self-assessment of student retellings.

A second-grade class views a prerecorded video of their teacher retelling a familiar story. They use smaller copies of the retelling rubric to rate the teacher's retellings. The teacher shows several versions of herself retelling, including a poor one and an excellent one so students can identify what constitutes high-quality retelling.

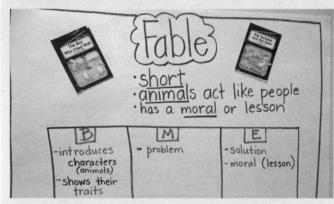

This very simple anchor chart helps students remember what differentiates a fable from other types of fiction. It hangs in the classroom library and includes samples of fables read aloud to the class.

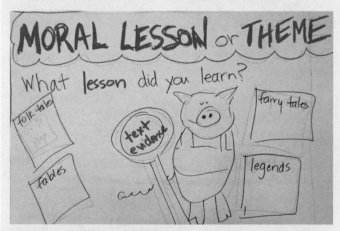

This is a plan for an upcoming anchor chart to be made with the class. The design was sketched in pencil ahead of time on plain white 8½-by-11-inch paper, and then color was added to make certain words pop. Pictures of book covers can be added as the teacher reads aloud different types of books to children in whole-group mini-lessons to teach about moral, lesson, or theme in literature.

Anchor chart about determining a story's central message or lesson. The word *theme* could also be added to the title.

Literacy Work Stations for Retelling Literature and Determining a Story's Central Theme, Moral, or Lesson

This portable buddy-reading station for kindergarten through grade one includes an "I Can" list made with the class, so students can remember what they're expected to do here. Partners read a book together, use a retelling card for support, and then write key details using pictures and words on a piece of paper folded in thirds and labeled BME. To differentiate, zip-top bags of books at different levels are marked with colored dots for different reading groups and stored in the container. All materials and procedures were used multiple times as part of whole-group instruction before this was moved to a station. Students can use this station over and over again. All you will have to change are the books for retelling, over time. Ask students for input on when new books should be added.

This station makes available differentiated bags of books with colored dots matching guided-reading groups. A differentiated retelling card marked with a yellow dot is provided for students in that group who need a simpler support for success.

A pair of students uses retelling cards from the core reading program to talk about and retell a familiar story in first grade. As you teach with new literature, add the retelling cards, too. It's okay to have stories and retelling cards from the past for students to revisit. The more they work with favorite stories, the more they'll remember them.

After reading a book with his partner, a kindergarten student retells the little book *Dot and Dan* in pictures and words. Then he uses his writing to retell: *In the beginning, Dot and Dan say, "Can we go?" In the middle, Dot and Dan make a mess. At the end, he takes the dog for a walk.*

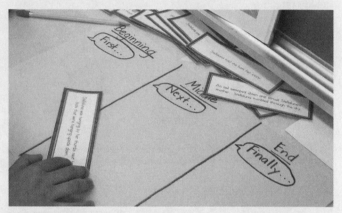

Students retell favorite stories from whole group using strips to sequence major events in order. Time order words *First, Next,* and *Finally* are written on a retelling board for support to effectively retell stories. Pictures from the book support vulnerable readers, too. Make new strips for retelling the beginning, middle, and end of stories during whole group. Then move them to this station for practice. Hole-punch the strips for a story and put them on a one-inch metal book ring along with the book.

Partners use retelling pieces along with a familiar book from read-aloud to retell a story at a retelling station. At any given time, there may be two or three different stories with matching retelling pieces at this station. Periodically, change out the books and matching retelling pieces as you teach with new materials. Keep some old favorites there, too.

Partners use a mini-anchor chart with retelling words on it for support at a portable listening station. They also have a recording sheet where they write about the characters, setting, problem, and solution.

Describing Characters, Settings, and Major Events in a Story

Stories contain interesting and amusing characters that often entertain and delight us. What young child doesn't love the antics of Clifford, the Big Red Dog or the heroic endeavors of Captain Underpants? When we read series books, we are able to interact with these favorite characters again and again. And in the process, we get know to them better. When we learn how to think deeply about characters and analyze them, we learn about what it's like to be human. We connect with characters that remind us of who we are and what we'd like to be (or not be). This, in turn, can lead to learning about human character or our own qualities.

Stories also include settings that can vary from the forest to the beach or the city during any season and across many time periods. We can travel in time and space through literature and take our students along for the ride! As they learn about setting, our children can deliberately choose to visit a new place or explore a historical or futuristic time.

Stories have plots, major events in which we follow characters into settings where they may encounter adventure, difficulty, funny situations, or even mystery. If we understand how stories are structured, we can better comprehend what we are reading and take away the most from this experience.

Sifting Through the Standard: Describing Characters, Settings, and Major Events in a Story	
What It Is	• Being able to identify and describe the characters, settings, and major events using key ideas from the story • Discussing how a character's traits, actions, and feelings influence what that character does and why • Comparing and contrasting characters, settings, and plots in stories by the same author, especially in a series
Why It's Important	• Describing characters, settings, and major events in a story aids reading comprehension of literature. • Reading research has shown that good readers attend closely to characters and setting when reading literature (Farstrup and Samuels 2011). • Understanding characters can help a reader make predictions about future events in a story, especially in series books. • Identifying a story's setting helps readers put themselves in that story's time and place to better understand what happens. • Describing major events in a story creates a "storyboard in the mind"—a visual of the big things that happened.
Prerequisites Needed	• Knowing the difference between fiction and nonfiction text • Knowing and expecting story elements (character, setting, plot or problem/solution) in literature • Understanding how to describe, using details to create a visual image
Academic Vocabulary	Kindergarten: • *identify* • *character* • *character actions* • *character feelings* • *setting* • *major/key event* • *story* First grade: • *describe* • *key details* • *plot (problem and solution)*

(continued on next page)

Sifting Through the Standard:
Describing Characters, Settings, and Major Events in a Story *(continued)*

Academic Vocabulary	Second grade: • *respond* • *character traits* • *character motivation* • *challenges* • *similarities* • *differences* • *main character* Third grade: • *how character actions contribute to the sequence of events*
Real-World Connections	• When we tell stories about our lives, we talk about who (characters, usually starting with ourselves) did what (events or actions) when and where (setting). • Relating story elements to students' favorite television shows and movies is a natural connection, too.
Examples of Test Questions	• "What motivated the character _____ to do _____?" • "What is the relationship between _____ and _____ in this story?" • "What can you conclude about the character _____?" • "The character (_____)'s mood changes from the beginning of the story to the end. How does this character feel at the beginning of the story? How does he/she feel at the end? Why does his/her mood change? Use details from the story to support your response." • "How did the setting influence events in this story?" • "Which event from the story completes this graphic organizer?"

Team Planning Tool:
Describing Characters, Settings, and Major Events in a Story—First Grade

Standard We're Teaching	**First grade:** Describe characters (and the reasons for their actions and feelings), settings, and major events (including plot or problem/solution) in a story, using key details.
Academic Vocabulary We'll Use and Expect to Hear	• *describe* • *characters* • *character actions* • *character feelings* • *settings* • *major events* • *plot (problem and solution)* • *key details*
Whole-Group Ideas	• Read aloud books (multiple times) with one or two strong, memorable characters. • Model how to read the beginning of a story and pick out details about the main character(s), including what the character looks like, and how he acts and feels (and why). • Create anchor charts about story elements, including one on character analysis, another on setting, and another about plot/major story events. • Use a graphic organizer, such as the circle map, to describe a main character in a story.

(continued on next page)

Chapter 5

Team Planning Tool:	
Describing Characters, Settings, and Major Events in a Story—First Grade *(continued)*	

Whole-Group Ideas	• Use conversation cards: "I think _____ feels _____ because _____. I think _____ did _____ because _____." • Model how to create speech and thought bubbles showing what characters feel and do in stories. • Do similar work with settings and key events. • Make a fiction beach ball, using a blank inflatable beach ball from a discount store, and write one of the following in each space: "describe a character"; "describe a character action and why"; "describe a character feeling and why"; "describe the setting"; "talk about the plot (problem and solution)"; "tell major events with key details." Model how to toss the ball to discuss story elements.
Partner Practice at Literacy Work Stations	**Character-analysis station:** Place books in a series along with a stick puppet or stuffed animal of the main character in a basket (such as Little Critter, Llama Llama, or Skippyjon Jones). Partners work together to describe the character using a graphic organizer and predict then discuss that character's actions and feelings as they read. They use a conversation card, too. In addition, they might write speech and thought bubbles about what that character feels and does and add those to a display around a character. **Creation station:** Have students create story-setting backdrops that include details important to the retelling of favorite stories. Be sure to include literature here, too, and information about setting. Encourage students to discuss how setting contributes to events in the story as they create. **Buddy-reading station:** Partners read a story and use the fiction beach ball to discuss story elements. **Listening station:** Partners listen to a story and then discuss it using the fiction beach ball.

Chapter 5

Lessons That Last: Whole-Group Mini-Lesson Plan for Describing Characters,	
Settings, and Major Events in a Story—First Grade	

Characters We Love

Focus: describing and analyzing characters (or setting or major events) from a story

Method to Maximize Student Engagement: a favorite story with a character (or memorable setting or events) kids will love and remember (series books are great for characters; use stories with varied settings over time; begin with events similar to those in kids' own lives); showing my thinking and jotting it on an anchor chart; turn and talk (kids describe a character, setting, or major events to someone sitting near them)

Materials: favorite story with a strong character, such as Llama Llama in *Llama Llama Red Pajama*; stick puppet or stuffed animal of that character; 18-by-24-inch white construction paper and colored markers for an anchor chart on character analysis; cutout picture of the character and a glue stick for a student to affix it to the chart; index cards for conversation cards

Model: how to think about and then jot down key details that describe what the character looks like, his or her feelings and actions, and reasons for them

Prompting for Independence:

• "Characters develop throughout a story. Read a part and then stop and think about what you just learned about the character. This can help you make predictions about what this character might do next."

• "What major event just happened? What did the character do and why? How do you think the character feels? Why?"

(continued on next page)

Lessons That Last: Whole-Group Mini-Lesson Plan for Describing Characters, Settings, and Major Events in a Story—First Grade *(continued)*

- "Describe the setting the author chose for this story. How does the setting add to the story?"
- "What were the major events in the story? We could use the major events to retell this story to someone."

Mini-Lesson Procedure:

1. Choose an interesting story that kids will enjoy with a strong character (or setting or events) with whom/which they can relate.

2. Tell students that thinking about a character (or setting or major events) can help them better understand what they read in a story. Label your anchor chart "Stories Have Characters" (or "Settings" or "Major Events/Plot"). Add to the chart as you read and think aloud about that particular story element. You'll want to do this across several days.

3. Show students the read-aloud book and matching stuffed animal or cardstock cutout and explain that stories have characters, settings, and major events. The author and illustrator often give clues about these elements on the front and back covers. Looking at the illustration on the title page sometimes tells a bit more. Look at them to see what you can find out before reading the book.

4. Look at the cover and title page, and think aloud about what you learn about the characters (there's a baby llama on the cover who looks scared, because his eyes are really big and he's holding a stuffed animal); setting (looks like it's bedtime because he's in bed); and major events (I think he is scared about going to sleep, and his mama will help him).

5. Then read aloud the text, a bit at a time, pausing to think with students about the main character. On the anchor chart, set up spaces for "describe character"; "character actions/why?"; and "character feelings/why?" Record your ideas (and those of your students) on the chart. Note: I did this on a dry erase board first to be sure the categories worked well. Later, I made a blank chart and laminated it so it could be used over and over.

6. Continue this procedure throughout the text, adding to the chart. On another day, you might make a second anchor chart titled "Stories Have Settings" and jot down what you want kids to remember about setting. Be sure to include "Where" and "When." Show how sometimes the setting changes in a story and how important it is to understand when this happens.

7. On yet another day, create an anchor chart with students with the theme "Stories Have Major Events" (or "Plots with Problems and Solutions"). Use a flow map graphic organizer to help kids keep track of major events.

8. When finished with any of the above, have kids share what they learned about characters, settings, or major events with the class.

9. Repeat these lessons with multiple pieces of literature to familiarize students with story elements and how understanding them can help them comprehend literature.

On-the-Spot Assessment: Ask students to share what they learned about characters, settings, or major events during whole-group lessons. You might put students' names on sticks in a cup and pull them out to be sure you are calling on all kids over time (and not just those with their hands up).

Connections to Whole-Group Mini-Lesson

Independent Reading Connection: Be sure all students are reading fiction when you're helping them think about characters, settings, and major events. Ask kids to think about the story element you have been teaching about during whole group. Then give them a graphic organizer or sticky note to jot down what they learned about either characters or settings or major events, depending on your focus. Have them share with a partner (or the class) what they learned.

Small-Group Connection: Use the same language (and anchor charts) as you taught with from whole-group instruction. Help students make connections between what was modeled in whole group and what you expect them to do with a bit of support in small group. Have them jot down notes on the same graphic organizers you modeled with from whole group to help students keep track of what they learn about characters, settings, and/or major events as they read fiction. Have them use their notes to describe those story elements after reading, too.

(continued on next page)

Connections to Whole-Group Mini-Lesson *(continued)*

Writing Connection: Help students use what they're learning about characters, settings, and major events to write their own narratives. Begin by having them tell stories and then write them down. They might use graphic organizers like those used in whole group and small group to help them think about their stories before writing them. Also, use read-aloud books from whole group as mentor texts to study how these authors describe characters, settings, and major events. Encourage your children to try this, too.

Evaluation: After ample instruction and practice, give students a new grade-level story to read independently. Have them use the graphic organizers you taught with to describe characters, settings, and major events in the story. Or have individuals tell you about the characters, settings, and major events in the story, and use a checklist anecdotal note form like the one in Figure 5.2. (This may work well if you have a standards-based report card.)

Figure 5.2 **Anecdotal Note Form for Describing Characters, Settings, and Major Events**

Student Name	Describes Characters (including key details about how they act and feel and why)	Describes Settings (how they contribute to the story and how they change in the story)	Describes Major Events (tells important parts in order)

Mentor Texts for Modeling:
Describing Characters, Settings, and Major Events in a Story

For characters:
- Llama Llama books by Anna Dewdney
- Skippyjon Jones books by Judy Schachner
- Fly Guy books by Tedd Arnold
- Little Critter books by Mercer Mayer
- Henry and Mudge books by Cynthia Rylant
- Frog and Toad books by Arnold Lobel
- Fancy Nancy series by Jane O'Connor
- *Henny* by Elizabeth Rose Stanton
- *Stand Tall, Molly Lou Melon* by Patty Lovell
- *Oddrey* by Dave Whammond
- *Wolfie the Bunny* by Ame Dyckman

- Elephant and Piggie series by Mo Willems
- *Ballet Cat: The Totally Secret Secret* by Bob Shea

For setting:
- *Owl Moon* by Jane Yolen
- *The Relatives Came* by Cynthia Rylant
- *Nana in the City* by Lauren Castillo
- Bats at the Ballgame series by Brian Lies
- *Thunder Cake* by Patricia Polacco
- *Cloudy with a Chance of Meatballs* by Judi Barrett

For major event/plot:
- *Elizabeth, Queen of the Seas* by Lynne Cox
- *Doctor Desoto* by William Stieg
- *Lily's Purple Plastic Purse* by Kevin Henkes
- *The Lorax* by Dr. Seuss
- *Nugget and Fang* by Tammi Sauer

Chapter 5

Teaching Tips for Describing Characters, Settings, and Major Events in a Story Across the Grades	
In Pre-K and Kindergarten	• Choose short stories with one main character with a memorable personality that appears in many series books (so kids really get to know the character well). • Use stick puppets of the main characters and setting backdrops to help kids remember these elements and aid them in retelling major events from the story.
In Grades One–Two	• Again, look for memorable characters that appear over and over again in series or simple chapter books. Start with books with one main character, and then move to books with two, such as Annie and Jack in the Magic Tree House books. • As you look at fairy tales, especially in second grade, help students identify good and evil characters, similar settings (forests and castles, *once upon a time*), elements of magic, and things in groups of three. • Help children use what they learn about characters and settings to make predictions about events in fiction. • Be sure to extend the work children do into describing how characters in a story respond to major events and challenges.
In Grades Three and Up	• Chapter books work well here, but so do picture books for analyzing characters. • Expose students to historical and science fiction, and examine what to expect in the settings of these genres (things that happened long ago in historical fiction and futuristic events in science fiction). • By fifth grade, kids should be comparing and contrasting two or more characters, settings, or events in a story or drama, drawing on details from the text (such as how characters interact in stories).

Sample Anchor Charts for Describing Characters, Settings, and Major Events in a Story

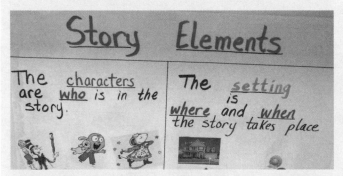

As students learn about characters in literature, new pictures of their favorite characters are added to this anchor chart in pre-K or kindergarten.

Young children use sticky notes with drawings and words to describe the character Sheila Rae on a circle map from www.thinkingmaps.com.

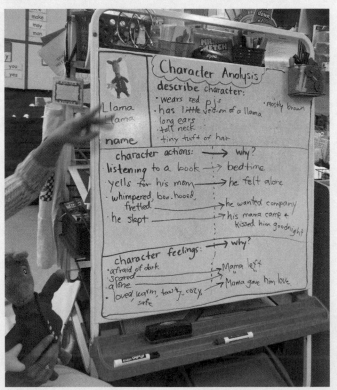

A first-grade class makes an anchor chart about the character Llama Llama during a read-aloud of students' favorite book, *Llama Llama Red Pajama* by Anna Dewdney. First, we describe the character. Then, we look at the character's actions and reasons for each one. Finally, we analyze the character's feelings and why he might have felt this way. This is later made into a blank laminated chart for partners to use at the character-analysis station.

"Do you think this story will have evil characters or good characters?" a second-grade teacher asks the class while referring to an anchor chart about story elements found in traditional tales.

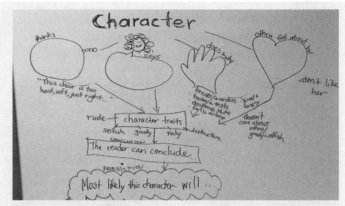

This sketch of a third-grade plan for an anchor chart on drawing conclusions about characters (*above*) provided the basis for the final anchor chart (*below*).

This third-grade anchor chart about setting includes more detailed information than charts for lower grade levels. This can help as students read genres such as historical fiction, fantasy, or science fiction.

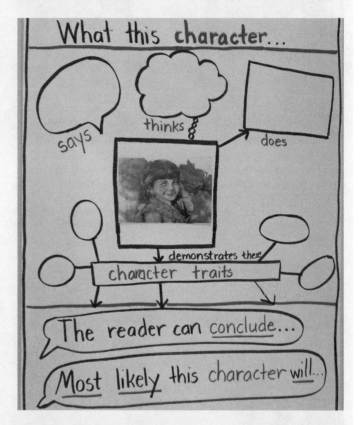

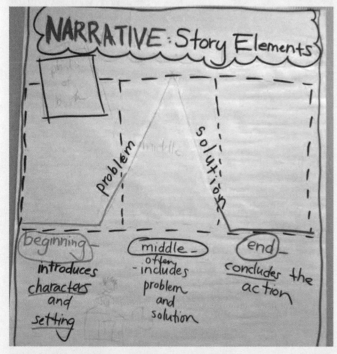

This plan for an anchor chart was made before teaching a lesson on story elements in second grade.

Character feelings with illustrations is used during whole-group lessons to help students move beyond happy, mad, and sad.

Chapter 5

Literacy Work Stations for Describing Characters, Settings, and Major Events in a Story

In response to listening to a recorded story, this student records what she now knows about its characters, setting, problem, and solution. Writing with a dry erase pen on a laminated graphic organizer attached to a file cabinet makes this fun. Note the "I Can" list posted here. Change the books at this station over time. Kids can record stories for their classmates to listen to, too.

Students can record what they learned about the characters, setting, or beginning, middle, and end of a story by choosing a graphic organizer in the classroom library. Each organizer is housed in a file folder with a copy of the graphic on the front. Having all materials at students' fingertips in this station makes it easy for kids to use them and reduces movement around the room that might distract others at work. Finished graphic organizers can be displayed on the bulletin board in this area. Plenty of books keep this station going all year long.

At a creation station, this student makes a poster of story elements to go with a story read in the core program collection taught in whole group. The poster is then displayed in the classroom library, encouraging others to reread the story. Change the books at this station periodically. Instead of making a poster, students might make a bookmark, write a book review, or write a song using story elements.

A large, laminated graphic organizer can be used by students to write down their thinking about setting as they listen to a recorded story together at the listening station. Just be sure you've taught with this graphic organizer in whole group before moving it to the station for independent practice! Again, simply change books or graphic organizers over time.

Kindergartners record in pictures and words what they learned about the characters and setting of a story at the buddy-reading station.

At a fiction buddy-reading station in first grade, students respond to questions about character, setting, and plot on sticky notes. The books and the question cards change periodically.

Partners read a Llama Llama book and then record their thinking on the character-analysis anchor chart made in whole group. Characters and books change over time.

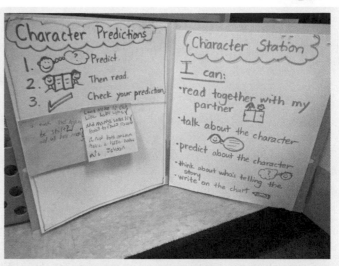

Supports at the character-analysis station remain there all year.

A pair of students chooses to read and act out a Llama Llama story at the character-analysis station.

Separate baskets hold a character stuffed animal (or a character's picture on a stick) along with books starring that character to use at the character-analysis station. Introduce new character baskets throughout the year.

Chapter 5

Acknowledging Differences in Characters' Points of View

A valuable lesson my dad taught me when I was young is that there are always (at least) two sides to a story. Understanding and acknowledging another person's point of view can help us get along better with each other both at home and in the world. Character education is sorely needed in many schools today because it is not always taught at home, but it can be tough to find extra time to teach this curriculum. If we focus on acknowledging points of view while reading literature, we can infuse our literacy lessons with character-building principles as well as improve reading comprehension and fluency.

Reading interesting stories with dialogue, captivating plays and reader's theater scripts, and sensory or even silly poems can help children think about points of view and read fluently as they speak in different voices for different characters. Fairy tales (original and fractured or retold) provide excellent opportunities for examining point of view. Lively discussions may ensue as children consider *The Three Little Pigs* or *Goldilocks and the Three Bears* from multiple points of view. Along with these traditional folktales, read aloud picture books such as Jon Scieszka's *The True Story of the 3 Little Pigs!* or Nancy Louwen's *Believe Me, Goldilocks Rocks: The Story of the Three Bears as Told by Baby Bear*. Then ask, "How does the story change when told from the perspective of the wolf versus one of the pigs, or Goldilocks instead of the three bears?" As students become third graders, this can be taken even further, when they are ready to discern their own point of view from that of the characters or narrator. This is sophisticated stuff that requires a firm foundation.

Take your time teaching kids to pay attention to points of view. Be sure *they* are using this academic vocabulary. We should not be the only ones in the classroom using these terms. As you read aloud, have young children say (or repeat), "The *author* is Jan Brett. She is telling the story with the words." Or "The *illustrator* is Paul Galdone. That means he did the drawings and an paintings in the book. Sometimes a person is an *author* and an *illustrator*." "Eric Carle wrote the words *and* drew the pictures." "Little Red Riding Hood is the *main character* in this story." And as you work with older students, "The *narrator* is telling the story here. He seems to be standing outside watching the characters. Now the story is being told from the *point of view of the wolf*. The wolf is hungry and wants to eat the little pigs, but they are working hard to stay away from him."

Sifting Through the Standard: Acknowledging Differences in Characters' Points of View	
What It Is	• Point of view is the perspective from which the story is told: who is telling it at any given point and conveying the opinion or feelings of the characters in the story. • Point of view is used in stories, essays, and poems to convey characters' feelings.
Why It's Important	• Knowing who is telling the story affects comprehension. We are given glimpses into characters through points of view. • Reading fluency (especially reading dialogue) is affected by identifying points of view. As we read and think about who is talking and what that character is like, we can use different voices and expression to read/talk like the specific characters in literature, including dramas, plays, and poetry. • As readers mature, it is important that they learn to differentiate between their own points of view and those of characters in a story, play, poem, or essay.
Prerequisites Needed	• Understanding the difference between *author*, *illustrator*, *character*, and *narrator*. These are all people related to stories and can be confusing to young readers. • Knowing which character a pronoun refers to in the text (for example, *Miguel was looking forward to seeing his dad that evening. He thought about the fun they would have together.* The narrator is telling this part of the story. *He* refers to Miguel, not Miguel's dad.) • Making personal connections helps us understand and engage with what we're reading.

(continued on next page)

Sifting Through the Standard: **Acknowledging Differences in Characters' Points of View** *(continued)*	
Academic Vocabulary	Kindergarten: • *author* • *illustrator* • *role in telling the story* • *play/drama* • *poem* First grade: • *who is telling the story* • *character* • *narrator* • *quotation marks* Second grade: • *character's point of view* • *dialogue* Third grade: • *your point of view* • *narrator's point of view* • *script* • *cast of characters* • *first person* • *third person*
Real-World Connections	• Point of view is perspective. It can be helpful in life to be able to consider different perspectives when making decisions. If we understand someone else's point of view, it can help us get along better with others. • Help kids think about point of view when this comes up naturally in the classroom. For example, when two children have a conflict, talk about their *points of view* to help them understand each other and resolve the problem.
Example Test Questions	• "Which of the following best describes the point of view of [character name]?" • "Which character is telling the story in paragraph ___? How do you know?" • "Is this part of the story told in first or third person? Use text evidence to show your thinking."

Team Planning Tool: **Acknowledging Differences in Characters' Point of View—Second Grade**	
Standard We're Teaching	**Second grade:** Acknowledge differences in the point of view, including by speaking in a different voice for each character when reading dialogue aloud.
Academic Vocabulary We'll Use and Expect to Hear	• *narrator is telling the story* • *the character _____ is telling the story* • *character's point of view* • *dialogue* • *quotation marks* • *play*

(continued on next page)

Chapter 5

Team Planning Tool:
Acknowledging Differences in Characters' Point of View—Second Grade *(continued)*

Whole-Group Ideas	• Using a projection device, do shared reading of plays, such as *12 Fabulously Funny Fairy Tale Plays* by Justin McCory Martin (2002).
	• Use character cards so everyone has a part to read.
	• Point out the text structure of a play and how to read it.
	• Model how to think about who is telling the story each time a new part is read.
	• Model how to think about each character's (or narrator's) point of view and make your voice sound like that character. Use point-of-view sticks made from a tongue depressor and a thought bubble taped to it labeled "C" or "N" (for *Character* or *Narrator*).
	• Make an anchor chart for point of view.
	• Make conversation cards for point of view. *I think _____'s point of view is _____ because _____.*
Partner Practice at Literacy Work Stations	**Drama station:** A pair of students distribute the character cards to go with a play, so they both have specific parts to read. Then they read the play together, using different voices and the point-of-view conversation cards to discuss the perspective of the different characters and narrator.
	Speech-bubble-writing station: Students choose a character from a story, drama, or poem and write what that person is thinking or feeling in a speech bubble in a selected part of the text after reading or listening to that piece of literature.
	Writing station: Partners work together to write their own plays, using a simple folk-tale such as *The Three Little _____s.*
	Buddy-reading station: Partners read a story together, using point-of-view sticks. They read a bit and think about who's telling the story; then they talk about that character's (or narrator's) point of view.
	Poetry station: Kids read poems written from the point of view of an animal or an inanimate object and identify point of view using conversation cards. Or they can write a poem from a particular point of view. For example, "Pretend you are a [spring flower, kite, cloud, and so on]." As a class, generate topics for this station.

First graders hold up the side of the card showing who is talking during a whole-group read-aloud. The letter C denotes a character and N, the narrator. The teacher can quickly check for understanding, plus students are readily engaged.

Chapter 5

Lessons That Last: Whole-Group Mini-Lesson Plan for Acknowledging Differences in Characters' Points of View—Second Grade

Character Cards and Point of View

Focus: noting different points of view in characters and speaking in different voices for each when reading dialogue

Method to Maximize Student Engagement: shared reading of a fun play; using different voices to go with each character; character cards to divide up parts among the class (each character's name written on a card)

(Note: Teach this mini-lesson multiple times with different pieces of literature, including plays, reader's theater scripts, stories with dialogue, sections of chapter books, and poems.)

Materials: play from *12 Fabulously Funny Fairy Tale Plays* by Justin McCory Martin (2002); character cards (index cards, each noting the name of a character from the drama or story); point-of-view anchor chart

Model: how to think about who's talking in the story and how to change your voice according to that character's point of view

Prompting for Independence:

- "Who is talking now? What is this character's point of view? How do you know?"
- "How would that character speak to show how he/she is feeling or what he/she is thinking? Make your voice sound like that emotion when reading."
- "Which character is telling the story? How does that affect the story? How might the story change if a different character told the story?"

Mini-Lesson Procedure:

1. Choose a play (or story or poem) that children will enjoy and connect to that has different parts and different points of view and dialogue, such as "The Popsicle Man"—based on "The Gingerbread Man"—from *12 Fabulously Funny Fairy Tale Plays* by Justin McCory Martin.

2. Explain that when we read a play (or dialogue), it's important to think about who's talking and to identify that character's point of view. That will help us understand the character and the action in the story as we read. Demonstrate how to use different voices for different characters based on what the author tells us about that character.

3. Refer to your point-of-view anchor chart as you demonstrate thinking about point of view for characters, such as Little Baby (who cries and has a baby voice) and Popsicle Boy (who speaks boldly as he evades those chasing after him).

4. Make the text accessible to all students by using a projection device to display the text of the play on a screen or whiteboard. Then read the names of the characters and distribute the character cards to groups of children, so that all students have a part to read collectively. (If you use this play, there will be Narrator, Little Baby, Popsicle Boy, Jump-Rope Girl, Boy on Bike, and Dog. Write each character's name on an index card.)

5. Do a shared reading of the play, with each group reading their part together chorally. As each character speaks, ask kids to think for a second about the character and his or her point of view and how he or she would sound.

6. When finished, have kids turn to a buddy and share what they liked about this play. Ask a few students to share with the class. Then have buddies tell each other what they learned about using point of view to read with different voices. Again, have one or two students share with the class.

7. Remind students to think about point of view as they read plays, stories, and poems. They can learn a lot about characters and their feelings as they consider point of view, and they can use the information to use different voices to read dialogue in literature.

On-the-Spot Assessment: Listen to students' responses. Are they using different voices that reflect the characters and their points of view?

Chapter 5

Connections to Whole-Group Mini-Lesson

Independent Reading Connection: Find plays (or reader's theater scripts, or stories with dialogue, or poems, depending on what you've modeled with) written on the independent reading levels of your class. Put kids in pairs or small groups and teach them how to make their own character cards that represent the parts played in the dramas. Then have them divide the cards between them and read the play. Remind them to think about point of view and use different character voices for each character. When finished, they may switch parts and read again.

Small-Group Connection: Over time, be sure to expose your students to reading plays (as well as other types of literature) in small group, too. Reading a play encourages students to think about point of view and use different voices when reading dialogue, which affects fluency.

Writing Connection: Work as a class to write a play, fracturing a simple folktale they know and love. For example, you might write "The Three Penguins." Provide a frame for support. See page 89 for ideas on how to do this.

Evaluation: Listen to students read a play or story with dialogue during independent reading time or small group. Use a rubric to evaluate how well the child understands point of view and reading dialogue with expression.

Mentor Texts for Modeling:
Acknowledging Differences in Characters' Point of View

- Plays, such as *25 Science Plays for Emergent Readers* by Sheryl Ann Crawford and Nancy I. Sanders or *12 Fabulously Funny Fairy Tale Plays* by Justin McCory Martin
- Reader's theater scripts, such as those from Benchmark Education
- Books in a series, such as *The World According to Humphrey* by Betty G. Birney. (This is a delightful series for third grade.)

- Books that tell folktales from different perspectives, such as *The True Story of the 3 Little Pigs!* by Jon Scieszka or *Believe Me, Goldilocks Rocks: The Story of the Three Bears as Told by Baby Bear* by Nancy Louwen
- *The Story of Fish and Snail* by Deborah Freedman
- *Winter Is for Snow* by Robert Neubecker
- *The Day the Crayons Quit* by Drew Daywalt
- *Duck! Rabbit!* by Amy Krouse Rosenthal
- *Voices in the Park* by Anthony Browne
- *Who Is Melvin Bubble?* by Nick Bruel
- *City Dog, Country Frog* by Mo Willems

Teaching Tips for Acknowledging Differences in Characters' Point of View Across the Grades

In Pre-K and Kindergarten

- Be sure to use the words *author, illustrator,* and *character* as you read aloud to students. Ask the children to use this academic vocabulary as they talk about books you're reading to them, too.

- Encourage students to use different voices when acting out stories that have been read aloud. Use retelling pieces or character masks to help them think about who's talking and how that character acts and feels.

(continued on next page)

Teaching Tips for Acknowledging Differences in Characters' Point of View Across the Grades *(continued)*	
In Grades One–Two	• Use plays, stories with dialogue, and poetry to teach your class about point of view. Fairy tales are a natural, since they include interesting, familiar characters, and many tales are available as told from different points of view. • Today, many children love to play video games. You can have them think about who's telling the story just like they think about who they are when playing a video game. When you're playing a game, you must think about point of view. If you are the target, you play the game differently from how you play it if you're the villain. • Give each child a card with an *N* (narrator) on one side and a *C* (character) on the other. As you read aloud, ask them to hold up the card to show who's talking (narrator or character) and discuss how they knew that and how the point of view changes throughout the piece of literature. • By second grade, writing fractured fairy tales can be fun for students. See photos of writing stations on page 97 for ideas.
In Grades Three and Up	• As students move into chapter books, there is a greater amount of dialogue (and less picture support) in literature. As much as we want students to make connections to the reading, they must learn to discriminate between their own point of view and those of the characters. They might still use the *N* (narrator) and *C* (character) cards as in grades one–two, but they also pause at places in literature to point to themselves and tell their point of view. • You might add a graphic organizer (see Figure 5.3) to your teaching that includes a character's point of view, the narrator's point of view, and the student's own point of view. • Continue to have students write fractured fairy tales and folktales to play with fiction elements and points of view. • Add the academic vocabulary *first person* and *third person* as directed by your standards. Make a conversation card that says *This part of the story is being told in _____ person. Text evidence that shows this is _____.*

Figure 5.3 **Graphic Organizer for Point of View**

Name_____ Title_____

Read and think about whose point of view is being given. Stop at the end of a chapter and write down a place in the text where you thought about point of view. Then jot down notes about that point of view under the column it matches. Was it the point of view of a character, the narrator, or your own point of view?

Text-Based Evidence and Page Number from Book	Character's Point of View	Narrator's Point of View	My Own Point of View

Sample Anchor Charts for Acknowledging Differences in Characters' Points of View

This pictorial anchor chart for kindergarten uses photos of children's book authors and illustrators from long ago and today. Note the pencil pointing to the words and the paintbrush pointing to the illustrations. Print the pictures in color ahead of time and gather two paintbrushes and pencils. Have the children help you attach the pieces to this anchor chart and refer to it often in reading and writing. Be sure kids are using the terms, too!

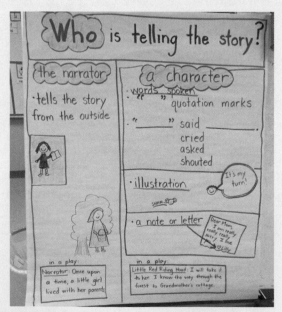

This anchor chart was made over several lessons in a first-grade classroom as part of mini-lessons on points of view. Shared reading was done to demonstrate how to read dialogue and pay attention to quotation marks. Students also noticed that sometimes the illustrator uses speech bubbles, notes, or letters to tell the story. We read stories and plays while making this anchor chart.

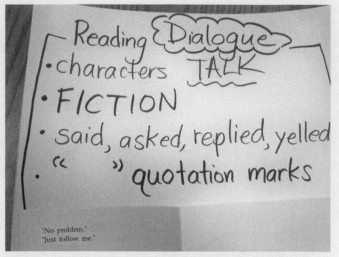

This anchor chart for reading dialogue was made quickly with a small group of students to assist them in guided reading. The teacher had not made an anchor chart in whole-group instruction. If just a few kids need this, it's okay to make the chart in small group; if most of the class needs support, make the anchor chart in whole-group instruction.

This point-of-view anchor chart from third grade includes examples of literature read aloud to illustrate first-person and third-person narratives.

Literacy Work Stations for Acknowledging Differences in Characters' Points of View

At the drama station, partners use character cards to determine who will read each part and use that character's voice while acting out the story or play. Change the plays periodically.

Students respond to a piece of literature read or listened to by writing something that a character might say in a speech bubble at the listening station or a writing station. Use paper with blank circles in place of the animals on the recording sheet, so kids can draw characters from any book.

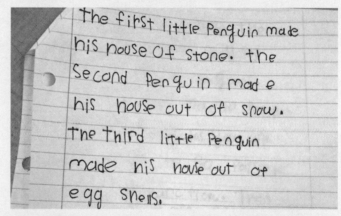

Students write fractured fairy tales based on *The Three Little Pigs* during writing workshop. They continue this work at a writing station in second and third grade. Various versions of *The Three Little Pigs* read aloud serve as mentor texts here. Supports (*pictured above*) have been used during whole-group instruction and are also placed at this station to help students remember story structure. Authors think about the different points of view as they write. Over time, use different folktales to fracture. Keep the story line simple to ensure student success.

Page 1 of a second grader's fractured fairy tale: "Once upon a time, there lived 3 little penguins and a mama penguin. One day the mama penguin said, 'Little penguins, you are old enough to go farther through Antarctica.' Then the little penguins set off to find a new home."

Page 2 continues . . . "The first little penguin made his house of stone. The second little penguin made his house out of snow. The third little penguin made his house out of eggshells."

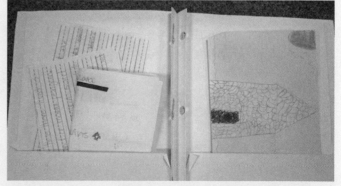

Students store their writing in a folder that they bring to the writing station as they write their fractured fairy tales in the same classroom.

At the buddy-reading station, partners read together and use narrator and character sticks in first grade (*left*) and conversation cards and a mini-anchor chart (*right*) to discuss point of view in third grade. Change literature periodically.

Digging Deeper

As you think about teaching students to read literature, start with your standards and academic vocabulary. The following questions can help you work as a team to plan for literacy work stations related to reading literature after you've read this chapter:

1. What ideas did you get for teaching literature from this chapter? What will you try first? How will you guarantee student success at literacy work stations related to teaching literature?

2. Work as a team (if you teach with others at your grade level) to plan for teaching a standard related to reading literature. Start with a standard from this book. Use the team planning tool to map the whole way, from writing down the standard to pulling out the academic vocabulary to discussing how you'll teach this in whole group, ending with creating materials that you can use in whole group and eventually at literacy work stations.

3. Make a video of your students working at one or more of their stations related to reading literature. Share with your team. Discuss why students are (or are not) successful at these stations. Or you might ask a colleague (someone who has an off period during the time your kids go to literacy stations, such as a literacy coach or a teacher from another grade level) to visit your classroom during stations time and jot down what she sees students doing and saying. Have that person ask kids, "What are you working on? What are you learning?" Then talk about what he or she found. It's helpful to have another set of eyes closely observe students.

4. Plan for an anchor chart related to reading literature *before* making it with your class. Do it as a team if you have one, and bring the anchor chart you make with your class back to the team to share it with them. (Remember that it might take several days to make a chart with your class.) Talk about how planning ahead helped the lesson flow. Share how you and your children are using the anchor chart in whole group, in small group, and at literacy work stations.

5. Try ideas from this chapter and then talk about the depth of students' understanding. Compare what you're doing now with what you used to do. What has helped your children understand literature more deeply?

6

Literacy Work Stations for Reading: Informational Text

Standards Covered in This Chapter	Lessons Described in This Chapter
Using Text Features to Locate Information	First Things First with Text Features to Find Information Info from the Illustrations
Identifying Main Topic/Main Idea and Key Details: Informational Text	Mapping the Main Idea and Key Details
Asking and Answering Questions: Informational Text	Question-and-Answer Sticks What's That Word Mean?
Comparing and Contrasting: Informational Texts on the Same Topic	Double Bubble Comparison

Young children are inherently interested in the world around them. They love exploring things such as puddles and bubbles and snails. Maps and globes are fascinating to primary students and open the possibilities of discovering new places. Little kids have questions about everything! "What's that? How's that work? Why?" Reading aloud informational text to children from a very young age builds their content-area knowledge and vocabulary, as well as feeds their natural inquisitiveness. Learning to read and write informational texts expands the world of the students we teach at all ages.

Begin by including lots of informational text in whole-group mini-lessons through read-aloud and shared reading to model what this kind of text sounds and looks like, and how to navigate its features and structures. Place informational texts in your classroom library in the "nonfiction" section, just like they'd be found in the school or public library. Dr. Nell Duke found in her seminal study in 2000 that the first-grade classrooms she observed spent an average of only 3.6 minutes per day with informational text. In addition, informational text made up less than 10 percent of classroom libraries and less than 3 percent of materials displayed on the walls and other surfaces in those same rooms. Yikes! In 2012, Yopp and Yopp discovered that narratives still constituted 77 percent of the books read aloud to children, with only 8 percent representing informational text. I strive to share an even mix of literature and informational text with students.

Duke and Bennett-Armistead's original (2003) framework categorized *informational texts* as those

- whose primary purpose is to convey information about the natural or social world;
- that make use of text structures, text features, and specialized vocabulary;
- that include books, newspaper and magazine articles, and Internet articles.

More recently, Duke (2014) has broadened her use of the term *informational text* to include the following:

- informative/explanatory—books and articles that convey information about the natural or social world; usually organized by topic; could include textbooks and field guides, too
- persuasive—texts that influence a reader's ideas or behaviors; examples include brochures, advertisements, editorials
- nonfiction narrative—tell stories of real events and include research in a story-like format; examples include historical fiction and fact-based stories
- biography—tell about the lives of real people and often include special text features such as time lines and important dates; often arranged chronologically; examples include memoir and autobiography
- procedural—texts that tell how to do something and include materials or ingredients lists in step-by-step sequence; examples include how-to guides and recipes

As you search for books to use with your students, think about the purpose of each kind of informational text and help students navigate the features specific to it. Be on the lookout for informational text that will interest and delight the children you teach. Connect to topics you are studying in science and social studies to build children's understanding of content-area knowledge. Search for books and articles with text features (such as headings, photos, captions, glossaries, and indexes) and that are organized by text structures, such as chronology, problem-solution, and cause-and-effect.

And as we're purposeful about reading more informational texts, be sure to use a wide variety, including history/social studies, science, *and* technical texts. Yopp and Yopp (2012) found that most informational text read-alouds in primary classrooms were books about animals, such as butterflies, owls, bats, and bears. Strive to expand your read-aloud repertoire to include informational texts about simple machines, rocks, magnets, history, communities, nutrition, ecology, design, light, and sound. Look at your science, social studies, and health curriculum, and include informational texts that match those topics. What a great way to integrate those content areas that sometimes get the short end of the stick in a crowded school day! Ask your school or public librarian for help in finding high-quality informational books that coordinate with content-area teaching.

There are many great reasons to use informational text as frequently as literature in teaching our children. Informational text is often the door through which struggling or reluctant readers, regardless of gender, enter the world of literacy. However, informational text is often a hook for boy readers, especially. According to research by Smith and Wilhelm (2002), boys tend to be better at information retrieval and work-related literacy tasks than girls are. Further, Smith and Wilhelm found that boys have much less interest in leisure reading than girls do, and are far more likely to read for utilitarian purposes than girls are.

This is exactly what I discovered as a classroom teacher: many of my students (especially boys) who had trouble with reading didn't choose to read for entertainment, but I could coax them to read for information—to find new facts about a topic of interest to them or to learn how to do something. My job was to help kids find a book they *wanted* to read, as well as to teach them *how* to read. Informational text was often critical to our success.

In this chapter on literacy work stations for reading informational text, I recommend we begin by taking a look at how much we're teaching with informational text. (Note that I'm including myself here!) Keep track of how many times a week you read aloud an informational text versus fiction. How often do you use books in which kids can read information about the natural or social world instead of stories in guided reading? Examine your classroom library: Does it include two areas, labeled just like the school or public library as "fiction" and "nonfiction" (as well as a leveled-book area), to help students choose informational text as readily as literature? Do the nonfiction books match what you're teaching in science and social studies this year?

Then plan for a science and a social studies station and/or an inquiry station; they tend to integrate informational texts naturally. Place as many informational texts at the listening station as you do stories. Technology-related stations, like computer and iPad stations, are another great place to include informational texts. You might have a newspaper station, a magazine station, and/or a biography station. (Even though biographies aren't classified as informational text, they are nonfiction and kids love them!) And remember to have an "I Can" list (that you make *with* students) to use at the writing station that includes opportunities for writing all kinds of nonfiction texts over time. See Figure 6.1 for an example.

Figure 6.1 Sample "I Can" List for Informational Texts

At the writing station, I can make . . .

- an information book
- a news article
- a how-to book

Use text features as you write information:

- title
- headings
- table of contents
- glossary

Just as in Chapter 5, there is a predictable structure to guide you through this chapter. As you read about teaching children how to read informational text,

the following headings will guide you through each section in a particular order to help you find the information you need: "Sifting Through the Standard," "Team Planning Tool," "Lessons That Last," "Connections to Whole-Group Mini-Lesson," "Mentor Texts for Modeling," "Teaching Tips," "Sample Anchor Charts," and then "Literacy Work Stations." Again, I didn't try to cover every single standard, but instead chose those "don't miss" ones, starting with the all-important "Using Text Features to Locate Information."

Using Text Features to Locate Information

Have you ever struggled with reading informational text, especially when you didn't know much about the subject? Pick up an organic chemistry text, and you'll probably find that you experience the same difficulties many of our students do: lots of new words and concepts, so much information that it's hard to determine what's most important, and diagrams, captions, and text boxes all over the page!

Reading informational text is a very different experience from reading literature. Understanding how to navigate text features is key to helping students comprehend science and social studies textbooks, technical pieces, and Internet and news articles. Text features steer us through informational text, helping us know what the author wants us to pay attention to—if we understand how to use those headings, bold words, and photographs with captions. Interestingly, text features, especially those incorporating bold print, colored fonts, large letters, or italics, jump off the page (when you know how to notice them).

Shared reading lessons with informational text provide the perfect opportunity to *show* students how to use text features. Be sure your class can *see* the text by using Big Books or enlarging articles via technology with a document camera or an interactive whiteboard connected to the Internet. As you model *how* to use text features, it will help students if you make and refer to an anchor chart like the one pictured on page 98.

Chapter 6

Sifting Through the Standard:
Using Text Features to Locate Information in Kindergarten–Grade Three

What It Is	Text features are used in informational text to help readers navigate large amounts of information. These text features include, but are not limited to, titles, headings, and subheadings; tables of contents and indexes; captions that accompany illustrations, maps, and charts; and bold print and glossaries. Digital text also includes electronic menus and icons. Illustrations, photographs, diagrams, charts, and maps are treated as text features in some state standards. In others, they are listed as illustrations.
Why It's Important	Each text feature has a specific importance that will help the reader if it is understood. *Titles, headings,* and *subheadings* help us make predictions about what the text is about. *Tables of contents* and *indexes* help us efficiently locate information we need. Nonfiction authors use *captions, illustrations, maps,* and *charts* to give us important information that's easier to understand in pictorial form. *Bold print* and *glossaries* help nonfiction readers understand important words related to the topic.
Prerequisites Needed	• Knowing that there is a difference between fiction and nonfiction. • Being able to sort literature from informational text (by the "look" of a book). Children as young as pre-K can help to sort books for the classroom library by realizing that nonfiction often has photos/ illustrations and gives information. • Understanding that illustrations are different from text, but that they work together to give information in nonfiction texts.
Academic Vocabulary	Kindergarten: • *front cover* • *back cover* • *title page* • *title* • *illustration/picture* • *predict/make predictions* First grade: • *text features* • *headings* • *tables of contents* • *glossaries* • *locate information* • *locate key facts* • *charts* Second grade: • *captions* • *bold print* • *subheadings* • *indexes* • *electronic menus* • *icons* • *preview text using text features*

Chapter 6

(continued on next page)

Sifting Through the Standard: **Using Text Features to Locate Information in Kindergarten–Grade Three** *(continued)*	
Academic Vocabulary	Third grade: • *search tools* • *key words* • *sidebars* • *hyperlinks* • *italics* • *maps* • *font/format*
Real-World Connections	• Throughout students' school careers, knowing how to use text features is necessary to comprehend content-area textbooks and online resources they will use to learn in a digital world. • As adults, we use text features daily as we read items such as magazines, news articles, menus, and train schedules, and navigate the vast resources available on the Internet.
Example Test Questions	• "Which chapter heading would most likely be above this text?" • "How does the author help the reader with unknown words in this passage?" • "In what part of the book would you find the meaning of the word _____?" • "The author includes a picture of a _____ to . . ." • "Which key words would best help a student find information about _____ on the Internet?" • "To find out which chapter in the science book is about _____, you would look in the . . ." • "The photograph best supports which idea from the selection?" • "The photograph of _____ is most likely included to . . ." • "Which part in the table of contents gives information about . . . ?"

Chapter 6

Team Planning Tool: Using Text Features to Locate Information—Second Grade	
Standard We're Teaching	**Second grade:** Use various text features (such as a table of contents, index, headings, captions) to locate key facts or information and explain how they contribute to and clarify a text.
Academic Vocabulary We'll Use and Expect to Hear	• *text features* • *table of contents* • *index* • *titles* • *headings* • *illustrations/charts/photographs* • *captions* • *key facts* • *information*
Whole-Group Ideas	• Shared reading of informational text, such as *Save Water* and Internet articles, and use tape flags labeled to signal text features. • Create an anchor chart on text features and how to use them. • Have kids spin a text-features spinner (with each space naming a text feature). They talk about how and what that particular text feature helped them learn about the topic of the text.

(continued on next page)

Team Planning Tool: Using Text Features to Locate Information—Second Grade *(continued)*

Partner Practice at Literacy Work Stations

Text-features station: When students are first learning about text features, you may want to have a station that focuses on this important skill. Here, partners use text features to preview the text. Have them use labeled tape flags to mark text features that help them make predictions about what they will read. Also provide a mini–anchor chart for students to refer to in naming the features. As they read, have them tell how the text features helped them understand what they read.

You might also use a news article cut up by text feature, as pictured in the photo on page 104.

Listening station: Have partners use text features to make predictions about what they will hear before they listen to recorded informational text. Encourage them to listen to a section and then stop the recording to discuss what they learned. Have them refer to the text features as they work here.

Buddy-reading station: Partners read one section at a time, using text features to preview the text. Again, include a mini–anchor chart about text features and labeled tape flags for kids to use. After reading, they might make up questions for each other about the text features. They can use the text-features spinner to choose a feature, such as table of contents, and talk about how the feature helped them understand what they read.

Computer or iPad station: Bookmark articles that correlate with science and/or social studies topics being studied. Have two students share one device and read an informational article together. Have them preview the text using text features. Remind them to name the features, such as *icons* or *electronic menus*, as they use them to locate information.

Lessons That Last: Whole-Group Lesson Plan for Using Text Features to Locate Information—Second Grade

First Things First with Text Features to Find Information

Focus: using text features to locate information or key facts

Method to Maximize Student Engagement: engaging text on topic of interest to students; using both print and digital information about the same topic to build and extend knowledge; manipulatives, such as labeled tape flags and a text-features spinner

Materials: informational text with lots of clear text features, such as *Save Water* by Kay Barnham; related digital informational text, such as the Water Sense Kids page from EPA found at www.epa.gov/WaterSense/kids/; labeled tape flags; text-features spinner; glue stick, blank paper, and markers for anchor chart; preprinted photos of text features for the anchor chart (from the text you'll read with them).

Model: how to first use titles, table of contents, and headings to predict what the text will be about; how to first use bold words and glossaries to determine word meaning; how to first use captions with illustrations and photographs to better understand concepts from the text.

Prompting for Independence:

- "*Text features* help readers understand and pay attention to important information in informational text."
- "*Titles* and *headings* tell us what the text will be mostly about. They are usually written in a special *font*. They may be *bold, colored, large,* or in *italics*. This is to help us pay attention to them, because they're really important. The author wants us to use these first!"
- "*Tables of contents* and *indexes* help us know what is included in the text and where to find it. The *table of contents* is in the front of a book. The *index* is in the back of a book. Read them first, before searching for information."
- "*Bold words* tell us to pay attention and look for what they mean. These same words and their definitions can usually be found in ABC order in a *glossary* in the back of the book."
- "*Illustrations, photographs, charts,* and *diagrams* along with *captions* give information related to the text. Be sure to read those, too. They will give you a deeper understanding of the topic you're reading about."
- "When reading information online, use *icons* and *electronic menus* to help you locate what you need."

(continued on next page)

Chapter 6

Lessons That Last: Whole-Group Lesson Plan for Using Text Features to Locate Information—Second Grade (continued)

Mini-Lesson Procedure: (Note: There are many text features, so this lesson will take several days to complete. Do a bit at a time, watching your class closely to see how much they can absorb in one lesson. Don't be afraid to take it slowly. Having a deep understanding of text features and how they help readers comprehend text will serve your students well for many years to come. The anchor chart photos that follow demonstrate how to teach about text features over time.)

1. Show the class the book you will read with them today during shared reading. Ask them what you should read first and why. ("Read the title, so we know what the book will mostly be about.") Point out that the author used large letters for the title, so that the reader will pay attention to it. ("The *title* of this informational text is *Save Water*. The *title* is written in large letters so we won't skip it! Read this first. Look at the *illustration* or *photograph* on the front cover, too. It gives us more information. It makes me think this book will be about ways we can save water. Water is really important, because we use it to keep clean.")

2. Have students talk to a buddy about what they already know about saving water, and then have a few share with the whole group.

3. Start to create an anchor chart with the class, titled "Readers Use Text Features to Locate Information." As you show the class the chart, ask them what they should read first (the *title*), what the important words are (*Text Features* and *Locate Information*), and how we know this (because the words are big and in *bold print*). Explain that as you read nonfiction text, it is very important to pay attention to text features. There are lots of them, so you're going to make a chart of them with the class over several lessons.

4. Make three columns under the chart's title and label these *Where?*, *What?*, and *Why?*. Tell the class you'll be looking for text features in informational text and paying attention to these three questions.

5. Then turn to the title page and read it together. Ask kids what they notice about this page. ("The *title* is in *bold print* again, and there's another *illustration* that gives us more information about what this book will be about. Rivers are water. We need to keep them clean . . .").

6. Have a student glue a photo of the book in the *What?* column. Draw an arrow to the title and label it as such. Write *where* titles are found and *why* they're included in the matching columns.

7. Next, turn to the *Contents* page of the book. Explain that this tells us what's inside the book. We should read it first, before we start reading the book. ("*Contents* means 'what's inside.' The *contents* of this marker is ink. The *contents* of my water bottle is water. The *contents* of this book is the information that is found here. It lists the page numbers to help us quickly find what we need. You don't have to read informational text in order. You can just go to the part you need.") Read the *Contents* page with the class, pausing briefly to discuss what they can find in this book, and where. Then have kids choose a section they'd like to read to get specific information. Use the *Contents* to find that page.

8. Add *Table of Contents* to the anchor chart along with the photo of that part of the book in the box labeled *What?*, and point out that it's also in the front of the book. Jot down the *Why?* to go with it.

9. Read a section of the book with the class, using the *Contents* page to find those pages. Ask kids what the author wants you to read first, and why. They may say the author wants people to read the title first. Tell them that these *bold words* are called the *heading* of this section and work just like a title. Always read the *headings* and use them to preview the text or make predictions before reading. If you read the *heading* "Saving water at school," have kids think aloud with you about what information or facts they might learn on these pages. Complete the *headings* part of the anchor chart with the class.

10. Then look at other text features on these pages and add them to the anchor chart as you delve into each one. Use the academic vocabulary in the "prompting for independence" language at the top of this lesson plan to help you make things clear for your students. Continue making the anchor chart with the class, as shown in the accompanying photos.

11. On another day, show students how many of these same text features are used in digital text. Use the article from the Environmental Protection Agency's Water Sense Kids page at www.epa.gov/WaterSense/kids/. Also point out the *electronic menu* and *icons* from the article as you read it together. Add these text features to the anchor chart, too.

On-the-Spot Assessment: Continue to read informational text with the class, referring to the text-features anchor chart as you do so. Use tape flags labeled with the names of the text features as you teach. Ask individuals to label various text features on enlarged text you read together (on Big Books, interactive whiteboards, or news articles). Have students tell how the text features helped them locate key facts or information.

Chapter 6

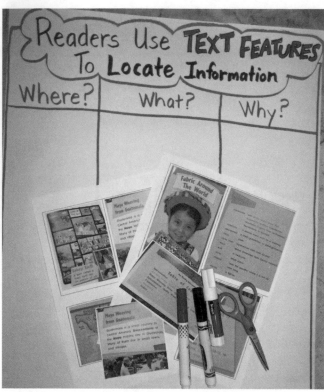

These materials were prepared before creating the anchor chart on using text features. The class added several items over a few days; the final anchor chart appears on page 111.

Chapter 6

Connections to Whole-Group Mini-Lesson

Independent Reading Connection: Be sure students choose informational text that is on their independent level. Have them work with a partner at first, so they can talk about the text features and how these help with locating information. Remind them to use the text-features anchor chart as they read and talk together. Ask them to share with the class how text features helped them read and understand informational text.

Small-Group Connection: Likewise, use informational text frequently in small group, just as you modeled in whole group. You might use the text-features spinner and/or labeled tape flags to talk about text features and how they help us find information.

Writing Connection: Writing their own informational texts can really cement students' understanding of text features. They will enjoy making their own books about topics of interest. Be sure to model how to use text features while writing your own informational text. Refer often to the text-features anchor chart as you write.

Evaluation: Give students grade-level informational text to read. Ask questions about the text features and how students used them to locate information.

The Common Core State Standards separate standards for text features into two different categories: those that deal with words and those that relate to illustrations. Other states include illustrations such as photographs, diagrams, and maps as text features. No matter where you teach, I think it's important to explicitly teach students how to extract information from the illustrations as well as the words. The following lesson is geared to kindergarten, where students can often get more information from illustrations than from words, but it can be adapted to other grade levels as well. Don't assume that third graders already use the illustrations in informational text; I have found that many older students, especially struggling readers, often skip the visuals and just read the words to get through the text faster.

Team Planning Tool: Using Information from Illustrations—Kindergarten	
Standard We're Teaching	**Kindergarten:** With prompting and support, describe the relationship between illustrations and the text in which they appear (e.g., what person, place, thing, or idea in the text an illustration depicts).
Academic Vocabulary We'll Use and Expect to Hear	• *illustrations* • *text/words* • *person, place, thing, or idea*
Whole-Group Ideas	• Read aloud informational books containing illustrations (such as photographs and drawings) that match the text (for example, sentences, labels, and simple captions). • Read and think aloud about how the illustrations go with the words/text, using a die-cut magnifying glass to point out the people, places, things, or ideas that are in both the text and the illustration.
Partner Practice at Literacy Work Stations	**Listening station:** Give partners their own magnifying glasses (without a lens or made from cardstock) to use while listening to a recorded informational text. As they listen, they place the magnifying glass on the part of the illustration that matches the words. After listening, partners talk about what they learned from the illustrations (and the words). **Buddy-reading station:** A pair of children read an informational text together, using the illustrations and the words (if possible). As they do so, have them place the magnifying glass on the illustration and talk about the people, places, things, or ideas in those photos or drawings. If they can, have them read the words and match them to the pictures. **Illustration station:** Students create illustrations to go with science or social studies concepts being studied and add words (sentence, labels, captions) to go with them. Place familiar books here for students to use for reference. Also include a word list that goes with the topic (with picture cues for support).

Lessons That Last: Whole-Group Lesson Plan for Using Information from Illustrations—Kindergarten

Info from the Illustrations

Focus: use information from illustrations to understand concepts and ideas from the text

Method to Maximize Student Engagement: read-aloud of a high-interest informational text with photographs/illustrations that tap into student interest; buddy talk about the illustrations; student participation using magnifying glass to show parts of the illustration that match the text

Materials: informational text with illustrations that match the text (*Things That Go!* by James Buckley, Jr.); index card and markers to make conversation card; magnifying glass with lens removed (or black tagboard die-cut magnifying glass)

Model: how to get information from illustrations and find words that match in the text

Prompting for Independence:

• "What part of the *illustration* goes with these *words* from the *text*?"
• "Find the *illustration* that goes with these *words*. How does the *illustration* help you understand the ideas the author is writing about?"
• "What person, place, thing, or idea is shown in this *illustration*?"

(continued on next page)

Chapter 6

**Lessons That Last: Whole-Group Lesson Plan
for Using Information from Illustrations—Kindergarten** *(continued)*

Mini-Lesson Procedure:

1. Show the class the front cover of the book you will be reading to them, and point out that on the *front cover,* the *author* makes up a *title* for the book and the *illustrator* creates the *pictures* or *photographs* or *illustrations.* *Illustrations* show the *people, places, things,* or *ideas* the *author* wants the reader to pay attention to. (There is a lot of academic vocabulary here. Refer to anchor charts you've made previously about parts of a book and author and illustrator to reinforce these terms. Samples can be found in Chapter 5.)

2. Read aloud the title *Things That Go!* Then ask the students to talk with a partner about the pictures or *illustrations* on the *front cover.* Call on several students to name what they see, using the sentence frame "I see an *illustration* of _____. It goes with the *words* _____. Write this on a conversation card, so it will support academic vocabulary now and can also be used later at a station (see photo). Have students come up to the book and put the magnifying glass on the part of the illustration they are noticing. It might sound something like this: "I see an illustration of a race car. It goes with the words *Things That Go.*" Or on the title page: "I see an illustration of a train. It looks really fast. It goes with the word *go.*"

3. Continue through the book in this way, reading the words and having kids look at the illustrations. Then have them buddy-talk about how the illustrations help them get information. Here's an example from the book: The teacher reads, "The first bicycles were hard to ride. Riders sat up high. They often fell off." A student might respond and point to the matching illustration: "I see an illustration of a bicycle. It goes with the word *bicycle.* The guy is up high. He might fall off."

4. Be sure kids understand how important the illustrations are in giving information. Help them see how the words and pictures match, too. Don't worry about naming the illustrations (for example, *diagram, time line, sidebar*). Instead, focus on the information given in the illustrations so students will look at them carefully.

5. One benefit of this kind of lesson is the content vocabulary you can develop through the illustrations. In this lesson, students also will learn the new words *machines, helmet, racers,* and *goggles* on the first few pages, using the illustrations and the words.

On-the-Spot Assessment: Observe children in this lesson and subsequent ones focusing on this same topic. Are they able to use the conversation card? Can they identify the illustrations versus the text? Are they seeing the connection between the words and the pictures? Are they using the information in the illustrations to deepen their understanding of the text? Are they learning new words and concepts?

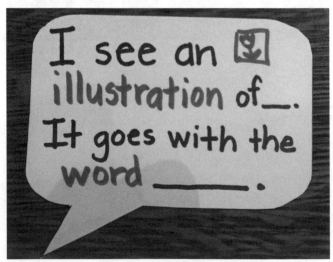

A conversation card is made with students to help them use academic vocabulary when thinking about how to use information from illustrations. The teacher refers to it over and over throughout lessons on this standard and helps children use this language as they respond.

Students take turns using a black tagboard die-cut magnifying glass to focus on the illustrations. They use the sentence frame from the conversation card to tell what they learned. Give support as needed to help kids use this academic vocabulary.

Connections to Whole-Group Mini-Lesson

Independent Reading Connection: Give informational text to pairs of students to "read" together. Encourage them to use the conversation card to point to illustrations and talk about them. Have them look for words that match, too. You might give each pair their own magnifying glass cutout to share when talking about the illustrations, to help them focus.

Small-Group Connection: Be sure to read informational text with students in guided-reading groups. Choose a book on their instructional level that they can read with just a little support. Before reading, tell them the focus of the lesson will be to use the illustrations with the words to get information. (See photo below for a sample focus board.) Then have children talk about the pictures and what they learn from them as well as the words.

Writing Connection: During writing workshop, model how to create illustrations that match the words as you write. Show kids how to add labels and captions to the illustrations. Explain that the illustrations give the reader additional information and clarify ideas. Help them match their illustrations to their words. Students can add labels and captions to illustrations at the writing station or an illustration station.

Evaluation: You might create an observation sheet like the one in Figure 6.2. Take notes on several students each day, jotting down what you observe them doing as readers of informational text. How do they gain information from the illustrations, and can they identify words versus the illustrations?

Figure 6.2 **Observation Sheet for Kindergarten Reading Informational Text**

Student Name/ Date	Can Identify Words	Can Identify Illustrations	How the Child Gains Information from the Illustrations

Mentor Texts for Modeling:
Using Text Features to Locate Information

- *Save Water* by Kay Barnham
- *Things That Go!* by James Buckley, Jr. Discover More Readers series
- *Amelia Earhart* by Caroline Crosson Gilpin
- *Fantastic Frogs* by Penelope Arlon
- *A Den Is a Bed for a Bear* by Becky Baines
- *Forest* by Sean Callery. Life Cycles series
- *Lions* by Sally Morgan. Animal Lives series

Use a dry erase board propped up on your small-group table with a plate stand so both you and your students can see it to help focus your guided-reading lessons. Read it together at the start of your lesson—"Get information from the illustrations"—and refer to it throughout the lesson. (Pictures are used to help young readers remember the focus.)

Teaching Tips for Using Text Features to Locate Information Across the Grades	
In Pre-K and Kindergarten	• Teaching our very youngest readers about text features begins with having them understand the function of the front and back covers and title pages. Focus on helping students use titles and illustrations/photographs/pictures to make predictions about informational text. • "Stay in your lane" with text features. Don't teach kids all the text features expected by third grade in pre-K or kindergarten. Be sure your students consistently identify and use titles and illustrations on the front and back covers and title page to get information. Help them extract information from the illustrations throughout the book, too, because it's likely they will not be able to read all the words in most informational text they encounter. • Give students opportunities to interact with the same books and online texts you've read aloud to them. They will do whatever they see you do and use the same language they hear you use. This can be done during independent reading time and at literacy work stations.

In Grades One–Two	• There are many text features included in informational text, so be strategic about which ones you spend the most time teaching. For example:
	
	  • Zero in on *titles, headings,* and *captions* and use them to preview text before reading.
	
	  • Also focus on how to use *bold words* and *glossaries* to determine words' meanings.
	
	  • Help kids learn how to read the *illustrations, charts,* and *maps* to more deeply understand the key information in the text. Explain that authors use these graphics to make the most important information clearer to readers.
	
	  • Teach one or two text features at a time. Organize your teaching of these features around their function (for example, *"Tables of contents and indexes help us find page numbers where information is"*).
	
	• Use electronic sources as well as print ones when teaching about text features.

In Grades Three–Four	• Review text features taught in kindergarten through grade two. When students are reading higher-level text, they will still need to use the same features covered in primary grades. However, as information becomes further removed from children's background knowledge, the task of reading informational text becomes more challenging, and kids may forget to apply what they've learned previously. • Teach students to continue to use *titles, headings, captions,* and *illustrations* to preview and make predictions, especially when reading content-area textbooks or doing research. • Expand into text features, such as *key words, sidebars, hyperlinks, fonts,* and *search tools*. • By the end of third grade, students should be using text features efficiently to find information. Beginning in fourth grade, the focus shifts from text features to *text structures* or how informational text is organized (chronology, comparison, cause/effect, problem/solution).

Sample Anchor Charts for Using Text Features to Locate Information

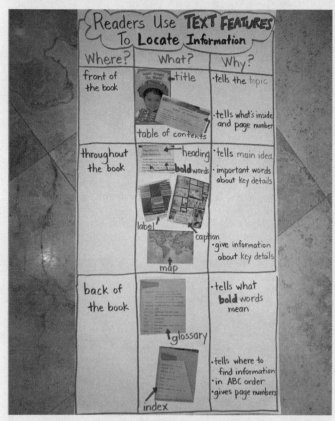

The "First Things First with Text Features to Find Information" lessons inspired this completed anchor chart on using informational text features.

This teacher has used old children's news magazines for samples on an anchor chart about informational text features. It is in the process of being added to over multiple lessons.

A kindergarten anchor chart helps students use titles and illustrations to make predictions about text.

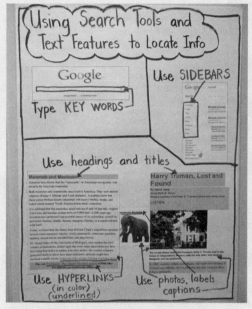

A third-grade class made this anchor chart about using text features and search tools to locate information efficiently.

Literacy Work Stations for Using Text Features to Locate Information

At this text features station, partners read informational text and mark features with labeled tape flags. A mini–anchor chart gives support. Substitute various informational text pieces over time.

At a listening station, young children use a magnifying glass to locate information in an illustration. Add new informational texts for kids to listen to over time.

At the buddy-reading station, a pair of students use a spinner to decide on a text feature to locate information. Change the spinner and the texts that kids work with over time.

Kids work together to read and look for text features in this informational text at the Big Book station. They use the sticky note labels to identify a text feature and talk about how the author used it to give information. They can share what they learned with the class during "sharing time" after stations, to encourage their classmates to do the same. Be sure to post your anchor chart on "How Authors Use Text Features" here for reference! Change out Big Books over time.

At this station, two kids share an iPad to do animal research. The mini–anchor chart reminds them about tools they can use as they search for information. Students may research various topics throughout the school year on the iPad.

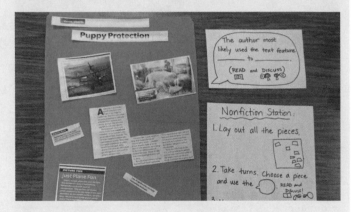

A news article written for kids in grade three is cut up by text feature (heading, illustration, caption, photograph, and so on). Partners work together to assemble the article and use the conversation card as they discuss the purpose of each feature. Directions were written with the class to help them remember what to do here. Add other news articles, over time, so kids have a variety to choose from. Putting each article in its own zippered plastic bag keeps things orderly.

Identifying Main Topic/Main Idea and Key Details: Informational Text

"What are you working on this week?" I ask Meghan, a first-grade teacher, in preparation for my visit to her classroom the following day.

"Main idea and details," she replies. "I usually introduce this concept with fiction books by Mercer Mayer. I cover up the title, read the book to my class, and then ask them what it was mostly about—the main idea. They usually come up with the title easily. From there, we move into main idea and details."

I picture this storybook-based lesson in my mind and examine it, thinking deeply about what we're really trying to do here. "I hate to be a weirdo," I tell Meghan, "but let me look at our standards to clarify exactly what we need to be teaching. I'm not even sure if this belongs with fiction or fits better with reading informational text." In the past, I often taught main idea and details with stories, but it was difficult for kids. I'm thinking that most of my successful lessons on main idea and details were focused on reading nonfiction.

Sure enough, it's right there in the Texas standards for reading informational text/expository text: "Students are expected to restate the main idea heard or read; identify important details in text." It's also in the Common Core State Standards under Reading Standards for Informational Text: "Students identify the main topic and retell key details of a text." It's nowhere to be found in the standards for teaching literature. Tomorrow, we'll begin teaching main idea using informational text, not literature.

As we examine read-aloud books for teaching main idea and key details, Meghan and I soon discover that not all informational texts will work well for these first lessons. Some books have too much information on lots of different topics in them; others have no headings and are just lists of facts. We decide upon a series called Animal Homes from Pebble Plus, because each book in that collection has a clear topic with headings and short text that we think her first graders will be able to read independently after we teach with them. We choose a book for read-aloud called *Birds and Their Nests* by Linda Tagliaferro. Other titles in this series include *Bees and Their Hives* and *Rabbits and Their Burrows,* which we'll place in the classroom library after introducing the first book in the series.

These informational texts help students learn facts about familiar animals, and the kids are able to make connections with them quickly, especially since they have been studying about habitats in science. Meghan and I decide to keep our eyes open for informational books on topics beyond animals to read aloud as we continue to teach lasting lessons about main idea and details. We'll be on the lookout for informational text related to magnets, simple machines, wants and needs, ecology, and nutrition, as these are first-grade science and social studies concepts we often struggle to find time to teach.

Sifting Through the Standard: Identifying Main Topic/Main Idea and Key Details: Informational Text in Kindergarten—Grade Three	
What It Is	Both the *main topic* and *the main idea* state the central idea of a sentence, paragraph, or text, which can make this confusing to students (and teachers). But the *main topic* tells *what* the text is about, usually in just one word or short phrase, such as *pirates, trees, community helpers,* or *things that go.* It is often a noun that is repeated throughout the text. The *main topic* is often the title or part of the title of an informational text.
	The *main idea* tells what the author is trying to convey as his or her message. The *main idea* is usually stated as one sentence that sums up the gist of the section, such as "The moon is different from the earth" or "Snakes hunt in many ways" or "Edgar Degas had early experiences with art." The *main idea* normally includes the *main topic* as the subject of the sentence.
	Supporting details support the main idea and tell how, what, when, where, why, how much, or how many. Some details are more important than others to communicating the main idea and are called *key details.*
Why It's Important	Reading informational text is very different from reading literature. Without understanding main ideas, informational text may seem like just a bunch of facts that are not related or easily remembered. Understanding how key details are connected to main ideas and topics will help the reader better understand the message the author is trying to convey.

(continued on next page)

Sifting Through the Standard: Identifying Main Topic/Main Idea and Key Details: Informational Text in Kindergarten–Grade Three *(continued)*

Prerequisites Needed	• Being able to classify or categorize objects or ideas is a prerequisite to understanding main idea and key details. Give kids objects or pictures and have them sort them into categories. Then have them tell the *main topic* of the items and how they are related. Food, furniture, colors, animals, and so on might be used for classifying. • To understand the difference between *main topic* and *main idea,* it will help if children understand the difference between a *word* and a *sentence.* • Determining importance is critical to understanding *main* or *key* "anything!"
Academic Vocabulary	**Kindergarten:** • *main topic* • *retell key details* • *words* • *illustrations* • *ways in which authors group information* • *front cover* • *back cover* • *title* **First grade:** • *main idea* • *author's purpose* • *important facts or details* **Second grade:** • *focus of the paragraph* • *order of events or ideas* **Third grade:** • *how key details support the main idea* • *supporting details* • *author's stated purpose* • *draw conclusions from the facts* • *support with textual evidence*
Real-World Connections	• You might use photos and have students come up with one word that describes the picture—that is, the *main topic.* Understanding the main topic can help kids name things. • I think it's important to read informational text to find information first and then discuss the main idea and key details. As adults, we do not typically read informational text to "find the main idea." Instead, we read to learn something or to gather information. We think about what it was mostly about as we reflect on what we read.
Example Test Questions	• "The main idea of this passage is _____." • "What is the main idea of paragraph 4?" • "The topic of this selection is _____." • "Which is *not* a key detail in the text?" • "Which key detail best supports the main idea in this passage?" • "Identify the main idea of this selection, citing key details as textual evidence from the passage."

Chapter 6

Team Planning Tool: Identifying Main Topic/Main Idea and Key Details: Informational Text—First Grade

Standards We're Teaching	**First grade:** • Identify the topic and explain the author's purpose in writing about the text. • Restate the main idea, heard or read. • Identify important facts or details in text, heard, or read.

(continued on next page)

Team Planning Tool: Identifying Main Topic/Main Idea and Key Details: Informational Text—First Grade *(continued)*	
Academic Vocabulary We'll Use and Expect to Hear	• *topic* • *author's purpose* • *main idea* • *important facts/key details*
Whole-Group Ideas	• Read aloud the book *Birds and Their Nests,* and use a partially prepared anchor chart for main idea/key details, using a tree map. • Write information on sticky notes and markers in different colors to show topic, main idea, and details as you read and think aloud.
Partner Practice at Literacy Work Stations	**Informational-text station:** Partners read informational text together and use the graphic organizer and colored sticky notes to discuss and write down the topic, main ideas, and/or key details. **Buddy-reading station:** Students read informational text and use the conversation card to tell about the topic and author's purpose. **Retelling station:** Partners reread informational texts read aloud in whole group and assemble the prewritten sticky notes from the lessons to restate the main idea and key details. They also use illustrations and/or words in informational texts to retell what they read.

Lessons That Last: Whole-Group Lesson Plan for Identifying Main Topic/Main Idea and Key Details: Informational Text—First Grade

Mapping the Main Idea and Key Details

Focus: identifying the main topic, main idea, and key details of informational text read aloud

Method to Maximize Student Engagement: informational text about a familiar topic being studied in science (birds and their nests); sticky notes for students to manipulate; buddy talk

Materials: *Birds and Their Nests* book; sticky notes in different sizes and colors; tree map drawn on a large chart (or dry erase board) with spaces that match the sticky notes (see photo on page 110); black marker and colored crayons; repositionable adhesive to create a sticky note from light green 4-by-6-inch paper

Model: how to read for information and then think about the main topic, main ideas, and key details

Prompting for Independence:

• "The *title* of the book or the *heading* of the section often tells the *topic,* or tells what the **text** is about. It is often just one word."
• "What was this section *mostly about*? That's called the *main idea.* It tells the big idea of what the author wants us to know."
• "*Key details* are important pieces of information that go with the *main idea.*"

Mini-Lesson Procedure:

1. Begin by looking at the front cover of the informational book. Ask the children if this book is fiction or nonfiction and how they know. ("This book is nonfiction because it is about something real and true; it has photographs.") At the top of a large piece of chart paper write "Reading Informational Text." Then read the title of the book together, *Birds and Their Nests,* and ask students to whisper to you one word that tells what they think this book will be about (birds). Write the word *topic* beside a shape drawn with green marker on a large chart or dry erase board, and then write *Birds* on a 4-by-6-inch piece of light green paper and affix it to the chart with repositionable adhesive to make a large sticky note. (See photos in the "Sample Anchor Charts" section that follows.)

(continued on next page)

Chapter 6

**Lessons That Last: Whole-Group Lesson Plan for Identifying
Main Topic/Main Idea and Key Details: Informational Text—First Grade** *(continued)*

2. Next, read aloud the first section of the book, starting with the heading *Building Nests*. After you've read this part, ask students to turn and talk to a buddy about what that part was mostly about. Give them the clue that the heading often tells this. Have them whisper to you what they think this section was mostly about (birds build nests). On the chart, draw several boxes with an orange marker under the green one and label these *main ideas*. Tell kids that main ideas are what the informational text is mostly about. Write "build nests" on a 3-by-5-inch light orange piece of paper and affix it to an orange square to show the main idea of this section.

3. Reread this section and ask students to think about the most important parts or *key details* as you read. Draw blue boxes under the orange ones for recording key details. As students tell you the most important information, write it on light blue sticky notes and place the notes in the boxes ("with mud, twigs, and grass"; "in many places like trees and buildings"; "in one day or two weeks or two months"; "using beaks and feet").

4. Then continue reading aloud another section and using the same process to record main ideas and key details.

5. To finish this lesson, have students retell what they read. Remove each sticky note from the chart, one at a time, starting with the main topic, and hand it to a child you know can read it. Then have the class retell by returning the sticky notes to the chart as students read them one more time.

On-the-Spot Assessment: Observe students to see if they are getting the gist of the main idea and key details from their discussion.

Connections to Whole-Group Mini-Lesson

Independent Reading Connection: Be sure students are reading informational text during independent reading as you teach about it, so you can observe and take anecdotal notes on their understanding. As you confer with individuals, ask them about the main topic, main ideas, and key details. Jot down notes to help you keep track of their comprehension. Use this information to plan further whole-group and small-group lessons on this key concept.

Small-Group Connection: Plan to use informational text in small-group instruction as well as whole-group lessons. Help children set purposes for reading for information before they read segments with you. Be sure they are thinking about main topics before reading. Guide their understanding of main ideas and key details during and after reading by giving them sticky notes just like you did during whole-group lessons. Help them use the notes to retell what they read.

Writing Connection: Young children love to make books! Teach them how to compose informational texts, using books you've read aloud as models. Help them write titles and headings (in bold print) that tell the main topic and main ideas. Show them how to plan key details before writing and include them through words, illustrations, and text features, such as simple diagrams or captions.

Evaluation: After ample instruction and practice, give students a short informational text to read, and have them use a preprinted tree map graphic organizer to write the main topic/main idea and key details.

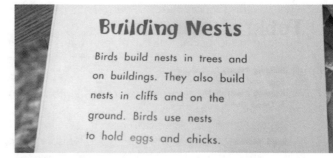

Building Nests

Birds build nests in trees and on buildings. They also build nests in cliffs and on the ground. Birds use nests to hold eggs and chicks.

This series from Pebble Plus was excellent for modeling for first graders how to think about topic, main idea, and key details. There was just enough information to read without it becoming overwhelming to young readers (and many students could later read it on their own, because it was familiar text). Headings in bold, colored fonts drew student attention to this text feature, which stated main ideas clearly. From there, we just had to think about the most important details.

Mentor Texts for Modeling:
Identifying Main Topic/Main Idea
and Key Details

- *Birds and Their Nests* by Linda Tagliaferro. Animal Homes series
- *What Happens to a Hamburger* by Paul Showers

- *Martin's Big Ideas* by Doreen Rappaport
- *Behold the Beautiful Dung Beetle* by Cheryl Bardoe
- *Handle with Care: An Unusual Butterfly Journey* by Loree Griffin Burns
- *No Monkeys, No Chocolate* by Melissa Stewart
- *What If There Were No Bees?* by Suzanne Slade

Teaching Tips for Identifying Main Topic/Main Idea and Key Details Across the Grades	
In Pre-K and Kindergarten	• Do sorts with familiar objects or photos, and have students name the *main topic* of each category. Use items from science or social studies to reinforce content-area information. Then have them tell *details* about the items. For example, if they sort winter clothing into a category, help them say, "The *main topic* is winter clothes. A *detail* is that we wear coats, mittens, and scarves in winter." • Remind students to always read/listen to the title first, because it usually tells the *main topic* of informational text. Help them pay attention to that word (or phrase), because it is often used over and over in the text. • As you share informational text with the class, model how to read a bit, then stop and ask kids to think about *details* that go with the *topic*. You might jot down the *key details* beside the words *what, when, where, why, how, how much,* and *how many.* Remind them that *key details* are really important things the author wants us to remember or understand. • Have students tell about details from the *illustrations,* as well as the *words.*
In Grades One–Two	• Try to choose informational texts that are organized into sections with headings to make it easier for students to identify main ideas, especially when they are first learning to think about *main ideas.* • Teach students the process of Read, Stop, Think as they read informational text. Show them the importance of stopping to think about information and what they've learned as they read a bit at a time. • Using a graphic organizer to record main topic, main ideas, and key details will take a lot of modeling! Don't expect students to do this independently too soon. Use the mini-lesson with sticky notes from this section multiple times with different books on a variety of science and social studies topics. This lesson can be used in small group, too, with children doing the reading (rather than the teacher, as in whole-group read-aloud). Note: The sticky notes are very helpful for teaching students how to retell informational text (since it is quite different from how to retell literature).
In Grades Three and Up	• It is still important to read aloud informational text to students and model how to think about main ideas and key details in upper grades. Use text from magazines, newspapers, and the Internet, as well as books that are on grade level or above. Use your science or social studies textbooks, too. • Over time, you will want to model finding main ideas and key details with informational text test passages, but that should not be your major source of modeling how to read informational text! • Begin with informational text about topics for which students have background knowledge, so children can focus on thinking about main ideas and supporting details. • If your students have difficulty identifying main ideas and supporting details, use suggestions from grades one–two to build their skill in doing so. Also give students text they *can* read independently to practice identifying main ideas and supporting details.

Sample Anchor Charts for Identifying Main Topic/Main Idea and Key Details

While modeling how to comprehend informational text, I read aloud a bit, demonstrated a think-aloud, and then wrote the topic on a large green sticky note and the main idea on a large orange sticky note (both made from plain paper and repositionable adhesive) placed on a tree map. I decided to write on a dry erase easel during this lesson for flexibility before making an anchor chart to use in future mini-lessons.

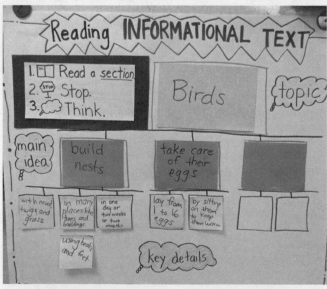

A completed anchor chart made with blank shapes outlined with colors to match sticky notes can be used for repeated mini-lessons on thinking about topic, main ideas, and key details of read-alouds. It can also be placed at the informational text work station along with books and colored sticky notes for student pairs to use independently of the teacher (over time). Note the process for how to read informational text in the black box at the top left-hand corner of the chart with picture support.

During a whole-group mini-lesson and read-aloud, students act out the process of how to read informational text: Read a section first (*top*), Stop (*center*), and Think (*bottom*). This kinesthetic activity helps them remember what to do as readers of news articles, informational books, and biographies.

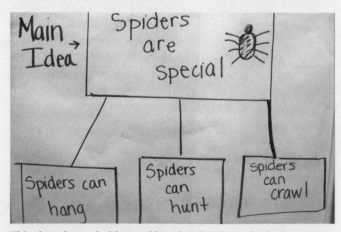

This chart for main idea and key details was made during science in a first-grade classroom.

Literacy Work Stations for Identifying Main Topic/Main Idea and Key Details

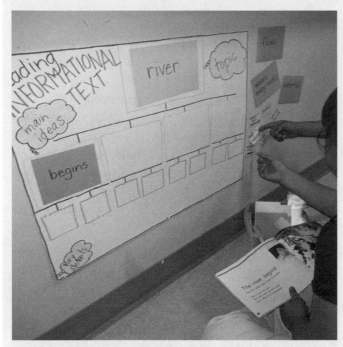

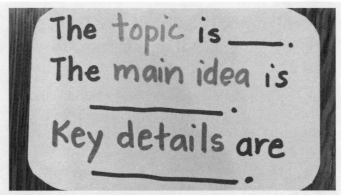

Partners work to place sticky notes on a large tree map to tell the topic, main ideas, and key details from informational text. They can use pieces you've read and worked with in whole group or read other informational text and create their own sticky notes. Vary texts. This is a station kids can use all year long!

Partners listen to informational text at the listening station. This conversation card is used to support talk about topic, main idea, and details. Change the text and provide a graphic organizer on which kids can take notes. Similar work can be done at buddy reading.

Students read, take notes on, and discuss topic, main idea, and key details at this newspaper work station in upper grades, where they work with laminated news articles at their reading level. Throughout the year, change the articles. Kids may even find some to add. Add different reading tasks here, too. For example, they might ask and answer questions or highlight new words they've found.

At this "info text" station, partners work together to reconstruct a cut-up news article, section by section. They use the title and headings to help them think about main idea and key details as they read each section. When finished, they summarize using the main idea and key details. News articles can be added or taken away over time. Use articles with headings, such as those from *Scholastic News, Time for Kids,* or online articles that you print and cut apart by sections.

Chapter 6

Asking and Answering Questions: Informational Text

Children must be taught, encouraged, and expected to ask thoughtful questions. Students need to be in a safe, risk-free community where the teacher models asking and answering questions, and children feel supported in doing the same. We have to beware of simply asking questions and rewarding students who give the correct answer or asking simple questions with yes/no answers. Questioning can be used for much more than checking on students' understanding. In a student-centered classroom, children are asking the majority of the questions and learning ways to search for answers.

Begin by asking good questions of your students. Model, model, model. Work with your colleagues to plan good questions. A good question is one in which we are made to think more deeply and search out answers. A good question sometimes has more than one answer. It requires more than a simple *yes* or *no* answer or just a one-word or phrase answer. Harvey and Goudvis (2007) refer to these as "thick questions."

Write out some of your questions for kids to see. Post these thick (deep) questions in your inquiry work station. Use prompts to help kids dig deeper, such as "How do you know?" or "Why do you think that?" or "Tell me more about your thinking." Planning several well-thought-out questions before teaching a lesson will allow you to give kids the time they need to think before answering. You might write the questions on sticky notes and put them in your read-aloud book or guided-reading lesson plan, so you're sure to remember them. When we've planned well, our lessons go faster, and we can give kids the "wait time" they need to think. Interestingly, *wait time* has come into vogue recently but has been around for many years. The importance of this practice was first described in Mary Bud Rowe's (1972) research. Stahl

(1990) updated the term to *think time,* which names just why this is so important to do!

Allow children to ask questions as you read aloud, even if it does take a bit longer to read the book. With modeling and guidance, this will teach students how to propel themselves through informational text with deeper comprehension. First, teach kids the difference between asking and telling (which will cut down on some of the wasted time we have all experienced in this situation). You might also post the focus for your lesson, such as "What causes a thunderstorm?" on the board (just until kids learn how to stay on topic). Tell students that the questions they ask should go with the topic of the informational text you are reading.

Each time someone asks a related question, point to your focus question and praise the child who stayed on topic. For example, "Corey asked, 'What are those big black clouds called?' which is a question about thunderstorms." Or, "Your question about where the animals go in a thunderstorm is a good one. Let's write that on a sticky note and place it on our inquiry board at the inquiry work station. This book doesn't talk about that, but perhaps you can find the answer in another book." Or, "You're telling about a time you were in a thunderstorm. That's telling, not asking. Let's jot down that idea, and some of you might want to write about a time you were in a thunderstorm during writing workshop."

Providing many opportunities for students to ask and answer questions when reading informational text will help them pay attention to key details and main ideas. Also model and expect students to ask and answer questions about new words as they read. (See Chapter 9 for additional ideas on teaching vocabulary.) Teaching children to read a bit, stop and think, and ask and seek answers to questions about information and new vocabulary will slow down their reading but lead to deeper understanding of informational text. It will set the stage for note taking and reading textbooks in later years as well.

Sifting Through the Standard: **Asking and Answering Questions: Informational Text in Kindergarten–Grade Three**	
What It Is	• Students using question words *who, what, when, where, why,* and *how* as they ask and answer questions to show understanding of key details in informational text • Students learning to ask and answer their own questions (not just answering a teacher's questions correctly) • Students learning to ask and answer questions about new words they encounter when reading informational text
Why It's Important	According to research done by the National Reading Panel (National Institute of Child Health and Human Development 2000), teaching students to ask and answer questions is one of the most effective ways to improve reading comprehension. When teachers ask questions about what kids are reading and give children immediate feedback, it improves comprehension. When children ask questions about what they read and subsequently search for answers, they are interacting with the text to construct even deeper meaning. Also, asking and answering questions about what unknown words mean helps students comprehend and use new vocabulary.
Prerequisites Needed	• Understanding that we read informational text to learn things • Understanding the difference between asking (questions) and telling (answers) • Being aware of end punctuation as signals for questions and answers • Realizing that you "don't know" something and using questions and answers to help you learn • Monitoring comprehension and developing "word consciousness" or knowing when to stop and ask and answer questions about what unknown words mean
Academic Vocabulary	Kindergarten: • *ask* • *answer* • *who, what, where, when, why, how* • *question* • *key details* • *unknown word* First grade: • *the word _____ means . . .* • *the phrase _____ means . . .* Second and third grade: • *evidence from the text* • *text evidence*
Real-World Connections	• Children are naturally curious. Be sure to encourage them to constantly ask questions and seek answers to them. • *What if, why,* and *how* questions promote deep thinking. Use these kinds of questions a lot! • If you are in an IB (International Baccalaureate) school, refer to the Learner Profile of "Inquirer"—*I am curious. I ask questions. I love to learn.* (Note: If you are not in an IB school, this is still an important trait to encourage!) • The structure of many informational texts is a question-and-answer format. Provide lots of informational books with this format to help students learn how to ask and answer questions when reading informational text.
Example Test Questions	• *Who, what, where, when, why,* and *how* questions abound on tests. • "What does the word _____ mean in paragraph ___?"

Team Planning Tool:
Asking and Answering Questions: Informational Text—Second Grade

Standard We're Teaching	**Second grade:** Ask and answer such questions as *who, what, where, when, why,* and *how* to demonstrate understanding of key details in a text.
Academic Vocabulary We'll Use and Expect to Hear	• *ask questions* • *answer questions* • *key details* • *question words: who, what, when, where, why, how*
Whole-Group Ideas	• Make an anchor chart with the class on asking and answering questions. • Read aloud and think aloud with informational text. Model how to ask and answer questions about what you're reading before, during, and after the reading. • Use punctuation craft sticks (see photo on page 124) and anchor chart as scaffolds for helping kids ask and answer questions about what they're reading. • Also model how to write question-and-answer books, using informational text as mentor text.
Partner Practice at Literacy Work Stations	**Buddy-reading station:** Partners read and take turns asking and answering questions about the informational text they're reading. They use the punctuation craft sticks to show whether they're asking or answering questions. **Inquiry station:** Students use sticky notes to jot down questions they have about topics being studied in the content areas and post them on a display board. Use one color sticky note, such as yellow, for all questions. Use another color, such as blue, for answers. That way kids can jot down answers and place them under the matching sticky-note question. **News article station:** As students read news articles together, they pause to ask and answer questions about the text. They may use punctuation craft sticks and sticky notes as they work. **Writing station:** Students may write question-and-answer books—informational text in question-and-answer format—using mentor texts as examples.

Lessons That Last: Whole-Group Lesson Plan for Asking and Answering Questions: Informational Text—Second Grade

Question-and-Answer Sticks

Focus: asking and answering questions, using *who, what, when, where, why,* and *how* to demonstrate understanding of key details in informational text

Method to Maximize Student Engagement: an informational text kids will connect to; over time, having students use punctuation craft sticks as they ask and answer questions

Materials: an informational text that invites curiosity and promotes inquiry, especially written in question-and-answer format to begin (such as the I Wonder Why series books by Barbara Taylor); 18-by-24-inch white construction paper, a large precut colored question mark, a glue stick, and printed cards that say *who, what, when, where, why, how* for an anchor chart; craft sticks with die-cut punctuation glued to the top of each (question marks and periods).

Model: how to read questions in headings in informational text and use question words to find answers using key details in the text; how to answer questions thoughtfully in sentences

Lessons That Last: Whole-Group Lesson Plan for Asking and Answering Questions: Informational Text—Second Grade *(continued)*

Prompting for Independence:

• "Some authors use questions as headings to help readers think about answers as they read. When I read, I ask questions all the time."

• "When we ask and answer questions about key details as we read, we understand the text better."

• "*Who, what, when, where, why,* and *how* are question words. When the word *who* is in the question, think about a person or creature in the key details. When the word *where* is in the question, think about places mentioned in the key details. The word *when* in a question tells the reader to pay attention to dates and times. Using *why* in a question cues the reader to pay attention to reasons; *how* alerts the reader that explanations or procedures will be given."

Mini-Lesson Procedure:

1. Choose a short, interesting piece of informational text that relates to something that interests students. Or you might use text related to what you're studying in science or social studies to maximize classroom time. Start with an informational text with question-and-answer format for good models of asking and answering questions, such as *I Wonder Why Zippers Have Teeth and Other Questions About Inventions* by Barbara Taylor. Other books in this series are good follow-up books.

2. Prepare visuals to use during the lesson (which will also be used in literacy work stations over time). These include the anchor chart materials listed above and the craft punctuation sticks. Be sure to read the text ahead of time, so you can gather objects that may be helpful in introducing students to new vocabulary in the book. When using the book mentioned above, I wore a skirt with a hook and eye and a jacket with a zipper.

3. Make an anchor chart about questions with the class. In front of students, write the title at the top: "Readers ask questions, read, think, and find answers." Then have a child glue the big construction paper question mark below. Tell kids that today you will be paying attention to questions the author wants to answer in informational text. Authors use *question words* to help us know which key details to think about when reading. Ask students if they know any question words. Have them help to glue these (preprinted) words inside the large question mark on the anchor chart—*Who, What, When, Where, Why, How*. Tell them that today as you read informational text, you want them to think about questions and answers. These will help them better understand what they read.

4. Preview the cover and table of contents of your read-aloud book with the class. Then ask them which questions they would like you to help them answer. Read aloud several segments to the class.

5. Before reading each section, point to the heading with a question, and point out that it's a question and how we know that. Ask students what the *question word* is. Then help them pay attention to that information. Explain that that is what the author wants us to focus on: the key details in the text she has written. For example, in the section, "Why do zippers have teeth?" the author wants us to pay attention to *why*. It may be helpful to use real objects or photos as supports for new vocabulary when helping kids find answers. You may want to show them a zipper on a jacket to point out the "teeth" and the "slider." Students may not know what a "hook and eye" is, so show that on an item of clothing, too.

6. As you read aloud, direct children's attention to the key details that answer the question they are trying to answer. Help them synthesize what they are learning by having them say the answer in a sentence. For example, "Zippers have teeth to make it easy to fasten clothing. Buttons take longer to use and leave spaces." As you ask a question, hold up the question mark punctuation craft stick. As you expect an answer, hold up the stick with the period on it.

On-the-Spot Assessment: Who understands the difference between a question and an answer? Which students can identify the question word (not just repeat the question) and find the key details that answer it? Are children paying attention to key details and not just finding interesting facts?

Connections to Whole-Group Mini-Lesson

Independent Reading Connection: Help students choose informational books they can read independently that have some questions in the headings. Have one-to-one conferences to see whether they are paying attention to questions and actively seeking answers. Children enjoy these kinds of books immensely and will want to share with others what they are learning!

Small-Group Connection: Be sure to use question-and-answer-type informational texts in guided reading groups, too. Guide students to pay attention to questions in the headings and think about the question word and key details the author wants them to think about. Over time, have students generate their own questions (like the ones in headings of familiar informational books) and answers about informational text using sticky notes. You might use cards with a question word (*who, what, when, where, why, how*) on each as cues to help students form questions. With older students, use test-question stems like those they'll have to answer on standardized tests to familiarize them with what these questions are asking. (The "Example Test Questions" sections in this book can help you get started.)

Writing Connection: Modeling for kids how to make their own question-and-answer books will help them write their own. This is a great way to have students apply the idea of asking and answering questions in informational text. Use read-aloud question-and-answer books as mentor texts. Teach students how to write the question in bold text and then have the text answer it, using key details.

Evaluation: Give students grade-level informational text to read that has headings with questions. Then have them answer the question using key details.

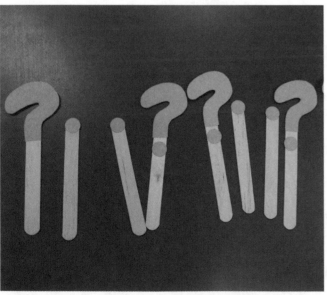

Die-cut question marks and periods are taped onto tongue depressors to create punctuation sticks that kids use to show if they are asking or answering a question. These are used in whole group and also at stations.

Just as it's important for students to ask and answer questions about information in the text, it's equally important for them to learn to ask and answer questions about new vocabulary they encounter. Beck, McKeown, and Kucan (2013) refer to this as "word consciousness." Be sure to spend time teaching kids to stop and ask, "What's that word mean?" when they come to unfamiliar words in the text, as demonstrated in the following lesson. When reading aloud, model what you do when you come across a word that's unfamiliar to you. Show that it's normal to not know the meaning of every single word you read, and that it's okay to stop and figure it out. If you model this with an iPad or tablet, you can show how to use the feature that looks up words for you. (Note: If you teach younger students and therefore know the meanings of all the words you read to them, you might want to share how you've stopped to figure out meanings of unfamiliar words in texts you've read at home.)

Team Planning Tool: Asking and Answering Questions About Words: Informational Text—Third Grade	
Standard We're Teaching	**Third grade:** Determine the meaning of general academic and domain-specific words and phrases in a text relevant to a grade three *topic* or *subject area* (ask and answer questions about what new words mean as encountered in texts).
Academic Vocabulary We'll Use and Expect to Hear	• *What does the word ___ mean?* • *What does the phrase _____ mean?* • *Text evidence*
Whole-Group Ideas	• Create anchor chart on finding meanings of unfamiliar words. • Model how to figure out what unknown words (especially when in bold or high-lighted print) mean while reading informational text. Also show how to use the glossary. • Model how to use the Frayer model (Frayer, Frederick, and Klausmeier 1969) to think deeply about new words. See Figure 6.3 for a sample graphic organizer based on the Frayer model.
Partner Practice at Literacy Work Stations	**Buddy-reading station:** Be sure to provide informational text at students' independent reading levels to use here. Have a recording sheet where they can jot down unknown words and what they think they mean, using text evidence and/or the glossary. Then have partners choose an important new word or phrase they learned (that they think they will use again and again) and use the Frayer model with this word or phrase to define and place in a community journal at this station. **Science or social studies station:** Provide informational text around topics in science and social studies your class has been studying. Have a trifold board labeled with the topic(s). Students make word cards with illustrations to add to the display. They can also play Guess My Word with the display board, giving clues to their partner to practice using the words. **Classroom library:** Provide "new word" bookmarks at the classroom library where kids can write down important vocabulary they learn as they read informational text. Challenge them to use these new words in their speaking and writing vocabularies.

Chapter 6

Figure 6.3 **Frayer Model**

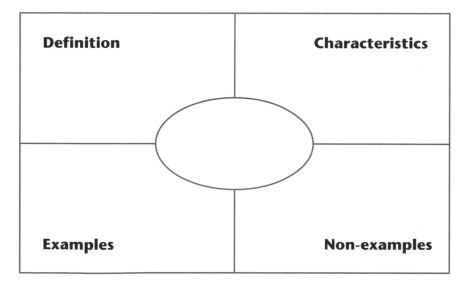

Lessons That Last: Whole-Group Lesson Plan for Asking and Answering Questions About Words—Third Grade

What's That Word Mean?

Focus: asking and answering questions to determine the meanings of content-area words and phrases in an informational text

Method to Maximize Student Engagement: an informational text related to science or social studies content being studied; highlighter tape to mark new words; opportunity for kids to make cards to add to a content-area word wall (related to topics of study in science or social studies)

Materials: an informational text with boldface words and a glossary (such as *Gravity* by Suzanne Lyons 2010); highlighter tape, precut and with an edge folded back and stuck on an index card for easy access; anchor chart on determining word meaning; 3-by-5-inch blank cards and markers for creating cards for a content-area word wall (may use a trifold board)

Model: how to monitor and think about new words and phrases while reading, using cues such as bold words, a glossary, and other words around the new word or phrase to determine its meaning.

Prompting for Independence:

- "Authors of informational text often use bold words to tell the reader to stop and pay attention."
- "When reading informational text, stop at bold words and ask, 'What does this word mean?' Then look around the word for help. Use other words, use pictures, think about another word that would make sense there, or use the glossary. Be sure you understand the word before you read on."
- "Sometimes when reading informational text, the author doesn't use bold print on new words. Use the same strategies that you would use on a bold word if you get to a word and don't understand what it means."

Mini-Lesson Procedure:

1. Choose a short, interesting piece of informational text that relates to something students are studying in science or social studies to maximize classroom time. Preview the book to be sure there are new vocabulary words that will give students opportunities to stop and figure out word meanings. Books with boldface words and a glossary are good choices for asking and answering questions about new words and their meanings (such as *Gravity* by Suzanne Lyons from Benchmark Education).

2. Plan for an anchor chart to use during the lesson; then display it in your whole-group area. Ahead of time, you might write the title on the chart ("What's That Word Mean?") and make cards that say "Stop," "Ask," "Look," and "Say." Also have a few text samples enlarged and printed from the book you'll be reading. These pieces can be glued to the chart as you make it with kids. (See accompanying photos in this section.) If you have a document camera, use it to project the informational text for all to see. Point to the anchor chart and read its title with the class. Take a minute to discuss the fact that informational text often has lots of new words and the importance of stopping to ask what new words mean as you read. Read aloud the book, one section at a time, pausing to think with students about the bold words and/or words they may not be familiar with. Encourage them to stop and ask, "What's that word mean?" and then follow certain steps to ascertain its meaning. As you model, use the words *stop, ask, look, say,* and have kids glue them to the anchor chart as you work through the process with several words from the text. Also have children glue samples from the text to remind them of how they figured out what words mean.

3. Here's an example: "As we read, pay attention to new words. The heading of this section is 'What Is Gravity?' Stop! I am already asking what a new word means: what is *gravity*? I'll pay attention, because the author will probably tell me." (Ask a student to glue the word *Stop* to the anchor chart at this point.) Then continue reading. "The text says, 'Stand up. Jump! What happens? Do you float in the air or fly through space? No! You quickly come back down. Gravity pulls you back to Earth.' The word *gravity* is a new word. *Float* might be a new word for someone, too. So let's pay attention to what both of those words mean here. Let's *ask*, 'What can we do to figure out what each new word means?'" (As you talk through this, add the word *Ask* to the anchor chart with your students.) Then show them ways to find the word's meaning by looking for clues. Add the word *Look* to the class chart along with examples of strategies to try and text samples, as shown on the chart on page 121.

(continued on next page)

Lessons That Last: Whole-Group Lesson Plan for Asking and Answering Questions About Words—Third Grade *(continued)*

Kids can help you glue these to the chart as you make it together. Some examples of strategies they might try are "Look at . . . [bold words, the glossary, words around it, the sentence before and after, the photos or illustrations]." Model how to use these strategies as you read the book with the children, pausing to figure out new word meanings. Add the strategies, one at a time, to the chart (as shown in the photos on page 129).

4. Continue to refer to and/or add to the anchor chart as you discover other ways to figure out new word meanings across mini-lessons using informational text. For example, we added the strategy "Say another word that makes sense here" as we came to a place in the text where that was the best thing to try.

On-the-Spot Assessment: The above lesson will need to be taught many times with various pieces of informational text. Keep using and referring to the anchor chart you've begun. Give students dry erase boards and markers. Do shared reading of informational text using a document camera or interactive whiteboard to enlarge the text. As you read together, stop and ask, "What does the word _____ mean?" Have students write the answer on their dry erase boards and hold them up, so you can quickly see what each student understands about how to find meanings in text.

Connections to Whole-Group Mini-Lesson

Independent Reading Connection: Be sure each student has an informational text, preferably with boldface words and a glossary on his or her independent reading level. Give kids small sticky notes and have them write a question mark on each one. Ask them to mark places in the book where they stopped and asked, "What does this word mean?" Have them also make a list of new words, their meanings, and how they figured them out. If students have iPads or tablets to use for independent reading, they can use the dictionary tool to retrieve word meanings. They still might jot down new words for which they learned the meanings.

Small-Group Connection: Likewise, give kids sticky notes with question marks to mark places where they stopped and asked, "What does this word mean?" Have them use the same recording sheet (that they used in independent reading) to write down what they learned about their new words.

Writing Connection: Model how to write informational text that includes boldface words and a glossary to help readers pay attention to important new words. You might choose boldface words to use from a list of science or social studies vocabulary students have been studying. This is a great way for student understanding of this vocabulary to go deeper.

Evaluation: After ample instruction and practice, give students informational text to read that includes questions about vocabulary.

Mentor Texts for Modeling:
Asking and Answering Questions About Information and/or Words: Informational Text

- *I Wonder Why Zippers Have Teeth and Other Questions About Inventions* by Barbara Taylor
- *Gravity* by Suzanne Lyons
- *Creature Features* by Steve Jenkins
- *Feathers: Not Just for Flying* by Melissa Stewart
- *Scholastic Discover More: My Body* by Andrea Pinnington
- *Tiny Creatures: The World of Microbes* by Nicola Davies
- *Buried Sunlight* by Molly Bang

Chapter 6

	Teaching Tips for Asking and Answering Questions About Information and/or Words: Informational Text Across the Grades
In Pre-K and Kindergarten	• Young children often confuse *asking* and *telling*. Be explicit by saying, "I have a question" or "This is the answer to my question." Likewise, have children use the words *question* and *answer*, too. For example, expect them to say something like, "I have a question. How does a snake eat a whole egg?" or "What is a hand grip?" • Use interesting, enlarged photographs to teach how to ask and answer questions. Write questions on sticky notes as kids ask them, and place them on the large picture. Help students find answers to these questions, too. • You might hold up the punctuation sticks to help students understand differences between asking and answering questions. Point out the way our voices sound different at the end when telling versus asking. But don't expect young students to use periods and question marks correctly as they write. They may experiment by placing these punctuation marks in their writing, but it takes lots of experience for punctuation to be used correctly. • Be sure to model thinking about unfamiliar words as you read, and encourage young children to ask, "What's that word mean?"
In Grades One–Two	• Model how to ask and answer questions as you read aloud informational text. Encourage students to do the same. Use sticky notes with question marks on them to show where in the text you had a question; then move it to the part of the text where it was answered. • Show how authors sometimes use questions to help readers think about the answers as they read. • Make charts with questions and answers your class has about informational texts as you read aloud. Then have them do the same as they read independently and at stations. • By first and second grade, expect children to use periods and question marks correctly as they write. • Teach kids to stop and ask questions about new words as they read. This "word consciousness" is a very important habit to establish at a young age! Children who are curious about words become children who use those words in their speaking, reading, and writing over time.
In Grades Three and Up	• Questioning has been referred to as the "strategy that propels readers on" (Harvey and Goudvis 2007). • Continue modeling how to ask and answer questions as you read informational text by using sticky notes. Show kids how to jot down questions that pop into your mind as you read on sticky notes and place them in the text so they stick out a bit from the edge of the page. Also show them how to move the sticky notes to the place in the book where each question is answered. Let them know that many questions will not be answered in just one text, which leads to inquiry and research projects using multiple texts. • Have a research station in your classroom where kids can post questions they have that have not yet been answered. Provide resources for them to use to search for answers (books, articles, online resources). • Use test passages with grades three and up that focus on word meanings. (There are lots of these kinds of questions on state tests.) But don't focus solely on test prep or having kids read test passages. • Be sure to make and use an anchor chart for determining what unfamiliar words mean.

Sample Anchor Charts for Asking and Answering Questions About Information and/or Words: Informational Text

This anchor chart was partially made by the teacher before the lesson (*top*) to save time with students. During a mini-lesson on asking and answering questions, students take turns gluing question words to the chart (*above*). This chart will be used over and over again throughout the year.

This finished anchor chart on asking and answering questions is used during a mini-lesson on reading informational text. The chart helps kids remember to ask questions and search for answers as they read. It also teaches them about question words.

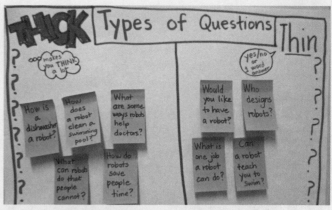

An anchor chart on asking questions from a second-grade classroom encourages students to ask deeper, or "thick," questions.

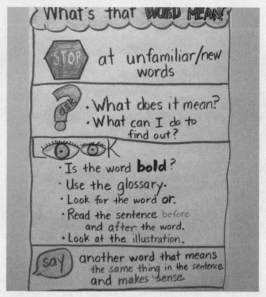

This anchor chart on asking and answering questions about unknown words was made over time with the class.

Literacy Work Stations for Asking and Answering Questions About Information and/or Words: Informational Text

Partners work together to ask and answer questions about an illustration at a question-and-answer station. They use question-word cards to help them think of questions. Change images, photos, and illustrations over time. Kids might write their questions on sticky notes and add them to photos for others to answer.

Chapter 6

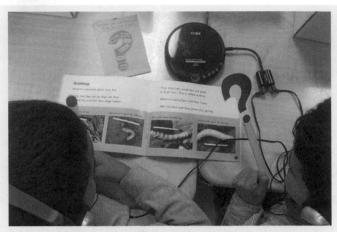

Partners use the mini–anchor chart about questioning to ask each other questions about the informational text they listened to at the listening station. Change the texts over time.

Kids can read informational texts together at the buddy-reading station. They use the punctuation sticks to ask and answer questions before, during, and after reading an informational text. They use the question-words anchor chart to help them use question words. Over time they might record a few of their questions and answers, as well as new words, in the community journal here.

Question Maker

1. Pick a passage you both agree on.
2. Read it together.
3. Write 5 or more questions.
4. Use TEST QUESTION STEMS.
5. Write questions on one side and answers on the other side.

Directions (top) were written by intermediate-grade kids for a question-maker station. They worked together to read a test passage and then wrote questions and answers to go with it (bottom). They used test-question stems (like those found on the standardized test) to help them.

Students read informational text at an "I wonder" station and write questions on yellow sticky notes. They help one another find answers and post them on blue sticky notes. This is a great way to extend learning about science and social studies topics. Questions will change along with the topics studied. Provide informational books at this station to help students answer questions.

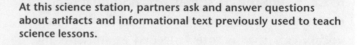

At this science station, partners ask and answer questions about artifacts and informational text previously used to teach science lessons.

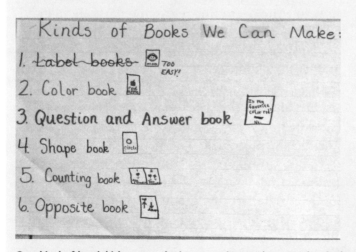

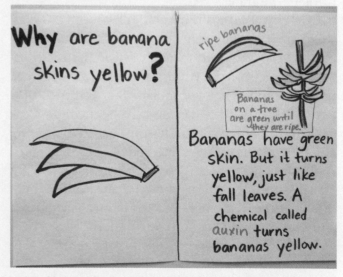

One kind of book kids can make is a question-and-answer book about topics of interest at the writing station (*left*). A sample like this one is made with the class and posted at the station as a model (*right*).

Comparing and Contrasting: Informational Texts on the Same Topic

"How do we find time to teach science and social studies?" is a question I'm frequently asked by teachers of young children. "At our school we teach only language arts and math in first grade. We were told not to worry about science." "Research? How can kindergarten kids do research?" These questions and comments cause me concern. How will we develop aspiring scientists and civic leaders unless we provide foundations for scientific and community-minded thinking in our primary classrooms?

Most of the reading and writing students will do in social studies and science involves informational text. Integrating read-aloud books on content-area topics during the reading block, combined with explicit instruction in comparing and contrasting ideas (via illustrations and words), is a great way to fit science and social studies into an often-crowded day. Likewise, teaching children to write about information they've learned from these same books during writing workshop is a way to integrate primary-style research into the classroom. An additional benefit of this type of teaching is the exposure to content-area vocabulary that is sorely needed as students move through the grade levels.

For example, in a third-grade classroom in Texas, we focused on the science standard "students are expected to observe *forces* such as *magnetism* and *gravity* acting on objects." This is a complex, abstract idea packed with science vocabulary that is difficult for young students to understand. To help children engage in the content of this lesson, I began by reading aloud two texts on the same topic, both titled *Gravity.* (This book was also used for the lesson on asking and answering questions about the meaning of unfamiliar words in the previous section.) We compared and contrasted the covers, illustrations, and text of the two books. *Gravity,* an informational text by Suzanne Lyons (2010), has a photo of an astronaut on the cover. A book with the same title by Jason Chin

(2014) is narrative nonfiction (information based on fact that is presented in a format that tells a story) and has a watercolor of an astronaut, Earth, and several floating objects on its cover. It also has factual information at the back of the book. Using two books on the same topic enabled us to dig deeper into the science concepts and content in both. Helping kids pay attention to ideas in both books laid a foundation for understanding the most important ideas about gravity. We also did science experiments, such as those found at www.brighthubeducation.com and www.pbslearningmedia.org, to further develop thinking about gravity. Children enjoyed these hands-on activities, which were recycled into a science station for further practice.

During read-aloud of the *Gravity* books, we used the double bubble map from Thinking Maps to first record similarities and differences in the information from the illustrations, starting with the front covers. In the past I'd used a Venn diagram to compare and contrast, but I found that the spaces were often too small, which made it difficult (for kids and myself) to write in. The color-coded double bubble map with larger, defined circles helped students look more deeply at how the illustrations (and ultimately the information) were alike and different. After examining illustrations, we read the words and compared and contrasted key ideas in the text. Later, I used the notes we'd written on the graphic organizer to model how to write beginning research reports about gravity during writing workshop.

Over time, we used this same technique to read and write about other science and social studies topics. Kids loved using the double bubble maps for reading and writing. We also used a Venn diagram in subsequent lessons, so kids would be exposed to that graphic organizer, which is often found on state tests.

This same type of compare/contrast reading lesson can be taught from pre-K through third grade. A detailed first-grade lesson comparing and contrasting information about monarch butterflies during a unit of study on life cycles is included in this section.

Sifting Through the Standard: Comparing and Contrasting: Informational Texts on the Same Topic	
What It Is	Examining two (or more) informational texts *on the same topic* to look for similarities and differences—in illustrations, descriptions, procedures, important points, or key details
Why It's Important	Marzano, Pickering, and Pollock (2001) found that helping students identify similarities and differences had the largest effect on student reading achievement of any reading strategy taught. Researchers have found this skill to be "basic to human thought" and consider it the "core of all learning" (Gentner and Markman 1994).
Prerequisites Needed	• The ability to classify or organize things into groups based on their similarities • The ability to identify important points in informational text, since students will now be expected to compare and contrast them
Academic Vocabulary	Kindergarten–first grade: • *similarities* • *same* • *differences* • *different* • *illustrations* • *descriptions* • *procedures* • *two texts on same topic* Second grade: • *compare* • *contrast* • *most important points* Third grade: • *key details*
Real-World Connections	• We constantly compare and contrast in our daily lives. Comparing and contrasting helps us make important decisions: Which is the best deal when buying a particular item? Which government official will I vote for? Which facts from several news accounts on the same event intersect, and what is being reported differently from different sources? • We need to compare and contrast the most important points and key details presented in two or more texts on the same topic to write or speak knowledgeably about a topic.
Example Test Questions	• "According to both articles, who _____?" • "Which of the following pieces of information is *not* found in both articles?" • "When comparing two texts, the authors both included information about _____." • "The author in the first text gave more information about _____ than the author of the second text." • "A key detail included in *both* articles is _____."

Team Planning Tool: **Comparing and Contrasting: Informational Texts on the Same Topic—First Grade**	
Standard We're Teaching	**First grade:** Identify basic similarities in and differences between two texts on the same topic (such as in illustrations, descriptions, or procedures).
Academic Vocabulary We'll Use and Expect to Hear	• *same* • *different* • *similarities* • *differences* • *topic* • *illustrations* *(descriptions, procedures)*
Whole-Group Ideas	• Examine cover illustrations of two texts on the same topic and discuss similarities and differences in the information given. • Use a double bubble map from Thinking Maps to compare and contrast information.
Partner Practice at Literacy Work Stations	**Classroom library:** Place a laminated double bubble map in the nonfiction section of the library for kids to use to compare and contrast two texts on the same topic. They choose a labeled nonfiction basket and use a magnifying glass to look at the illustrations (or descriptions or procedures over time). **Compare-and-contrast station:** You might place objects here that are related to science or social studies topics being studied (for example, monarch butterflies, or rocks and minerals). Have kids use the double bubble map or a Venn diagram to compare and contrast the items. Add texts on the topics over time, too, to be used for comparing and contrasting. **Science station:** Kids asked whether we could have a butterfly station after this initial mini-lesson! We put informational books from read-aloud and other butterfly books there along with the double bubble map.

Lessons That Last: Whole-Group Lesson Plan for Comparing and Contrasting: Informational Texts on the Same Topic—First Grade

Double Bubble Comparison

Focus: identifying similarities in and differences between cover illustrations in two informational texts (eventually do the same with other illustrations in the book, and then descriptions)

Note: also teach lessons on identifying similarities in and differences between procedures using other books

Method to Maximize Student Engagement: a topic that kids are interested in, particularly in science or social studies; buddy talk; double bubble map with precut laminated circles that kids can take on and off

Materials: two nonfiction books on the same topic, *The Journey: Stories of Migration* by Cynthia Rylant and *Monarchs Migrate South* by Melissa Burke; three magnifying glass die cuts, laminated and labeled "Illustrations," "Descriptions," and "Procedures" (see photo on page 129); dry erase board and markers; die-cut colored circles, laminated and attached with Velcro to a large piece of chart paper for follow-up lessons

Model: how to get information from the illustrations (as well as the words) in informational texts

Lessons That Last: Whole-Group Lesson Plan for Comparing and Contrasting: Informational Texts on the Same Topic—First Grade *(continued)*

Prompting for Independence:

- "The writer uses *illustrations,* or pictures, as well as words to give *information* in *nonfiction* books."
- "We can look for and notice *similarities* and *differences* in the *illustrations* in two books on the *same topic*. If we see things that are the *same,* it means the ideas are really *important. Differences* are often seen in the *details*."
- "*Similarities* are things that are the *same. Differences* are things that are *different*."
- (Over time, substitute the words *descriptions* and *procedures* for *illustrations*.)

Mini-Lesson Procedure:

1. Choose two informational texts on the same topic, preferably related to something you're studying in science or social studies. Draw the circles for the double bubble map on a whiteboard, using different colors for each section as shown in the photo.

2. Ask students to tell one another what they'll expect to find in informational text. Have them use the words *informational text* in their response. For example, "I expect there will be facts in *informational* text. When I read *informational* text, I think there are things that are real."

3. Tell them that today you are going to look at the *illustrations* in informational text (and point to them). Explain that illustrations are the pictures, not the words, and that in nonfiction the illustrations give information that we should pay attention to. Show the magnifying glass labeled "Illustrations" and how you are paying attention to them by peering through it.

4. Show students the two covers and ask them what the topic is (*monarch butterflies*). Write the name of the illustrator of each book in a circle, as shown in the anchor chart photos. Talk about how Cynthia Rylant's book uses drawings and Melissa Burke's uses photographs for illustrations, and fill in the appropriate circles on the double bubble map. Then have kids talk to a buddy about what they see that's the same or different in the illustrations or pictures and the information they give them.

5. Call on children to tell you what they noticed with their partner, and jot down notes on the graphic organizer.

6. When finished, have kids reflect on what they learned about looking for similarities and differences in the illustrations of two informational texts on the same topic. ("The illustrators use some of the same details in two books. I know a lot more about how a monarch butterfly looks, because we studied what was the same. Monarch butterflies have orange wings with black edges and white polka dots.")

7. On another day, use a double bubble map where kids can physically manipulate the circles. Before the lesson, make large die-cut circles in three different colors and laminate them, as shown in the photo on page 129. Attach the circles to a large sheet of chart paper with Velcro, so they can be moved around and reused. Show students the books and magnifying glass from the previous lesson, but this time show illustrations from sections on the same topic, such as where or how monarchs migrate. Ask kids to talk to their partners about similarities and differences in the illustrations and the information they give. Then chart their ideas on the circles, using a dry erase marker, and attach the circles to the chart with Velcro.

8. After charting, take the circles off the double bubble map, one at a time, and hand them to individual children. Ask the child to read what the circle says as you talk about similarities and differences in the illustrations. Then ask students to rebuild the double bubble map, reading each piece as they put it back on the chart paper with Velcro.

9. Repeat this procedure on several more days, looking at *descriptions* in the two texts about the same topic. Use the magnifying glass die cut labeled "descriptions." Repeat the procedure with different texts and different topics, looking through the lens of *illustrations, descriptions,* or *procedures* over time.

On-the-Spot Assessment: Pay attention to students' responses in whole group. Do they understand similarities and differences in illustrations of informational text? Descriptions? Procedures? This will take lots of exposure for some children.

Connections to Whole-Group Mini-Lesson

Independent Reading Connection: Buddy reading will work best for this. Put students in pairs and help them find two informational texts on the same topic. If you work with illustrations, the reading level isn't critical. But when you move into comparing and contrasting descriptions and procedures, be sure the books are at their independent reading levels. Have partners read and talk about a section of their two texts through the lens of *illustrations, descriptions,* or *procedures,* depending on the focus of your mini-lesson. Make the double bubble map available for them to use while talking. Some will use it to scaffold their talk, and others will write on the map.

Small-Group Connection: You might use a double bubble map in small group after introducing it in these whole-group lessons. Use the map while reading two informational texts on the same topic across several lessons to help readers get information from the illustrations, descriptions, or procedures.

Writing Connection: Model how to take information from two books on the same topic and use it to write your own little book about that topic. This is the foundation for research. Over time, you might even look at two students' writing about the same topic and discuss similarities and differences in their illustrations, descriptions, or procedures. See Chapter 8 for more ideas.

Evaluation: After ample instruction and practice, give students two pieces of informational text on the same topic and have them identify similarities in and differences between the illustrations, descriptions, or procedures. They might use a double bubble map to tell or write what they noticed.

Mentor Texts for Modeling:
Comparing and Contrasting: Informational Texts on the Same Topic

- *Gravity* by Suzanne Lyons; *Gravity* by Jason Chin
- *The Journey: Stories of Migration* by Cynthia Rylant; *Monarchs Migrate South* by Melissa Burke
- *Giant Pandas* by Gail Gibbons; *Giant Pandas from China* by Allan Fowler
- *A Little Book of Sloth* by Lucy Cooke; *Sloths* by Julie Guidone
- *Owen and Mzee* by Isabella Hatkoff; *A Mama for Owen* by Marion Dane Bauer
- *Frogs* by Nic Bishop; *Frogs* by Seymour Simon
- *The Beetle Book* by Steve Jenkins; *Beetles* by Cheryl Coughlan
- *Egg: Nature's Perfect Package* by Steve Jenkins; *An Egg Is Quiet* by Diana Aston

Teaching Tips for Comparing and Contrasting: Informational Texts on the Same Topic Across the Grades	
In Pre-K and Kindergarten	• Have students classify objects or pictures related to the informational texts they will read. They must be able to sort items into those that have similarities in order to compare and contrast information. • Start small with informational text topics children know and love, such as animals, vehicles, food, and families. • Focus on comparing and contrasting illustrations from two texts on the same topic to start. Over time, examine descriptions and/or procedures from the texts. • Model how to do "kindergarten-style research" using ideas from Chapter 8.
In Grades One–Two	• Begin with lessons on comparing and contrasting illustrations from two texts on the same topic. • Over time, move into comparing and contrasting descriptions and procedures from two texts about the same thing. • Model with a color-coded double bubble map several times and give kids lots of opportunities to use them on their own, too. • Teach students how to write research reports using information from the double bubble maps or Venn diagrams. See Chapter 8 for more ideas. • Use these same techniques to help students compare and contrast literature (characters, settings, plots), as well as informational text.
In Grades Three and Up	• Continue to have students compare and contrast illustrations, descriptions, and procedures at these grade levels. Also move into having them compare and contrast the most important points presented by two texts on the same topic. • Help students use their understanding of similarities and difference in two texts on the same topic as they read informational text and apply that understanding to doing research.

Sample Anchor Charts for Comparing and Contrasting Informational Texts on the Same Topic

Modeling how to look closely at cover illustrations in one of two texts on monarch butterflies during a read-aloud related to a topic of study in science. We used the double bubble map on a large dry erase easel to compare and contrast information from both books (*see below*).

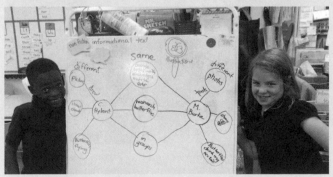

First graders exude pride about what they learned in comparing and contrasting the front covers of two different books about monarch butterflies in a mini-lesson using read-aloud of informational text. A blank double bubble map was then used in multiple follow-up lessons.

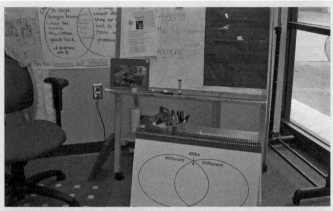

Compare-and-contrast was taught using a Venn diagram in this classroom, with a commercial laminated chart and hand-drawn charts. Students used these same charts at informational text–related listening and buddy-reading stations, too.

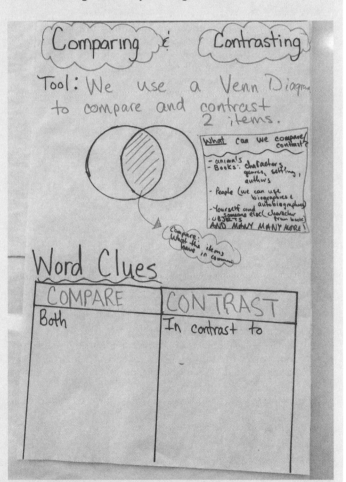

This compare-and-contrast anchor chart with a Venn diagram was made with intermediate students. The graphic organizer was used to familiarize children with the way it often looks on standardized tests.

Literacy Work Stations for Comparing and Contrasting Informational Texts on the Same Topic

Chapter 6

First graders work together comparing and contrasting the same book used in whole group on monarchs at the butterfly (science) station. We made an "I Can" list together for the class to use here. Change out topics and related books here, such as *magnets* or *light and sound,* as you teach with these throughout the year.

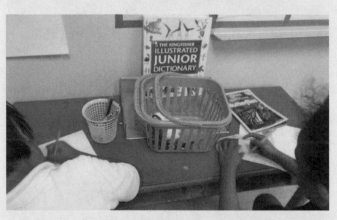

A student chooses to write an informational text about monarch butterflies at the writing station in the same classroom. Anchor charts on how to write informational text should be posted on the wall at this station. (See Chapter 8 for more writing ideas.)

Partners work with the double bubble map, using laminated movable colored circles on which they write how illustrations are similar and different. This was done multiple times in whole group with a variety of texts.

A pair of boys compares and contrasts two I Spy books using a double bubble map after it was introduced in the whole-group lesson with books about monarch butterflies.

Kindergarten students compare and contrast real worms and gummy worms at a science station. They use paper folded in half and write/draw about real worms on one side and gummy worms on the other.

Digging Deeper

By now, you are probably thinking about how to process all the information in this chapter on literacy work stations related to reading informational text. Take one standard at a time and play with ideas related to it. Use the questions below to help you and your grade-level team (if you have one) plan for deep work with your students related to informational text standards.

1. Keep a record of how many fiction and nonfiction texts you read aloud to your class for several weeks. Is there a balance of literature versus informational text? Then examine the nonfiction titles. How many are narrative nonfiction versus informational text, according to the description at the beginning of this chapter? What topics have you been reading aloud about? Are most of the texts about animals? Or are you expanding to include books about concepts such as simple machines, rocks, magnets, history, communities, nutrition, ecology, design, light, and sound? Do your informational text read-alouds match what you've been teaching in science and social studies? If not, you'll want to adjust accordingly.

2. Discuss with colleagues how to teach students about using text features in informational text. This would be a good vertical team topic, so you can build from one grade level to the next. Use ideas from this chapter to refine your teaching of text features. Compare what you've done in the past with what you're noticing that students learn from these lessons. Create opportunities for students to practice working with text features at stations, and share your ideas and results.

3. What did you learn about teaching main idea and details in this chapter? Share any "aha" moments with your colleagues. Try some of the lessons, and share results with your grade-level team if you have one.

4. Skim the chapter after reading it thoroughly. Look for academic vocabulary that is used across lessons with informational text, such as *front cover*, *title*, and *illustrations*. What other academic vocabulary jumps out at you that must be reinforced over and over when students read this kind of text? Which ideas from this chapter will help you teach and have students use this academic vocabulary? Share examples with colleagues after you've tried them in your classroom.

5. Asking and answering questions is an important standard to teach in your classroom. Take a close look at the kinds of questions both you and your children are asking. Work with colleagues to create higher-level-thinking questions before teaching lessons in whole group and small group. Keep those questions in front of you as you teach, but be flexible, too.

6. Series books are mentioned throughout this chapter. Talk about the importance of using informational-text series. Take a field trip to the school library or each other's classrooms or even a children's bookstore and examine the informational text you're reading aloud. Strive to find strong informational-text series to read aloud to your students.

7. Look at the literacy work stations you currently have set up in your classroom. At which ones are students working with informational text rather than reading literature? Be sure there is a balance. Implement ideas from this chapter to increase opportunities for kids to practice reading, writing, listening to, and speaking about informational text at stations.

8. Work with your grade-level team to discuss teaching students to compare and contrast informational text using two books on the same topic. This is different from comparing and contrasting two topics and requires close examination of how authors and illustrators treat the same topic. What did you learn by trying lessons using the double bubble map from this chapter? How did you move this to literacy work stations, and what results did you observe?

7

Literacy Work Stations for Reading: Foundational Skills

Standards Covered in This Chapter	Lessons Described in This Chapter
Learning Letter Names and Sounds	Name That Letter or Sound or Word
Identifying High-Frequency Words	Highlighting High-Frequency Words
Developing Phonological and Phonemic Awareness	Sound by Sound
Using Chunks and Word Families	Chunks and Word Families
Recognizing Long-Vowel Patterns	Lots of Long-Vowel Patterns
Reading Long Words (Syllabication)	Studying Syllables with Haiku

Even if you teach third grade, please read this chapter! Learning how letters and words work continues to be important in pre-K through third grade to establish a foundation for reading and writing. Use the chart above to find sections that match what students in your class need, regardless of their age or grade level, and use the ideas found there.

Children come to us with varying understanding of letter names and sounds in pre-K and kindergarten. Some can segment and blend sounds, some recognize and write their names and several other words, and others scribble write or make mock letters. By the end of kindergarten, students are expected to know all the letter names and sounds and to be able to decode consonant-vowel-consonant words (such as *dog, bat, win, leg*) within text (not just in isolation), as well as recognize twenty to fifty high-frequency words.

In first grade, phonics expands to more complex sounds and combinations, including consonant blends (*bl, tr, sw, cr, fl,* and so on) and digraphs (*ch, sh, wh, th*). Many other sounds must be learned, including long-vowel patterns (*ai, a-silent-e, ay, eigh*), vowel-plus-*r* combinations (*ar*, *er*, *ir*, *or*, *ur*), and combinations of letters, such as *ou*, *ow*, *augh*—just to name a few! By second grade, children must read with high levels of fluency and accuracy. And from second to third grade, phonics instruction shifts to the study of more complex blends and digraphs (*str*, *spl*, *thr*, *sch*) and multisyllabic words, including those with prefixes and suffixes. It's a tall order to teach all of this and to be sure that reading comprehension takes precedence so that children don't become "word callers"—kids who can say the words but have little to no idea what they have just read.

Most primary teachers have lots of phonics materials and resources in their classrooms. Schools (or individual teachers) often purchase or make phonics, rhyming, high-frequency word, and fluency games and activities. Phonics workbooks abound. It can be tempting to just put these materials on a shelf or worksheets in a tub for kids to choose from during stations time. But what I've observed is that giving students these materials doesn't guarantee that they will develop the skills written on the box or folder. Sometimes, students spend more of their time matching puzzle pieces or cutting and pasting than thinking about the sounds the letters make or the meaning of the words they're working with. Or they work with a skill in isolation and have difficulty applying the sounds or words to the reading and writing of their own texts.

Brittany invited me into her classroom to look at her ABC and word-study stations. "Will you please help me better use all these word work resources?" she asked. "I bought a lot of these because they matched skills for my grade level. I put them on a shelf, and kids choose from them during literacy work stations. But they aren't always effective, especially for students who don't already know the sounds or words."

We began by looking at Brittany's data. She used a flexible reading groups folder to keep track of her guided-reading groups, as described on pages 24–25 in *Making the Most of Small Groups* (Diller 2007). Together, we discussed the specific needs of kids in each group, based on their reading levels and district assessments. Then we jotted down notes about the kinds of practice that would be best for each group (on a large sticky note) and placed it in that group's section in the folder. (See the photo top right for an example.)

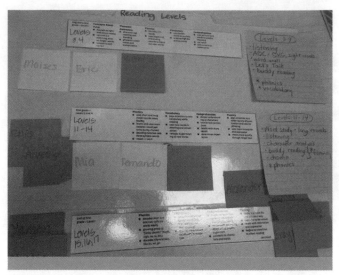

Using a guided-reading folder, as described in my book *Making the Most of Small Groups,* we put each child's name on a small sticky note to go with what to focus on at that reading level. Then to the right, we placed a large blue sticky note that told what kind of practice those kids needed at literacy stations and discussed the specific phonics element for each small group.

Next, we zeroed in on what each group of kids needed to work on regarding phonics. For example, the readers who were struggling most in Brittany's class who were also English language learners needed to work with CVC (consonant-vowel-consonant) words. Brittany had those three children (reading on DRA2 Levels 3–4 or the end of kindergarten level, even though they weren't kindergartners) play a commercial matching game with pictures of CVC objects and words at a word-study station. However, I observed them simply making puzzles with this commercial matching game rather than working with words.

Brittany realized that her students would focus more on the words if she used these puzzles as part of small-group instruction and changed the task slightly (before students used them at a word-study station). So, in small group, we showed students how to work together to name a picture, stretch out the sounds, and then write each sound in an Elkonin box with a dry erase marker. Afterward, they checked their work by looking at the matching word written on the back of the picture card. We also modeled how to use a familiar ABC chart for help with sounds if needed. See the photos on the next page for a before-and-after sample. Then, we placed these materials at the word-study work station in a green basket, since this was Brittany's green group.

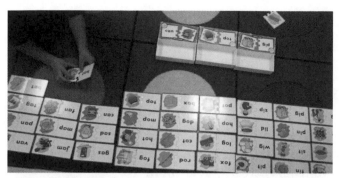

Before: Commercial word-study materials include CVC words to match pictures. Students were simply using puzzle shapes to match many of them.

After: We used just the puzzle pieces with pictures (shown in this photo) and discarded the matching word pieces. Students chose a dry erase strip with Elkonin boxes drawn on it. They named the picture and wrote the CVC word with a dry erase pen, writing a letter in each box as they stretched out the word. Then they checked their spelling by looking at the word on the back of the card. An alphabet chart provided support for letters and sounds, as needed.

Likewise, we differentiated word study for Brittany's most advanced readers who needed to work with multisyllabic words. Instead of having them do isolated word work, we had them apply word study to their writing. Working with these two students in small group, we asked them to choose a piece they'd written in writing workshop and look together for words they weren't sure they'd spelled correctly. Here's the routine we decided on:

1. Use a yellow crayon to circle a word you think might be misspelled.
2. Say the word aloud, clap the syllables, and draw a box for each syllable on a dry erase board.
3. Write each word part (syllable) with a dry erase pen in a box. | fam | i | ly |
4. Use a beginning dictionary to look up the word and check its spelling.
5. Cross out the misspelled word and write it correctly on your draft.

At this differentiated word-study station, advanced partners work with a piece from writing workshop, helping each other spell words using the five-step routine described in this chapter.

As we looked at the needs of Brittany's guided-reading groups, we organized her phonics resources to match her students' needs and made plans to teach with them in small group before moving them to word-study stations. We got rid of materials she didn't need—recycling outdated things or games that were missing pieces and donating duplicates to new teachers. We labeled each remaining word-study material (and a corresponding basket) by the phonics element it reinforced (*beginning consonants*, *short vowels*, *consonant blends*, *word families*, *prefixes and suffixes*, and so on) and placed it in Brittany's small-group area, ready for use in small group before moving it to a word-study station.

This chapter will focus on how to get the most out of your instruction and the subsequent partner practice of foundational skills, including work with letters and sounds, phonics patterns and syllabication, high-frequency words, and fluency. Know that the purposeful work you do around letters and sounds, high-frequency words, and phonics will increase students' fluency in reading and writing, especially if you move from isolated work to having kids practice and apply these skills in authentic reading and writing! As you read this chapter, reflect on your state standards, your school's curriculum, and the differentiated needs of your students; then use materials you already own to transform student work with these foundational skills.

Chapter 7

Learning Letter Names and Sounds

Standards for print concepts are found in pre-K through first grade across North America. They build a foundation for helping young children look at print and how it works. Along with reading from left to right and top to bottom, students must learn to print-match by pointing to one word at a time, recognizing that spoken words are represented by letters written in a particular order to create a message.

One very important aspect of print awareness is the identification of letters, including their names and sounds. Give emerging readers opportunities to point to an ABC chart with both upper- and lowercase letters printed and to sing along as they name the letters. If this is done in whole group, it can also be moved to an ABC station where students repeat the activity on their own, as pictured in this section. This chart could also be added to writing resources for individuals, table groups, or the writing station. Repeated use of ABC charts can help students learn the names (and eventually the sounds) of the letters.

Be sure to use the academic vocabulary *uppercase* or *capital* letters and *lowercase* letters, instead of *big* and *small* letters, to avoid confusing students (for example, the lowercase letter *d* is a tall letter, which some children may think of as *big*). Begin by teaching letter names. Research by Kim et al. (2010) has shown that children who know the names of letters learn letter-sound relationships more readily than those without letter-name knowledge. Also, work with students to help them understand that letters are different from words and actually make up words.

Pre-K and kindergarten kids will benefit from singing the traditional ABC song as they point to various ABC charts in whole group as well as at an ABC station.

Sifting Through the Standard: Learning Letter Names and Sounds	
What It Is	• Identifying the name and sound of each of the twenty-six letters of the English alphabet (or the twenty-eight letters in the Spanish alphabet) • The ability to also use the sounds when reading words in connected text • Putting letters and words in alphabetical order
Why It's Important	• English is an alphabetic language. (Spanish and French are alphabetic languages, too.) We must know letter sounds to decode words when reading. • Naming letters is helpful when talking about print and when writing. (For example, *Jazmine's name starts with the letter* J. *When writing the word* like, *begin with the letter* l.) • Knowing letter sounds helps children decode and write.
Prerequisites Needed	• Recognizing one's name in print is helpful in learning about letters. A young child's name is his or her most powerful piece of print. It is the first word most children learn to read and write. • Being exposed to print through books, signs, names, and so on is helpful. It will stimulate curiosity in children about letters and the sounds they make.
Academic Vocabulary	Kindergarten: • *uppercase letter* • *lowercase letter* • *word* • *letter name* • *letter sound* • *vowel* • *short vowel* • *long vowel* • *consonant*

(continued on next page)

Chapter 7

Sifting Through the Standard: Learning Letter Names and Sounds *(continued)*	
Academic Vocabulary	First grade: • *ABC order* • *letter sequence*
Real-World Connections	• The traditional ABC song will give young children a context for learning about letters. As adults, many of us still sing this song in our heads as we use alphabetization to look for books in a library or search our iTunes catalog or try to find the seasonings we need at the grocery store. • The alphabet is everywhere. Help students identify letters in their environment—on food packages, on signs, and in the classroom.
Example Test Questions	• "Which words have the same beginning sound?" • "Which words sound the same at the end?"

Team Planning Tool: Learning Letter Names and Sounds	
Standards We're Teaching	**Kindergarten:** Students are expected to identify upper- and lowercase letters; recognize the difference between a letter and a printed word.
Academic Vocabulary We'll Use and Expect to Hear	• *uppercase letter* • *lowercase letter* • *word* • *letter name* • *letter sound* • *vowel* • *short vowel* • *long vowel* • *consonant*
Whole-Group Ideas	• Sing and point to letters on several different printed ABC charts using different ABC songs. • Build the alphabet arc with the class, using magnetic letters as kids name them. • Place children's name cards on the word wall, one at a time, and use them as points of reference for letter names and sounds (where applicable). • Build name puzzles on a pocket chart and name the letters. • Use magnetic letters to sort by letters with circles or sticks, etc.
Partner Practice at Literacy Work Stations	**ABC station:** Use a familiar ABC chart and point to each letter, using one-to-one matching, while singing an ABC song. Alternatively, use an alphabet arc and magnetic letters, taking turns naming each letter (and its sound) while placing it in the appropriate spot on the arc. Students might do letter sorts, too. **Names station:** Partners work together to build names, using name puzzles and a pocket chart and/or magnetic letters. They identify each letter as they build the name. **Word-wall station:** Students work together to read the names on the word wall using a pointer. They can also point to each letter in a name and identify it. They can identify words and letters, as well as uppercase and lowercase letters.

Chapter 7

Lessons That Last: Whole-Group Mini-Lesson Plan for Learning Letter Names and Sounds

Name That Letter or Sound or Word

Focus: identifying letters, including lowercase and uppercase (and vowels and consonants over time); recognizing the difference between letters and words

Method to Maximize Student Engagement: student names and their photos on name cards to be added to a word wall; reading simple Big Books about the children that include their names, and identifying letters and words; matching letters by manipulating them.

Materials: low, interactive, word wall designed as a grid in or near the whole-group teaching area (see Chapter 2 for ideas on how to set this up); labels for each section with an easy-to-read uppercase and matching lowercase letter and a photo or picture that starts with that sound; a name card that represents each student (large typed black print and matching student photo); Big Books about your students; chopsticks with a black foam or cardstock letter glued to each one (for matching to print)

Model: how to look at print; noticing letters (how many letters, naming them, saying their sounds, identifying them as upper- or lowercase); comparing letters; naming letters; identifying sounds; the difference between letters and words

Prompting for Independence:

- "Caden's name begins with an uppercase letter. It matches this uppercase letter on our word wall."
- "This is a letter. This is a word. A word is made of letters."
- "This is a lowercase letter. Show me another lowercase letter."
- "Let's look at the letter *Cc*. Show me the uppercase letter. Point to the lowercase letter."
- "Show me a letter. Point to a word."
- "Find a word that starts with the letter ___. Find a word that starts with the sound ____."
- "Find a name that starts like _____."

Mini-Lesson Procedure:

1. Have students sit on the floor by the word wall for this mini-lesson. It's important to place the word wall in or near the whole-group teaching area so that you can easily help students make connections between letters and words you're reading and writing together.

2. During the first few weeks of school, introduce one or two students' names each day. (Before this lesson, type each child's name on a card with black letters large enough to be seen across the room and add the child's photo.)

3. Show the class a name card, read it together, and then point to each letter as you name it—*Blake, B, l, a, k, e.* Then make the sound of each letter, as you point to it—/b/, /l/, /a/, /k/. (If a letter is silent, say so. *"The e is silent and doesn't say a sound at the end of* Blake.*"* Likewise, if a letter makes a sound other than the one it makes in Standard English, tell students so. *"Juan starts with* J. *In Spanish, the letter* Jj *says /h/, but in English* Jj *says /j/."*) You might have students write the name in the air as you name the letters together again. Point out that a name begins with an uppercase letter and is made up of lowercase letters, too.

4. Add the name card to the word-wall space that begins with the first letter. For example, *Blake* would go in the *Bb* section.

5. As you add another name, repeat the procedure and then compare it with other names already on the word wall. *"Brooke also starts with* Bb. *What's the same in these words? What's different?"*

6. Also make name puzzles that students can place in a pocket chart as part of whole group and eventually at a names station as well. (See photos on page 148 for an example.)

On-the-Spot Assessment: Involve all students whenever possible in whole-group mini-lessons, and pay attention to what children are connecting to. Which children already can identify the letters in their names by using the letter name and/or sound? Which can identify the letters in the names of others?

Connections to Whole-Group Mini-Lesson

Independent Reading Connection: Provide simple alphabet books for students to read on their own. Encourage students to point to and read the letters on each page. Have kids make the sounds of the letters, too, if they know them. Model this during read-aloud before asking students to do it on their own.

Small-Group Connection: Use name puzzles in small group to reinforce letter learning, especially with students who have trouble remembering letter names and sounds. Do letter sorts.

Writing Connection: Model and then give children opportunities to write things using each other's names. For example, they might write lists of friends. Or they may write a note to or a card for a classmate. They might even write a little book about a friend. See the photos for examples.

Evaluation: Use letter-identification assessments, such as the one found in Marie Clay's *Observation Survey* (2005).

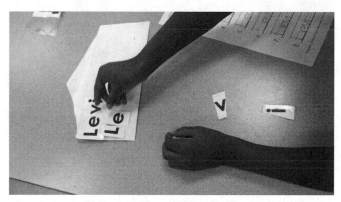

New kindergartners work with building and writing their names at a names (or word study) station. Prior to this, they met in a small group with the teacher to use the name puzzles for learning letter names and sounds.

Mentor Texts for Modeling:
Learning Letter Names and Sounds

- *A, My Name Is Alice* by Jane Bayer
- *Alphabet Under Construction* by Denise Fleming
- *Alphabet Mystery* by Audrey Wood
- *LMNO Peas* by Keith Baker
- *The Alphabet Tree* by Leo Lionni
- *Alphabet Trucks* by Samantha Vamos
- *Chicka Chicka Boom Boom* by Bill Martin, Jr.
- Personalized ABC books with photos can be made for and with struggling students using online sites such as www.shutterfly.com

Teaching Tips for Learning Letter Names and Sounds Across the Grades	
In Pre-K and Kindergarten	• Anchor letter learning to children's names. This is the first word most kids learn to read and write, and it gives purpose and context to letter learning for those that find it difficult.
	• There are many activities geared to helping young children learn letter names and sounds. Choose those that focus on what students know and build from there.
	• It will be helpful to work with just several letters at a time. Link what the child knows to the new. For example, "You know the letter *n*. The letter *r* looks almost like that. It has a stick and a little curve and is in Roberto's name."
In Grades One–Two	• Most students will leave kindergarten knowing their letters and sounds. However, for those who don't have a firm grasp on these concepts, meet these children where they are. Use ideas from this section in small group with them.
	• You might make individual ABC books with students who need help learning their letters and sounds. Use a word and picture on each page that has meaning for the child. Make this over time for the student.
In Grades Three and Up	• You may have English language learners who need to learn the letter names and sounds in English. Build on their home language, pointing out similarities and differences as you work with them to learn English. For example, *"In Spanish, many of the letters look the same but have different names. Some letters make different sounds (i says ee in Spanish, but I/ĭ in English)."*

Sample Anchor Charts for Learning Letters and Concepts About Print

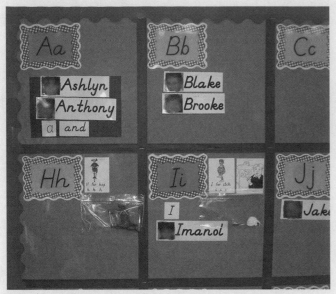

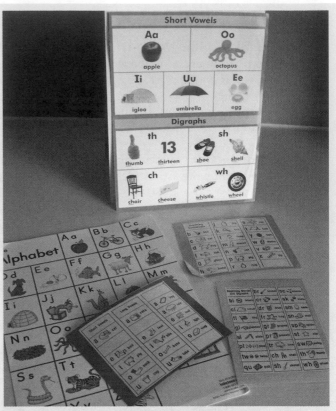

The word wall in pre-K, kindergarten, and first grade is an anchor for helping students learn about letters and sounds. Children's names and photos are added to the word wall, one per day, in kindergarten to provide meaningful anchors for letter learning. The teacher uses each student name to teach letter names and beginning sounds. I've found I can often teach the majority of letters and sounds this way. Pictures of a matching action can be added over time to add a kinesthetic element to letter learning, accompanied by an ABC song like "Alphardy" by Dr. Jean Feldman.

Alphabet charts showing both upper- and lowercase letters and a matching picture for the beginning sound make strong anchors for students' learning letters and sounds. These are from a variety of sources, including *Words Their Way* (Bear et al. 2011).

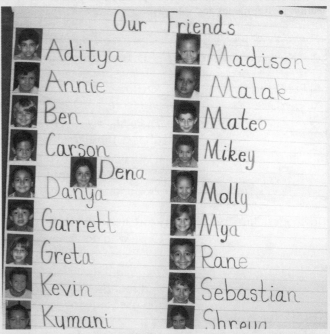

A low, interactive word wall is created on a large dry erase board at the front of the classroom in the whole-group teaching area. There is a space on a grid for each letter of the alphabet with a picture clue and the uppercase and lowercase letters represented to help students with letter learning. This also becomes a word-wall station during independent learning time.

The names anchor chart shows each student's name with the first letter written in red to draw attention to the first sound. Each child's photo is included as a support to reading the name. This chart was made with the class during the first week of school. The high-frequency word *and* is highlighted in two names later in the year.

Literacy Work Stations for Learning Letters and Concepts About Print

An automotive drip tray divided by green tape provides a large magnetic area on which students can sort lowercase and uppercase letters. An ABC chart is provided as a support for partners working on this task. Other letter-learning materials, such as alphabet puzzles, are in the baskets to the left. Change the categories for sorting the letters as you introduce other ways to look at letters. For example, include category cards that say *letters* and *words* or *vowels* and *consonants* after you've taught with them in whole group.

This pair of students works together on the side of a file cabinet marked as a grid to sort magnetic letters by feature, such as letters with sticks, circles, or tails. This work helps children just learning about print to pay attention to letters' distinguishing features. Don't start with all these sorting categories. You might begin with circles, sticks, and dots. As this task becomes easy, add other categories, as shown.

Partners share an alphabet-matching mat and take turns saying the next letter that goes on the mat as they drag the letter to the mat to match. For example, after *C* the next child will say and find the letter *D*. Over time, children do the same letter-identification task with lowercase letters.

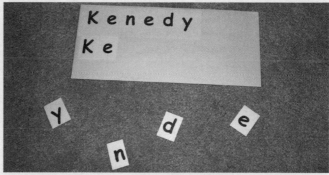

A name puzzle is made from an envelope and letters typed and printed on cardstock. One copy of the child's name is glued onto the top of the envelope and then laminated; copies of the individual letters are kept inside the envelope. Students can match the letters and name them. The child's picture can be added for extra support. Students who need to feel the shape of the letters to better discriminate among them can use magnetic letters. You might add last names to the puzzles over time. Have children begin with their own names and then work with those of friends, especially if they are having trouble learning letter names and sounds.

Students listen to a recorded ABC song as they follow along and point to each letter on a familiar alphabet chart at this listening station. Use other ABC charts and other alphabet songs at the station, over time, to help children become flexible with the letters of the alphabet. ABC videos work well, too.

Two students work together on a letter-identification task. First, one child reaches into a brown paper bag with sandpaper letters in it. He describes the letter. *("It has a stick and a circle.")* Then they both try to guess the letter. Finally, they match the letter to a large, familiar alphabet chart, as shown in the picture. They say the letter and its sound along with the objects it matches. For example, "*B* says /b/ like in *bear.*" Then the other student reaches into the bag and describes the letter she chooses, they guess it, and so on.

Provide a basket of ABC books in the classroom library for students to read there. Likewise, children might make ABC books at the writing station.

Identifying High-Frequency Words

Many teachers use the terms *high-frequency words* and *sight words* synonymously. However, they are not exactly the same. *High-frequency words* are the words found *most frequently* in the texts we read. *Sight words* are words we can read quickly and easily. For an adult reader, almost every word in text is a *sight word* because it can be read automatically.

The most commonly used high-frequency word lists in schools today are the Dolch word list and the Fry word list or some hybrid of the two. The Dolch (1936) list contains 220 words (excluding nouns) most often found in text. It was geared to students in grades one–three. The words came from those used most often by young children in their oral language before first grade and in beginning readers.

The Fry word list, which was last updated in the 1990s, contains 100–1,000 words (depending on the list you use). It was intended for students in grades one–six. The words were taken from the *American Heritage* list (Carroll, Davies, and Richman 1971), which ranks the frequency of words taken from materials used in grades three–nine. According to Fry and Kress (2006), the twenty-five most frequently used words in text make up 33 percent of reading material, the 100 most frequently used words make up 50 percent of text, and the 300 most frequent words constitute 65 percent of

what students read. (Both the Fry and Dolch lists can be found in the online appendix at www.stenhouse.com/gilappendix.

Regardless of the list you use, learning high-frequency words is very important for beginning readers. When children can read high-frequency words such as *A, I, the, to, see,* and *like* quickly and easily in simple, repetitive text, they gain access to print (especially when those words are the first in a sentence).

Whole-group shared reading of Big Books, poems, and other enlarged text containing high-frequency words you are teaching empowers students in early grades to have an "I can do it" spirit when it comes to reading. As a class, chorally read Big Books or poems that have repeated words and phrases (containing the high-frequency words you are teaching) and supportive pictures. You might also use a document camera to project similar little books onto a screen or large whiteboard for whole-group shared reading activities.

Another useful teaching strategy is to have your class read poems together, copied line by line onto sentence strips placed in a pocket chart. Then ask individual students to remove the sentence strips from the chart one at a time (*"José, please find the part with the word* here*"*) and work together to rebuild the poem in the pocket chart as the class rereads it together. This kind of work can help young readers look more closely at print. (I recommend black print on white sentence strips to mirror text found in books. You can cut the poem apart line by line, phrase by phrase, or even word by word in some parts. Think about what you want children to focus on.)

Read the same Big Books and poems multiple times throughout the week, so that kids become familiar with them. After reading, have students find those high-frequency words by pointing to them with a pointer, circling them with Wikki Stix, or using removable highlighter tape. Later, partners can use the same materials at a Big Book station or a poetry station.

Likewise, using the routine of morning message or daily news written for and/or with your children can provide additional exposure to the same high-frequency words. See photos in this section for a sample. This can be turned into a morning message or daily news station where partners work together to reread the message and find high-frequency words. Kids can also use high-frequency words while composing their own morning message or daily news for their classmates to read on a large piece of laminated paper.

To help students connect their learning of high-frequency words to shared reading and writing routines, I highly recommend that you post a high-frequency word wall in or near your whole-group teaching area. One kindergarten teacher told me that his kids learned

more high-frequency words than ever before when he used this approach. As his class read Big Books and poems together, children could easily point to the high-frequency words they found on the word wall because it was right there!

Patricia Cunningham's (2012) seminal work on word walls and predictable text in *Phonics They Use* provides many simple activities for working with high-frequency words. For example, teach three to seven high-frequency words a week. Post them on your board and have students read and spell them daily. Play games such as Guess My Word with them. Give clues in the form of "I'm thinking of a word that…[has three letters, begins with *s*, or rhymes with *blue*]." Students write a word from the list on a dry erase board or piece of paper and change their guess as you give more clues.

To maximize learning, Isabel Beck (2010) recommends teaching high-frequency words in conjunction with a systematic approach to phonics instruction. Knowing letter sounds can help children learn high-frequency words more easily. Many high-frequency words, such as *had, in, that, be, and, is, she,* and *but* are easily decodable. Other high-frequency words (such as *you, was, said,* and *would*) should be memorized, but using phonics clues can help children remember these words and read them quickly and effortlessly.

Sifting Through the Standard: Identifying High-Frequency Words	
What It Is	• Learning to quickly identify and read words that are found most often in text • The Dolch word list and the Fry word list are two respected sources of high-frequency words. • It is important to expose students to high-frequency words as they appear in the text they read. Do *not* teach children these words in alphabetical order (as they may be found in some lists).
Why It's Important	• Knowing how to read high-frequency words frees up the brain to comprehend. • Being able to read some words quickly gives children confidence as readers, especially if they can read the first word in a sentence. • Some of these words are not easy to sound out, because they follow irregular patterns (for example, *you, the, of, said*). • Knowing some words helps students "check" or monitor their one-to-one matching as they read.
Prerequisites Needed	• Identifying a word versus a letter is helpful. • Letter identification (names and sounds) can help students apply the alphabetic principle to high-frequency words they are learning. (Many high-frequency words, such as *in, he, with, up, not,* and *can* are decodable.)

Sifting Through the Standard: Identifying High-Frequency Words *(continued)*	
Academic Vocabulary	Kindergarten (and up): • *high-frequency words* • *word-wall words*
Real-World Connections	• These words are the most frequently used in text, so there is tremendous relevance in learning them. • Attaching meaning to high-frequency words is important to help children remember them. For example, *Manuel* is *kind. Stephanie* is *funny.* We like to *play.* We like to *sing.* We like to *eat.*
Example Test Questions	• "Read these words quickly. " Note: In today's testing environment, children are often given limited amounts of time to complete the test. Being able to read high-frequency words fast and fluently will help them finish within time constraints as well as free up their brains for comprehension.

Team Planning Tool: Identifying High-Frequency Words	
Standard We're Teaching	**First grade:** Students are expected to identify and read at least 100 high-frequency words from a commonly used list.
Academic Vocabulary We'll Use and Expect to Hear	• *high-frequency word*
Whole-Group Ideas	• Teaching with five–seven high-frequency words written on individual cards (to be placed on word wall) each week • Shared reading of Big Books and/or poems that contain these high-frequency words (poems may be written line by line on sentence strips and used in a pocket chart) • Using pointers and highlighting tools to find words in these texts
Partner Practice at Literacy Work Stations	**Big Book station:** Pairs of children read familiar Big Books together. They highlight high-frequency (word-wall) words as or after they read. **Poetry station:** Partners work together to build a poem, using sentence strips in a pocket chart. They match high-frequency words to those on the word wall. **Word-wall station:** Students work together to read the words on the word wall using a pointer. They can also play Guess My Word using dry erase materials and giving each other clues, such as *"The word has four letters. The word starts like your name . . ."* **Word-study/high-frequency station:** Partners play games with high-frequency words, such as Our Pile, My Pile, Your Pile. They put high-frequency word cards facedown on a pile and take turns flipping them over, one at a time. The goal is to both say them fast so the cards go on "our pile." If someone says it first, it goes on "my pile" or "your pile," depending on who read it first. **Daily news (or morning message) station:** Two kids work together to reread old daily news or morning messages. They can edit them or search for high-frequency words and phonics patterns being studied. They may also write their own messages on a laminated chart, using high-frequency words.

Lessons That Last: Whole-Group Mini-Lesson Plan for Identifying High-Frequency Words

Highlighting High-Frequency Words

Focus: identifying and reading high-frequency words in isolation and in text

Method to Maximize Student Engagement: shared reading of Big Books and poems; using highlighting tools to identify high-frequency words

Materials: Big Books and poems containing high-frequency words being studied this week; highlighting tools (pointer, highlighter tape, bubble wand, Wikki Stix, or magnifying lens); nearby high-frequency word wall

Model: how to identify and read high-frequency words in text

Prompting for Independence:

- "These words are in lots of books, so it's important to learn to read them fast."
- "Where can we find that word? Where did we see that word before?"
- "That's a word-wall word."
- "Use the first sound to help you get started."
- "If you can read _____ here, you can read _____ here."

Mini-Lesson Procedure:

1. Introduce this week's high-frequency words by reading them together. Explain that these words are found often in text and need to be read quickly.

2. Then have the children stand, read one word at a time, and spell it with movement. Have them reach to the sky if it's a tall letter and squat down if it's a short letter. For example, you'd stand, read, and spell the word *the* like this: "The—t [reach high], h [reach high], e [squat down], the."

3. Next, read a Big Book or poem containing as many of those high-frequency words as possible. Tell your class to be on the lookout for these words, because they are in many texts. You might come up with a signal (for example, put your hand on your head, touch your nose, or pull your ear) to use when they read one of these words.

4. After reading, talk about the text to be sure students comprehend (and aren't just searching for high-frequency words).

5. Then have them take turns coming up to the Big Book or poem to highlight and read high-frequency words. They might use highlighter tape, a magnifying lens, or a bubble wand.

6. Reread these Big Books and poems throughout the week and have students continue to use a variety of highlighting tools to find the high-frequency words.

On-the-Spot Assessment: Take note of which children find and read the high-frequency words easily. Plan to work with children in small group who are having difficulty reading and remembering them.

In whole group, we read and spell the high-frequency word *here,* squatting down for the small letters *e, r,* and *e.* (We reached for the sky as we spelled the tall letter *h.*)

Connections to Whole-Group Mini-Lesson

Independent Reading Connection: Encourage students to be on the lookout for the high-frequency words being studied in their books during independent reading. They might each have a high-frequency word list in their book bag or box to which they add tally marks as they find these words in text.

Small-Group Connection: Choose little books for guided reading that contain several high-frequency words that children in that group need to practice. Then start the lesson by having kids build those words with magnetic letters (or letter tiles). Remind them that these words will be in the book they are reading today, and they should try to read them fast.

Writing Connection: As you model writing in whole group, be sure to try to integrate the high-frequency words you've been teaching. As you use one of the words, point to the list or the word on the word wall and tell kids, "That's a high-frequency word. Point to where you can find it." Remind students to look on the word wall for these words to be sure to spell them correctly. You might also write "predictable charts" with your class, using a sentence stem with one or more high-frequency words in it. They can reread these charts at a predictable chart station and add to them, too. Make Big Books with your class using the same high-frequency words.

Evaluation: Show each individual student a list of ten to twenty high-frequency words that have been taught and have the student read them to you quickly. Or use high-frequency word assessments periodically, as required by your school system's core curriculum.

The focus of this small-group lesson for beginning readers is the high-frequency word *we*. The teacher has written the focus of the lesson on a dry erase board to remind the children to point under the word *we* as they read. She has chosen a guided-reading book with the word *we* on several of the pages. Students also built the word *we* with magnetic letters at the start of the lesson.

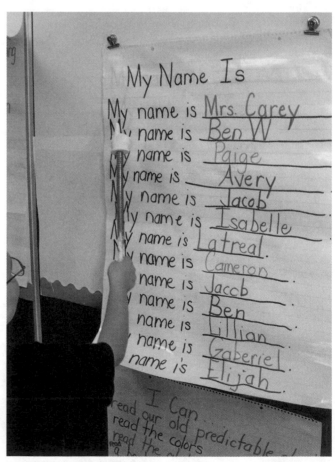

Predictable charts that use high-frequency words are written as a class and then reread by partners at a predictable-charts station.

Mentor Texts for Modeling:
High-Frequency Words

- Simple series books such as *No, David!* by David Shannon
- *Cat the Cat, Who Is That?* by Mo Willems

- *Me I Am!* by Jack Prelutsky
- *Go, Dog, Go!* by P. D. Eastman
- *A Fly Went By* by Mike McClintock
- *First the Egg* by Laura Vaccaro Seeger
- *I Went Walking* by Sue Williams

Teaching Tips for High-Frequency Word Work Across the Grades	
In Pre-K and Kindergarten	• Begin with words most frequently needed for writing as well as reading, such as *I*, *like*, *love*, *can*, *a*, *the*, *mom*, *me*, and *my*. Add these words to your word wall (after starting with children's names). Make connections between high-frequency words and students' names. For example, "*My* starts like *Michael*; *can* rhymes with *Dan* and has the same letters at the end." • Look in leveled books your students will be reading to choose high-frequency words needed. Double-check them with your district list (or the Dolch or Fry list found in the online appendix) to be sure they are truly high-frequency words. • Don't send home a list of 100 words kids need to learn at the beginning of the year. It can be very frustrating for both parents and children. It's best to send home word lists as you're teaching with them.
In Grades One–Two	• Link high-frequency words studied across the day. For example, help students find these words in the shared reading of Big Books and poems as well as in their guided-reading and independent-reading books. Use the same words in modeled and shared writing, and expect students to spell them correctly in independent writing. Remind the children, "That's the same word we read/wrote in_____." • Study no more than seven new high-frequency words at a time. That's the largest number of chunks of new information the brain can handle at once. • Don't give kids long lists of high-frequency words to memorize (or big packs of flash cards). Have them work with smaller numbers of words they need, especially if they're having trouble learning them.
In Grades Three and Up	• Most students in upper grades probably won't need to work with high-frequency words, but some may. If several children need practice with certain words (that you notice they are constantly misspelling or reading in error), teach those high-frequency words in whole group; if just a few kids need to learn particular high-frequency words, work with those words in small group. • When working with high-frequency words, engage all areas of the brain by having students say the word (auditory), look at the word carefully (visual), and touch, make, or write the word (kinesthetic).

Sample Anchor Charts for Identifying High-Frequency Words

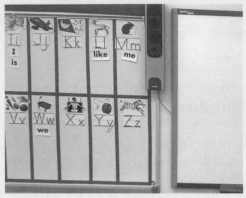

A high-frequency word wall in pre-K through grade two is one of the best anchors for helping students learn high-frequency words. Try to find a space for it in or near your whole-group teaching area, so it is easy for you and your students to make connections to it during shared reading and writing routines. Add three to seven words to the word wall weekly. Add words you know your children will need for what they're currently reading and writing. You might use a large whiteboard. Make a grid on the wall with colored tape to help students focus on words that begin with a certain letter. Use uppercase and lowercase letters and a picture clue for that letter's beginning sound.

The first-grade word wall for high-frequency words (*above*) uses a bulletin board and wall space that wraps around a corner by the whole-group teaching area. The second-grade word wall (*below*) is made of laminated 8½-by-11-inch colored construction paper on which the teacher writes high-frequency words with a dry erase marker. Note that vowels are in a different color to help them stand out.

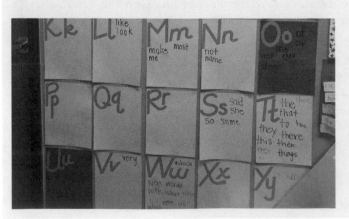

Literacy Work Stations for Identifying High-Frequency Words

Pairs of children reread familiar Big Books and look for high-frequency words. In this photo, they match words on sticky notes. Over time, add Big Books with different high-frequency words being studied. Keep old favorites here, too.

At the Smartboard station, students can pull down high-frequency words and pictures to make sentences. Periodically, change high-frequency words for students to work with here. Keep words children need additional practice with as well, so there are several tasks to choose from.

Partners reread familiar poems and mark high-frequency words being studied with precut colored highlighter tape. (This can also be done in Big Books.) Add new poems and keep old favorites. Add new high-frequency words to highlight as you teach them. Keep old words students need additional practice with.

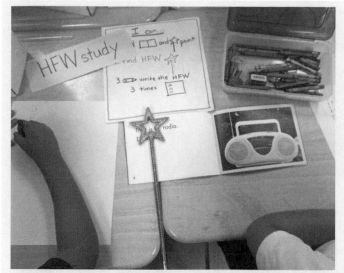

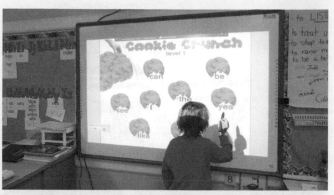

At this Smartboard station, partners take turns pulling down high-frequency words as they listen to each word being read. Provide several games here, so students can work on a variety of word-study tasks. Over time, change the high-frequency words children work with at this station, and keep old ones here, too. This station can be used for spiral review.

At a word-study station, children work in pairs to reread familiar books (from whole or small group) and use a small wand to locate high-frequency words being studied (*above*). Then they "rainbow write" the words three times using different-colored crayons. They can also build the high-frequency words in multiple ways shown in the "I Can" list (*below*). Add new high-frequency words as they are taught. Keep old words here that children need to practice. You might have differentiated bags of word cards for students in different reading groups. Place a colored dot on the bag to show which group should work with those words.

Children build familiar poems, such as "Rules Rap," at the pocket-chart or poetry station. Store cut-up sentence strips with the poem copied onto them in a small brown envelope that has the poem on the front of it for visual reference. Over time, add new poems with new high-frequency words being taught. Keep old favorites here, too.

Daily-news items using students' names can be recycled into a station by simply displaying old messages written with your class. Add highlighter tape for children to mark high-frequency words being studied. Add a blank, laminated piece of chart paper and dry erase markers with which children can write their own daily news. Keep a variety of daily-news messages here for them to read and work with. Encourage students to use word-wall words as they write daily news or morning messages.

At this computer station, students work with high-frequency words. They can hear a word, read it, and type it, as well as read text in which it is embedded. Differentiate for individuals, based on the high-frequency words they need to practice.

At the word-wall station, these boys work together to read the word wall and then search familiar books for the same words. Here they discover the high-frequency word *one* in a favorite book. Add new high-frequency words to the word wall weekly. Children can search for these words in different books over time.

Developing Phonological and Phonemic Awareness

"Why are phonological awareness and phonemic awareness important?" is a question teachers sometimes ask. "And what exactly is the difference between the two terms? Isn't it kind of like phonics?" Often, I notice that phonics lessons are being taught without regard for phonological awareness. Or the terms *phonics* and *phonological awareness* are used interchangeably.

Phonological awareness involves playing with the sounds of language (for example, rhyming, alliteration, and the segmenting and blending of syllables); it includes phonemic awareness, or manipulation of the smallest speech sounds, which lays the foundation for phonics. (See Figure 7.1.) Kids who can take apart and put together spoken (not printed) words, sound by sound, have a foundational understanding of how words work—which ultimately will help them decode and spell words. Students who struggle with phonics often do not possess phonological or phonemic awareness.

Let's take a glimpse inside Tamara's first-grade classroom to see this foundational work in action. Tamara begins her whole-group mini-lesson by telling the chil-

dren that they will be learning about how vowels work in words. Every word has at least one vowel sound in it, and they will listen for those particular sounds as they play a (phonemic awareness) game. The class quickly recites the vowels and their sounds as their teacher points to the vowels on the word wall. She tells them that they will work together to do a sound sort of picture cards with items that have different short-vowel sounds. Tamara plans to repeat this picture sort with her class for several days until she is sure most of the students can do it pretty well. At that point, she'll move the picture sort of these sounds to a word-study station where partners work together to sort them in the same fashion.

This wise teacher knows that if her students can't isolate and hear the difference between the vowel sounds in spoken words, it will be difficult for them to map the letters onto the vowel sounds when both reading and writing these words. The class reads each picture together and then segments the sounds of the word, moving their left hands down their right arms, pausing to say each sound and paying attention to the vowel sound—*hat, /h/a/t/*—as that picture card is subsequently placed into a pocket chart and sorted into the corresponding category; there are pockets for each short-vowel sound. The students are engaging in phonemic awareness—working with the smallest speech sounds—through hearing sounds (not reading words at this point). Then students make a short-vowel-sound anchor chart with Tamara, who draws pictures (instead of writing words) of an item to help the class remember each sound. She elicits their responses and makes a simple chart, as pictured in this section.

After the sound sort for phonemic awareness, Tamara will move into a phonics lesson on how to spell words with these short vowels—but only after she is sure that children have a foundational understanding of the differences in the sounds of short vowels. (See "Phonics: Using Chunks and Word Families" later in this chapter for additional ideas on how this phonemic awareness work is extended into the phonics portion of this lesson.)

Figure 7.1 **This drawing represents the phonological awareness continuum and includes the pieces that lay the foundation for phonics.**

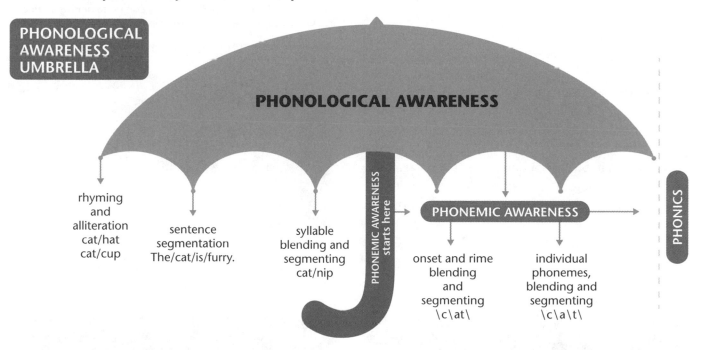

First graders engage in a picture sort of items by short-vowel sound (*a, e, i, o, u*) during whole-group instruction. This can be done in a pocket chart or on an interactive whiteboard.

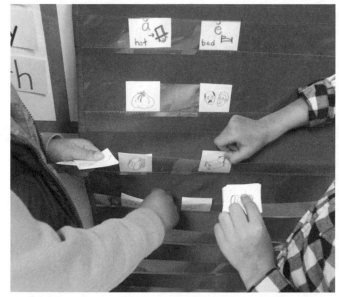

At a word-study station, partners work together to "read" each picture and then sort them by the short vowel sounds. The word is written on the back of each card, which makes this word work self-correcting and provides kids with immediate feedback. Kids can record their work by drawing quick sketches of the things they sorted and trying to write the word to go with each picture. Over time, change out photos and/or sounds being studied (e.g., consonant blends, long vowel sounds, vowel plus *r* patterns, chunks like *-tion* or *-able*, and so on).

Likewise, during writing workshop, Tamara begins with phonological awareness as she models how to write her message. After she thinks aloud about her idea, she plays with her first sentence and puts one finger in the air for each word. Because some children still forget to leave spaces between their words, she draws a yellow line with crayon on her paper to represent each word and places a space between the lines. In terms of phonological awareness, she is modeling how to segment a spoken sentence into words (sentence segmentation).

Today, Tamara says, "I want to write about going to the pumpkin patch this weekend. My first sentence might be *My family went to see pumpkins on Saturday.* Or I could write, *We just had to get a pumpkin when we spied them in the patch!* That's a lot of words! I'll put a yellow line for each word on my paper and say each word again to help me remember my sentence."

After that, she shows students how to use high-frequency words from the word wall and stretches out words, sound by sound (phonemic awareness again!), as she writes her message in front of the class. She'll model writing another sentence or two and then encourage students to use these same strategies to write on their own during writing workshop and, subsequently, at the writing station. Over time, she'll place samples of writing here to remind children what they *can* do as writers.

How to segment words is modeled during phonemic awareness work in whole-group reading. This is also done during writing to show how to segment words to help write their sounds in order.

The teacher also models how to segment sentences, word by word, by drawing a yellow line for each word she plans to write with a space between them. She stretches out words as she writes as well, using phonological awareness as a tool in spelling.

Sifting Through the Standard: Developing Phonological and Phonemic Awareness	
What It Is	• *Phonological awareness* is an umbrella term that refers to an understanding of *spoken* (not printed) words and includes an awareness of syllables, rhymes, and individual speech sounds (phonemes) • Encompasses phonemic awareness or the ability to manipulate the smallest speech sounds (*cat is /c/at/ or /c/a/t/*) • Developed through the ear; an aural activity • Instruction and related literacy work stations involve listening and working with pictures and/or objects, not printed words.
Why It's Important	• Phonological awareness lays the foundation for later work with phonics, which relates to learning letter-sound relationships in books and other texts. (Note: Phonics involves associations between sounds and how they are represented in print.) • As when students learn to rhyme, phonological awareness prepares them to manipulate smaller units of speech, down to *phonemes*—the smallest unit of speech. • Phonological awareness also affects children's writing. Being able to orally segment words and later, syllables, can help writers transform their spoken words into printed ones.
Prerequisites Needed	• Phonological awareness is playing with language, so the only real prerequisite is that children have both receptive language (words they've heard) and expressive language (words they use to communicate orally).

	Sifting Through the Standard:
	Developing Phonological and Phonemic Awareness *(continued)*
Academic Vocabulary	Kindergarten: • *sentence, word, syllable* • *rhyming words* • *rhyme or sounds the same at the end of the word* • *count, blend, segment sounds* • *first/beginning, middle, final/ending sounds* • *add, substitute sounds* First grade: • *long- and short-vowel sounds*
Real-World Connections	• Young children love to play with language, especially words that rhyme or sound the same in some way. • Play sound games with their names. Call them to line up by saying a word that rhymes with a child's name: "Line up if your name rhymes with Jack. Yes, that's Zach!" • Nursery rhymes are loved by young and old and are a great base for teaching about rhyming.
Example Test Questions	• Having phonological awareness will help students with decoding and spelling, which affects what they will be able to do as fluent readers and writers in testing situations.

	Team Planning Tool:
	Developing Phonological and Phonemic Awareness
Standards We're Teaching	**First grade:** Blend sounds, including consonant blends, to produce single- and multi-syllable words; segment the individual sounds in one-syllable words.
Academic Vocabulary We'll Use and Expect to Hear	• *blend* • *segment* • *sounds* • *consonant blend* • *word*
Whole-Group Ideas	• Blending sounds and segmenting words with a hand puppet and a list of words for the teacher to use with the class in blending and segmenting work • Have students use their hands and arms to blend sounds and segment words. Then use Elkonin boxes to push sounds they hear in words to demonstrate the order of the sounds.
Partner Practice at Literacy Work Stations	**Listening station:** Students listen to sounds being blended and use either their hands and arms or Elkonin boxes to physically demonstrate hearing the same sounds in order. They orally try to make a word or break it apart, sound by sound. **iPad station:** Children use technology apps, such as Reading Magic 1 from Preschool University, to blend and segment sounds. **Sorting station:** Pairs of students work together to sort pictures representing words with a certain number of sounds (two-sound words, three-sound words, four-sound words, and so on). **Writing station:** Kids segment words as they write messages at the writing station. They may use their bodies or Elkonin boxes placed here to stretch out words they want to write in their stories, notes, and cards.

Lessons That Last: Whole-Group Mini-Lesson Plan for Developing Phonological and Phonemic Awareness

Sound by Sound

Focus: blending sounds, including consonant blends, to make words; segmenting one-syllable words into phonemes

Method to Maximize Student Engagement: having all students use their left hand and right arm to blend and segment sounds; use of a puppet to make the work playful; having kids use counters and Elkonin boxes for pushing sounds (saying a word slowly and pushing a counter into a box to represent each sound in order)

Materials: hand puppet; list of words to blend and segment; Elkonin boxes (pictured on page 164) and counters to push sounds

Model: how to blend and segment speech sounds in words

Prompting for Independence:

- "Blend the sounds together, in order, to make a word."
- "Let's take a word apart, sound by sound."
- "Move your hand down your arm as you say each sound. Blend the sounds together."

Mini-Lesson Procedure:

1. Gather your class on the carpet and show them the puppet on your hand.

2. Then talk to the puppet about the sound game you're going to play: "Mr. Monkey, let's play a game with the class. You tell me the sounds, and we'll blend them together to make a word."

3. Continue in this way, pretending that the puppet is telling you sounds to blend into words. Use a word list, like the one in Figure 7.2. Model using your left hand to move down your right arm, saying each sound. Then show how to blend the sounds to make a word.

4. Do similar work with segmenting words. Have the puppet "tell" you a word, and then model how to break it apart sound by sound, moving your left hand down your right arm. Have students do the same thing with the words you give them.

5. There are several ways to add an Elkonin boxes component to this activity. Here are two of them:

   - Give each child a laminated cardstock strip and several counters. Then have them push the counters into individual boxes in order as they blend or segment sounds.

   - Use a larger Elkonin box drawn on a large dry erase board (or interactive whiteboard) with magnetic counters (or virtual counters) that students take turns pushing into the boxes for others to watch as they blend and segment.

6. After this phonemic-awareness work, you might move into phonics by writing (or having kids write) a letter in each box to represent each sound in order.

On-the-Spot Assessment: Were the students able to blend sounds to make words? How did they do with segmentation? Be sure phonemic awareness is in place before moving into adding letters to the sounds.

Figure 7.2 **Word List for Sound by Sound (Blending and Segmenting Phonemes)**

up	tap	wish
on	set	chin
sun	mop	shop
big	fit	whip

Connections to Whole-Group Mini-Lesson

Independent Reading Connection: Although students are not practicing phonological awareness as they read on their own, having this foundational skill helps them decode.

Small-Group Connection: Work with students who need extra support with developing phonemic awareness by repeating the whole-group lesson. Use the same words or a different list, depending on your students' needs. Give them Elkonin boxes and counters to push sounds as they blend and segment. If the group really is struggling, you might use small objects or pictures for support. Have them blend sounds and segment words that match the pictures. Be sure to use one-syllable pictures and objects, such as *cat, brick, mouse, tree,* and *sled* when having children segment words.

Over time, have them write letters that represent the sounds they hear in the Elkonin boxes as they move into phonics work. Start with short-vowel words.

Writing Connection: Model how to segment words, sound by sound, as you show the class how to spell words during modeled writing in writing workshop. Encourage children to do the same as they write on their own during independent writing and at a writing station.

Evaluation: Pay attention to which children are successfully blending and segmenting sounds during whole group. Make note of those who are struggling, and work with them in small group as well.

Mentor Texts for Modeling:
Phonological and Phonemic Awareness

Rhyming books:
- *Llama Llama Red Pajama* by Anna Dewdney
- *Brown Bear, Brown Bear* by Bill Martin Jr.
- *My Truck Is Stuck* by Kevin Lewis
- *There's a Wocket in My Pocket* by Dr. Seuss
- *The Seven Silly Eaters* by Mary Ann Hoberman
- *Down by the Bay* by Raffi
- *Silly Sally* by Audrey Wood
- *Stick and Stone* by Beth Ferry
- *One Big Pair of Underwear* by Laura Gehl

Alliterative texts:
- *Four Famished Foxes and Fosdyke* by Pamela Duncan Edwards
- *Some Smug Slug* by Pamela Duncan Edwards
- *Chicken Cheeks* by Michael Ian Black
- *Princess Pigtoria and the Pea* by Pamela Duncan Edwards
- *If You Were Alliteration* by Trisha Speed Shaskan
- *A Piggy in the Puddle* by Charlotte Pomerantz

Books that play with sounds:
- *Clang! Clang! Beep! Beep! Listen to the City* by Robert Burleigh
- *Zoom! Zoom! Sounds of Things That Go in the City* by Robert Burleigh
- *Tap Tap Boom Boom* by Elizabeth Bluemle
- *Squeak, Rumble, Whomp! Whomp! Whomp!* by Wynton Marsalis
- *Cock-a-Doodle-Doo, Creak, Pop-Pop, Moo* by Jim Aylesworth

Teaching Tips for Phonological and Phonemic Awareness Across the Grades	
In Pre-K and Kindergarten	• Favorite rhyming books read over and over are great anchors for learning how to rhyme. Use the Mentor Texts list in this section for starters.
	• Use familiar objects and pictures during phonological awareness work. If children can't easily identify pictures of things such as jacks, remove them. Focus on the rhyming (or sound) work rather than on vocabulary development here.
	• Play with a hand puppet to make and break apart spoken words and encourage children to have fun playing along. Talking to Mr. Monkey about words makes it a lot more fun than just reading a list of words to segment to the class.
	• The key to phonological awareness work is to make it joyful and not monotonous.

In Grades One–Two	• Review rhyming in these grades as you work with word families. Hearing sounds in these words will help children transfer letter/sound knowledge to the ending part of the word more easily. Ditto for listening for words with the same beginning sounds before moving into phonics of words with the same sounds. • Be sure to have students work with blending consonant blends as well as single-consonant sounds. • Kids in these grades often have difficulty with consonant blends at the start of words, hearing *pr* as /p/er/ in *pray* rather than /p/r/ay/. When asked for words that start like *pray*, they will sometimes say *purple*. Or they'll spell *pretty* like they say it—*purty*. Check if students can hear the *sounds* in these spoken words.
In Grades Three and Up	• If students are still having trouble with decoding, check their phonemic awareness by simply having them blend and segment words they hear. Take the decoding task away and see if they can add, delete, or substitute sounds. If they have difficulty, do some phonological awareness work with them in small group before doing related phonics work. • When modeling writing in front of more advanced writers, model how to pronounce words and segment syllables as you break apart words to write them.

Sample Anchor Charts for Developing Phonological and Phonemic Awareness

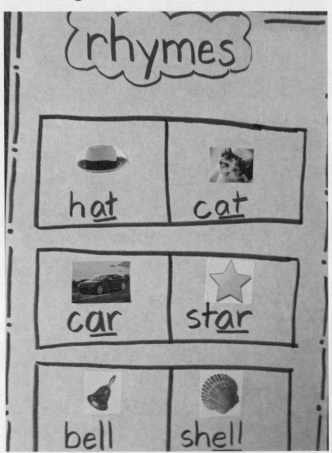

This anchor chart for rhyming uses pictures of rhyming objects on it at the beginning of the year. At a later date, when word families were studied, words with the rhyming part underlined were added.

This anchor chart was made with students to help them listen for sounds in words. An Elkonin box is used to represent a space for each sound in three-letter words.

Literacy Work Stations for Developing Phonological and Phonemic Awareness

These two students work together at a listening station where they listen to recorded sounds and play Sound Bingo. They mark the space matching the picture of the sound they hear. Different cards can be used over time.

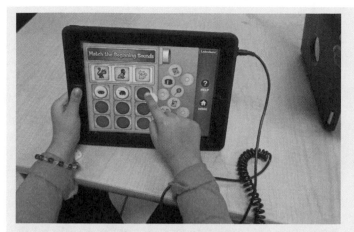

One of the best ways to move phoneme work into a literacy station is through technology. Students can listen, record themselves, and get immediate feedback at a computer or listening station for this kind of work. Ask your tech specialist to recommend some good apps.

At this station, students sort objects that begin with a particular sound into a tub with a mat divided into thirds and labeled by letter. The teacher provides containers with three different letters (using an uppercase and lowercase magnetic letter for each) and matching objects to sort. Use different objects and letters over time.

Young children do a picture sort for beginning sounds (*above*). A conversation card they might use is shown below. Use different picture cards and letters over time. Do the same kind of work with ending sounds or middle sounds as you introduce them to students.

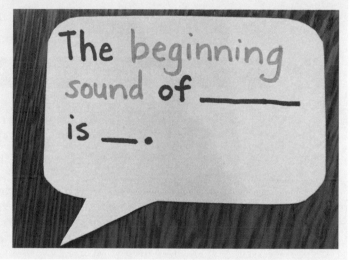

The beginning sound of ____ is __.

Using Chunks and Word Families

Whereas phonological awareness lays a foundation for *hearing* sounds in words, phonics is where students learn to *apply letters to* sounds. At first, children learn to decode CVC (consonant-vowel-consonant) words, like *mat*, *big*, and *sun*. From there, they should work with words that include consonant blends and digraphs, reading words like *plan*, *stem*, *ship*, and *with*. You might have students work with magnetic letters, letter tiles, or dry erase materials as they blend individual sounds (and eventually consonant blends and digraphs) to read short-vowel words in isolation; also provide opportunities for students to practice reading little books that contain words with the phonics pattern in guided and independent reading.

Children should be able to decode simple CVC words, sound by sound, in text by the end of kindergarten or at Fountas and Pinnell Level C or DRA2 Levels 3–4. Once children can do this, it is important to help them begin blending *chunks* or parts of words, using common phonograms, such as *-at*, *-ick*, and *-ot*. Instead of blending /n/o/t/ as individual sounds, it is more efficient to blend /n/ with /ot/ to read *not*. Likewise, blending /pl/ and /an/ to read *plan* will promote reading fluency and allow children to think more deeply about what they read, using their brainpower for comprehension rather than decoding.

Teaching students about word families between Fountas and Pinnell Levels C and D or DRA2 Levels 4–6 can help them read words with these patterns quickly and easily. If they can read *mop,* they can read *top* and *stop* and *crop.* In addition, if children can hear and produce rhyming words orally, they are much more likely to be able to understand how word families work when learning how to read at these levels.

Many times, I visit kindergarten classrooms where teachers are making long lists of words in a word family when children cannot yet read those words. There is a difference between hearing or producing rhyming words and reading those words, although the two skills are strongly linked. Although it may not hurt children to see lists of rhyming words, it does not guarantee that they will be able to read them in isolation or in the context of reading books. I think it's best to wait until many students are approaching end of kindergarten reading levels to teach the whole group about word families in print, because children will be better able to readily apply this skill in reading at that time.

In addition, I believe it is critical to use the whole-part-whole model when teaching phonics. Be sure to start with the *whole* by using high-quality read-alouds and shared reading of engaging literature and informational texts. Then move to the *part* or teaching phonics skills in isolation to show what those letters represent. Finally, move it back to the *whole* again where kids read and transfer those phonics skills while reading and writing connected text. Reread poems, Big Books, and other enlarged text (project any text with a document camera so all students can see it), and have kids search for words with those patterns in them. Do shared writing and morning message where students apply these phonics patterns to their writing. This last step of taking it back to text is the one where phonics will stick for many students.

Sifting Through the Standard: Using Chunks and Word Families

What It Is

- A *chunk* is a part of a word the student knows that can be used to decode a longer word, including phonograms, such as *-at, -ick,* and *-um.* Consonant blends (for example, *sl, tr, spl*) and consonant digraphs (*ch, sh, wh, th*) are also chunks.
- A *word family* contains words that share an ending called a *rime* or a commonly used phonogram (a group of letters that stand for a sound).
- *Onset* is the consonant sound (or sounds) that comes before the *rime,* which includes the vowel and the letters to the right of it in a one-syllable word; for example, in *hand,* the onset is *h* and the rime is *-and.*
- The *chunk -and* can also be used to decode longer words (for example, *handy, outstanding*).

Note to teachers: The terms *onset, rime,* and *phonogram* are for you to use. Use the terms *chunks* and *word family* with your students.

Why It's Important

- Thirty-eight common phonograms, or rimes, are the most useful for students to learn and make up 654 different words (Fry 1998). See Figure 7.3 for a list of them.
- Decoding by reading *chunks* or parts of words is more efficient than reading each individual sound.

Prerequisites Needed

- Phonological awareness: hearing and producing rhymes before studying word families will enable children to more easily decode words with these rhyming parts or chunks.
- Phonemic awareness: when children can first hear these bigger sound chunks, it becomes easier for them to map letters onto sounds and to understand that words are made of parts (Diller 2007).
- Knowing beginning sounds and blends will help students blend these with rimes to create word families.

Sifting Through the Standard: Using Chunks and Word Families *(continued)*

Academic Vocabulary	Kindergarten: • *sounds* • *blend* First grade (and up): • *word families* • *chunks* • *word parts* • *spelling pattern*
Real-World Connections	• Connect each *chunk* or word part to something students know, such as a picture of *rain* for the chunk *-ain*. • Take phonics from the part to the whole. After kids look at a phonics pattern in isolation, invite them to add words they find in their own reading to the chunk and the word-family anchor charts by using sticky notes (if an error is made, the note can easily be removed from the chart).
Example Test Questions	• "Find the word _____." • "Which word rhymes with ___?" (Students are looking at printed words here.)

Team Planning Tool: Using Chunks and Word Families

Standard We're Teaching	**First grade:** Decode words with common spelling patterns (e.g., *-ink, -onk, ick*).
Academic Vocabulary We'll Use and Expect to Hear	• *decode* • *spelling pattern* • *word family*
Whole-Group Ideas	• Read aloud a poem or book with a common spelling pattern. See the "Mentor Texts for Modeling" list for ideas. • Make an anchor chart with the class using a common spelling pattern from the 38 Most Common Phonograms chart in Figure 7.3. • Ask students to write words with this spelling pattern, one at a time, on dry erase boards as you dictate words to them. • During Morning Message and Daily News, leave blank spaces for the spelling patterns you've been teaching for kids to fill in. • Have students do word hunts as they read familiar text. Ask them to find words with the spelling patterns you are studying and write these on sticky notes to add to the anchor charts.
Partner Practice at Literacy Work Stations	**Big Book station:** Partners read familiar Big Books and highlight words with the spelling pattern (rime) you've been studying. **Poetry station:** Do the same as above with familiar poems. **iPad station:** Students work with word family apps, such as Abitalk Phonics Word Family. Have children work with the short vowels that represent the 38 Most Common Phonograms. **Word-study station:** Partners build words with chunks (spelling patterns), changing the beginning letter to make new words. Have them go on word hunts in familiar books and write words they find that have the same spelling pattern. **Writing station:** Post spelling pattern anchor charts at this station and encourage partners to help each other check their writing to be sure they spelled words with these patterns correctly. They might use a highlighter pen to mark words with the spelling patterns studied.

Chapter 7

Lessons That Last: Whole-Group Mini-Lesson Plan for Using Chunks and Word Families

Chunks and Word Families

Focus: using chunks to decode new words

Method to Maximize Student Engagement: reading a Big Book or poem with the chunk in it; creating and referring to a class-made anchor chart and then connecting it to the previously read Big Book or poem with that chunk; students take turns highlighting words with the chunk in it

Materials: anchor chart for a chunk or word family, such as *-ill*; Big Book or poem with several words containing that chunk; index card and markers; highlighting tape or tool, like a flyswatter with a hole cut in it or a magnifying glass with the lens removed

Model: how to use a known word part to read and write new words

Prompting for Independence:

- "If you can read *-ill*, you can read *fill*."
- "Find a part you know. Use that part to read the new word."
- "If you can write *will*, you can write *still*."

Mini-Lesson Procedure:

1. Gather your students on the rug and read a poem or Big Book with words in it containing the chunk you will study today.
2. Then create a word family anchor chart together for that chunk.
3. Read the word family anchor chart together for *-ill* or another useful chunk they need. (See Figure 7.3 for the most commonly used phonograms.) Be sure to refer to the picture cue you've included to help them remember the sound being studied. For example, use a hill for a chart on the *-ill* word family.
4. Then do a shared reading of the poem or Big Book that contains words with this chunk. Tell students that you picked this book especially for them so they can practice reading new words with that chunk and be on the lookout for more words to add to the *-ill* family.
5. Read the text with enthusiasm, making sure students comprehend it. If students get stuck on a word, look for a known chunk (such as *-ill*) to help them decode it.
6. Then reread the text, pausing each time they notice a word with the *-ill* chunk. Help them realize that if they can read *-ill*, they can easily read any word with this part in it.
7. On another day, revisit and reread the word-family anchor chart. Then make a task card from a 3-by-5-inch index card. Write *-ill* on it with a picture of a hill. Read the poem or Big Book from the previous lesson again. Then ask individuals to go to the text and highlight a word with this pattern, using highlighter tape that is precut and placed on a laminated file folder. Read each word with the class. Add any favorite new words to the anchor chart for *-ill*.
8. Invite students to be on the lookout for more words with *-ill* as they read at school and at home. Show them how they can add another word to the chart using a sticky note.

On-the-Spot Assessment: Can students find and read words in the word family you are studying? Are they able to read the rime pattern as a chunk instead of saying each individual sound in a word? Pay attention to how children transfer this understanding to small group, too.

Connections to Whole-Group Mini-Lesson

Independent Reading Connection: Encourage students to be on the lookout for words containing chunks you are studying from word families. They might write these words on individual small sticky notes.

Small-Group Connection: Revisit specific anchor charts for word families and chunks before students read a new book if they need practice with any of them. You might also have students work with magnetic letters to make words containing certain chunks, and ask them to change the first letter to make new words.

Then have them read books that include words with those particular chunks. Also set the purpose for reading and have students read to understand (not just to find words with a particular phonics pattern). Remind kids that you'll be watching to see how they use these chunks as they read. You might give students several small sticky notes and encourage them to write down any words they found that use these chunks. The words can be reviewed and added to the chart at the end of the lesson.

Writing Connection: Writing a morning message or daily news with your class is a great time to model using chunks and word families to write new words. Leave blanks for the parts of words you want students to help fill in. For example, your message might say, "To___ we w____ learn about all kinds of f___ in science." (*Today we will learn about all kinds of fish in science.*) As students think about the missing word parts, have them refer to the word-family anchor charts in your room that help them solve these words. They might also use a highlighter pen to mark the chunks after the message is complete. These powerful examples can help students as they write independently.

During small-group instruction, you might do interactive writing and share the pen with a few children to write about a book you've read in that group. I often have children read a book one day and write about it the next. This helps kids connect reading and writing and gives them opportunities to apply new sounds they've been learning about with the support of the teacher in a small-group lesson. As you share the pen, encourage students to write *chunks* of words rather than just individual letters. Again, they might highlight chunks to pay closer attention to them.

A teacher uses morning message as a whole-group routine. She leaves blanks for word parts so students can think about what makes sense and apply phonics elements being studied. Leave blanks for chunks that match the word families you are studying.

In small group, this child uses her fingers to look at a part she knows when problem solving on the new word *Nana* and glances at a nearby anchor chart on chunks. Encourage students to refer to these class-made resources for help as they read.

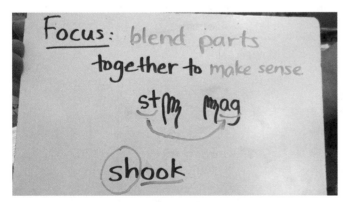

This focus board used in guided reading reminds students to look for chunks in words and blend them together when decoding unfamiliar words. The teacher displays this small dry erase board at the start of the small-group lesson and reminds kids how to use this strategy. She then supports them in practicing it as they read the new book.

Mentor Texts for Modeling: Using Chunks and Word Families

- *Poem of the Week* by Betsy Franco
- *Dan the Flying Man* by Joy Cowley
- *Cat on the Mat* by Brian Wildsmith
- *Splat the Cat* by Rob Scotton
- *The Magic Hat* by Mem Fox
- *Jake Baked a Cake* by Gerald Hawksley
- *The Singing Mermaid* by Julia Donaldson

Chapter 7

	Teaching Tips for **Using Chunks and Word Families Across the Grades**
In Pre-K and Kindergarten	• Focus on anchor charts for beginning and ending sounds and blends. • Create rhyming charts with pictures (see pages 163–164 for ideas). • Move to word families only when students can *hear* rhymes and can blend sounds in CVC words.
In Grades One–Two	• Start with the list of the thirty-eight most common phonograms as shown in Figure 7.3. • Teach short-vowel patterns before long-vowel patterns. • Don't teach too many word families at once. • Provide several strong examples of words from a word family on the anchor charts (that most kids can read) instead of listing every possible word you can think of when creating these with your class. • Pictures create strong anchors for children to remember chunks. Be sure to use them to provide a scaffold for all students who might need them. Ask them for their ideas of a picture that will help them remember.
In Grades Three and Up	• Students with a shaky understanding of phonograms will probably have trouble decoding longer words. A chunk like *-ap* is used in longer words, such as *happiness*, *wrapping*, *strapped*, and *grapple*. Don't assume that older children know these chunks, usually taught in first grade, if you notice that they are having difficulty. You might make simple anchor charts with pictures for parts they have trouble remembering. See the "Syllabication (Reading Long Words)" section in this chapter as well.

Figure 7.3 **Thirty-Eight Most Common Phonograms in Rank Order Based on Frequency (Fry 1998)**

• *ay*	• *unk*	• *ew*
• *ill*	• *ail*	• *ore*
• *ip*	• *ain*	• *ed*
• *at*	• *eed*	• *ab*
• *am*	• *y*	• *ob*
• *ag*	• *out*	• *ock*
• *ack*	• *ug*	• *ake*
• *ank*	• *op*	• *ine*
• *ick*	• *in*	• *ight*
• *ell*	• *an*	• *im*
• *ot*	• *est*	• *uck*
• *ing*	• *ink*	• *um*
• *op*	• *ow*	

Sample Anchor Charts for Using Chunks and Word Families

An anchor chart for the phonogram -ank includes a few pictures of things the students suggested to help them remember this chunk.

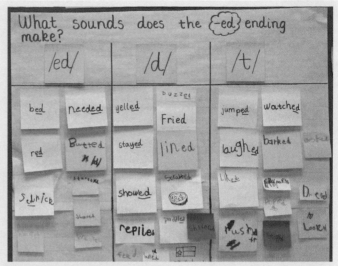

This phonics chart was made with students and hangs near the small-group teaching area for easy reference during lessons. It focuses on the sound that -ed can make, especially at the end of words. This chart was made with advanced kindergartners as part of small-group instruction to extend their learning beyond word families. Students have added words found in their books to the charts, which helps them take ownership for the learning of these chunks. Adding a picture clue for each word family would help students remember each sound.

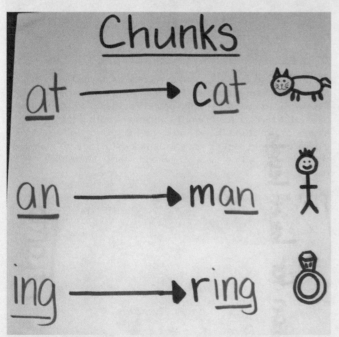

This anchor chart was made in whole group with first graders to help them remember several useful chunks they need to know to read beginning words. The teacher began with -at and added -an when students were familiar with the first chunk. Later, -ing was written on the chart. Note the use of color to help students pay attention to the important parts of the chart. Each chunk is written in red and underlined. The teacher wrote one chunk at a time and then asked students to name something with that chunk in it. For example, kids named cat for the -at chunk. Then the teacher drew a simple, quick sketch to illustrate the example and help students remember the representative sound. These word parts were used to create word families.

Early in the year, charts for the sounds sh- and th- were made with the class. Note how students make the sound along with pictures and examples of words with those sounds. Over time, the anchor charts for word families were added, one at a time, with word and picture samples.

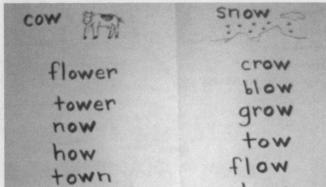

Here's an example of an anchor chart with a more sophisticated chunk, -ow, that represents two sounds. The picture cues help students think about the different sounds these two letters can make. Again, students can use sticky notes to add words they find in their reading to the chart.

Literacy Work Stations for Using Chunks and Word Families

Students work with word families and chunks at a word-study station. Kids reread familiar books and use sticky notes to add words with these phonics patterns to the matching shapes (*star* for -ar, *ball* for -all, and so on). Change the phonograms students search for over time. Put their sticky notes into word-family books made of big construction paper with the picture and chunk on the page. They can practice reading the words on the sticky notes.

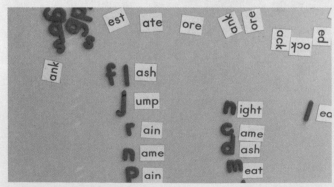

At this word-study station, a pair of students builds words using chunks and magnetic letters. It is useful to have each chunk on a tile (rather than having students work with individual letters) so students can build words more efficiently. Have kids go on a word hunt in familiar books to find other words with these patterns. Change the chunks over time. Have students record the words they made and illustrate them to show meaning.

At this word-study station, students can build word-family words with magnetic letters on a file cabinet. They can also add new words to the word-family posters as they read. And they can read a teacher-made word-family book with photos (the –*each* book is pictured here) and write the missing letters on the laminated pages using a dry erase marker. Change the patterns students work with over time. Keep old chunks here that they need to work with longer.

Partners take turns writing beginning sounds to make word-family words on a shared laminated board. They also read familiar books to find other words with that pattern.

This student reads and then finds CVC words, which he writes in Elkonin boxes. Most of the words are truly CVC words (with short vowels); a few are just three-letter words. The teacher will help him clear up this confusion during small group as they continue to work on CVC patterns. Adapt the word hunt to any phonics pattern with which students need to work (for example, -ot, -ap, -in).

At this poetry station, the teacher tapes each laminated poem she's taught with to a wire coat hanger. Students work together, reading the poem and circling words that contain the chunks being studied with a dry erase pen. Change the poems over time. Include old favorites with chunks students need to practice over and over again. Add highlighter tape or other tools for students to find the chunks they see.

Two girls read together at a poetry station. They can read this familiar -ish poem and highlight words with that pattern. Or they can read other poems for fluency and comprehension. Every week new poems are added that match the word families being studied. Students can read the new poems and old favorites here. Change the poems over time, using ones with the chunks you are studying.

These kids at computer work stations are reading stories with phonics patterns they need to practice. Use different stories with phonics patterns being studied here over time.

Recognizing Long-Vowel Patterns

As students are able to decode short-vowel patterns, begin to move your instructional focus to long vowels. At this point, children can't just listen to the sounds to figure out how to read and write words. Now they must look carefully at the way words are spelled as they read and write.

Long-vowel sounds can be represented by a variety of phonics patterns. Continue to work with students in much the same way you did when working on short vowels, but emphasize noticing the *pattern of the letters* used to make that long-vowel sound. For example, long-*e* can be spelled with *e-e, ee, ea, y,* or just an *e.* Long-*a* can be represented by *a_e, ai, ay, ei, eigh,* or just plain *a.* It takes a lot of reading to understand and remember which words use which long-vowel patterns.

You might check to find out if students can *hear* the difference between short- and long-vowel sounds by doing picture sorts before working with long-vowel patterns in print. If phonological awareness is in place, proceed to phonics. If you notice that students don't hear the difference in sounds, work on it until they do. Then move into the phonics segment of your reading lesson. Don't just assume kids can hear the difference between short and long vowels. Some will see a word with an *a* in it and simply make the long-*a* (or short-*a*) sound.

In whole group, students sort photos of objects with the short-*a* sound from those with the long-*a* sound before working with a long-*a* phonics pattern to make sure they can hear the difference in these two sounds. Then the class reads aloud a poem, "The Sale" by Betsy Franco, with these sounds and finds examples of short-*a* words and long-*a* words. Later, these same materials can be used at a poetry (or word study) station in exactly the same way. Students can sort the pictures, read the poem, and locate short- and long-*a* words. Add other poems with short- and long-vowel patterns being studied over time. Change the photos used to sort particular vowel sounds, too.

Use the ideas from this section to teach about other phonics patterns involving vowels, such as vowel-plus-*r* (for example, *bird, car, heard, purse, form*) and what I like to call the "funky chunks" in phonics, such as *-ou, -ough, -ow, -oy, -oi,* and *-augh.* Make anchor charts with strong exemplars to help students remember these patterns, move from whole to part to whole when teaching them, and give children opportunities to practice reading and writing connected text with words using these varied vowel patterns.

Sifting Through the Standard: Recognizing Long-Vowel Patterns	
What It Is	Long vowels can be spelled in many different ways. See the long-vowel patterns chart in Figure 7.4 for reference.
Why It's Important	Students often confuse long and short vowels when reading in English. If they learn to recognize long-vowel patterns and the sounds they represent, children will be able to decode words more readily while reading, which affects comprehension.
Prerequisites Needed	• Children need to be able to hear the difference between short- and long-vowel sounds in oral language (before looking at these vowel patterns in printed text). If they can hear these sounds, they will more readily be able to transfer them to print. • It will be helpful for students to have a grasp of decoding short- vowel words before moving into the study of long-vowel patterns. Look at their writing. If they are spelling short-vowel words correctly but are mixing up long-vowel patterns (for example, spelling *seet* for *seat*), they are ready to study long-vowel patterns.

Sifting Through the Standard: Recognizing Long-Vowel Patterns *(continued)*		
Academic Vocabulary	Kindergarten: • *vowels* • *consonants*	First grade (and up): • *short-vowel sounds/patterns* • *long-vowel sounds/patterns* • *final-*e • *vowel teams*
Real-World Connections	The brain is a natural pattern seeker. Children will enjoy searching for patterns that long vowels make in the texts they read.	
Example Test Questions	• "Which word in this text is *not* spelled correctly?" • Reading tests are often timed, and reading fluently will allow students to navigate text efficiently and use more brainpower for comprehension, which is the goal of all reading.	

Figure 7.4

Long-Vowel Patterns				
Long-*a* patterns	**Long-*e* patterns**	**Long-*i* patterns**	**Long-*o* patterns**	**Long-*u* patterns**
a *a-e* *ai* *ay* *eigh* *ey (they)*	*e* *e-e* *ee* *ea* *y (pretty)* *i (pizza)*	*i* *i-e* *ie* *igh* *y (my)*	*o* *o-e* *oa* *oe* *ow (snow)*	*u* *u-e* *ue*

Team Planning Tool: Recognizing Long-Vowel Patterns	
Standard We're Teaching	**First grade:** Know final-*e* and common vowel team conventions for representing long vowel sounds.
Academic Vocabulary We'll Use and Expect to Hear	• *long vowels* • *final-*e • *vowel teams*
Whole-Group Ideas	• Read poems, Big Books, and other enlarged text with long-*e* words in them, and have students pay attention to words with that long-vowel pattern. • Model how to use highlighting tools, such as highlighter tape, magnifying glasses, or bubble wands, and use word cards with long-*e* for sorting. • Create anchor charts for long-vowel patterns, one chart for each long vowel.

Team Planning Tool: Recognizing Long-Vowel Patterns (continued)

Partner Practice at Literacy Work Stations	**Word-study station:** Kids do word sorts for long-*e* patterns, including words with *e_e, ee, ea, e,* and *y* at the end, and *i*. Also have them go on word hunts in familiar books looking for other words with these patterns.
	Buddy-reading station: Pairs of kids read together and then look for words with long-*e* patterns. Have them copy words onto lists and color-code the patterns they find.
	Poetry and/or Big Book station: Partners read familiar poems and/or Big Books and highlight words with long-*e* patterns. They use the conversation card to discuss which letters make the long-*e* pattern in each word.
	Writing station: Students write and pay attention to how they spell long-*e* words. Or they might work together to edit one of their pieces of writing together, searching for long-*e* words.

Lessons That Last: Whole-Group Mini-Lesson Plan for Recognizing Long-Vowel Patterns

Lots of Long-Vowel Patterns

Focus: find words with long-*e* patterns

(Note: Similar lessons can be taught with other vowel patterns, such as other long vowels, vowel-plus-*r* combinations, and so on.)

Method to Maximize Student Engagement: shared reading of an engaging poem; highlighting devices to find long-*e* words

Materials: poem with long-*e* words; marker; document camera; conversation card

Prompting for Independence:

- "Find words with long-*e* patterns."
- "What letters represent long-*e*?"
- "Look at the word carefully. Long-*e* is spelled differently in different words."
- "What patterns do you notice for long-*e*? Look for them in books you read."

Note: Use this same type of lesson multiple times for long-*e* patterns. Also use this kind of lesson for each long vowel over time (*a, e, i, o,* and *u*).

Mini-Lesson Procedure:

1. Gather your students on the rug and read aloud a poem with long-*e* words in it. Read it once for enjoyment and then a second time asking kids to listen for words that have a long-*e*.

2. Then show them the text using a document camera. This time, read it with them and ask them to look for words with long-*e*.

3. Have individuals underline the words on the board you are projecting onto. Then have them circle the letters that represent the long-*e* pattern.

4. Make an anchor chart showing the ways long-*e* can be represented in words. Add to it over time as you read more texts with long-*e* words.

5. Add a conversation card that says, "The long-vowel pattern in _____ is ___" to use during additional whole-group lessons on this and other long-vowel patterns, as well as at a literacy work station, over time.

6. Tell students to be on the lookout for more words with long-*e* patterns as they read at school and at home.

On-the-Spot Assessment: Can students find the letters representing the vowel pattern you are studying? Can they read words with this vowel pattern quickly and accurately in text during whole group and small group?

Connections to Whole-Group Mini-Lesson

Independent Reading Connection: As students read on their own, they pay attention to long-*e* words. Have them make a list of long-*e* words they found, writing the words in columns following the different ways long-*e* is spelled.

Small-Group Connection: Have children who need to focus more on decoding review ways long-*e* is spelled before reading. Review the anchor chart made with the whole class. Then remind students to think about the ways long-*e* is spelled if they come across any of these words in that day's books. You might have them jot down long-*e* words on small cards after they've read and sort these words as a group.

Writing Connection: Think aloud about the long-*e* patterns you are using to write a message as you write in front of the class. Encourage students to think about how long-*e* words are spelled as they write, too. Remind them to use the long-*e* anchor chart and pay attention to long-*e* words and how they are spelled as they read and write.

Evaluation: Analyze running records to see whether students can decode long-*e* words in the context of reading connected text. Also look at their writing to see whether they're spelling long-*e* words correctly. Students' writing can give us strong clues about what they understand about how words work.

Students do a picture sort, listening for short and long vowel sounds before reading in a small-group lesson. Note the focus on the small anchor chart that was made with the children. Pictures anchor their knowledge of sounds before decoding.

Mentor Texts for Modeling:
Recognizing Long-Vowel Patterns

Books that play with long-vowel patterns:

- *Sheep in a Jeep* by Nancy Shaw
- *Kate and Nate Are Running Late* by Kate Egan
- *Where Is the Green Sheep?* by Mem Fox
- *The Nice Mice in the Rice* by Brian Cleary
- *Here Comes Silent e!* by Anna Jane Hays

Teaching Tips for Recognizing Long-Vowel Patterns Across the Grades	
In Pre-K and Kindergarten	• Use familiar objects and pictures during phonological awareness work with short- and long-vowel sounds. Develop a strong foundation for hearing vowel sounds in words. This will help students with decoding long-vowel words later. • Focus on decoding short-vowel words in these earliest grades.
In Grades One–Two	• These are the grade levels where there should be a strong focus on long-vowel patterns. • Start the study of long-vowel patterns with silent-*e* words, such as *cake*, *line*, and *hope*. You might show students how the short-vowel sound in some CVC words can be changed to a long-vowel sound simply by adding a silent *e* to the end of the word (for example, *cut* to *cute*; *plan* to *plane*; *mop* to *mope*). • The study of long vowels should focus on visual patterns. Children must read lots of print to remember these varied long-vowel patterns and which pattern goes with which word. Word sorts and word hunts provide effective practice with this skill.

Teaching Tips for Recognizing Long-Vowel Patterns Across the Grades

In Grades Three and Up	• If students are still having trouble decoding long-vowel patterns in upper grades, remove the decoding task and see whether they can isolate the vowel sound in *spoken* words or *pictures* of objects (for example, "What is the vowel sound in *snack*?"). Can they identify the vowel as long or short? (*Snack* has the short-*a* vowel sound.) Can they change the vowel sound from short to long (*snack* to *snake*)? Do this kind of work before doing related phonics work to be sure students can *hear* the sounds.
	• Give these students plenty of practice with looking for long-vowel patterns in the texts they *can* read. They will have to pay close attention to print to master reading long-vowel patterns.
	• When modeling writing in front of more advanced writers, model how to listen for and write long-vowel sounds thoughtfully. For example, when writing the word *neighbor,* say, "*Neighbor.* I can clap two parts—*neigh, bor. Neigh* is the first syllable. I hear the long-*a* sound. There are many ways to write the long-*a* sound, so I'll look at the anchor chart for long-*a* and think about what that word looks like when I've seen it in print."

Sample Anchor Charts for Recognizing Long-Vowel Patterns

Here is one of the first phonics-related anchor charts made with students about long-vowel patterns. In this example, kids are learning about the "bully *e*" and how he says, "Hey, vowel! Say your name!" Clear exemplars are added with the class over time, and the teacher refers to these charts often during reading instruction.

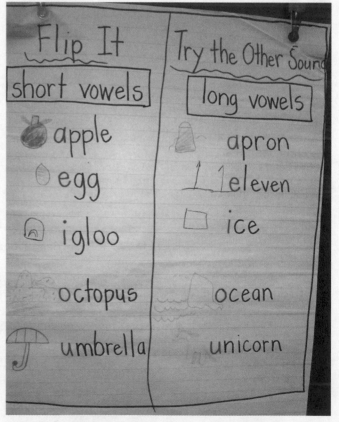

This anchor chart for short- and long-vowel sounds was made with the class and illustrated by students. It can be used during small-group lessons and at literacy stations to help children remember the difference between short- and long-vowel sounds.

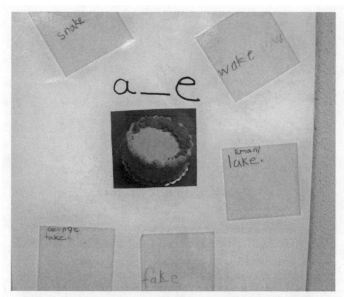

Small charts like this one were made by the teacher. Kids found words during shared and independent reading that they added to the chart with sticky notes. The picture helps anchor the sound.

These anchor charts for long-vowel patterns (and words we love) are displayed on a board behind this first-grade teacher's small-group table. She can easily refer to it when teaching about long vowels during a guided-reading or writing lesson.

This anchor chart of long-o patterns was made over time with the class. Students paid attention to the different ways long-o was spelled in texts they were reading.

Literacy Work Stations for Recognizing Long-Vowel Patterns

After modeling how to read and find words with long-vowel patterns in text, allow students opportunities to create their own circle maps, as pictured at left, writing words found in their own reading that have these patterns. Having kids write the vowels in a different color (or underlining the vowels) will help them pay attention to long-vowel patterns. Change the vowel patterns that students work with over time.

At this spelling station, children give each other a spelling test with words from this week (or from previous weeks for spiral review). The child on the left is "playing teacher" and reads one word at a time to the child on the right. He writes the word on the front of the teacher's desk (or a dry erase board) with dry erase markers, using black for the consonants and red for the vowels, helping him pay attention to the long-vowel patterns in these words. They take turns being the "teacher" and dictating words for each other to spell.

Children read familiar poems and highlight words with long-vowel patterns, adding them to a community journal at the poetry work station. They use a conversation card that reminds them to look for words with a particular pattern. Change the poems over time. Students need a lot of practice reading words with long-vowel patterns to remember them.

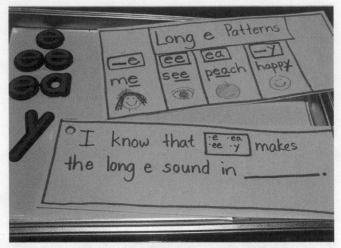

Various materials help children work with long-*e* patterns. Vowel teams are made by affixing foam letters to clear packing tape and then cutting around the edges (rather than having kids work with individual letters). Mini-anchor charts and conversation cards are used in whole group first and then moved to this word-study station. Partners find words in familiar books and write them on this cookie sheet covered with dry erase paper. They use the conversation card to discuss the various ways long-*e* is spelled. Similar materials can be created to go with other long vowels.

Small anchor charts for various long-vowel and other phonics patterns are posted by the writing station as a spelling support for students as they write here. Continue to add phonics patterns that children need support for spelling.

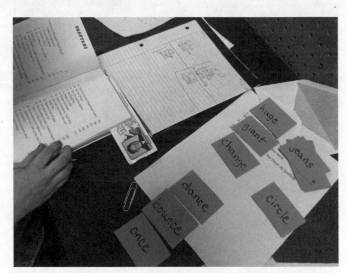

Students work with their spelling words at this word-study station. Each spelling word is written on a card; then partners work together to sort the cards by spelling pattern. Then they write the words by pattern and underline the pattern with a red pencil. They also hunt for words with those spelling patterns in familiar books. Spelling patterns change from week to week, but kids can still work with old words and old patterns for spiral review here.

Reading Long Words (Syllabication)

"What is the one thing that this group of students needs to help them move forward as readers?" I ask teachers this question often as we plan guided-reading lessons together. The answer from many intermedi-ate-grade teachers is, "Decoding longer words. My kids often freak out when they see a really long word, and they just take a few sounds and make up a word!"

This all-too-common problem of children who are reading significantly below grade level occurred recently in a guided-reading group with fifth graders reading on a third-grade level. The teacher told me she'd taught her kids about prefixes and suffixes, but it wasn't enough. This group needed a straightforward approach for breaking down longer words. We chose a nonfiction leveled book titled *Dangerous Professions of the Past* by Julie Haydon (2003) for the four boys in this group, because this high-interest text provided opportunities for them to decode longer words. I began the lesson with an honest conversation with the guys: "Do you ever kind of choke when you get to a long word when you're reading?" They all responded with nods. "What do you do when you come to a long word?" I continued.

"I try to spell it out," said one young man.

"I try to break it apart," responded another.

I told them that we'd focus on decoding long words as they read, and wrote the word *dangerous* on a small dry erase board. The boys took turns using a colored dry erase marker to circle big parts they knew. One student circled *-gerous* and said, "ger-i-ous." I suggested he look at the beginning of the word first. We erased the circle and he quickly said, "Ooh, I see it." and circled *danger-*. I asked another boy to circle another part, and he drew a red line around *-ous,* but hesitated. I encouraged him to try it and he said, "-us?" Finally, I showed the boys how to blend the sounds together in sequence and make a word that makes sense. They easily read *dangerous* at this point. We continued this process with several other long words in the text, and then I reminded them to do that as they read that day. I showed them how to use their fingers to frame parts of words and blend them together (since they can't circle words in their books) and told them I expected them to try it that day.

As they read silently and took notes using a circle map for comprehension, I had each boy whisper-read a bit to me to see how his decoding was going. They did really well and didn't need much support. After reading, we discussed what they read, and I had them show me long words they encountered and strategies they used to decode them. I ended the lesson by reminding them to decode long words by breaking them apart, looking at the first part, and blending the parts in sequence to make a word that makes sense.

When I debriefed with their teacher, she was pleased to see how well the boys had read and comprehended. She realized that she'd done a lot of work in isolation on decoding longer words with the class in

whole group but had never given them the opportunity to transfer the skill to reading connected text with her for guidance. She saw the power of guided reading and how to help her most struggling students apply what she'd been previously teaching in isolation.

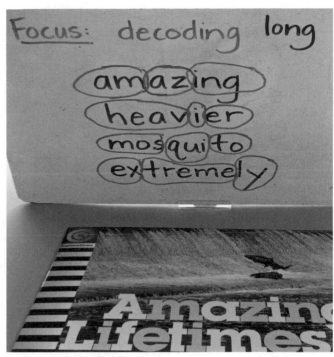

Decoding long words is the focus of this guided-reading lesson for third graders who need help with phonics. Before reading their new book, they circled syllables and then read the parts in sequence to make a word they understood.

A student's circle map for note taking from this lesson is pictured above. Comprehension should be the goal of all reading, even if the focus of the lesson is decoding long words!

Chapter 7

Sifting Through the Standard:
Reading Long Words (Syllabication)

What It Is	• Syllabication is breaking a word apart, syllable by syllable. Students as young as first graders must understand that every syllable (or word part) must have a vowel sound in a printed word. For example, the word *pillow* has two syllables or parts. Each syllable has one vowel sound.
	• There are *closed syllables* that end with a consonant and make a short-vowel sound (for example, *mat, rab-bit*).
	• There are *open syllables* that end with a vowel and make a long-vowel (for example, *he, ba-by*).
	• There are also *final stable syllables,* such as *ap-ple, ta-ble,* and *puz-zle.*
Why It's Important	As students grow as readers, they will encounter longer words. Learning how to break these words into parts, or syllables, will help them decode more advanced vocabulary efficiently.
Prerequisites Needed	• Again, phonological awareness is critical. Students must be able to hear a word and clap its syllables, or parts, before being able to decode longer words in print. Blending and segmenting words orally, syllable by syllable (without seeing them in print) is foundational to decoding long words.
	• Knowing vowel sounds, especially more complex vowel patterns (such as *ow, eigh, or,* and *au*) will help students decode longer words, too.
Academic Vocabulary	First grade: • *syllables* • *open syllable* • *closed syllable* • *final stable syllable* Second and third grade: • *prefix* • *suffix*
Real-World Connections	• As language develops, children use increasingly complex vocabulary. The words become longer and are typically multisyllabic. Kids *love* big words! Exposing them to learning how to decode long words, syllable by syllable, will help them tackle new words in both their reading and writing.
	• Many words in the English language come from other countries. Helping students listen for and identify vowel sounds in syllables will assist them in decoding those long words. (For example, *pi-zza* and *pi-an-o* are from Italian and different vowel sounds that are different from those used in North America today.)
Example Test Questions	• "Which word in this text is *not* spelled correctly?"
	• Decoding long words efficiently and effectively can help students both with finishing a timed reading test on time and with vocabulary-related questions.

Team Planning Tool: Reading Long Words (Syllabication)—Third Grade	
Standard We're Teaching	**Third grade:** Decode multisyllabic words.
Academic Vocabulary We'll Use and Expect to Hear	• *syllable* • *multisyllabic words* • *prefix* • *base word* • *suffix*
Whole-Group Ideas	• Read together an engaging text using a document camera, pausing at multisyllabic words (especially those that contain prefixes and suffixes) as needed to decode them. • Model how to use a colored pen to circle known word parts, preferably from left to right, and then blend parts in sequence to make words that make sense. • Demonstrate how to words by putting together prefix, base word, and suffix cards on a pocket chart. • Create an anchor chart on syllables, including sounds and parts that come from other countries. • Model reading and writing of haiku to further explore syllabication (line one has five syllables, line two has seven syllables, and line three has five syllables). • Teach how to play the game Syllable Brainstorm, using content-area topics (see photo in the section on literacy work stations).
Partner Practice at Literacy Work Stations	**Word-study station:** Pairs of students work together to build words using parts or syllables. They match prefix, base word, and suffix cards to make words. Be sure they check the spellings with an online dictionary such as www.dictionary.com. They can also go on word hunts to find multisyllabic words using familiar books. **Poetry station:** Have pairs of kids work together to read and write haiku. This is a fun way to work with syllables. **iPad station:** StickyWords is a free app that students can use to create haiku. **Research station:** Provide multisyllabic words (harvested from read-alouds or content areas) that have word parts or letter sounds from other countries. Have students research the origin of these words and place them in a little book to use as a reference tool at the writing station. **Writing station:** Have kids work together to check their writing for multisyllabic words. They might work together to use a dictionary to check their spelling of long words. **Buddy-reading station:** Have students practice reading texts with longer words in them, especially texts they've read with you in guided reading. This will aid their fluency and should improve their comprehension as they can think more about what they read. **Syllable brainstorm station:** Kids choose a topic card (brainstormed with the class related to topics studied, such as rocks and minerals or communities) and record related words that have one, two, three, or four syllables on folded paper.

Lessons That Last: Whole-Group Mini-Lesson Plan for Reading Long Words (Syllabication)

Studying Syllables with Haiku

Focus: decoding long words

Method to Maximize Student Engagement: shared reading of engaging text with multisyllabic words; word hunting; building long words from the text in a pocket chart with syllable cards

Materials: haiku, informational text related to science and social studies topics being studied; document camera and colored markers for circling word parts in text; parts of words copied onto syllable cards

Prompting for Independence:

- "That's a long word. Break it into parts or syllables in sequence and then blend them to make a word that makes sense."
- "Look for parts you know. Use your fingers to read each part in order."
- "Read the prefix first. Then blend it with the base word. Add the suffix at the end."

Mini-Lesson Procedure:

1. Before class, prepare several "syllable cards" by writing parts of long words from the text (of the haiku you'll use in this lesson) onto cards. Include parts that will make some of the long words from the book, for example, *grass, hop, per, ten, fin, ger, ed, clothes, pins, mo, tor, cy, cles*. Place these in a pocket chart with labels for "closed syllables," "open syllables," and "final stable syllables."

2. Project a poem from a book of haiku onto the board in your whole-group area. (I used *Guyku: A Year of Haiku for Boys* by Bob Raczka [2010]). Give students some background on why you selected the book, focusing specifically on long words that you will practice decoding, or reading part by part, with them.

3. Read the title with the class, showing the parts of the word by using your fingers to look at each part and then blending the parts together. Explain that haiku is a type of three-line poem that has a pattern of a certain number of syllables—five, seven, five. Make a small anchor chart on haiku, as pictured in the photo on page 187. Tell students that haiku is fun to read because of its rhythm but that haiku very rarely rhymes; instead, haiku poets have to pay special attention to syllables in the words they choose.

4. As you begin to read the first section about spring, tell students that there will be some longer words they might have to break into parts or syllables to read quickly and easily. When you reach these words, have volunteers circle syllables they can read, one at a time, and then blend them together. Also show students how to use their fingers to break apart long words into syllables as you read together. Do this with words such as *grasshopper, ten-fingered, clothespins,* and *motorcycles* when you reach them in the text.

5. After reading a section of the book or a few poems, hand out the syllable cards to students and have them read their syllable using what they know about open and closed syllables. Then have students work together to build words from the book with the syllable cards. (Create an anchor chart on open and closed syllables with your class, if needed.)

6. Repeat this process with words from other haiku. It might take several mini-lessons to do so. This is word study that will take multiple sessions for some students to do effectively and efficiently.

7. Use other books to do similar mini-lessons with decoding long words, syllable by syllable in text.

On-the-Spot Assessment: Can students find and blend syllables within long words to decode them accurately? Are they able to identify and use what they know about open, closed, and final stable syllables to decode multisyllabic words? Observe for this behavior in small-group guided reading time, too.

Connections to Whole-Group Mini-Lesson

Independent Reading Connection: Remind children that as they read self-selected books, they will probably encounter long words. Tell them that it's okay to use their fingers to read long words, syllable by syllable, to make them make sense. Suggest that they record several words they were able to decode when using this strategy. Have them share their words with a buddy or the whole class after reading.

Small-Group Connection: This is a skill to transfer to guided reading, too. Use the ideas shared in this section's introduction to have children decode longer words with a little support as needed from you. Again, after reading and discussing the text, have students share long words they read correctly and tell how they decoded them.

Writing Connection: As you write a piece (a story, some informational text, or even a haiku) with your class, model how to say a long word, one syllable at a time, as you write it. For example, "As I write about the benefits of being a friend, I'll write *benefit* one part at a time. *Ben-e-fit*." You might even clap the parts of a long word, syllable by syllable. Ask students to do the same thing, thinking about how the word sounds and looks as they clap or tap it syllable by syllable.

To encourage children to take risks in using longer words, which will help both their reading and writing of these words, you might have a "multisyllabic word challenge." After they write, give kids a highlighter to mark words with three or more syllables in their writing and share them with a partner or the class. Allow them to use an online dictionary to check their spelling.

Evaluation: Pay attention to students as they read and write long words. Are they decoding and encoding words syllable by syllable to read and write words that make sense? Or are they using a few letters and sounds and making up words that don't look right or make sense?

Mentor Texts for Modeling:
Reading Long Words (Syllabication)

Books that play with syllables:
- *Dangerous Professions of the Past* by Julie Haydon
- *Guyku* by Bob Raczka
- *Dogku* by Andrew Clements
- *Hi, Koo!* by Jon Muth
- *Won Ton* by Lee Wardlaw

Teaching Tips for Reading Long Words (Syllabication) Across the Grades	
In Pre-K and Kindergarten	• In the early years, work on phonological awareness of syllables in words. All work should be done aurally, or through the ear. Have kids blend and segment syllables, beginning with their names and words representing familiar objects. Play games with syllables, such as "Line up if you hear the syllables in your name—*Dan-ny*. Show me your *pa-per, cray-on, eye-brow*," and so on.
In Grades One–Two	• Be sure that students can *hear* syllables before you work with them in print. Continue work similar to that done in pre-K and kindergarten. • When you introduce print, focus on two-syllable words. Teach the concepts of closed syllables (*pen-cil*), open syllables (*ba-by*), and stable final syllables (*ta-ble*). • Do syllable sorts with word cards on a pocket chart as part of whole group and then move them to a word-study station for practice. • Use the whole-part-whole method when working with decoding two-syllable words. You might read aloud a poem or short book with two-syllable words in it (whole). Have students listen for two-syllable words. Then work on decoding some of those words in isolation (part). Finally, have students help to read the whole text, applying what they've learned about decoding two-syllable words in context (whole).
In Grades Three and Up	• Once students can easily decode two-syllable words, move to longer words. Build from two- to three-syllable words (for example, *end-ing* to *un-end-ing*; *a-ble* to *dis-a-ble*; *hap-py* to *hap-pi-ness*). • Have children circle parts they know in longer words and read those parts in sequence to make a word that makes sense. • Again, use the whole-part-whole method for decoding long words. Be sure to show students how to decode multisyllabic words within the reading of a text; don't just do this in isolation.

Sample Anchor Charts for Reading Long Words (Syllabication)

Literacy Work Stations for Reading Long Words (Syllabication)

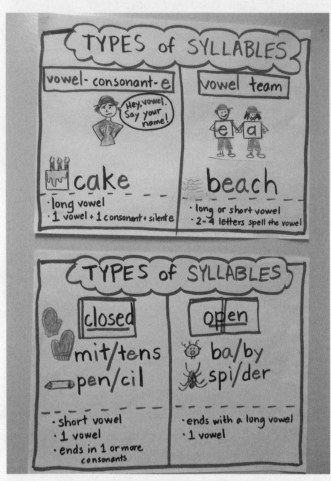

This anchor chart on open and closed syllables helps children remember how to decode longer words.

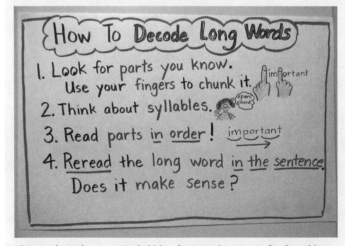

This anchor chart reminds kids of strategies to use for breaking down big words.

Students sort photos of classmates and their names on cards by clapping the number of syllables in the names at this word-study station. Over time, have students sort by open and closed syllables. Add last names as well after kids can successfully recognize and clap a larger number of syllables.

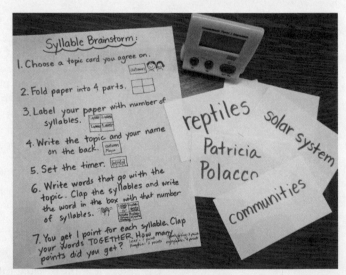

Third graders play Syllable Brainstorm using directions written with the class. They brainstorm words on topic cards that are changed periodically and use them to write related multisyllabic words. Change topic cards to reflect content areas of study or other topics of interest (for example, states of matter, communities, weather, winter, and Valentine's Day).

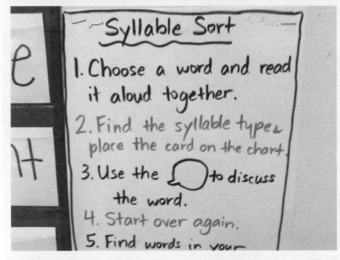

Partners work together at this haiku station to read and write their own haiku. Note the mini-anchor chart for haiku with a colored adhesive dot under each syllable. We gave kids small colored dots to check their syllables in the haiku they wrote and posted on index cards.

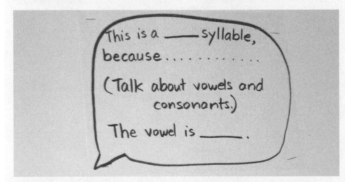

Intermediate kids sort word cards by syllable type (*top*). They can also add word cards here using words they find in familiar rereading of text (*middle*). Directions and a conversation card keep kids focused on the word study (*bottom*).

Three students build words together using prefix, suffix, and root-word cards. They take turns choosing cards and trying to make words. During the last five minutes at this word-study station, they check the words they built on an online dictionary to be sure they are real words. They get one point for each card they use correctly and try to beat their score from the last time they worked here.

Digging Deeper

1. Look at the phonics and word-study materials you have in your classroom. Organize them to match the needs of your students. Get rid of things you don't need. Label phonics materials by category, such as ABCs, word families, long vowels, and so on. Plan to teach with these differentiated materials in small group before moving some of them to literacy work stations for those students. Make a flexible-groups folder for word study like the one on page 142.

2. Examine commercial phonics materials you have. Are there too many cards? Does the task involve more puzzle-like matching than focusing on the letter or phonics work? Can you make over some of these materials to better meet the needs of your students?

3. Who needs letter learning in your class at this time of year? Do those children know the letters in their names? Plan for ways to best meet the needs of these (and other) students who need to work on letter identification through instruction and related literacy work stations. Share ideas with colleagues on your grade-level team.

4. Are the words your students are working with truly high-frequency words that they need right now? How are you introducing the words and connecting them to text like Big Books and poems? How are your students practicing them (in isolation and/or in connected text)? Use ideas from the section in this text and share the results with your team.

5. Do you have students who struggle with phonics? How is their phonological awareness? What will you try from this chapter to better meet their needs with instruction and related literacy work stations practice?

6. Using examples from this book, make anchor charts for word families with your class. Share them with your colleagues. How did the process go? Are your students paying better attention to and transferring their knowledge of word families in both reading and writing?

7. Examine your students' reading and writing of long-vowel (and other vowel) patterns. Do the same with multisyllabic words. Discuss ideas you'll try from this book. Share what you learned with others on your team.

8

Literacy Work Stations for Writing

Standards Covered in This Chapter	Lessons Described in This Chapter
Writing Opinions	Give Your Opinion
Writing Informational Texts	Informative Writing: From Topic to Introduction (Third Grade)
	Making Stuff: Invitations, Lists, or Information Books (Kindergarten)
Writing Narratives	Fractured Folktales
Focusing on Conventions of Writing	Hit the Target with Punctuation
Doing Research	Interviews and Note Taking (Kindergarten–Grade One)
	Gathering and Organizing Information (Grades Two–Three)

It's midyear as I enter Tina's room filled with second graders working happily at literacy work stations. Today, I'm focusing on the writing her students are doing during stations time. I turn my attention to the writing station—a small table thoughtfully positioned near a bulletin board with writing-related anchor charts and student writing samples displayed. It's near the word wall, too, so children can easily access high-frequency words they may need to spell as they write. I'm pleased to see a pair of students working diligently, composing stories and letters.

One girl is wearing finger puppets of a princess and a frog and is writing a story about them. She proudly shares her piece with me: "Once upon a time, there was a beautiful princess. She lived with her grandparents in a stone castle in the woods. One day her grandfather accidentally turned a spell on her . . ." She knows the language of story because she's heard many fairy tales—both in literature (at school) and in movies (at home). "I got my idea from the movie *Shrek*," she tells me with a smile, and goes right back to writing.

Her partner is writing a letter to thank someone who has donated materials to their classroom through www.donorschoose.org. "Dear Susan, Thank you for the things you gave our class. We love the new books for our classroom library . . ." The teacher will mail these handwritten letters to Donors Choose in appreciation for the generous donation of books given to her second graders.

At another writing-related station, students are writing facts on a graphic organizer as they read informational text. "We're at the research station," this pair tells me. "We're learning about pandas. Did you know that pandas eat bamboo at least twelve hours a day? They live in China, but you can see them at some zoos." These kids are exuberant about what they're learning. Right now they're jotting down notes. They tell me they're making a page for a class book of animal facts. They'll apply text features, including a heading, illustrations, and captions.

At a technology station, a pair of children works on an iPad to create a digital story using the free Puppet Pal app. First, they choose characters and a background. Then they tell a story and record it on the iPad. They've decided on a fairy godmother and a dragon for characters and a cave containing a pot of gold as the background for their story. I listen as they begin: "Long ago there was a magical kingdom. Two kids named Jayson and Lauryn went there and met a fairy godmother. They had a wish to find gold . . ." This class has been studying about fairy tales, and their understanding of the genre is reflected in the story the kids tell. They will share the beginnings of their oral stories with the class via the iPad during Sharing Time after literacy work stations and small-group time today. On another day, they may write a traditional paper book about this story, too.

Writing is alive in many forms in this classroom, because the children have a sense of purpose and audience thanks to their teacher's thoughtful planning. These students also have a rich store of writing experiences beyond work stations. Tina writes with them during writing workshop every day. She shows them how she decides what to write about and how she chooses her words. She models how she organizes her ideas and shows the class how to reread and think about what her readers might want to know. Tina uses high-quality children's literature and online resources as mentor texts to show how other writers construct their texts, too.

Although Tina often feels crunched for time and sometimes feels uncomfortable writing in front of her students, she makes time and takes the risk. By doing so, this class is filled with writers who view themselves as fellow authors. They are learning to read as writers and write as readers.

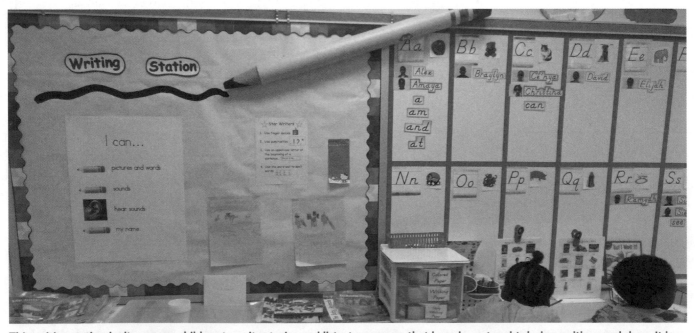

This writing station invites young children to write stories and lists, two genres that have been taught during writing workshop. It is placed near the word wall, so writers can easily access it to help them write words they know. All the materials they need are at their fingertips. An "I Can" list and anchor charts provide support.

We used the teacher's desk (because she used her small-group table as her workspace) as a writing station. Kids loved it! We placed it near a wall so there would be lots of space for anchor charts about writing to be posted there as reminders. The writing station was also placed near computers, which kids can use to compose while here.

This kindergarten writing station is near the word wall and has great tools to help kids: word cards about topics, alphabet charts for sounds, tactile letters to support letter formation. The "I Can" list helps kids remember what they can do here.

Second graders sit on crates to write at a table at this inviting writing station. Writing anchor charts and dictionaries provide support.

Writing Opinions

Down the hall from Tina, I visit a kindergarten classroom where children are voicing their opinions about books in the classroom library. "*Superheroes* is one of my favorites," announces Jesse as I stop by this literacy station.

"Why do you like this book?" I ask him.

"My teacher read it to us, and now I can read it. It's about superheroes. I love Batman!"

Young children like Jesse can write about why certain books and topics are their favorites in kindergarten and first grade. This kind of writing will eventually lead to second- and third-grade opinion pieces about issues and topics students at these ages care about. It's important to help children find interesting topics about which they want to voice their opinions. For example, share local news stories that may produce items of interest, such as saving a park, donating to fight children's cancer, or cleaning up a nearby stream. Read aloud op-ed pieces; write your own persuasive pieces in front of the class to provide strong models. Finally, and most important, be sure that students' opinion writing is shared with its targeted audience to have the greatest effect.

Chapter 8

Sifting Through the Standard: Writing Opinions

What It Is	• Students write their preferences and opinions about books and topics of interest. • Kids must give reasons that support their opinions, beginning in kindergarten. • They are required to use linking words and phrases to support those opinions starting in second grade. • Students should learn the organizational structure of writing an opinion piece: 1. Introduce the topic or book. 2. State your opinion. 3. Give reasons for your opinion. 4. Closure
Why It's Important	• The ability to voice one's opinion is helpful when trying to persuade someone about an idea or a cause. • To best interpret what is read, it is important to read facts and form one's own opinion but also to identify the perspective of the author on timely issues.
Student Prerequisites	• For young children, telling and then writing about a *favorite* (pet, food, book, and so on) is typically easier than giving an *opinion about a topic*. • If children can practice *telling* their opinions, they will develop voice in which to *write* their opinions. • It will be helpful if children know what a fact is. Facts can be used to support opinions. • Learning to distinguish others' opinions (points of view) will help students form their own opinions over time.
Academic Vocabulary	Kindergarten: • *favorite* • *topic* • *opinion* First grade: • *reason* • *closing* Second grade: • *support* • *linking words* • *concluding statement or section* Third grade: • *introduction* • *point of view* • *organize* • *connect opinions and reasons* • *persuade*
Real-World Connections	• In the real world, book reviews usually contain readers' opinions about the books they've read. Ditto for restaurant, movie, product, and game reviews. • The opinion pages of newspapers and magazines are some of the most commonly read pieces in those publications. Decision makers in government, corporations, and nonprofits often read opinion pages (op-ed) to understand where the general public stands. • Political campaigns and advertisements include opinions. • Writing to persuade others is an important life skill. For example, I've written letters for everything from persuading a children's author to visit my classroom for free to receiving compensation for lost luggage.

Sifting Through the Standard: Writing Opinions *(continued)*	
Example Test Questions	• "Write about your favorite _____." • "Write your opinion about ____ and give reasons to support it." • "What is your opinion about _____?" • "Persuade someone to read a book you've recently read."

Team Planning Tool: Writing Opinions—First Grade	
Standard We're Teaching	**First grade:** Write opinion pieces in which they introduce the topic or name the book they are writing about, state an opinion, supply a reason for the opinion, and provide some sense of closure.
Academic Vocabulary We'll Use and Expect to Hear	• *favorite* • *topic* • *opinion* • *reason* • *closing*
Whole-Group Ideas	• Read aloud favorite first-grade books. • Read book review samples. • Make anchor chart on opinions and how to write them. • Make topic cards with the class. • Model how to tell your opinion about a topic. • Model how to write an opinion.
Partner Practice at Literacy Work Stations	**Give-your-opinion station:** Use topic cards and take turns stating an opinion about a topic with a partner. (For example, "My opinion about ____ is _____.") Then kids write their opinions to share with the class. **Writing station/classroom library:** Write a book review about a favorite book and tell reasons why others should read it. Post the reviews in the classroom library. Write other kinds of reviews (restaurant, movie, product, game reviews).

Lessons That Last:
Whole-Group Mini-Lesson Plan for Writing Opinions—First Grade

Give Your Opinion

Focus: stating an opinion and providing supporting reasons about a book or topic of interest

Method to Maximize Student Engagement: read aloud books that kids really love and will have strong opinions about; choose topics that kids will have strong feelings about; partner talk

Materials: favorite books to read aloud, sample book reviews, topic cards, chart paper and markers for anchor chart, paper and pencils for students

Model: how to tell and then write opinions about books or topics

Prompting for Independence:

• "One of my favorite books is _____ because _____."
• "My opinion about _____ is _____."
• "One reason for my opinion is_____."
• "Why do you think we should _____? Give reasons to support your opinion."

Lessons That Last:
Whole-Group Mini-Lesson Plan for Writing Opinions—First Grade *(continued)*

Mini-Lesson Procedure: Note that this mini-lesson will take several days and must be repeated multiple times with different books and topics.

Writing About Favorite Books/Book Reviews:

1. Share reviews of a book that's a class favorite, using reviews such as those found online at goodreads.com, and explain how you sometimes use them to help you decide whether to read certain books. Also share kid-friendly sites, such as www.spaghettibookclub.org and www.dogobooks.com, which have book reviews written by children.

2. Explain that people often write book reviews to influence others to read (or not read) the books they've read.

3. Make an anchor chart about how to write a book review. (See samples in the photos.)

4. Tell about a book, and then model how to write a book review.

5. Have students do the same with books they love.

Writing Opinions About Topics:

1. Introduce the idea of opinions by sharing something you feel strongly about. Explain that an opinion is what someone thinks about a particular thing, event, or person. An opinion is something you believe or feel strongly about. It is helpful to use facts to support your opinion. Tell the class that you are going to talk (and eventually write) about your opinions. For example, "I think that _____ has the best football team!" Or "I believe that the cafeteria should serve only healthful food."

2. Make an anchor chart about opinions, as pictured on the next page.

3. Select a topic of interest and relevance to your students. Model how to tell your opinion to a partner, and then listen to your partner give his or her opinion.

4. Then work with the children to make topic cards of things kids might give their opinions about. First graders may come up with the following: sports, games, TV shows, what time they have to go to bed, books, and so on. Write each topic on a 3-by-5-inch index card that kids can later illustrate. (Connect the term *topic* to previous learning about reading informational text. You might tell students that a *topic is something or someone that people talk or write about.*)

5. Have students work with partners to choose a topic card and share their opinions with one another about that topic orally. Ask several students to volunteer their opinions with the class orally.

6. On another day, share your opinion about a topic of interest, such as favorite foods, with your students. Model how to write your opinion about this topic, step by step:

    a. Introduce your topic.
    b. State your opinion about the topic.
    c. Give a reason for your opinion.
    d. Close with a strong ending.

7. Have students tell their opinion about this topic to a partner. Then have them write their opinions and share them with the class.

On-the-Spot Assessment: Listen to students as they verbally tell their opinions. Do they do this in an organized way, naming the topic or book, giving an opinion about it, supporting the opinion with a reason, and then ending with some sense of closure? Are they able to do the same in writing? Use a rubric (see Figure 8.1 for a sample) to guide your observations.

Figure 8.1 **Rubric for Writing Opinions**

Student: _____ Date: ____ Orally___ Written___	Yes	No	Somewhat
1. Introduces the topic or book title			
2. States an opinion about the topic or book			
3. Gives a reason for the opinion			
4. Ends with a strong closing			

Connections to Whole-Group Mini-Lesson

Independent Reading Connection: Have students read and then tell a partner their opinions about the book they're reading. Do they like it? Why or why not? Would they recommend it to a classmate? Why or why not?

Small-Group Connection: You might have a small-group meeting to help students who need support with telling their opinions. Let them practice with your help. Likewise, you might meet with a small group of students who need help with writing their opinions and write an opinion together.

Whole-Group Reading Connection: Read aloud books and book reviews in which opinions are given. Websites like spaghettibookclub.org and dogobooks.com are kid-friendly. Also help students identify opinions that characters have in the books you read aloud.

Evaluation: Use a rubric like the one in Figure 8.1. Have students evaluate their own writing and that of a partner before you do so.

Kids thought about topics about which they had opinions, and I wrote their ideas on "topic cards" made with index cards and a black marker. Later, students illustrated the topics and used them at the writing station to continue writing opinion pieces.

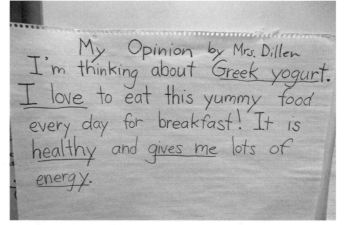

I modeled how to write an opinion piece about one of my favorite foods, Greek yogurt, referring to our anchor chart as I wrote step by step.

I'm making an anchor chart titled "Give Your Opinion" with the class.

Kids talk in pairs about their opinions using topic cards. I overheard things like, "My opinion about sports is that baseball is my favorite. I think the Astros are the best team" and "I think dogs make the best pets, because they love to play and make me happy." This talk helped them rehearse what they would write *before* independent writing.

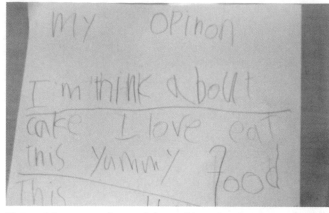 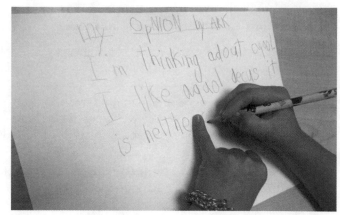

Pictured is some student opinion writing after my first modeling in the fall. On the left, an English language learner wrote "My Opinion. I'm think about cake. I love eat this yummy food. This happy yummy yummy." On the right side, a struggling reader wrote "My Opinion. I'm thinking about apples. I like apple because it is healthy." These kids took risks as writers (and didn't need to just fill in the blank), because of good modeling, talk as rehearsal, and time to write.

Mentor Texts for Modeling:
Writing Opinions

- *Earrings!* by Judith Viorst
- *The Greatest Dinosaur Ever* by Brenda Guiberson

- *What's Your Favorite Animal?* by Eric Carle and friends
- *I Wanna Iguana* by Karen Kaufman Orloff
- *Hey, Little Ant* by Phillip Hoose
- *A Pig Parade Is a Terrible Idea* by Michael Ian Black

Teaching Tips for Writing Opinions Across the Grades	
In Pre-K and Kindergarten	• At these grade levels, focus on having kids *talk* about their *favorites*, giving reasons why they like particular books, foods, activities, and so on. • Encourage the youngest students to use the words *favorite*, *opinion*, and *reason*. • To start, you might use the sentence frame "My favorite _____ is _____ because _____." However, do not limit children to only this language. • As you read aloud, model how to talk about why a book is your favorite. For example, "*No, David!* is one of my favorite books. I love the way David Shannon shows the main character getting in trouble all the time." Or, "I think Pete the Cat is funny. He's one of my favorites because of the way he's always singing songs."
In Grades One–Two	• Begin with book reviews and expand to restaurant, movie, product, or game reviews. • Give kids lots of opportunities to *tell* opinions before they write them. As you read aloud, share and invite opinions about characters and what they do, say, and feel. Be sure to support your opinions with reasons, especially those backed by facts. • Chart connecting words with students, including *because* and *also*. • Collect and display samples of strong introductions and endings for opinion pieces to help students improve their writing. • Help kids think about who their audience is as they write opinions. What will influence this audience? What does this group or individual care about?
In Grades Three and Up	• Show students op-ed pieces found in the editorial section of the newspaper. Share pieces with opinions about topics of interest to your class. *Time for Kids* is a great resource to use with your students. • Sense of audience is important to develop as students move up the grade levels. Ask kids to think about who will read their opinion pieces and encourage them to write to influence that audience. • Chart connecting words with students, including *because*, *also*, *therefore*, *since*, and *for example*. • Look for opinions when reading historical or scientific informational text with your class. Examine the voice with which the author writes and discuss biases the author may have as reflected in his or her opinion. Talk about the author's point of view, too.

Sample Anchor Charts for Writing Opinions

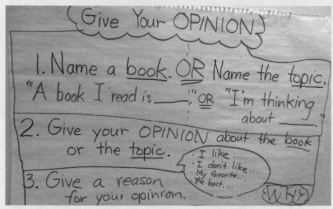

A finished anchor chart lists steps on how to give an opinion about a topic.

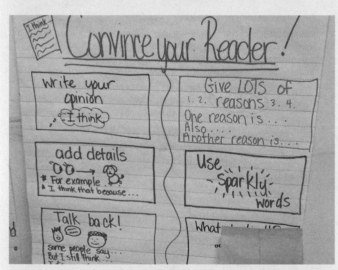

An anchor chart titled "Convince Your Reader" helps children successfully write opinions in second grade. Posting this near the writing station will remind kids how to write opinions and give more structure to the writing they do there.

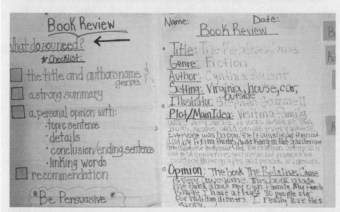

This book review (*right*) was written with the class and serves as an anchor chart for kids at the writing station. They can write book reviews about some of their favorite read-alouds or books they've read on their own. The anchor chart (*left*) on how to write a book review reminds kids to include a personal opinion.

Literacy Work Stations for Writing Opinions

These topic cards were made in whole group and then illustrated by students. They are now placed in the writing station along with the "Give Your Opinion" anchor chart and sample. Kids continue to write opinions with a partner or on their own. If they write independently, they read and get their partner's feedback. New topic cards can be used over time.

There are two options for response after listening to books at this listening station. Children can write a book review or make a circle map about a character. Change the books listened to at this station periodically.

Three second-grade boys write book reviews at the writing station. Note the anchor chart for how to write a book review posted here. Change the focus from writing a book review to writing a review of a restaurant, movie, television show, game, or product. Provide modeling before asking all students to write these types of reviews.

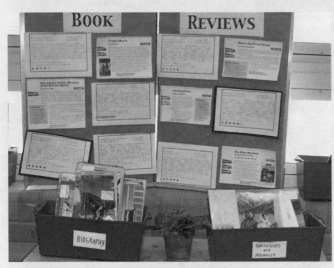

Students' book reviews are posted by the classroom library. Children use the reviews to help them choose their "next read" books.

Intermediate students write persuasive letters at this writing station. A sample letter made during whole group provides a model displayed here. Note the use of sticky notes labeling the parts of the letter. Kids manipulate the sticky notes during whole group (and at the writing station, if they choose to) to identify the parts of a persuasive letter. This helps them remember to include each part and think about its purpose. You might include a list, made by the class, of who to write to and post it here.

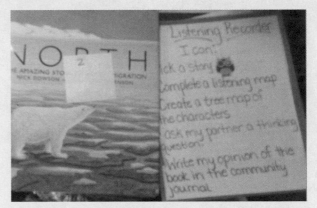

One option on the "I Can" list at this listening station is to write an opinion about a book in the community journal after listening to it.

Writing Informational Texts

"We've been studying natural disasters in science, so it seemed like a good fit to have my class write information pieces about tornadoes, hurricanes, and glaciers," David, a third-grade teacher, told me as we planned together. "But it was so hard for the kids! Even though they got to choose a natural disaster to read and write about, it was like pulling teeth."

As I worked with David's class, I saw firsthand why this writing assignment had been so difficult. Many of his third graders speak English as a second language, and, fortunately, most have never experienced natural disasters. I asked him to show me some of the informational texts he'd read aloud. "Unfortunately," he admitted, "most of the informational text we've read has been in the form of test passages." He explained that his class had done a brief study of (and could identify) text features in informational text, but he hadn't shown them how to apply these features to their writing. In addition, David admitted that writing often takes a backseat to reading instruction in his classroom because of time (and testing) constraints. David was open to recommendations for helping his kids write informational text.

My colleague Dr. John O'Flahavan, from the University of Maryland, taught me that students must *consume* many texts within a genre (through reading) before we can expect them to *produce* writing in that same genre. I looked through several students' book boxes and saw that the majority of their books were fiction. A close look at David's third-grade classroom library revealed that there were many more books in the fiction section than in the nonfiction baskets. A first step for David would be to consistently read aloud authentic informational texts about a variety of topics. (I recommended he scour his school library or possibly the public library to find informational texts matching his class's interests, as well as social studies and science topics of study.) He could revisit text features, this time paying attention to how *writers* used them to relay information to readers. He'd also help students identify the *topic* of each read-aloud text and pay attention to how the writer *introduced* the topic. I recommended that David create an anchor chart with his class about how authors write informational texts, including a section on the *introduction* and *topic sentence*. This would strengthen his students' reading and writing of informational text.

Another lesson I shared with David from John O'Flahavan's work (O'Flahavan, Grabowsky, and McCraw 2012) was the notion of *reconstructing* text, much as artists do when learning to paint. John had witnessed artists at the National Art Gallery painting their own copies of the masters' works as part of their studies and got the idea of having children reconstruct text in much the same way. Pure brilliance! I showed David how to take two test passages on different topics and cut them apart, paragraph by paragraph. I also cut out the title or headings, illustrations, and captions for kids to sort and put back together like a puzzle. As they sorted with a partner, they'd discuss what went where and why. They'd also use tape flags to label the parts—"title," "introduction," "topic sentence," "illustration," "caption." He'd have to model and show kids how to do it on the document camera first, but I knew they'd engage with the task readily and learn how informational text is constructed in a hands-on way.

You'll notice that different standards use slightly different terms: *informative*, *explanatory*, *expository*, and so on. Because these all fit within the larger genre of informational texts, I've decided to use that term—informational text—throughout the chapter for clarity and simplicity. Of course, as you are planning with your colleagues using your school's set of standards, you'll want to adapt the terminology to suit your needs.

Sifting Through the Standard: Writing Informational Texts

What It Is	• Students learn how to write about a topic in an organized fashion that includes an introduction, some facts and related points, and a sense of closure. • Young students may write lists, captions, invitations, or letters. • This genre also includes responses to literary or informational texts.
Why It's Important	• This genre contains most of the writing people do within their lifetime. • Learning to write information in a clear, concise way is a key to communicating with others. • Donald Graves (1989) explains that "the ability to recount a process is the forerunner of one of the most difficult kinds of writing: directions. Recounting a process is the foundation of observation and recording in sciences such as chemistry, physics, and biology."
Student Prerequisites	• It is helpful to have heard lots of informational text read aloud before being expected to write this kind of text. • Students who have a solid understanding of what a *fact* is will be better able to write informational text successfully. • Learning to talk about and stay on a topic will help children be able to write about that topic in an organized fashion. • Understanding the difference between a narrative or story and an informational text will help students focus on information rather than writing a story about a topic.

Sifting Through the Standard: Writing Informational Texts *(continued)*

Academic Vocabulary	Kindergarten: • *information* • *topic* • *lists* • *captions* • *invitations* First grade: • *name a topic* • *facts* • *focus* • *closure* • *letter (date, salutation, closing)* • *comments* • *response* Second grade: • *introduce a topic* • *definitions* • *concluding statement* • *concluding section* Third grade: • *convey ideas and information clearly* • *topic sentence* • *main idea* • *develop a topic* • *illustrations* • *details* • *explanations* • *organize related information into paragraphs* • *linking words or phrases*
Real-World Connections	• Most of the writing we do in our day-to-day life is informational writing. We write lists and invitations. We write to convey information in memos, e-mails, letters, and invitations, to name a few. • Young children love to write notes and letters to communicate with others. List writing is one of the easiest kinds of writing for them to do and teaches them to focus on one topic. • Writing directions is a more difficult type of writing but is often used by technical writers, such as those who write manuals to go with appliances, cars, and so on.
Example Test Questions	• "Write an informational text about _____." • "Write a letter telling someone about _____." • "Write a response to the text you just read. Include _____ in your response."

Team Planning Tool: Writing Informational Texts—Third Grade	
Standard We're Teaching	**Third grade:** Write informational texts to examine a topic and convey ideas and information clearly; introduce a topic and group related information together; include illustrations when useful to aiding comprehension.
Academic Vocabulary We'll Use and Expect to Hear	• *informational text/informative text* • *convey ideas and information clearly* • *topic sentence* • *main idea* • *develop a topic* • *illustrations* • *details* • *explanations* • *organize related information into paragraphs*
Whole-Group Ideas	• Reread and have kids help to label parts of informational texts used during previous read-alouds. Focus on *title, topic sentence, introduction, illustration, caption,* and eventually *conclusion.* • Model how to reconstruct a cut-up informational text, thinking aloud about how and why the author wrote it. Then have kids add tape flag labels as per above. • Model how to start writing a narrative and a separate informational text about the same topic using two different charts on topics kids know lots of information about.
Partner Practice at Literacy Work Stations	**Writing station:** Continue to write informational texts from writing workshop. With a partner, read over informational text writing you've done. Post and discuss the following: "Can the reader identify the topic in the first sentence? Is there an introduction? Is the information conveyed clearly?" Work together to revise and edit. **ABC book station:** Work with a partner to make a page for an ABC book on a topic studied in science/social studies and predetermined by the class. Include a title, introduction, and facts or information about something related that begins with that letter. For example, if studying natural disasters, children might write, "*Aa* is for avalanche" or "*Tt* is for tornado." See photos for a sample. **Genre examination station:** Partners work together to examine informational text and identify topics, introductions, and, over time, conclusions. Also examine how facts and information are organized. Students can read and label informational books with tape flags. They can also reconstruct cut-up informational texts, discuss them, and label the parts. Copies of related social studies and science book texts would work well for this.

Lessons That Last: Whole-Group Mini-Lesson Plan for Writing Informational Texts—Third Grade

Note: You will need to teach multiple mini-lessons for this genre! (It is not a seed that germinates quickly.)

Informative Writing: From Topic to Introduction (Third Grade)

Focus: informative writing

Method to Maximize Student Engagement: ask students for topics they both know about and care about; get student input on how your writing sounds

Materials: chart paper, markers, familiar informational text that has been read aloud previously, anchor chart on text features

Model: how to determine a topic and write an introduction to a piece of informative writing

Prompting for Independence:

- "My topic is _____. I chose this topic because _____."
- "The title of my informative piece is going to be _____. This tells what it's mostly about."
- "First, I'll write the introduction to my piece. Let's look at how other authors wrote their introductions to help get started."

Mini-Lesson Procedure:

1. Gather the class in the whole-group meeting area and tell them you will be starting to write an informative piece today.

2. Begin by looking at several familiar informational texts that you've previously read aloud to your students. (Be sure they have an introduction of some sort.)

3. Show several introductions from books and think aloud about how the authors started their writing. For example, showing the book *The Seven Continents* by Wil Mara (2005), say, "This author started to write with a question to hook the reader. He writes, 'Do you know you live on a continent?' which informs me that his writing is going to be about continents." Use another book, such as Chris Butterworth's *How Did That Get in My Lunchbox?* (2011), and show how he began: "This author introduces his topic with the words . . . 'One of the best parts of the day is when you lift the lid of your lunchbox to see what's inside. Your parents have packed it with lots of tasty things to eat. They probably got all the food from a grocery store—but food doesn't grow in stores.' I know the topic is food and where it comes from."

4. Brainstorm and make a list of several topics students could write about. Think aloud how to choose a topic that you both know about *and* care about. Narrow it down. Students may say things like *skateboarding,* which is too broad. Help them think about a smaller slice, like *skateboarding tricks.* (For example, we narrowed *art* to *painting tools* and *football* to *two Texans players.*)

5. Choose a topic for your modeled writing. Write a title at the top of the chart paper and think aloud about why you chose these words. "How to Prepare for Thanksgiving is my topic. It tells exactly what I'll write about."

6. At this point, you might end the day's mini-lesson and have students work in pairs or small groups to browse informational texts they've been reading, identify titles and topics, and then generate topics they might want to write about. From there, they can each tell their topic and write a matching title.

7. The next day, review the topic and title you wrote in front of the class in the previous lesson. Then quickly write the beginning of a story related to your topic on another piece of chart paper to show kids the difference between a story and an informational text. See the photo for a sample.

8. Then return to the informational piece you're writing. Explain that it's not a story but will contain organized information about your topic. Think aloud about your introduction as you write in front of the class. Explain that the introduction should tell the reader what you're writing about. This is often called a *topic sentence* because it includes the topic, or what you're writing about.

9. After you've written the introduction, have students add sticky-note labels to your modeled writing. Include labels for "title," "introduction," and "topic sentence." Tell them you expect them to use these when writing their own informative pieces.

**Lessons That Last: Whole-Group Mini-Lesson
Plan for Writing Informational Texts—Third Grade** (continued)

10. Before they write, have students work with partners and tell each other their topic and title, helping them narrow or edit if needed. Then give them paper and have them write just the introduction to their informative piece.

11. After they've written, ask students to read just their introduction and have the class identify the topic. After a few have modeled, have students work with a partner to do the same.

12. Recap by reviewing what students learned about writing informative text today.

On-the-Spot Assessment: Think about the following: Were students able to choose a topic they knew about and cared about? Did they write a title that named the topic? Did they write an introduction that clearly introduced the topic? Did they write an informational piece or a story?

Connections to Whole-Group Mini-Lesson

Independent Reading Connection: Be sure students have informative/explanatory texts in their independent reading materials and choose them to read. Have them use sticky notes to label the introduction and topic sentence in a book or section. Have them use a different-colored sticky note to write down the topic.

Small-Group Connection: When reading in small group with students, use some informational texts with them over time. Before they read, have children predict the topic from reading the title or heading. Also have them read the introduction and tell how the topic is introduced to the reader. Help them read like writers and notice how the author organizes information. One way to do this is to help them read headings, bold words, and captions before reading a particular section of text. Then show them how to do that in their own writing during writing workshop.

Whole-Group Reading Connection: As you read aloud informational texts in whole group, ask students to name the genre and differentiate them from stories. Model how to use text features the writer has included to make predictions and to glean information. Show kids how to use these same features as they write.

Evaluation: Create a rubric with the class and use it to evaluate their informational text writing. See Figure 8.2 for a sample.

Figure 8.2 **Sample Rubric for Writing Informational Texts—Grades One–Three**

Student: _____ Date: _____	Yes	No	Somewhat
Includes a title that names the topic			
Begins the piece by naming or introducing the topic			
Uses facts or details or steps to convey information about the topic			
Groups related information together, including illustrations when useful to aid comprehension (third grade)			
Uses linking words and phrases (such as *also, another, and, more, but*) to connect ideas within categories of information (third grade)			
Ends with a concluding statement or section			

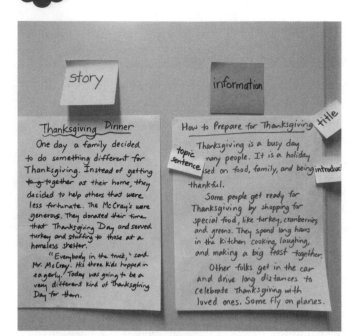

Writing informational texts should begin in kindergarten. Our youngest writers can be successful as we allow them to "make stuff," as Katie Wood Ray (2003) so brilliantly advises in her book *About the Authors*. Four- and five-year-olds love making lists with words and pictures. They will make cards and invitations and books galore. This type of work is foundational in learning how to write nonfiction and will often become a favorite of even the most reluctant writers. The photos on pages 208–211 show examples of the rich writing students can do at stations across grade levels.

Modeled writing in third grade—the start of a narrative piece on the left and an informational piece on the right—is used to show the difference between genres. Sticky notes label the "title," "topic sentence," and "introduction."

Team Planning Tool: Writing Informational Texts—Kindergarten	
Standards We're Teaching	**Kindergarten:** Students are expected to dictate or write information for lists, captions, or invitations; use a combination of drawing, dictating, and writing to compose informative/explanatory texts in which they name what they are writing about and supply some information about the topic.
Academic Vocabulary We'll Use and Expect to Hear	• *information* • *list* • *caption* • *illustration* • *photograph* • *invitation* • *what I'm writing about (topic)*
Whole-Group Ideas	• Read aloud books with examples of lists, captions, or invitations in them. • Show examples of real-life lists or invitations you've made or received and discuss their purposes (lists help us remember or organize things around a topic; captions give more information about an illustration; invitations ask us to attend an event for a special purpose). • Model how to write a list, a caption, or an invitation. • Have kids write their own lists around topics. • Provide illustrations or photos for which kids can add captions. • Have students write invitations for school (or home) events.
Partner Practice at Literacy Work Stations	**Writing station:** • Students work alone or with a partner to write lists, captions, or invitations. • They may also make informational textbooks about a topic of interest.

Whole-Group Mini-Lesson Plan Template for Writing Informational Texts—Kindergarten

Making Stuff: Invitations, Lists, or Information Books (Kindergarten)

Focus: writing a list or invitation or caption focused on one topic

Method to Maximize Student Engagement: shared writing about topics of interest to your students for authentic purposes (for example, an invitation for parents to attend a school event; a list of materials needed for a class project; captions to go with photos of things your class has done together)

Materials: real invitations or lists or information books with captions to use as models; large paper folded or cut to look like an invitation or list or caption; enlarged photos of your class engaged in something they love to do (playing on the playground or eating a snack) for which you can write captions

Model: how to organize information by writing a list, an invitation, or a caption for a specific purpose

Prompting for Independence:

- "We can make a list to organize information that we want to remember."
- "Write a word (or words) at the top of your list to name the topic or what you're writing about."
- "We can write a caption to give more information about an illustration or photograph."
- "We can make an invitation to ask someone to attend an event, like a party or a play."

Mini-Lesson Procedure:

1. Gather the class in the whole-group area and show them examples of the type of writing (list or invitation or caption) you will expect them to write.

2. Name the kind of writing you want them to pay attention to and point out how it's organized. For example, "This is a list. The words at the top tell what it's about—Thanksgiving food. Then the foods are listed or written below the name of the list. Everything on my list tells something my family will eat for Thanksgiving dinner. Here is another list. The words at the top say 'People in My Family,' so that tells what it's about—all the people in my family. It's a list of the names of everyone in my family. It has words written under each other in a list form."

3. Model how to write a list (or invitation or caption) related to something of interest to your students. Ask them for their ideas of topics. Think aloud how you decided on your topic and named it (for example, "I'll make a list of food I need to pick up at the grocery store today. I'll call my list *Groceries* so I remember what it's about"). After modeling, give kids a chance to try it on their own. For example, ask students to tell you what they'd like to make a list of. Then give them paper and have them make their own lists.

On-the-Spot Assessment: Pay attention to which students can stay on topic, demonstrate understanding of the genre they're writing, and organize ideas.

Connections to Whole-Group Mini-Lesson

Independent Reading Connection: Give kids little books that include captions, lists, or even invitations. If you don't have any available, you might construct some with students during writing workshop, reproduce them, and make them available for independent reading.

Small-Group Connection: In small group, either read or write these kinds of texts with children. You might do interactive writing where you share the pen with group members to create lists of something kids read about, add captions for photos, or write invitations for upcoming events.

Whole-Group Reading Connection: In whole group, read aloud informative/explanatory texts that include lists or captions. You may find invitations as part of some picture book stories, as noted in the list of mentor texts.

Evaluation: Can students write lists, invitations, and/or captions? Use the rubric in Figure 8.3.

Figure 8.3 **Sample Rubric for Writing Informational Texts—Kindergarten**

Student: _____ Date: _____ List/Caption/Invitation Dictated____ Drawn_____ Written_____	Yes	No	Somewhat
Uses correct form (list/caption/invitation)			
Stays on topic			
Uses facts or details or steps to convey information about the topic			

Mentor Texts for Modeling:
Writing Informational Texts

- *The Seven Continents* by Wil Mara
- *How Did That Get in My Lunchbox? The Story of Food* by Chris Butterworth
- *How to Make Bubbles* by Erika L. Shores
- *The Life and Times of the Peanut* by Charles Micucci

- *How to Wash a Woolly Mammoth* by Michelle Robinson
- *How to Babysit a Grandpa* by Jean Reagan
- *Everyone Can Learn to Ride a Bicycle* by Chris Raschka
- *Walk On! A Guide for Babies of All Ages* by Marla Frazee
- *How to Teach a Slug to Read* by Susan Pearson

Teaching Tips for Writing Informational Texts Across the Grades	
In Pre-K and Kindergarten	• Children in the earliest grades should be exposed to many informative/explanatory texts through read-aloud. Be sure to tell kids that these are informational books (not stories), so they learn the difference. • Young children love to make stuff! Model and then have them create lists, invitations, and captions around topics and events of interest. • Young kids can make informational books if you study this with them. See examples in the literacy work stations photos that follow.
In Grades One–Two	• Again, expose kids to this genre through read-aloud. Point out the kind of text (informative or explanatory) you are reading aloud and how it is constructed, paying special attention to the *topic, headings, introduction, organization,* and *concluding statement/section.* • Model how to write a variety of texts, including letters and responses to literature. • Help students choose and narrow topics they will write about, and use mentor texts to show them how authors do this as well.
In Grades Three and Up	• Reading aloud many informative/explanatory texts and using them as mentor texts will be valuable as your students continue to learn how to write these kinds of pieces. • Use mentor texts to show how authors narrow and organize their topics. Show how they add illustrations and captions to give additional information without lots of extra words. • Have kids look for examples of how authors both introduce and conclude pieces of writing on a topic. Show them how to use these same techniques in their writing. • Above all, model, model, model with your own writing in front of the class. Take risks to show students how you choose a topic, narrow it, write an introduction, organize information about the topic, and use a concluding statement or section. Break this up into multiple lessons. Don't expect students to include all of these in one writing session to start!

Sample Anchor Charts for Writing Informational Texts

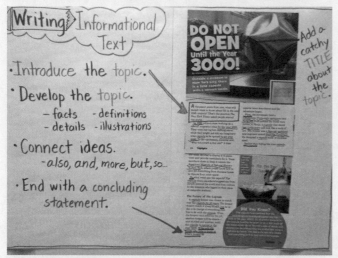

This anchor chart was made with the class to help students remember how to write an informative text.

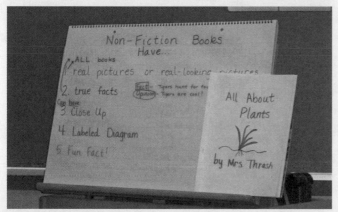

An anchor chart for writing nonfiction books was made with kindergartners.

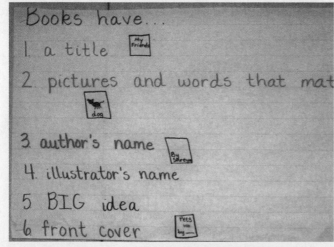

An anchor chart for how to make books is displayed at the writing station. It is also used during writing workshop to help kids remember what to include when making a book.

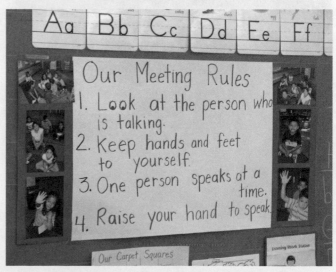

Procedural anchor charts like these were made with the class and serve as models for how to do things in school, as well as models for writing procedures.

This anchor chart for writing a letter was made with the class in whole group. Sticky notes label the parts of a letter. As students learned about this new genre, they manipulated the sticky notes to learn the academic vocabulary associated with writing letters.

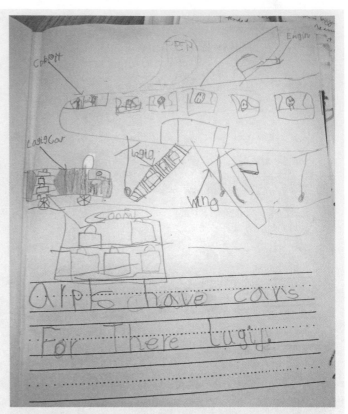

A kindergartner writes an informational book about airplanes. Look at the text features he's used! His teacher connected reading and writing of informational text, and the result is amazing.

Literacy Work Stations for Writing Informational Texts

This child uses word cards with photos on a clothesline, which can be removed while writing lists at Thanksgiving. Word cards change seasonally.

This "I Can" list includes samples of the kind of writing young authors can choose to do at the writing station. Add student writing samples or class models as you teach how to write a letter or a story, and so on.

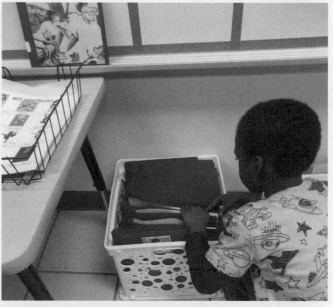

Partners write daily news on this laminated chart. They "play teacher" here, as they write their own news for their classmates to read and respond to. Over time, students may draw lines for their friends to fill in the missing parts of words using phonics elements being studied.

The teacher in this classroom places a crate with a folder in it for each child by the writing station. This way kids can keep working on pieces from writing workshop at this station.

Students write informative texts about the solar system at this science station. Provide books related to topics being studied for reference. Change out science topics as you study them. Do the same at a social studies station.

A student discovers he loves to write when given the opportunity to read and write his own Who Would Win? books at the writing station. This series by Jerry Pallotta inspired him to use facts and write his own books. Use mentor texts like these to inspire kids to add their own books to a series of informational texts.

At the writing station, a student continues to write informational text about penguins, working on a piece from writing workshop. This child incorporates the text feature of a diagram based on the modeling and anchor charts provided in his classroom. His teacher will encourage him to add other text features, such as a heading or caption, as he thinks about how best to communicate information to his readers. This kind of writing can be done all year. Topics can change along with what's being studied in science or social studies. Allow children to continue to write about things they've already studied for spiral review and deeper understanding.

At this writing station, first graders write lists early in the year. Note the sample lists made with the class in whole group posted as models along with a handwriting chart for support.

Partners work on an ABC book at this station. The class has brainstormed words from A to Z that go with a content-area topic of study (e.g., Michigan, magnets, electricity). When kids come to this station, they make an individual page that will be added to a class book. Kids will enjoy making ABC books all year long on a variety of topics.

Kindergarten kids love making stuff at the writing station. Early in the year lists and cards are good choices. This student makes a list of her classmates.

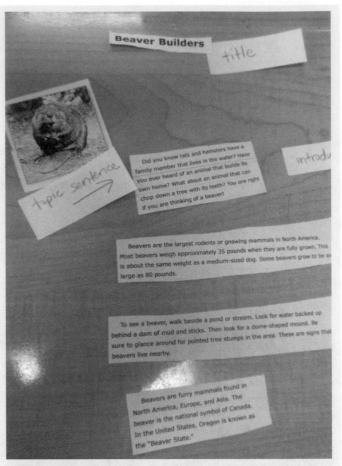

Intermediate-age kids work together to reconstruct cut-up informational text test passages. They label parts of the text (for example, "title," "introduction," and "topic sentence") to familiarize themselves with the way tests are constructed. (Tests are a genre unto themselves!)

Young writers use store advertisements to make wish lists for holidays and birthdays at the writing station. Change the kinds of lists kids write over the year according to the season (such as favorite sports teams or players, things we do in winter, signs of spring, and people we love).

Students at this writing station decided to write notes to the principal, one of their favorite people at school. With your class, make a list of people kids can write notes to and post this at the station.

After learning how to make how-to books in writing workshop, kindergartners suggested we have a how-to station. We made a portable station with how-to books that were commercially published and student-made. Children loved reading and writing their own how-to books here. For variety, we added materials kids needed to make things from selected how-to books at this station.

Writing Narratives

In the picture book *Rocket Writes a Story* (Hills 2012), the author tells a story about a dog named Rocket who collects words and wants to write his own story. However, Rocket gets stuck looking at a blank page because he doesn't know what to write. Sound familiar? This happens to professional writers as well as students!

Rocket's story unfolds with the help of a wise character, the little yellow bird, who tells Rocket that he might want to write about his experiences and reminds him that writing stories takes time. The little yellow bird urges Rocket on with questions about his story and gives him time to develop his ideas. This is what wise teachers do as well.

Teachers who read to and write stories with their students will develop readers *and* writers of stories. But it takes time and attention, just like growing plants in a garden. My friend Heather did this in her kindergarten classroom. She consistently read and reread stories to her class. They made charts of what they noticed that authors did in these stories and then wrote their own. Early in the year, their stories were told mostly in pictures. But by the end of the year, as you'll notice in the photos, these young writers were using words and drawings to tell stories, often echoing the language of the authors they'd studied closely. This class wrote daily. Heather modeled by writing in front of her kids, she conferred with students every day, and they closed writing workshop with Sharing Time, when several children shared what they wrote with the class.

Kindergarten writing the first week of school consists mostly of drawing to tell a story.

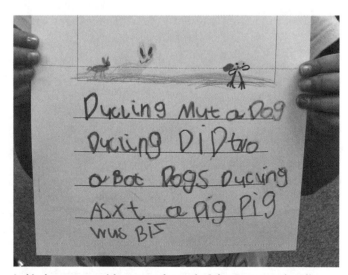

In kindergarten writing near the end of the year, words tell most of the story. "Duckling met a dog. Duckling didn't know about dogs. Duckling asked a pig. Pig was busy."

Sifting Through the Standard: Writing Narratives

What It Is	• Students are expected to write narratives that tell stories that include several sequenced events in order as well as thoughts, actions, and feelings. Stories should include a beginning, middle, and ending and feature characters, settings, problems, and solutions. • This genre may include personal narratives, such as what Lucy Calkins (2003) refers to as "small moments" and/or imaginative stories.
Why It's Important	• Writing down our stories can help us understand the events of our lives and help others understand us. • Writing narratives is a form of creative expression. • Learning to write narratives can help kids learn to sequence events and fill in details, which is helpful in informative and academic writing, too.
Student Prerequisites	• Oral language (or telling stories) is an important prerequisite for writing stories. • It is important for students to have heard many stories so that they are familiar with narrative elements and can mimic the language of stories in their writing. • Young children's knowledge of some letters and sounds can help when recording words to go with drawings that tell their stories.
Academic Vocabulary	Kindergarten: • *story* • *events* • *in order* • *sentences* First grade: • *narrative* • *sequenced events* • *details* • *closure/closing* • *beginning* • *middle* • *end/ending* • *characters* Second grade: • *temporal words* • *details that describe thoughts, actions, and feelings* Third grade: • *real or imagined experiences* • *plot* • *climax* • *narrator* • *situation* • *dialogue* • *introduction and transition words*
Real-World Connections	• Everyday people write texts, e-mails, and online postings that tell the stories of their lives and what they do, think, and believe. • Many people enjoy reading stories written by authors. These stories are written in a multitude of genres, such as historical fiction, mystery, folktales, fantasy, drama, humorous fiction, and narrative nonfiction. Some of your students may grow up to become novelists or journalists!
Example Test Questions	"Write a clearly developed narrative about a time that you had an adventure."

Team Planning Tool: Writing Narratives—Second Grade	
Standard We're Teaching	Second grade: Write narratives in which they recount a well-elaborated event or short sequence of events; include details to describe actions, thoughts, and feelings; use temporal words to signal event order; and provide a sense of closure.
Academic Vocabulary We'll Use and Expect to Hear	• *narrative/story* • *folktale or fairy tale* • *sequenced events* • *details* • *beginning, middle, ending* • *characters* • *temporal words* • *details that describe thoughts, actions, and feelings*
Whole-Group Ideas	• Read aloud multiple versions of familiar folktales or fairy tales, explaining that these stories are based on life events. Then model how to write your own version of one of these tales (sometimes referred to as "fractured folktales"). For example, you might write *The Three Little Chickens and the Big, Bad Fox.* • Make anchor charts on narrative writing and story structure (see photos).
Partner Practice at Literacy Work Stations	**Writing station:** Continue to write fractured folktales or fairy tales from writing workshop. Post samples of narrative writing and anchor charts here for students to use as resources. **Drama station:** Have students read and act out one another's fractured folktales or fairy tales here.

Lessons That Last: Whole-Group Mini-Lesson Plan for Writing Narratives—Second Grade

Fractured Folktales

Focus: write narratives (fractured folktales or fairy tales)

Method to Maximize Student Engagement: use familiar folktales or fairy tales students choose as models for writing; partner writing

Materials: chart paper and markers; graphic organizer and anchor charts; simple puppets to accompany folktales read aloud (such as *The Three Bears*, *The Three Little Pigs*, *Cinderella*, *The Little Red Hen*)

Model: how to write a fractured folktale or fairy tale using a beginning, middle, and ending and events sequenced in order

Prompting for Independence:

• "A narrative or story includes a beginning, middle, and ending."
• "Start your narrative with words that introduce it, such as *One day*, *Once upon a time*, and so on."
• "Introduce your characters and setting in the beginning, and use details to describe thoughts, actions, and feelings."
• "Include events told in sequential order that let the reader know what happens first, next, and so on."
• "Use temporal or time-order words, such as *next*, *then*, *later*, and *finally* to let the reader know the order in which events happened in your story."
• "Use a strong ending to let the reader know how the story finishes."

Chapter 8

Lessons That Last: Whole-Group Mini-Lesson Plan for Writing Narratives—Second Grade *(continued)*

Mini-Lesson Procedure:

1. Read aloud a familiar folktale or fairy tale that students might like to write their own version of. For example, stories like *Cinderella, The Three Little Pigs,* and *The Little Red Hen* have many retold versions that can be used as examples. Have students pay attention to the characters and setting as you read aloud. Use a graphic organizer, such as the one in the photo below, to jot down ideas for your own story.

1. Model how to write the beginning to your own fractured folktale or fairy tale, thinking aloud about the words you're choosing as you write. For example, "I'll begin with *Once upon a time,* because that tells the reader it's a folktale or fairy tale. I'll include the names of my characters and the setting to let the reader know who is in my story and when and where it takes place."

2. Have students work with a partner to write the beginning to a fractured folktale or fairy tale. Give them a graphic organizer to help plan their writing (see photo below left).

3. On another day, model how to write the middle of your fractured folktale or fairy tale. Model how to use temporal words to show the order of events in your story as you add them. Then give partners time to work on theirs, too. Confer with students as they write, helping them add details. (You might do this for several days.)

4. Finally, model how to write the ending of your story. Use mentor texts as models while you write this important part. Then have partners work together to finish their stories. Have them share their stories with each other.

5. Publish students' stories and place them in the classroom library for their classmates to read and enjoy. You might place some in the drama station with finger puppets, so students can reread and reenact these stories.

On-the-Spot Assessment: Do students have a sense of beginning, middle, and end as they write together? Are they able to add details in order and use temporal words to signal event changes? Are they adding details to show how characters think, act, and feel?

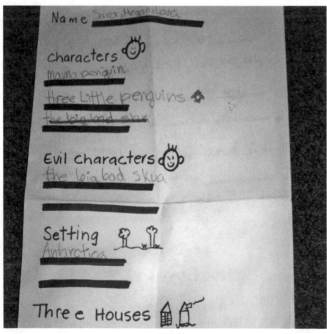

One group's plans for writing a fractured folktale in second grade are shown on a graphic organizer. They'd read many versions of *The Three Little Pigs* before planning and worked on this writing during writing workshop. Some kids also chose to work on these pieces at the writing station.

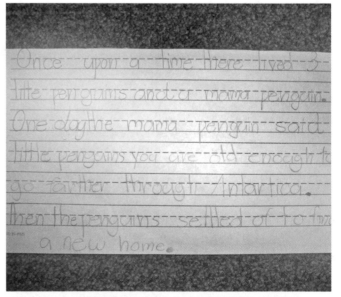

The first page of one group's fractured folktale reads, "Once upon a time there lived three little penguins and a mama penguin. One day the mama penguin said little penguins you are old enough to go farther through Antarctica. Then the penguins settled off to find a new home."

Connections to Whole-Group Mini-Lesson

Independent Reading Connection: Have students read folktales or fairy tales as part of their independent reading while they are writing in this genre. Remind them to pay attention to the details and temporal words the authors use. They might mark some of these with tape flags to refer to as they write.

Small-Group Connection: Have students read and pay attention to how writers craft narrative stories through details, time-order words, beginnings, middles, and end parts. You might also meet with a small group that needs support in writing their narratives.

Whole-Group Reading Connection: As you read aloud narratives, point out techniques writers use to help students see that the story is just beginning, that a new event is occurring, or that a character thinks/acts/feels a certain way. Point out details that enhance the setting or action. Help children read like writers and then try some of these same techniques in their own writing.

Evaluation: Use a rubric like the one in Figure 8.4 to evaluate student writing of narratives. Ask children to use this rubric, too, to self-evaluate.

Figure 8.4 **Rubric for Writing Narratives**

Student: _____ Date: _____	Yes	No	Somewhat
Title names the story clearly			
Begins the narrative by introducing characters and setting			
Includes well-sequenced event or series of events			
Uses temporal or time-order words to signal sequence of events			
Includes details that show how characters think, act, or feel in the story			
Sense of closure at the end			

Mentor Texts for Modeling:
Writing Narratives

- *Rocket Writes a Story* by Tad Hills
- *Ralph Writes a Story* by Abby Hanlon
- *Arthur Writes a Story* by Marc Brown
- *The Best Story* by Eileen Spinelli
- *Library Mouse* by Daniel Kirk
- *Little Red Writing* by Joan Holub

For fractured folktales and fairy tales:

- *The Three Little Pigs* by James Marshall
- *The Three Little Javelinas* by Susan Lowell
- *The Three Little Wolves and the Big Bad Pig* by Eugene Trivizas
- *Ninja Red Riding Hood* by Corey Rosen Schwarz
- *The Other Side of a Story* by Nancy Loewen
- *Goldilocks and the Three Hares* by Heidi Petach
- *Jim and the Beanstalk* by Raymond Briggs

Teaching Tips for Writing Narratives Across the Grades	
In Pre-K and Kindergarten	• Do repeated read-alouds of stories over time, so students learn the language of stories. • Give young children many opportunities to *tell* their stories. Write them down. Enlist the help of other adults for student dictation, if possible. • Encourage children to draw to tell their stories. If they learn to add details in drawing, eventually they will learn to add details in writing, too. • Encourage students to write more than simple "I like ____." sentences. They are capable of so much more! Model how to use the language of story, have kids tell their stories, and then have them draw and write them.
In Grades One–Two	• Children's written stories will become more story-like as they gain more facility with writing and hear more stories. • Continue to give children opportunities to *tell* stories before they write them down. You might use a "storytelling chair" where one child tells a story (or part of a story) to the class before writing. This same chair can be used as the "author's chair" where a student shares writing from that day with the class at the end of writing workshop. • Help students write and then read their writing. Teach them this pattern that writers use! • Model how to add details and use temporal words to more fully develop the writing of narratives in these grade levels. With permission, use students' writing as models for the class, and help kids add details that readers would like to know more about.
In Grades Three and Up	• At these levels, we see the introduction of imaginative writing of stories (not just writing about their own lives). Be brave, and model writing your own imaginative stories in front of your class. • Ask your students to help you make up characters and settings, and write class stories together in whole group. Have fun playing with events and adding dialogue, details, and so on. • Focus on word choice, especially transition words that help to connect events. • Help students continue to use picture books as mentor texts, especially to study how authors craft story beginnings and endings. • Beware of using only story prompts with children at these grade levels. Although state test writing is usually of the "prompt variety," giving students many experiences to write their own stories will help them grow as writers (not just test-takers).

Sample Anchor Charts for Writing Narratives

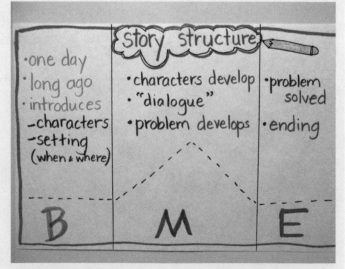

Here's an anchor chart focused on how to write a personal narrative. It could be displayed along with writing samples of personal narratives at your writing station.

This story structure anchor chart is built over time with second or third graders to help them develop characters, settings, and events as they write stories with well-organized beginnings, middles, and endings.

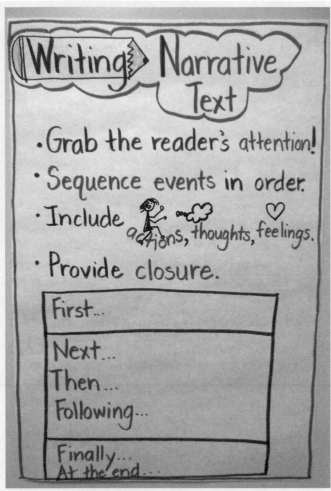

This "Writing a Narrative" anchor chart includes academic vocabulary kids need when both reading and writing narratives.

Literacy Work Stations for Writing Narratives

Providing photos can help students get started writing their own stories. Photos offer more support than story starters printed on cards. Children can tell a story to their partner about the photo first and then write. Change the photos periodically. Take pictures of your students or have them bring in their own from home.

Young children can write books telling about their lives. A kindergarten student wrote and illustrated an "I Am book" at the writing station. These pages read," I am nice. I am good." Encourage young writers to use high-frequency words when writing stories about themselves (for example, "I like . . ."; "My mom . . ."; "One day . . ."; "One night . . .").

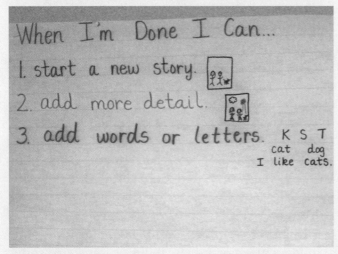

An anchor chart made over time reminds kids of what they can do if they think they're finished with a piece of writing.

A young writer uses little stuffed animals for inspiration in writing her own story using these characters at the writing station. She acts out the story and then writes it. Change the stuffed animals periodically or use finger puppets.

Partners in this intermediate class write an add-to story. One pair of children starts the narrative, and other pairs add to the story as they come to the writing station. Letting kids write on large chart paper with different kinds of markers keeps interest high.

Use mentor texts in writing workshop, and allow kids to write their own versions of stories with favorite characters at the writing station. The first page of this child's *Tacky the Penguin* story begins with "Sun on the iceberg." He experimented with literary language because he'd been exposed to many, many stories through read-aloud at school and at home. We provided a date stamp and had kids stamp the book cover each day they continued on this piece. Simply getting to stamp their cover encouraged kids to continue working on a book beyond a day or two.

Focusing on Conventions of Writing

"Why don't my kindergarten students use spaces? How can I help kids remember to use capital letters and periods? What about spelling?" are questions teachers of primary children often ask. I believe that the first step in writing for young children is to help them get their ideas on paper. From there, we can focus on writing conventions.

Think about all that's involved when a youngster writes. First, he must think of an idea (which is why teachers often tell kids what to write about). Then he must think about which words he'll use. Next, he must figure out which letters make the sounds that represent those words, remember how to form those letters, write the letters in the order he hears (or remembers seeing) them, and remember what he wanted to say in the first place! Throw in having to use capital letters at the beginning of sentences and for names, as well as end punctuation along with spaces and neat handwriting, and some kids are on total overload.

If we can help children get their ideas on paper and *then* work on writing conventions, we may see better writing in the long run. As I learned from Ralph Fletcher (2001, 2007) many years ago, one way to do this is to plan for a balance of writing mini-lessons on writing craft (how to get words on the paper) and writing conventions (how to spell words, capitalize, and so on). Writing conventions are for the reader, so having a sense of audience is critical. As you write in front of your students, think aloud about your readers. Show that you're putting periods at the ends of sentences to show readers where to stop, so they can better understand what you're writing. For example, "I'll write, 'Last weekend Chloe learned how to go down a sliding board.' Chloe is my granddaughter's name, so I'll use a capital *C* to show my readers that this is a name. Also I'm putting a period at the end of the sentence, so my readers will know to stop there."

I've found it helpful to focus on just one or two conventions at a time when I'm teaching writing conventions in a mini-lesson. Marcia Freeman (2013) recommends helping kids "hit the target" for these conventions after you've modeled. I often post a target with a strip telling what I expect kids to do as they write that day. Then I walk around the room during independent writing time and put a small dot sticker on places in children's writing where they've used that convention correctly and "hit the target." During Sharing Time after students write, I ask several kids to share their writing and show how they hit the target for that writing convention that day. Moving the same target to the writing station can help students focus on continuing to try to use that convention as they write.

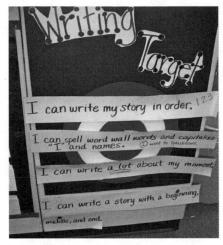

Make a writing target and post it in or near your writing station as a reminder to children of specific conventions you want them to practice using when writing.

Sifting Through the Standard: Focusing on Conventions of Writing	
What It Is	• Capitalization, punctuation, spelling, handwriting, and spacing make up writing conventions. • Sometimes the acronym CUPS (capitalization, usage, punctuation, spelling) is used to remind students to use conventions, especially in intermediate grades.
Why It's Important	Writing conventions are for the reader. They clarify meaning for the person reading a text. If words are spelled conventionally, standard language is used, and handwriting is legible, it's easier to read a message. Punctuation helps readers know where the writer wants them to stop.
Student Prerequisites	• Children must see and understand the importance of writing conventions in order to apply them. • A sense of audience is critical to caring enough to use writing conventions. • Young children must understand word boundaries to use spaces between words. They must know the difference between upper- and lowercase letters to capitalize. • Kids should be able to identify punctuation marks and their purposes before using them in their writing.
Academic Vocabulary	Kindergarten: • *capital letters* • *capitalize* • *first word in a sentence* • *uppercase letter* • *lowercase letter* • *spelling* • *sounds, letters* • *punctuation* • *end of sentence* • *first name, last name*

Sifting Through the Standard: Focusing on Conventions of Writing *(continued)*

Academic Vocabulary	First grade: • *date* • *comma* • *words in a series* • *spaces* • *spelling pattern* • *period, question mark, exclamation mark* Second grade: • *holidays* • *product names* • *proper noun* • *titles and initials in names* • *geographical terms* • *greeting of letter, salutation* • *closing of letter* • *apostrophe* • *contraction* • *possessive* • *reference material* • *dictionary* • *margin* • *declarative, interrogative, exclamatory sentences* Third grade: • *title* • *address* • *historical period* • *company name* • *coordinating adjectives* • *quotation marks* • *dialogue* • *direct speech* • *suffix* • *base word* • *cursive*
Real-World Connections	• In the real world, writing conventions matter! Without standard conventions, messages may be misunderstood and the writer may be perceived as uneducated or incapable of working at higher levels. • Judgment of one's ability is often based on the outward signs of one's spelling, handwriting, usage, and punctuation (or lack of it).
Example Test Questions	• "Which word in this sentence is *not* spelled correctly?" • "Which sentence has no punctuation errors?" • "Which words in this sentence should be capitalized and why?"

Chapter 8

Team Planning Tool: Focusing on Conventions of Writing—Second Grade

Standards We're Teaching	**Second grade:** The student will recognize and use punctuation marks, including ending punctuation in sentences, apostrophes and contractions, and apostrophes and possessives; use commas in greetings and closings of letters, dates, and to separate items in a series.
Academic Vocabulary We'll Use and Expect to Hear	• *punctuation marks (comma, apostrophe)* • *ending punctuation (period, question mark, exclamation mark)* • *greeting and closing of a letter* • *items in a series* • *contraction* • *possessive*
Whole-Group Ideas	• Read aloud familiar stories as mentor texts to show how authors use punctuation marks to communicate messages clearly. (*Punctuation Takes a Vacation* is a great book to use as an introduction.) • Create punctuation anchor charts to help kids understand *how* authors use punctuation. Model writing to show how to use a particular type of punctuation and place an example on a "target." Ask kids to "hit the target" in their writing, and place a small colored dot on a place where they did that when they write independently. • Use sentence strips to build sentences with your class and have kids add cards with punctuation to the sentences in a pocket chart.
Partner Practice at Literacy Work Stations	**Writing station:** Students may continue to write pieces from writing workshop here, paying attention to their punctuation usage. Post a target here with the punctuation they are expected to use. Students may also work together to read one another's writing, stopping at punctuation. The writer listens to see whether the message, as punctuated, is what he or she intended. Partners work together to fix punctuation to reflect the author's message. Using colored pencils for editing one's work makes this task more appealing. Students might also add small cohesive colored dots to their partner's paper to show where that child "hit the punctuation target." **Punctuation station:** Provide written messages that lack punctuation on sentence strips in a pocket chart. (Kids can make these, too.) Have physical punctuation marks available that students can add to the sentences. Make apostrophes and commas by gluing single pieces of elbow macaroni to small pieces of sentence strip. Use foam die cuts of periods, question marks, and exclamation marks, too. Have students place these physical punctuation marks at appropriate places on the sentence strips and then practice reading the sentences as punctuated. **Big Book station:** Partners spin a spinner to identify a particular punctuation mark (period, question mark, exclamation mark, comma, apostrophe). Then they work together to use highlighter tape to mark that kind of punctuation throughout the Big Book. Finally, they read the Big Book together, paying special attention to that mark of punctuation. For follow-up with their own writing, children may then reread a piece of writing they've done, highlighting that same mark of punctuation and reading it to be sure they've used it correctly.

Chapter 8

Lessons That Last: Whole-Group Mini-Lesson Plan for Focusing on Conventions of Writing—Second Grade

Hit the Target with Punctuation

Focus: using end punctuation to create clear messages in writing (Note: This lesson focuses on end punctuation and will need to be repeated multiple times. Teach similar lessons for other forms of punctuation—apostrophes, commas, and so on.)

Method to Maximize Student Engagement: physical punctuation models for students to manipulate; interesting text in which the author has used a variety of punctuation marks; student choice of topics for writing; "hit the target" dots

Materials: mentor texts for read-aloud; chart paper, markers, physical punctuation models, target and small, colored adhesive dots; anchor chart on punctuation made with the class

Model: how to use punctuation while writing (end punctuation)

Prompting for Independence:

- "Listen to where your voice stops."
- "End punctuation tells the reader where to stop."
- "Punctuation tells the reader how our writing should sound."
- "Punctuation adds rhythm and voice to our writing."
- "How do you want to say that? With excitement? Use an exclamation mark. As a question? Use a question mark."

Mini-Lesson Procedure:

1. Read aloud a mentor text, such as *Yo? Yes!* and show students how the author intentionally used punctuation to tell us how to sound when we read. Point out that writers use a variety of end punctuation to create meaning and give voice and rhythm to their writing. Use an anchor chart created with students to discuss the purpose of various end punctuation marks.

2. Next have students work with partners to buddy-read familiar text and *read like a writer*. Ask kids to think about why the author used those end punctuation marks and if a variety of punctuation was used. Have them think about the rhythm of the piece, too, and how it sounds.

3. Bring the class back to the carpet and have several students share how end punctuation marks helped them as readers. They might show a few samples they liked.

4. Then on a magnetic dry erase board, write together several sentences about things your class has been studying. You might write about a topic from science or social studies. (Try to include a variety of sentences to show how to add voice and rhythm to your writing.) As you write in front of the class, don't use any end punctuation or capital letters to show sentence beginnings. The children will probably quickly stop you! Have them explain where and why end punctuation (and accompanying capitalization) needs to go. Provide physical punctuation marks (die-cut them from foam and add magnetic tape to the back) and have kids place them on top of your writing. Show them how to edit
for capital letters, too.

5. Use a target and tell kids you want them to "hit the target" for end punctuation as they write today. Add the words *end punctuation* to the target. Give students the option of writing a new piece or rereading and checking an old piece of their writing. Tell them to especially pay attention to end punctuation. Remind them to think about how they want the writing to sound when someone reads it.

6. While students write independently, circulate among them and affix small, colored adhesive dots to a few places in their writing where they "hit the target" for end punctuation. You might read those spots aloud and ask the child if that's the way he or she wanted it to sound.

7. At the end of writing workshop, ask several students to share their writing and show how they used end punctuation to create meaning and add voice to their pieces.

On-the-Spot Assessment: Did the children use end punctuation to signal sentence boundaries? Did they use a variety of end punctuation to create voice?

Connections to Whole-Group Mini-Lesson

Independent Reading Connection: Remind students to pay attention to end punctuation as they read on their own. (This will help with reading fluency, too.) Have them read like a writer and examine how authors use a variety of end punctuation to create voice and rhythm in their writing.

Small-Group Connection: You might meet with a small group who needs extra support on using end punctuation. Using the writing of one child at a time, have the group read the piece as it is punctuated. Ask the writer if that's how he or she intended it to sound. Have the group help that student add end punctuation as needed. Take turns using different children's writing.

Reading Connection: In guided-reading groups, remind students to pay attention to end punctuation as they read to help them sound like the writer intended. This can aid reading fluency. Tell them to move their eyes quickly across the page to the end punctuation to sound more interesting.

Evaluation: Create and use a rubric with your class for editing for end punctuation. See Figure 8.5 for a sample.

Figure 8.5 **Sample Rubric for Editing for End Punctuation**

Student: _____Date: _____	Yes	No	Somewhat
Uses end punctuation correctly to show where sentences end			
Uses variety of end punctuation to create rhythm and voice			
Capitalizes the first word in a sentence			

Mentor Texts for Modeling:
Conventions of Writing

Punctuation:
- *Yo? Yes!* by Chris Raschka
- *Punctuation Station* by Brian Cleary
- *Moo!* by David LaRochelle
- *Hurry! Hurry!* by Eve Bunting
- *Punctuation Takes a Vacation* by Robin Pulver
- If You Were a Period . . . series by Nicholas Healy
- *Exclamation Mark* by Amy Krouse Rosenthal

Capitalization:
- *The Case of the Incapacitated Capitals* by Robin Pulver
- *If You Were a Capital Letter* by Trisha Speed Shaskan

Spelling:
- *Where's My T-R-U-C-K* by Karen Beaumont
- *Word Wizard* by Cathryn Falwell
- *Silent Letters Loud and Clear* by Robin Pulver
- *Take Away the A* by Michael Escoffier
- *E-mergency* by Ezra Fields Meyer

Teaching Tips for Focusing on Conventions of Writing Across the Grades	
In Pre-K and Kindergarten	• Insist that children answer and speak in complete sentences. If they can't speak in sentences, they'll never be able to write sentences! Help them by having them repeat information in a sentence if they need support. • Show students how writers use punctuation at the end of sentences to show how it should sound. Model how to use end punctuation, and expect students to experiment with it. • Don't be surprised if young children put a period at the end of each line as they write. This is often what the little books they're reading look like! Show them how to place the punctuation to show the reader where to stop. Use cut-up sentences and play with putting a period in different places to see how it sounds. • Help children learn and apply letter-sound knowledge to "spell" words as they write. Set them up for success by accepting what they *can* write. Standard spelling will come as students develop and are taught how to spell in first grade and above. • Work on letter formation (as opposed to handwriting on the lines) with young children. Teach them how to form letters from left to right and from top to bottom. They should use big muscles first (standing at an easel or large board to practice or writing in the air with a finger) and then move to small muscles by writing on paper. • Spacing between words is difficult for many beginning writers. If they don't have one-to-one print matching of words (or counting objects), they will not understand the need for spaces. By the end of kindergarten when children read at DRA Level 3 or Fountas and Pinnell Level C, they should be expected to use spaces in their writing.
In Grades One–Two	• Expect children in these grade levels to correctly spell high-frequency words you've been teaching with on your word wall. When most of the children can spell the word correctly in their writing, remove the word from the wall to make room for other words. • Teach children to use a yellow crayon or yellow pencil to circle words they're unsure of spelling. After they write, they can return to those words and use a beginning picture dictionary to spell them. • Children are expected to learn a wide range of punctuation and capitalization at these grade levels. Take it slowly. Model, model, model by writing in front of your students and showing them how to use different kinds of punctuation and capitalization. • Use mentor texts and help children look carefully at how authors use punctuation and capitalization. Create anchor charts with your class, and include examples from text for children to use as visual references. • Be sure students have real audiences for their writing (beyond you as the teacher). Having a sense of purpose and audience can help writers pay attention to writing conventions. • Give students opportunities to compose using technology as well as writing on paper. Those with improving keyboarding skills may write with more ease on a tablet or computer.
In Grades Three and Up	• If a strong foundation for writing conventions hasn't been built by the time children reach upper grades, look back at what should be done in earlier grades and start there. Meet kids where they are. • Expect students to speak and write in sentences. • Have kids use a colored pencil for circling words they're unsure of spelling and for editing for punctuation and capitalization. • Create anchor charts with your class with clear examples from books you've read together that show how writers use various types of punctuation or capitalization. Don't put too much on each chart. See samples from the following section. • As a class, create and use rubrics for your expectations for writing conventions. • Again, a sense of audience is critical for students in upper grades. If children know someone other than the teacher is reading their writing, they may pay more attention to writing conventions. Harness the power of the peer through peer editing and writing to and for each other! • With permission, use student writing as models for editing for writing conventions. Teach children how to pay close attention to how they've used spelling, punctuation, capitalization, and handwriting for the purpose of communicating with others. • At these grade levels, many children will be able to compose more readily with technology. This may help some students with writing conventions. However, teach them not to rely too heavily on spelling-check and auto editing programs to be correct. They still need to reread their writing before sending it to the appropriate audience.

Sample Anchor Charts for Focusing on Conventions of Writing

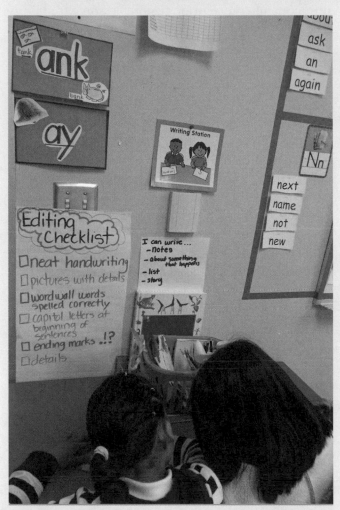

This editing checklist anchor chart is posted at the writing station and is an easy-to-use, meaningful reference for children as they write here.

Punctuation	Look Like?	What it makes your voice do...
Comma	,	pause with a high pitch
Quotation	" "	read like the character might talk
Exclamation	!	Excitement, voice elevates
Question	?	voice elevates, exception waiting for answer
Hyphen	—	pause and the continue
Ellipsis	. . .	drag it out
Parenthesis	( )	Lowering the voice - an aside
Semicolon	;	PAUSE and then continue
Period	.	STOP and take a breath

A punctuation anchor chart was made over time with this intermediate class. The name of the punctuation mark, a sample of what it looks like, and what it makes your voice do are written down as each new punctuation mark is added.

Literacy Work Stations for Focusing on Conventions of Writing

Partners build sentences on sentence strip frames (e.g., *I like _____. _____ likes _____.*) using environmental print, student names, and high-frequency word cards. Then kids add a punctuation card to the end of the sentence and practice reading it the way it's punctuated. Add sentence strips that say *Do you like _____?* and *Does _____ like _____?* and question mark cards. Change sentence frames to include new high-frequency words.

Students build sentences using individual word cards and punctuation cards at this pocket-chart station, too. The teacher can see children's work from her small-group table, so she can monitor students' developing punctuation usage. If she notes errors, she can help these students with this skill during small-group time. Kids might use an iPad to take a photo of their sentences and share them with the class during Sharing Time. This provides a perfect opportunity for helping kids with sentence structure and punctuation.

When We Conference
1. Listen
2. Honest and kind and respectful
3. Tell something we like
4. Make a helpful suggestion.

The anchor chart for how to confer was made with first graders, and they often used it during writing workshop and at the writing station.

Doing Research

What is research? The literal translation of this word is to "search again." That sums it up pretty simply! Research is more than just writing a report. When we research, we ask questions we're curious about, seek out valid resources, and search to find the best answers. By consulting a variety of sources, including people, print, and technology, our knowledge base deepens. As a result, we then can share or apply what we've learned in some way.

Research has traditionally been reserved for springtime in many primary classrooms, possibly because research seems to take a long time to do! Depending on how research is approached, it can be a lengthy process, leaving time for students to do only one research project a year. However, given the depth and complexity of what children are required to learn in today's world, I believe we should devote more time to helping children learn to *think and act as researchers* as part of our day-to-day learning. Project-based learning is one approach for engaging young children in research that is meaningful to them. As described by Lilian Katz and Sylvia Chard (1989, 2014) project-based learning is "an in-depth investigation of a topic worthy of investigation in the students' immediate environment." Nell Duke (2014) says that the times are ripe for project-based learning to engage students fully in reading and writing informational text.

Whether or not you use project-based learning, consider your current stance toward primary children doing research and ask yourself these questions: "What opportunities exist for my students to research throughout the school year? What might my children be interested in learning about? What resources could we explore together to help my kids find answers to their own questions, deepen their knowledge bases, and expand their vocabulary? How can we conduct interviews, read books and online texts to find information we need, and share what we learned?"

When I taught first grade, my class, filled with children reading below grade level, was most excited about learning when we were seeking answers to questions they had come up with. One day during a particularly unsuccessful whole-group reading lesson, I found my students focused not on my instruction but instead on a spider that had spun itself down from the ceiling to the carpet where we'd gathered. "Ooh, look at it. It's a spider!" one child exclaimed, distracting the entire class. I tried to get them back on track, but the spider just dangled in front of our eyes. I must admit it was mesmerizing.

I abandoned the lesson for a few minutes and focused on my children. My struggling students' eyes lighted up as they began asking questions. "I wonder what kind of spider it is. Does it bite? What's that thing it's hanging from?" In that moment, I decided that we would continue to read and write, but we'd read and write about spiders. I asked the children what letter we'd need to look under to find information about spiders, and they responded, *"S!"*

Off to the library we went. We found the nonfiction section and checked out a bunch of books about spiders. As time presented itself over the next few days, I found ways to read these books aloud, teach what I needed to, and help students find the answers to their questions. We created displays of what we were learning about spiders in the form of labeled diagrams, wrote pages for our own books about spiders, and observed spiders in their natural habitat around the school, including a giant orb weaver nestled in a bush by the parking lot outside our door.

My most poignant memory is of Christopher, a child reading at one of the lowest levels in my class, who was reading (the pictures, not the words) on his own and exclaimed, "Ms. Diller, Ms. Diller, I found it!" When I went to him, he pointed to a photograph of a spider and painstakingly read the caption under it, sound by sound. "It's a *drrr-aaag-llli-n,*" he said. "That thing the spider was hanging from. I found it in this picture!" Sure enough, I hadn't been able to find the term used to describe the thread a spider hangs from, but this child had done it independently. We added the word *dragline* to a label on our class diagram of a spider. Christopher was a researcher!

	Sifting Through the Standard: Doing Research

What It Is	• To research is to gather information to answer a question or to investigate a topic in depth.
	• As researchers we ask a question, seek an answer from multiple sources, and present the answer.
	• Research may involve any of the following:
	  • conducting interviews in person or on the phone
	  • writing letters, texts, or e-mails to experts for information
	  • reading and viewing information online
	  • reading print books and articles

Why It's Important	• Human beings are naturally curious. When we learn how to actively search for answers to our questions, we continue to grow and learn. • Researching helps students deepen their understanding of topics and terminology valued by a discipline, especially in science and social studies. It expands our view of how the world works.
Student Prerequisites	• Children will need to understand what a question is (it asks and doesn't tell). • Understanding what the word *topic* means will be helpful when conducting research. • Knowing how to read and write informational texts will support children's research work. • Keyboarding skills will assist in being able to locate information online. • Children will need to know how to extract information from visuals as well as print.
Academic Vocabulary	Kindergarten: • *question* • *explore* • *topic* • *information* • *sources* • *favorite authors* • *opinion* • *research* • *record* First grade: • *relevant* • *interview* • *experts* • *text features (table of contents, index, and so on)* • *locate information* • *notes, charts, diagrams* • *visual display* • *dramatization* • *results* • *presentation* Second grade: • *observations* • *organize* • *summarize*

Academic Vocabulary	Third grade:
	• *conduct research projects*
	• *build knowledge*
	• *print sources*
	• *digital sources*
	• *multiple sources*
	• *data*
	• *online sources*
	• *reference texts*
	• *sort evidence*
	• *categories*
	• *narrow a topic*
	• *formulate questions*
	• *generate a research plan*
	• *surveys*
	• *encyclopedia*
	• *skim and scan*
	• *author, title, publisher, publication year*
	• *paraphrase in your own words*
	• *plagiarism*
	• *valid and reliable sources*
	• *draw conclusions*
	• *written explanations*
Real-World Connections	• Research is done in many places, such as schools and universities; communities; hospitals; oceans, forests, and other outdoor environments; and even in outer space.
	• Most career fields, including technology, medicine, design and construction, teaching, engineering, writing, and entertainment (to name a few), require workers to conduct or use research.
	• The skills used in research are valuable in many areas of life. For example, narrowing our focus on a topic can be applied to focusing our attention on something we need to get done. Interviewing skills can be used to help us be more comfortable with talking to new people we meet. Research requires organizing information, and being organized is a huge life skill.
Example Test Questions	• "The following paragraph is an excerpt from a student's report about _____. After reading the paragraph, you will identify details that are unnecessary and explain why they should be removed."
	• "In the space below, identify the sentences from the paragraph that are unnecessary, and briefly explain why each one should be removed."

Team Planning Tool: Doing Research—Kindergarten–Grade One

Standard We're Teaching	**First grade:** Students (with adult assistance) are expected to gather evidence from available sources (natural and personal) as well as from interviews with local experts.
Academic Vocabulary We'll Use and Expect to Hear	• *question*
	• *research*
	• *gather evidence*
	• *sources*
	• *interview*

Team Planning Tool: Doing Research—Kindergarten–Grade One *(continued)*	
Academic Vocabulary We'll Use and Expect to Hear	• *expert* • *notes, charts, diagrams* • *visual display* • *dramatization* • *results* • *presentation*
Whole-Group Ideas	• Show video interviews of children's book authors, such as the ones with Bill Martin, Jr. (author of *Brown Bear, Brown Bear*), at www.readingrockets.org/books/interviews/martin or Judy Schachner (author of *Skippyjon Jones*) or Jacqueline Woodson (author of books featuring African American families, including *The Other Side*) at www.nbclearn.com/portal/site/learn/writers-speak-to-kids. • Invite into the classroom local experts who can help answer kids' questions about a topic of interest. • Model how to ask questions and how to take notes (use chart paper). • With permission, record interviews so kids can view them again and again. Provide ways to present what was learned.
Partner Practice at Literacy Work Stations	**Observation work station:** Have objects or books around topics of interest to kids (for example, shells, rocks, butterflies). Students record observations and jot down questions on sticky notes about their wonderings. **Research work station:** Partners work together to find answers to the questions generated at the observation station with books and sources provided by the teacher. If they are working on any kind of project-based learning, work toward that can be done here as well. **Interview work station:** Partners view interviews of children's book authors and jot down notes in pictures and/or words about what they learned. They share this information with the class after stations time. They may also interview each other and record their findings at this station. **Writing station:** Students work on writing informational text to report what they found through their research. They might make an "All about ___" book or create a visual display to show what they learned.

Lessons That Last: Whole-Group Mini-Lesson Plan for Doing Research—Kindergarten–Grade One

Interviews and Note Taking (Kindergarten–Grade One)

Focus: learning about interviews—how and why

Method to Maximize Student Engagement: video interviews of favorite children's authors; opportunity to interview each other; visits from local experts about topics of interest to kids; opportunity to doodle and take notes

Materials: video interviews for class to view; clipboards, paper, and pencils; local expert contacted and scheduled to visit or Skype

Model: how to ask questions about a topic of interest to an expert (or each other)

Prompting for Independence:

• "An expert is a person who knows a lot of information about a topic. I know a lot about teaching writing, so I'm an expert at teaching writing. I'm also an expert at knowing a lot about my family."

• "What are you an expert on? What do you know a lot of information about?"

**Lessons That Last: Whole-Group Mini-Lesson Plan
for Doing Research—Kindergarten–Grade One** *(continued)*

- "What information would this expert be able to share with us that nobody else could?"
- "When we interview someone, we ask them questions and write down the answers."
- "Think of a question that will give us the information we need."
- "Let's record what we learned from our source by drawing and/or writing notes."
- "We can present the information we learned from our research."

Mini-Lesson Procedure:

1. Choose a favorite book of your class and ask if students would like to learn about how the author wrote that book. (The interview with Bill Martin, Jr., about *Brown Bear, Brown Bear* is a very good one with which to begin this lesson.) Tell the students that today they're going to learn how to do research and find out answers to questions they may have. Tell them that sometimes we can do *interviews* to do research. Then show your class a video of that author being interviewed. Point out that someone will ask the person a question, and then the person answers. Show the clip so students can see the process.

2. Next, tell the children that when you *interview* someone to do *research*, you take *notes* to *record* what you learned from your *source.* Watch the video again, pausing as needed, and model how to take notes by drawing and/or writing words.

3. Talk about how everyone is an expert on something. We are all *experts* on ourselves, so we could interview each other about who we are and what we like or don't like. Generate a short list of several questions children could ask each other in interviews.

4. On another day, review what research is and the purpose and procedure for interviewing. Then model how to conduct an interview with a child. Ask questions and record what you learn. Use chart paper to do this.

5. Then pair students and have them interview each other. Make a chart of sample questions they might come up with and how they might record what they learn.

6. Finally, as a class, help students think about questions they'd like to research around something of local interest. Arrange for a local expert to visit your classroom, and through shared writing create a list of interview questions for him or her. When the expert visits, help the students use their questions and take notes to maximize their learning. Have kids then share with others what they learned.

On-the-Spot Assessment: Do the children understand what an interview is and its purpose? Which students can generate questions about topics? How are your students doing with recording what they have learned through interviewing?

Connections to Whole-Group Mini-Lesson

Independent Reading Connection: Challenge children to think about interview questions they would ask the authors of books they're reading independently.

Small-Group Connection: You might meet with small groups or pairs of students to help them locate information in print or online resources and record what they learned. Or you may help students with group projects and how to present what they learned.

Whole-Group Reading Connection: Use ideas from the section on reading informational texts from Chapter 6. Think aloud about the research questions the author might have had and how he went about the process of researching to find answers to include in his writing.

Evaluation: Use a rubric created with your students to evaluate how they used interviews to ask questions and gather information about a topic. See Figure 8.6 for a sample rubric.

Figure 8.6 **Sample Rubric for Interviewing and Research**

Student: _____ Date: _____	Yes	No	Somewhat
Demonstrates understanding of how interviews are used in research (to ask questions of an expert and record answers)			
Can develop focused questions around a topic			
Can record answers to questions generated in an interview			
Presents information learned through interviews with others			

Team Planning Tool: Doing Research—Grades Two–Three	
Standard We're Teaching	**Grades Two–Three:** Collect and organize information about the topic into a short report.
Academic Vocabulary We'll Use and Expect to Hear	• *topic* • *collect information* • *skim and scan* • *use text features* • *take notes* • *paraphrase in your own words* • *plagiarize* • *organize information* • *category* • *report*
Whole-Group Ideas	• Generate a question with the class to use for modeling the research process. • Gather books and online resources related to the research question. • Model how to read or view and take notes using sticky notes and a large sheet of construction paper on which to record the question and headings.
Partner Practice at Literacy Work Stations	**Research station:** Have books and technology on hand for kids to use to research topics of interest. (Know their questions ahead of time to help gather resources.) They work together to take notes on sticky notes and organize them. **Writing station:** Kids help each other use their notes to write a short report about the topic they've researched. This can be an extension of writing workshop and can be connected to topics studied in social studies or science.

Lessons That Last: Whole-Group Mini-Lesson Plan for Doing Research—Grades Two–Three

Gathering and Organizing Information (Grades Two–Three)

Focus: gathering and organizing information to answer questions about a research topic (for example, "Why do bees buzz?")

Method to Maximize Student Engagement: using sticky notes and arranging them in categories

Materials: books and online resources about the question (for example, resources about why bees buzz); document camera; sticky notes; 12-by-18-inch construction paper; markers

Model: how to collect and organize information about a topic that will be used to create a short report

Lessons That Last: Whole-Group Mini-Lesson Plan for Doing Research—Grades Two–Three *(continued)*

Prompting for Independence:

- "I'm skimming and scanning this book on [bees] to find information about [why bees buzz]. I'm searching for answers to my question."
- "I'll use the table of contents and index in books to help me find answers to my research question quickly. That way I don't have to read the entire book, which will help me stay focused on my research topic."
- "This information answers my question, but I don't want to plagiarize. So I'm paraphrasing the information; I'm writing it in my own words by jotting down notes."
- "I'll write one bit of information on this sticky note and place it under my original question: ['Why do bees buzz?']. Putting sticky notes together with information about the same question will help me organize my information."
- "This is interesting. The information doesn't exactly answer my question, but it does help me better understand the answer. It's a diagram of [a bee and its body parts]. I think I'll include something like this when I share what I learned. I believe it will help the reader of my research."
- "While I'm doing my research, I'm formulating some new questions. One of my new questions is ['How does a beekeeper do his or her job?']. I'll write this question on a sticky note and put it on the back of my paper. I might do research about that topic later."
- "This is kind of a fun fact. It's related to my research question. I'll include it in a text box as a 'fun fact.' I'm going to make a place in my folder for this and label this section 'Fun Facts.'"
- "I'm going to write the author, title, publisher, and publication year of my source on a sticky note, so I can keep track of where I got my information. I'll write the names of websites I use, too."

Mini-Lesson Procedure:

1. Before this lesson:
   a. Work with students to formulate a question they'd like to research.
   b. Gather several kids' books about the topic to use for modeling how to collect and record information about the question.
   c. Experiment with key words to search online for answers to the question and possibly bookmark helpful websites.
2. Write the class research question at the top of a large piece of construction paper using a dark marker, and tell kids you're doing it to keep focused on your research.
3. Now use a document camera and model how to skim and scan books on your topic to find answers to your question. Think aloud as you look at the table of contents and index pages to locate information quickly. Show students that some books won't have anything helpful in them. This doesn't mean they're bad books; they're just not what you're looking for.
4. When you find information related to your question, stop and read it aloud. Then take a sticky note and model how to take notes using your own words, reiterating that you're doing this so you aren't plagiarizing.
5. Place the sticky notes on the large piece of construction paper; you'll show students how to organize them in a separate mini-lesson (see photo on next page).
6. It will probably take several mini-lessons to model the process. Be sure to also model it with online resources. Model how to keep looking for information in multiple sources, because you often learn even more than you expected.
7. In another mini-lesson, begin to show students how to organize their notes. Fold or divide the large paper into sections (resembling a tree map), and ask them to help you manipulate the sticky notes, placing them in categories that make the most sense. For example, in answering the question "Why do bees buzz?" our categories were *wings, shaking, finding food,* and *angry bees.* We also created a category of "Fun Facts." Finally in another mini-lesson (or several), model how to take these sticky notes and use them to create a research report. Create headings for each group of sticky notes. (See photo on next page.) Show students how to write an introduction and a few sections with information, as well as a concluding statement or section. Add visuals and text features as they write informational text. See the photo for the beginning of our finished research report.

On-the-Spot Assessment: Observe students to see whether they understand why you don't have to read the whole book to find information to answer a research question. Are they able to identify where and how to find information quickly in nonfiction texts? Also, are they able to help you paraphrase information from the sources? Can they manipulate the sticky notes into categories that make sense?

Notes about why bees buzz are written on sticky notes and organized on a large piece of construction paper in categories with headings added. This work was done in whole group with the class using multiple resources.

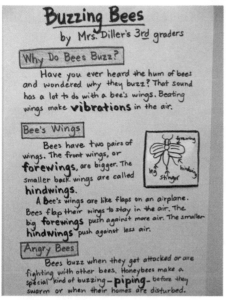

This is an example of modeled writing of a research report done with the class.

Connections to Whole-Group Mini-Lesson

Independent Reading Connection: Give students opportunities to read lots of informational text during independent reading time as they search for answers to their own research questions. Provide sticky notes for them to take notes.

Small-Group Connection: You might meet with small groups or pairs of students who need support to help them skim and scan print materials for information to answer their questions. Or you might meet with them to organize their sticky notes into categories. Finally, some groups may need guidance in using their notes to write about what they learned in a brief report.

Reading Connection: Remind students and keep modeling how to use text features to quickly locate the information you're searching for when researching. Titles, contents, indexes, headings, and visuals such as charts, diagrams, and photos with captions can be very helpful.

Evaluation: Create and use a rubric with your students. See Figure 8.7 for a sample.

Figure 8.7 **Sample Rubric for Collecting and Organizing Information for Research—Grade Three**

Student: _____ Date: _____	Yes	No	Somewhat
Formulates a research question to guide information search			
Uses tables of contents and indexes to efficiently locate information on the topic of the research question			
Takes notes that relate to the research question			
Writes notes in own words without plagiarism			
Organizes notes in categories related to research question			
Uses notes to write brief report or create presentation related to research findings			
Documents sources using title, author, publisher, and publication year for each source, as well as cites websites			

Mentor Texts for Modeling:
Doing Research

Some sources for online video interviews of children's book authors:

- www.readingrockets.org/books/interviews
- www.nbclearn.com/portal/site/learn/writers -speak-to-kids
- www.teachingbooks.net

Collect *text sets* for students to use when conducting research. Be sure the books are on levels where children can read the words and/or the visuals. Ask your school or public librarian for help.

In the above example, the texts I used for modeling included the following:

- *Bees: A Kids' Book About Bees* by Jared Johnson
- *What Do You Know About Bees?* by Carol Miller
- *Bee: A Picture Books for Kids* by Jen Marie Mueller

I also used the following websites when modeling how to do research about bees buzzing:

- www.wonderopolis.org
- www.highlightskids.com
- www.buzzaboutbees.net
- www.whyzz.com

Teaching Tips for Doing Research Across the Grades	
In Pre-K and Kindergarten	• Cultivate a spirit of curiosity in young children. When they wonder aloud about things, write down their questions and talk about where they could find answers. Then help them find that information in books, online, or from experts. • Model how to research all year long! • Integrate field trips and site visits with research. If you're going to the zoo, formulate questions the students would like answered while there. It's a perfect opportunity to do in-person interviews! If you're studying about local food and where it's grown, invite a gardener to your class and interview him or her; then take a visit to that person's garden or farm. Seek grant funding, if necessary. One possible source for donations is www.donorschoose.org. • Integrate author studies with research. Help children explore several titles by an author and express their opinions about them. Use author interviews to teach children more about the writing process (including the fact that interviews are part of research).
In Grades One–Two	• If you start by selecting a research topic for all children, don't limit it just to a particular animal, what it looks like, what it eats, and its habitat. Although this kind of research report may be a starting point for some children, move beyond it over time. • Find out what your kids have questions about. Keep a Wonderings board where you and your class can post things they wonder about. Here are a few things kids recently inquired about in primary classrooms: "Are there more trees like pine trees that don't lose their leaves?" "Why is the ocean salty but rivers aren't?" "How did last names start? "Why weren't women allowed to vote long ago?" "How do they make crayons?" Use these questions for research. • Use search engines geared for kids and their research (such as askkids.com, kidrex.org, about.com, yahooligans.com, and sweetsearch.com). • Bring in experts whenever possible and teach kids how to interview them. Call on people you know, including school personnel and family members.

Teaching Tips for Doing Research Across the Grades *(continued)*	
In Grades Three and Up	• Don't focus just on animals for research topics. Help students formulate questions, especially related to what they're learning about in social studies, science, and health, or community events. • Research skills take time and practice to develop. Model, model, model, especially how to take notes and organize them! Think aloud every step of the way. • Share your own research processes with your class. For example, if you're buying a new car, share how you've read reviews of cars, talked to others about their vehicles, visited car lots, done online searches, and so on. Let students know that people do research all the time. • Present a variety of ways for students to share what they learn, including reports, posters, dramatizations, videos, trailers, PowerPoint presentations, brochures, and so on. • Think aloud about what makes a source reliable and valid. Especially when searching for online resources, point out what to look for. For example, "There is no publisher shown for this book even though it's being sold online. *Highlights for Kids*, NBC, and *Time for Kids* have been in business for a long time; they are reliable sources."

Sample Anchor Charts for Doing Research

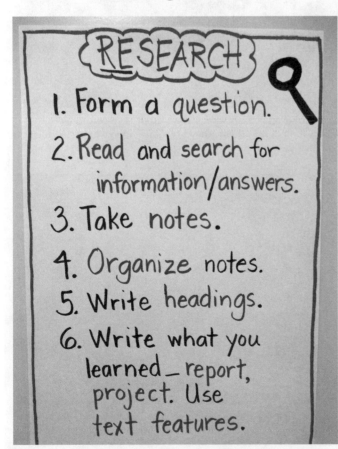

An anchor chart on research for third grade lists steps to take. Start with just the first step and teach kids how to formulate good questions. Then add the next step to the chart, and so on. This chart was made over many lessons throughout the year.

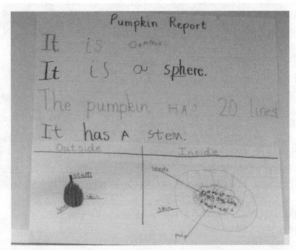

This kindergarten report serves as an anchor chart for early research writing. It was composed with the students using interactive writing (shared pen) and is based on their observations of a pumpkin in the fall. Informational text features of labels, a drawing, and a diagram are included. This chart was placed at the observation station for kids to use as reference.

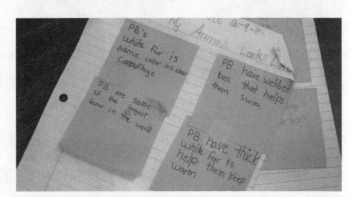

Second graders learn to do research with sticky notes. Here's a sample the teacher did with the class.

Literacy Work Stations for Doing Research

First graders read informational text and take simple notes at this nonfiction station. The emphasis here is on note taking, not report writing. Topics studied and the books provided are changed during the school year.

Second graders take notes as they read informational text in the classroom library. This is part of the research they do in their classroom.

Kindergartners use magnifying glasses to examine fall leaves at this observation station. An "I Can" list made with the class reminds kids of what they can do here. Things kids observe change throughout the year.

This "I Can" list is used at a second-grade observation station. Objects to observe are coordinated with topics of study. Or students bring in items to observe, including personal collections (with parent permission).

At a third-grade observation station, students record their observations about shells. They use informational books, including field guides. Students create their own field guides over time.

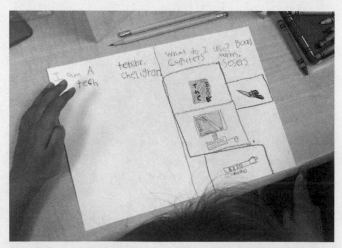

A pair of first graders works together to make a page for a question-and-answer book at this writing station. They use a guided-reading book as a model. On the left side, they write, *I am a teacher. I teach children.* On the right side, they write, *What do I use? Books, computers, markers, scissors.* Add other question-and-answer books, and have kids write a question as a heading on each page and answer it with information in the text.

Students use a tree map for note taking at this research station. They also write short reports using this information. Ongoing practice should take place all year long.

A pair of intermediate students does online research using iPads. They work together to read and take notes. This work continues throughout the year. Students need many opportunities to read informational text and take notes online.

Digging Deeper

Now that you've considered many options for both writing instruction and writing work stations, take a look at what you and your colleagues can do to set up stations for writing and/or tweak existing ones. Here are some things to ponder and discuss as you do so:

1. Do you have a writing station in your classroom? What does it look like and what do students do there? Where is it placed? Why? Reflect on these questions with your team. Visit one another's rooms to get ideas of how to set up stations for writing.

2. As you visit one another's classrooms, also consider the following: Are models and samples of writing posted for students to use as reference at the writing station? (A wall, a bulletin board, cabinet doors, or a trifold board works well for display purposes.) Where did those models come from? What supports are provided? Can you tell what's expected (without asking the teacher)? Is the work student generated? Look at anchor charts throughout this chapter. Which of them will you use as models for what you're teaching in writing?

3. Examine your state standards for writing instruction. What have you modeled well? How are you connecting writing standards to what students are doing at stations? Work with colleagues to use the team planning tool from this chapter to plan writing instruction and related partner practice at writing stations.

4. Have you moved what you've been teaching students to do as writers during writing workshop into writing stations? Or have you given kids story starters and told them to write? For the highest quality of writing and greatest transfer, think about what you've been modeling and what you expect your students to do as writers. Post clear expectations for writing at the writing station. Allow students to continue writing pieces from writing workshop at the writing station.

5. I'm often asked if students should write at *every* station. I believe that writing should be included as part of a station if it helps to deepen students' understanding. Which stations in your classroom invite kids to write to help them think more deeply? Are there any stations where you've had kids write to "prove" they did something there? Reflect on these questions with a colleague. Be intentional about the writing students do in your classroom, especially while they are at work stations.

6. In your classroom, do you spend more time helping students craft their writing ideas or working on writing conventions? Strive to have a balance, since writers need both. Which ideas from this chapter will you use for modeling *how* to write (opinions, informational text, or narratives)?

Chapter 8

How will you move that work to writing stations? Which ideas from this chapter will you incorporate to help students with writing conventions?

7. How do you incorporate research in your classroom? Start by looking at the research standards for your state. Use ideas from this chapter to plan ways to help children think like researchers all year long. Share successes and struggles related to research work with your colleagues. Help each other increase research opportunities in reading *and* writing on a regular basis.

8. Scan this chapter to find ideas on how to help your students *read like writers* and *write for readers*. Plan ways to incorporate one or two of these ideas into your instruction and eventually into a writing-related station. Share with colleagues what you tried and artifacts from work you and your students did as a result.

9. What is the quality of the writing your students are doing at writing-related stations? What can you and your students do to help them improve their writing? (For example, ask whoever worked at the writing station to share what they wrote with the class as part of Sharing Time at the end of stations time; model, model, model whatever you expect students to be doing as writers; be sure you have clear expectations generated *with* the class posted.) Try some of these techniques and share the results with your colleagues.

9

Literacy Work Stations for Speaking, Listening, and Language

Standards Covered in This Chapter	Lessons Described in This Chapter
Speaking to Describe Things or Tell Stories	Let's Talk
Listening to Texts and Following Spoken Directions	Listen Closely Listening Games
Using Correct Grammar and Parts of Speech	Looking for Verbs
Expanding Vocabulary	Vocabulary Card Retelling

Oral language is the foundation of all reading and writing children will do. It is defined as the system through which we use spoken words to express knowledge, ideas, and feelings. In 1970, British educator James Britton made the profound statement, "Talk is the sea upon which all else floats" (164), which is often paraphrased as "Reading and writing float on a sea of talk." His theories on language and literacy shaped the progressive teaching of writing to young children in school.

Speaking, listening, and language must be fostered from early childhood through adolescence. Although one important component of oral language is vocabulary development, children must also learn how to pro-

nounce words, how to combine them to sound grammatically correct, and how to speak according to their situation (for example, at home versus at school). These are often sources of difficulty for students learning English as a second language, hindering their literacy development (August and Shanahan 2006).

Children who leave kindergarten and first grade able to say, "I *predict* that the *topic* of this *nonfiction* book is dinosaurs" or "The *character* feels *shy*, because she is new to this school" or "My mom *forbids* me to stay up late. I have to get *plenty* of sleep" are children who will most likely become strong readers and writers. Through listening and speaking, they have learned the vocabulary and language structures they'll need while mapping sounds to decode and make meaning of text. Likewise, because writing is *talk written down,* these children will probably write more engaging, interesting pieces. Most likely, these are also the students who will succeed on standardized tests in grades three and above.

As an educator for almost forty years, I have often seen the power of oral language to transform a struggling reader or writer into a successful one. Alex was a second grader who had difficulty decoding words. Although he'd been taught phonics rules, he had difficulty applying them. The first time I asked Alex to read a book to me, he told me he couldn't read it because he hadn't heard it read aloud. If he'd heard a book, he'd remember the gist of the story so that when he read it on his own and came to unfamiliar words, he'd use beginning sounds and think about what made sense. Fortunately, this child had strong oral language skills, including a well-developed vocabulary.

Over time, I taught Alex strategies for solving unfamiliar words. It was especially helpful for him to use chunks of words and blend those *in sequence* to make a word that *made sense.* When he used his strengths of vocabulary and language, coupled with a few tools for decoding, he began to read a variety of stories and informational texts with increasing independence. Oral language was a crucial piece; it enabled this child to make meaning.

Similarly, I've met students with strong oral language skills who struggle with spelling but take risks as writers to get their messages on paper. Their confidence in speaking pushes them forward to record their ideas, even with unconventional spelling. For example, Jessica, a first grader, wrote the following journal entry:

I got a godn snak for my buth day. It is green. I have kreks to fed it.

She described her birthday gift as a green "garter snake" and said she has "crickets to feed it." She could have used simple words to write, "I got a snake. It is green. I like it." But because this child had strong oral language, she used more advanced vocabulary and complex sentence structure in her writing. A few days later, Jessica continued to take risks as a writer in this entry: "Yestrday my dad stat kolg. Wen did you go to kolg? He kam home lat last nite. He brot some books home thet didt hav pekchs." Even though she struggled with standard spelling of these more advanced

words (*started, college, late, brought, pictures*), Jessica used them because this is how she spoke. Her language gave her confidence as a writer.

Oral language development begins at birth as humans are surrounded by voices. Babies as young as six weeks old coo and play with sounds. Between twelve and eighteen months of age, toddlers begin naming objects and people using single words, like *mama, dada, juice, shoes.* As they approach age two, they start to string words together to make meaning—*Tea hot. More cookie. Go bye-bye.* By the time they enter kindergarten, children are able to converse in more complex sentences to communicate with others.

I constantly name things in my toddler granddaughter's environment and encourage Chloe to repeat what I say, even if it's an approximation. When she points to her puppies and says, "Og," I say, "Yes, those are dogs. Chloe has two dogs, Meat and Toby. Let's count your dogs. One, two." I also sometimes hear her jibber-jabbing away with vocalizations that sound much like sentences in their intonation. She is playing with language that will eventually become words and sentence strings. I listen to her in wonder and remember that learning to talk requires time, exposure, and practice.

Our children need the same things at school—to be surrounded with language, bathed in rich vocabulary, and given opportunities to use words and sentence structures they've heard. It's our job as teachers to accept students' approximations and scaffold them as they attempt to use new vocabulary and speak in more complex sentences in Standard English.

One way to do this is by expecting children to speak in sentences (with support, as needed) during whole- and small-group instruction. Yes, it's quicker and easier to accept one- or two-word responses, but a stronger foundation is built when children become accustomed to speaking in sentences. For example, when I recently asked kindergartners about things the boy liked in the little book *Things I Like* by Isabella Rivas (2009), they responded with one- or two-word answers: *Pizza. Some water. Grapes. Flowers.* When I asked them to give me a sentence (and provided scaffolding), the children spoke using more complex language, such as "The boy liked bread" and "He likes flowers, so they put some on the table." When a student said, "He gots some water," I said, "Yes. He got some water. At school we say, 'He *got* some water.'" I then gave the child a minute to repeat this "school" way of talking.

As children progress from kindergarten through third grade, it is important to create structure that provides norms that encourage students to talk about what they're learning. Sentence frames, such as the "conversation cards" I've included in this book, help students develop *accountable talk,* which Michaels, O'Conner, Hall, and Resnick (2002) have found helps students move beyond completing tasks to developing conceptual understanding—a much deeper learning goal. Accountable talk helps students learn to ask for and furnish evidence to support their thinking as they read, write, and talk together.

We need to give students as many opportunities as possible to speak so that they will develop oral and academic vocabulary. A silent classroom isn't necessarily an effective, well-run classroom. One of the reasons I believe literacy work stations are so important and successful is that children are allowed and expected to talk with partners during this independent learning time. In this chapter, we'll take a look at ways children might develop speaking, listening, and language at stations.

Speaking to Describe Things or Tell Stories

When looking at the literacy needs of students, especially in the early grades, I recommend that teachers examine children's oral language development along with reading and writing. For those students who need more practice in building oral language, try setting up a "Let's talk" station. This will give them opportunities to practice talking with each other in sentences to expand their language and vocabulary.

I first got the idea for this station while working in schools with a high concentration of low-income students in Denver. Because there were many ELL students who needed oral language development, the schools had purchased a program from Mondo called "Let's Talk About It," which included flip charts of large photos related to science and social studies. These charts were used in whole- or small-group instruction to stimulate conversations with children about what they saw in the pictures. For example, when students examined a photo of a girl exploring flowers in a spring garden, with teacher prompting they said things like, "The girl is in a garden. She's looking at pink flowers. I think the flowers smell sweet." They also added handwritten labels to the photo using sticky notes, and they often wrote about the picture, too.

After the flip charts and sticky notes were used during instruction, they were recycled into a "Let's talk" station for partners to use independent of the teacher. The familiar photos and vocabulary labels provided appropriate prompts for children's talk. At this station, children could talk about, label, or write about the photos.

Even without the Mondo oral language kit, you can do similar work with children in whole- or small-group settings. Use photos you already have and provide prompts to help kids speak in sentences. Make a "Five Senses" anchor chart, as pictured below, and prompt kids by asking them to tell what they see or might hear, smell, taste, or feel if they were in the picture. Use sticky notes to create vocabulary labels for items in the photos. Kids will enjoy manipulating the labels (which provide scaffolds for speech).

You might borrow fine-art prints from a local art teacher or download them from online art museums. Real objects, especially related to science and social studies topics (such as rocks and minerals; maps and globes) can also be used to promote conversation. During a study of butterflies, we used a wordless photo book picturing all kinds of specimens. The possibilities are endless. Move the materials you've been teaching with into a "Let's talk" station, and ask your students for ideas of things they'd like to talk about, too.

To add an extra dimension to "Let's talk," add a recording device, such as an iPad or a digital voice recorder. Children record themselves talking and then play it back to listen to their language. Listening to themselves speak gives students valuable feedback and motivates them to talk. I found that when kids get to record themselves, they are really excited about producing even more oral language.

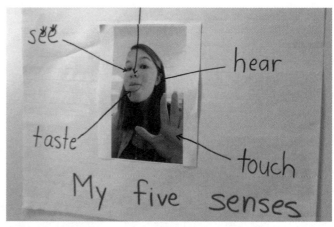

Make a "Five Senses" chart with kids to use during whole- and small-group lessons. Also provide a small copy for them to use at the "Let's talk" station.

Sifting Through the Standard: Speaking to Describe Things or Tell Stories	
What It Is	Speaking is an important part of oral language development. We speak to give information, to express ideas or feelings, and to ask questions. Talk can take the form of discussions, conversations, or oral reports. The word *talk* originates from the German for "tale" and "tell."
Why It's Important	• Kids love to talk! Whenever we can harness that talk for learning, time will be used more efficiently in the classroom. • Children who can express ideas and stories cohesively when speaking usually read and write in similar ways. • Children who verbally use more mature speech (in both words and sentence structure) typically read and write at higher levels than students with less developed oral language.
Student Prerequisites	• Listening is a prerequisite to speaking. It is important to hear advanced vocabulary spoken in order to learn to speak those same words. This helps with pronunciation and syntax as well as comprehension. • It is helpful for native Spanish speakers to understand cognates, or word derivatives. For example, if a Spanish-speaking child uses the word *inevitable* in Spanish, a connection can be made to that same word (with a different pronunciation) in English.
Academic Vocabulary	Kindergarten: • *describe* • *people* • *places* • *things* • *events* • *details* • *text* • *topic* • *use a complete sentence* First grade: • *ideas* • *feeling* • *information* • *tell stories* • *retell stories* • *in order* • *conversation* • *sensory details* Second grade: • *facts* • *descriptive details* • *clarify* • *conversation* • *coherent sentences* Third grade: • *report* • *understandable rate* • *eye contact* • *enunciation* • *volume* • *visual media* • *organize ideas chronologically* • *clear and concise*

Sifting Through the Standard: Speaking to Describe Things or Tell Stories *(continued)*	
Real-World Connections	• In everyday situations, speaking clearly to communicate is an important life skill. People who can express themselves well typically are more successful in relationships both at work and at home. • Speaking effectively is an important leadership skill.
Example Test Questions	• Although speaking is usually not formally tested, it does affect how children score on tests of reading comprehension, writing, and vocabulary. • A study by Justice, Mashburn, and Petscher (2013) found that poor comprehenders in fifth grade (that is, those with poor reading comprehension despite good decoding abilities) had evidenced weak language skills as early as fifteen months of age compared with their age-matched peers who went on to become good comprehenders and poor decoders. • The NELP report (2008) found that early language skills were predictive of later reading comprehension development but much less predictive of early decoding skills.

Team Planning Protocol: Speaking to Describe Things or Tell Stories—First Grade	
Standard We're Teaching	**First grade:** Speaking audibly and using appropriate language, recite poems, rhymes, songs, and stories, with careful attention to sensory detail when describing people, places, things, and events.
Academic Vocabulary We'll Use and Expect to Hear	• *describe* • *people* • *places* • *things* • *events* • *sensory details* • *use a complete sentence*
Whole-Group Ideas	• Model how to describe people, places, things, and events using sensory details (provide objects, fine-art prints, and photos for kids to describe). • Make lists of words on anchor charts that describe using the five senses. • Read and recite poetry together.
Partner Practice at Literacy Work Stations	**"Let's talk" station:** Kids work with partners to orally describe familiar objects, photos, or fine-art prints. They can record their voices on an iPad or other recording device and then listen to themselves. **Poetry station:** Students read familiar poems together and practice trying to recite them from memory. **Writing station:** Children write poems of their own using sensory details. They don't have to rhyme but should use language that tells what the writer sees, hears, smells, tastes, or feels (as in touch) when observing an object, people, or an event.

Lessons That Last: Whole-Group Mini-Lesson Plan for Speaking to Describe Things or Tell Stories—First Grade

Let's Talk

Focus: speaking in complete sentences; using sensory details to describe people, places, things, and events

Method to Maximize Student Engagement: use of an interesting object, photo, or fine-art print to describe; anchor chart made with students, including sensory details; cube to toss with a word and matching picture label on each side: "people," "place," "thing," "event," "action," "idea"; opportunity to record speech and listen back via iPad or other media

Model: how to describe people, places, things, and events using details related to our five senses while speaking in sentences

Prompting for Independence:

- "Describe the _____ using sensory details about what you see, hear, touch, taste, or smell."
- "Tell us more. What else do you notice? What else could be happening?"
- "Use a sentence. I'll help you get started. 'I think you could hear . . .'"

Mini-Lesson Procedure:

1. Show the class an interesting object, a photo, or a fine-art print of something they could describe using sensory details. For example, you might display a colorful pumpkin in the fall or a bouquet of spring flowers. You might use a photograph of something your class enjoyed doing together, such as going on a field trip or taking a walk around the school. Or you might borrow a fine-art print from a local art teacher or museum (or simply use an image in the public domain found online). For this lesson, I'm using Georges Seurat's painting *A Sunday Afternoon on the Island of La Grande Jatte.*

2. Tell children they'll take turns describing or telling about what they see (and hear, smell, taste, feel). You might make an anchor chart with the five senses on it (as pictured on page 241) and encourage kids to look at the painting/object/photo and tell what they see or might hear, smell, taste, and feel (if they touched it).

3. You might also use a cube with the sides labeled "people," "place," "thing," "event," "action," and "idea." Take turns tossing the cube and having children describe what they touched. For example, if they touch the word *people,* they might say, "There are many people in the painting. I see lots of families, and they're dressed up like on Sunday. I hear many people talking in soft voices and just relaxing." Keep going around the room inviting others to add comments to the first one. "There are people of all ages—moms and dads and children. The women are wearing long skirts, so I think this is long ago." "Almost everyone is wearing hats, not like today." Or if they touched *event,* they might say, "Maybe it's a holiday in the summer. Lots of people have umbrellas to protect themselves from the sun, which is probably hot. There are smells of hot dogs cooking at a stand away from the water. Maybe they'll have fireworks when the sun goes down."

4. You could also use sticky notes to record specific vocabulary you'd like students to use when working with these photos or objects. Use advanced vocabulary (for example, *relaxing, finest apparel, protect, stand*). Have students manipulate the notes to label the items, and use those words when speaking.

5. Record the language of your class by using a recording device, such as an iPad. Then play it back for all children to hear. Have students point to the part of the body they're using when they sense something said. For example, when they hear, "I smell . . . ," they point to their noses.

On-the-Spot Assessment: Are students able to describe using sensory language? Are they speaking in complete sentences? Which students need scaffolds to speak in sentences or to extend their ideas?

Connections to Whole-Group Mini-Lesson

Independent Reading Connection: Invite young children who can't read all the words in their books to tell the story using the pictures. Have them describe what they see and experience in the illustrations, using sensory details. For students who need encouragement, you might provide an iPad for recording and playing back.

Small-Group Connection: Do this same activity with children who need additional support in small group. Use objects, photos, or fine-art prints and toss the cube, much as you did in whole group, or use wordless picture books as included in the "Mentor Texts" section. With a smaller group, children have more opportunities to speak. Record and play back their language. Use the "Five Senses" anchor chart, too, to encourage sensory language.

Writing Connection: During writing workshop, model and give kids opportunities to write about the same objects, photos, and art prints they have talked about. Then move these and related objects, photos, and prints children have talked about into the writing station. After students have described them orally, it will be easier for them to write about them. Likewise, model how to add labels or sentences to the wordless picture books you have used in small group. Students might use these books at the writing station and add labels and sentences to pages using sticky notes.

Evaluation: Use a rubric, such as the ones in Figures 9.1 and 9.2, to evaluate how students' speaking is improving. Teach children how to self-evaluate as they listen to recordings of themselves, too.

Figure 9.1 **Sample Rubric for Speaking to Describe Things or Tell Stories (for Teachers)**

Student: _____ Date: _____	Yes	No	Sometimes
Verbally describes people, places, things, events, and actions that appropriately match objects, photos, prints, and pictures			
Includes sensory details while describing verbally			
Uses increasingly complex vocabulary in verbal descriptions			
Oral sentence structure is becoming more complex when describing			
Speaks clearly and audibly while describing			
Speaks in complete sentences			

Figure 9.2 **Sample Rubric for Speaking to Describe Things or Tell Stories (for Students)**

Student: _____ Date: _____	Yes	No	Sometimes
I describe people, places, things, events, and actions.			
I describe what I see, hear, smell, taste, and touch.			
I use big words.			
I speak so others can hear and understand.			
I speak in complete sentences.			

A small group works on oral language by using a cube (pictured on page 249) to prompt student talk.

Mentor Texts for Modeling: Speaking to Describe Things or Tell Stories

Use wordless picture books, such as the following:

- *The Snowman* by Raymond Briggs
- *Chalk* by Bill Thomson
- *Pancakes for Breakfast* by Tomie dePaola
- *The Farmer and the Clown* by Marla Frazee
- *Journey* by Aaron Becker
- *Hunters of the Great Forest* by Dennis Nolan
- *Flashlight* by Lizi Boyd
- *Hank Finds an Egg* by Rebecca Dudley
- *The Girl and the Bicycle* by Mark Pett

- *Unspoken* by Henry Cole
- *Draw!* by Raul Colon

Use fine-art prints, such as the following:

- *A Sunday on La Grande Jatte* by Georges Seurat, 1884
- *Starry Night* by Vincent van Gogh, 1889
- *The Great Wave Off Kanagawa* by Katsushika Hokusai, 1829–32
- *American Gothic* by Grant Wood, 1930
- *Ram's Head White Hollyhock and Little Hills* by Georgia O'Keeffe, 1935
- *Self-Portrait with Monkey* by Frida Kahlo, 1938
- *The Apartment* by Jacob Lawrence, 1943

Teaching Tips for Speaking to Describe Things or Tell Stories Across the Grades

In Pre-K and Kindergarten	• Young children need many opportunities to talk to peers and adults. • When reading aloud, be sure to stop and give kids the chance to turn and talk to a partner about what you've read. This encourages active listening and improves speaking as well as comprehension. Then ask several students to tell what they talked about with their peer. • Young children often call out to make comments or ask questions during read-aloud. Teach students to raise their hands and take turns, but don't discourage them from asking questions.
In Grades One–Two	• Students in grades one and two need lots of chances to talk, too. A silent classroom is not one where active learning is occurring. • Literacy work stations give children the opportunity to talk with one another about what they're doing and learning. Be sure partners are working *together* and not just sitting side by side doing work. Their collaboration invites conversation. • Provide an iPad or digital recording device at the "Let's talk" station, to increase students' motivation to speak and to provide accountability.

Teaching Tips for Speaking to Describe Things or Tell Stories Across the Grades (continued)	
In Grades Three and Up	• Big kids like to talk, too! Just because they're older doesn't mean their oral language has fully developed. • Continue to provide objects, photos, prints, and topics for students to describe and discuss. Connect the objects to content-area learning to develop language that will help students as they read and write. Teach them to use accountable talk by asking one another to support their ideas with evidence. Accountable talk charts are good visual reminders to help develop deeper thinking and language. • Continue to provide recording devices at talking stations. Older students also enjoy recording themselves and listening to their language. • At these levels, kids should expand their talk to orally reporting on topics. You might include a news-reporting station where students practice orally summarizing current events and presenting the news items to the class.

Sample Anchor Charts for Sensory Language for Speaking

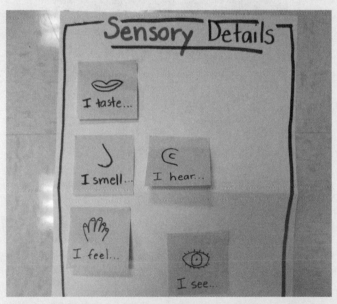

This simple anchor chart is an interactive one. Sticky notes with the five senses can be removed and used on text.

This anchor chart with reminders for speaking clearly and audibly was made with intermediate students.

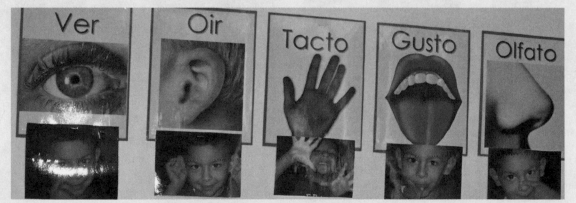

Another anchor chart for using the five senses to observe and describe people, places, events, or objects uses student photos and can be personalized for your class. This one was developed in a bilingual classroom.

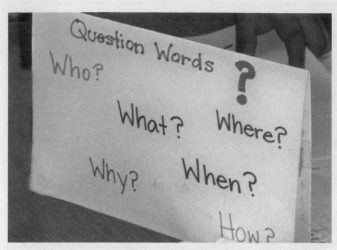

Tent-folded tabletop charts on groups of student desks help kids with accountable talk for questioning. The other side of the chart includes a small version of the anchor chart shown to the left.

The "I Can" list reminds kids what to do at another "Let's talk" station. They can label the photo, talk about the picture, or make up a story about it.

Literacy Work Stations for Speaking

Partners take turns talking about the large photos. They take a clothespin (with a red or green colored dot on it) each time they speak. This encourages equal turn-taking. One child takes red; the other green. The "I Can" list helps them remember their choices at this station. Change photos students work with over time. Use photos of familiar places and activities around the school or from field trips your class has taken. You can also borrow fine-art prints from your art teacher or a local art museum.

At this "Let's talk" station, partners use a wordless book of photos to talk about butterflies, a science topic of study. They record themselves on an iPad and then listen to the recording.

An Easi-mic can also be used for young children to record and then play back their talk.

Kids use a prompting cube with a fine-art print for oral descriptions. It can be labeled "people," "places," "things," "actions," "color," and "size." A similar cube could have parts of speech ("names/nouns," "actions/verbs," "describing words/adjectives") on it for older students. The cube can be tossed to prompt children's talk at oral language stations. Each face has a word/picture cue to remind kids what to discuss: people, places, actions, things, size, color.

An 8½-by-11-inch photo of the forest is masked by a piece of plain paper the same size but folded in fourths. One quarter has been cut out to make a viewing space. Kids work together, observing and describing one-fourth of the photo at a time. They fold another piece of white paper in fourths and use it to write their observations.

At an observation (or science) station, partners use hand lenses to observe natural objects such as shells, rocks, and leaves, and then talk with each other about what they notice. The five senses cards remind them to observe using sight, sound, touch, smell, and taste. Kids love wearing lab coats, too! Children can also read related science books or write about what they observe here. Over time, change out observation objects so they correspond to science topics of study for your grade level. You might add a recording device—such as an iPad—to record student conversations, too.

Students use an app for speaking (Tell About This) on the iPad. They click on a photo, which reads them a prompt, such as "Describe your favorite farm animal," and then record themselves talking. They can play back their recording. This can be used before kids write at the writing station or at the iPad station for speaking. Puppet Pals and Chatter Kids are great apps for this, too.

Listening to Texts and Following Spoken Directions

The majority of standards within the Common Core Speaking and Listening strand focus on speaking. But there are several references specific to listening (for example, listening to others and taking turns speaking about the topics and texts under discussion, gaining the floor in respectful ways, and listening to texts read aloud or to information presented orally or through other media). Other states have separate listening standards that add following oral directions to those mentioned above.

Many adults (and kids) are better at speaking than listening. Watch people having conversations. Are they listening to each other or waiting for their turn to speak? How do you feel when you are interrupted by an adult or a student? Children can benefit from being taught how to listen carefully—to each other and to texts read aloud. It's a life skill worth spending time on!

Likewise, it's difficult for many students (and adults) to follow spoken directions, especially those that include several steps. Recently, I had an opportunity to figure out why this is such an important skill. I was traveling alone in an unfamiliar city at night and went to a movie. Alas, my cell phone died during the film, and I didn't have a charger or GPS in the car. Panic descended on me as I realized I'd have to ask someone how to get to my hotel and then try to *remember* those oral directions.

I listened very carefully to the parking attendant who gave me directions. Then I followed the advice I'd

recently given a teacher whose kids were struggling to follow multistep oral directions: repeat the steps, one at a time, while visualizing the steps in order, and this will help you remember what to do. Fortunately, it worked! And it reinforced for me how important it is as we rely more and more on technology and automation to teach students how to listen effectively.

Because of the importance of listening both at school and in life, I've included two different kinds of listening work to do with students in this section: listening for information and listening to follow directions. Please examine your specific state standards and adapt the following ideas to meet the needs of your students.

Sifting Through the Standard: Listening to Texts and Following Spoken Directions

What It Is	• Lundsteen (1979) considered *hearing* a physical act and *listening* a mental act.
	• To listen is to give attention to things we hear. Listening is an active process in which we take notice of and act on what others say.
	• As we listen, we choose to respond to advice or a request.
	• When we listen, it's important to make meaning from what's being said before we respond.
	• State standards include several components of listening:
	1. listening to others and taking turns
	2. listening to texts and information presented orally or through other media
	3. listening to step-by-step directions
Why It's Important	• People have a basic human need to be heard and understood.
	• Listening has been estimated to make up as much as 55 percent of oral communication.
	• Listening well affects our job effectiveness as well as the quality of our relationships with others.
	• Listening comprehension precedes reading comprehension. If a child has difficulty making inferences when text is read aloud, that student will most likely have trouble inferring while reading as well.
Student Prerequisites	• In order to listen, students must be able to hear. Auditory acuity and processing is important.
	• Although it may not be a prerequisite, removing auditory distractions (for example, background music, the roar of a classroom air-conditioning unit) can help students listen more carefully.
Academic Vocabulary	Kindergarten: • *conversation* • *rules for discussion* • *take turns* • *listen to others* • *listen attentively* • *speak about the topic being discussed* • *clarify understanding* • *follow directions* • *sequence* • *in order* • *two-step directions*

Sifting Through the Standard: Listening to Texts and Following Spoken Directions *(continued)*

Academic Vocabulary	**First grade:** • *speak one at a time* • *build on others' talk* • *clear up confusion* • *clarify information* • *restate directions* • *give instructions* • *sequence of events* **Second grade:** • *gaining the floor* • *respectful* • *linking comments* • *further explanation* • *three-step directions* • *four-step directions* • *multistep directions* **Third grade:** • *make eye contact* • *face the speaker* • *stay on topic* • *elaborate* • *series of related sequences*
Real-World Connections	• Listening is required at school, at home, and in the workplace. • Listening is needed to learn a language. Young children listen before and as they learn to speak. • Three of Stephen Covey's *7 Habits of Highly Effective People* (1989) relate to communication and listening, including Habit 5, "Seek first to understand, then to be understood."
Example Test Questions	Some standardized tests, such as the Iowa Test of Basic Skills, have a listening component in kindergarten through grade two. Students listen to short scenarios followed by comprehension questions, all presented orally. They must follow directions and think analytically.

Team Planning Tool: Listening to Texts and Information Presented—Third Grade

Standard We're Teaching	**Third grade:** Determine the main ideas and supporting details of a text read aloud or information presented in diverse media and formats, including visually, quantitatively, and orally.
Academic Vocabulary We'll Use and Expect to Hear	• *determine main idea and supporting details* • *view and listen to information presented in multimedia* • *conversation* • *elaborate* • *ask for clarification*

Team Planning Tool: Listening to Texts and Information Presented—Third Grade (continued)

Whole-Group Ideas	• Read aloud informational texts or show short videos related to what you're studying in science and social studies. • Model how to do close viewing of a video (or close listening to a text). Show the video several times and have kids use clipboards and paper to take notes. Do the same with multiple read-alouds of a text. Set a different purpose for listening or viewing each time (for example, pay attention to the illustrations, or the use of text features, or the use of music).
Partner Practice at Literacy Work Stations	**Listening station:** Students listen to a recorded nonfiction book. They might listen to it two times for different purposes, taking notes each time on a clipboard or recording sheet. Then they have a conversation about what they learned, taking turns and elaborating on their ideas each time they listen. As they listen, provide text-dependent questions to have them cue into: • First listen—the gist of what it's about (main idea and key details) • Second listen—craft and structure (repeated words; who the author is) or knowledge and ideas (find evidence that the author . . .) **Viewing station:** Have partners view preselected videos (related to science and social studies), watching and listening to them several times. Provide text-dependent questions to guide their viewing and conversations. **Writing station:** Students might write about what they learned from viewing or listening at the above stations. They could also share this information with classmates in a community journal (a spiral notebook that the whole class shares) that others could add to.

Lessons That Last: Whole-Group Mini-Lesson Plan for Listening to Texts and Information Presented—Third Grade

Listen Closely

Focus: how to listen to texts or speakers or videos

Method to Maximize Student Engagement: interesting books, audio recordings or podcasts, videos, or live speakers to share that have information related to topics being studied in content areas and/or of interest to students

Model: how to listen carefully to information being presented and take notes to answer text-dependent questions or to clarify understanding; how to think more deeply while listening or viewing closely (by examining text through various lenses, such as the words, illustrations, music, and so on)

Prompting for Independence:

• "Listen carefully to the gist of what the author/speaker is telling us. What is the main idea? What are the key details?"
• "Pay attention to repeated words the author/speaker uses. What do these words tell us about the message the author/speaker is communicating?"
• "Think about how the speaker/author organized the information."
• "Ask yourself (or each other) questions. What did you understand? What was confusing? Listen again and talk with each other to answer those questions."
• "When listening, listen to how the reader/speaker used her voice to tell important parts."
• "When viewing, notice the illustrations or images that were used. Why do you think the illustrator/videographer included them? What did you learn from the illustrations or images?"
• "When viewing, listen to any music used. Describe the music. Why do you think the videographer used that music?"

**Lessons That Last: Whole-Group Mini-Lesson
Plan for Listening to Texts and Information Presented—Third Grade** *(continued)*

Mini-Lesson Procedure:

1. Choose the text, audio, video, or speaker carefully. Select something *short,* so students will be able to focus and take something of *depth* from this experience. Be sure the material is at least on grade level or a bit above and will *add to* students' knowledge of topics. (I used an online video about dinosaurs from the American Museum of Natural History at www.amnh.org.)

2. Tell the class you will be viewing (or listening to) something you think they'll find interesting. Relate it to something you've been studying. For example, say, "We are learning about types of organisms that lived long ago and about the nature of their environments. When the environment changes, some organisms survive and reproduce or move to other locations, or even die. The video we'll watch today is about dinosaurs and is produced by the American Museum of Natural History." Don't tell them too much about the topic, because you want them to listen and pay close attention to the video.

3. Show them the short video. (The trailer I've used, "Dinosaurs Explained," is a minute and twenty-three seconds in length.) Before they view, ask them to just listen and watch and see if they can figure out the gist of the video. After watching, have students turn and talk to a partner about the key ideas they took from listening. Then have a few students share with the whole class.

4. Now ask them to watch (or listen again). This time have them pay attention to the words being said. Have them listen for repeated words, words they think are important, or words they didn't understand. You might give them clipboards to jot down their thinking and may need to model how to do it. Again, have them talk with partners and then share with the group.

5. Finally, have them watch (or listen) one more time and pay attention to the music (or the illustrations). Ask, "How would you describe the music? Why do you think the videographer used this music?" Be sure to let them talk with partners and share with the class.

6. After they've viewed (or listened) several times, have them answer text-dependent questions about the information. Then have them summarize what they learned.

On-the-Spot Assessment: Were students able to pay attention to the particular aspects you asked them to tune in to (such as words, music, or illustrations)? What did you notice about their understanding of the topic? Did it deepen with increased opportunities to listen? Did partners take turns speaking and listening to each other?

Connections to Whole-Group Mini-Lesson

Independent Reading Connection: You might have students choose related informational texts to read independently following the above lesson. Ask them to make connections with the information they listened to or viewed. They might engage in reading the information several times to take deeper meaning from it.

Small-Group Connection: For students who need extra support in listening and/or viewing, occasionally teach lessons like the one from whole group with just them. Help them engage in a collaborative conversation with each other about what they learned.

Writing Connection: Model how to take notes while viewing. Create viewing guides, as needed, to help students pay attention to particular things while listening or viewing. (A sample is provided in Figure 9.3.) Kids might also use these notes to summarize what they learned orally and/or in writing.

Evaluation: Use a rubric like the one in Figure 9.4. Take notes in the spaces provided. Don't just check *yes* or *no*.

Chapter 9

Figure 9.3 **Sample Viewing Guide for Video**

_____   _____
(student name)   (video title)

1. Gist: I think a key idea from the video is _____

_____.

2. Words: Important words, repeated words, new words are _____

_____.

3. Illustrations or images: From looking at the images I learned _____

_____.

   I think the videographer included these images to _____

_____.

4. Music: This music sounded _____.

   I think the videographer used this music to _____

_____.

Figure 9.4 **Sample Rubric for Listening to Texts and Information Presented**

	Yes	Somewhat	No
Content: Student listened and determined the main ideas and supporting details of a text read aloud or information viewed.			
Attentiveness: Student faced the speaker, made eye contact, and focused attention.			
Communication: Student stayed on topic and added to the conversation.			
Critical listening: Student got deeper meaning from close viewing or close listening and elaborated on ideas.			

**Team Planning Tool: Listening to and Following
Spoken Directions—Kindergarten**

Note: This lesson can easily be adapted for students in other grade levels by expanding the number of directions given at a time, in order. For example, in first or second grade, use three- or four-step spoken directions, depending on your state's standards and students' needs and skill levels.

Standard We're Teaching	**Kindergarten:** Follow oral directions that involve a short related sequence of actions.
Academic Vocabulary We'll Use and Expect to Hear	• *follow directions* • *in order* • *in sequence*

Team Planning Tool: Listening to and Following Spoken Directions—Kindergarten (continued)	
Whole-Group Ideas	• Play listening games, such as Simon Says. Give children oral directions, one or two steps at a time. For example, "Clap twice, then touch your head" or "Point to your eyes, then touch your toes."
	• Give students materials and then give oral directions for making something simple. Give one or two directions at a time. For example, "Glue a red heart in the middle of your paper." (After students do this, give the next direction/s.) "Now glue a small pink heart onto the red heart. Next, glue the tiny white heart onto the pink heart. Decorate the rest of the paper however you wish."
Partner Practice at Literacy Work Stations	**Listening station:** Students listen to a recording of step-by-step instructions. Give one- or two-step directions at a time. Then pause and give children time to do that before recording the next direction (or two). You can record physical movements for them to follow. Or the directions could be an art-type project. Students could also give their partner directions to follow, step by step.

Lessons That Last: Whole-Group Mini-Lesson Plan for Listening to and Following Spoken Directions—Kindergarten

Listening Games

Focus: listening to follow one- or two-step directions

Method to Maximize Student Engagement: read-aloud books about listening to directions; active movement games, like Simon Says, or giving directions (one or two at a time) to make something

Model: how to actively listen by focusing eyes on the speaker and not talking while directions are being given

Prompting for Independence:

- "Listen carefully. I will give you directions and then you will follow them."
- "Look at the speaker and be ready to listen. I will give you two directions at a time. Think about doing one thing and then the next. Picture what you will do in order. Ready?"

Mini-Lesson Procedure:

1. Gather the class on the carpet and tell them they'll be learning how to listen and follow directions. Read aloud a book about listening, such as *Listen Buddy* by Helen Lester (1997). Discuss the importance of learning to listen. Talk about what it means to listen actively. You might make an anchor chart with students on being a good listener. Remind them to listen with their ears, eyes, and brains.

2. Play a listening game, such as Simon Says. Have the class stand. Start by giving one-step and then two-step directions. Tell them to do the actions only if you say "Simon Says." If they don't follow directions, they'll be out and have to sit down. The object of the game is to follow directions and stay standing.

3. For example give one-step directions such as, "Simon says touch your nose. Simon says rub your belly. Simon says jump two times. Now jump just one time." If students jump when you didn't say "Simon Says," they must sit down.

4. Continue playing the game, varying directions as you go. Be sure to sometimes give two-step directions, such as, "Simon says touch your shoulders and then touch your toes." Other ideas: blink your eyes three times; clap twice; clasp your hands in front of you; shrug your shoulders; touch your elbows; flap your arms like a bird four times; reach for the sky; squat down low; wiggle your nose; make the sound of the letter *b*; march in place one-two-three; bend to the left; raise your right foot.

5. On other days, give one- and two-step directions orally that instruct students to make drawings or build things. For example, give kids paper and crayons. Then give directions such as the following:
   - Draw a big, blue circle in the middle of your paper.
   - Write your name inside the circle. Use a green crayon.
   - Draw stripes inside the circle. Use a yellow crayon.
   - Draw a black string hanging from the bottom of the circle. Pretend this is a balloon and draw someone holding on to it.

On-the-Spot Assessment: Pay attention to who is listening and following one-step directions. Who is following two-step directions?

Connections to Whole-Group Mini-Lesson

Independent Reading Connection: Children who struggle with reading or learning English will benefit from time spent listening to recorded texts. Periodically, you might allow these students to listen to recorded books during independent time. You might record some books about listening such as those in the mentor text list.

Small-Group Connection: Have children who have trouble following directions work on this in small group. Try some of the same types of activities from whole group with children who need support. Review habits of active listening and then work with them to build their attention for directions. Keep the directions simple; try to help kids visualize what they are supposed to do before they attempt to do two-step procedures.

Writing Connection: Teach children how to write simple one- and two-step directions. They can then try to read and follow one another's directions.

Evaluation: Keep a simple checklist noting who can follow one-step or two-step oral directions.

Mentor Texts for Modeling: Listening to Texts and Following Spoken Directions

- *Listen Buddy* by Helen Lester
- *Press Here* by Herve Tullet
- *Tap the Magic Tree* by Christie Matheson
- *Touch the Brightest Star* by Christie Matheson
- *Tap to Play* by Salina Yoon
- *Telephone* by Mac Barnett
- *Pass It On* by Marilyn Sadler

Mentor Videos for Modeling:

- "Dinosaurs Explained" (Trailer), 1:23, from www .amnh.org and found on amnh.tv. 2012. (Series of short videos on dinosaurs and other topics.)
- "The History of Gargoyles," 3:48, from www .watchknowlearn.org (from Meet Me at the Corner Virtual Field Trips).
- "Waterfalls," 2:23, from www.nps.gov/shen/ planyourvisit/waterfalls.htm (information about visiting Shenandoah National Park in Virginia, particularly about waterfalls and safety).
- "Hummingbirds," 2:05, from http://video .nationalgeographic.com/video/hummingbirds (interesting information about this incredible bird).

Note: You might search YouTube videos for clips to share with your students.

Teaching Tips for Listening Across the Grades	
In Pre-K and Kindergarten	• Remind children of the habits of being a good listener during read-aloud time (and throughout the school day).
	• Provide opportunities for children to listen to recorded books at a listening station, too. These can be used for listening comprehension and vocabulary development.
	• Giving a child a microphone, even if it's a toy from a dollar store, can help him project his voice, which, in turn, can help other students to listen.

Teaching Tips for Listening Across the Grades *(continued)*	
In Grades One–Two	• Continue reading aloud to students across the grades daily. Think aloud and ask questions to help students develop strong listening comprehension. This will provide a foundation for their reading comprehension, over time. • Have students listen to stories and informational texts multiple times for different purposes to help them think more deeply about these texts (as part of whole group and at a listening station). • Teach children how to view videos and listen for important ideas and words used.
In Grades Three and Up	• Note taking is an important skill for intermediate students to learn. It will help them be active listeners and pay attention to what's most important. • Using recorded information such as videos and/or inviting speakers to your classroom can set the stage for having real purposes for listening. • Having students work in literature discussion groups also provides authentic opportunities for kids to listen to one another. This is a great place for them to learn to take turns respectfully, how to share the floor, and how to build on others' ideas during discussion.

Sample Anchor Charts for Listening

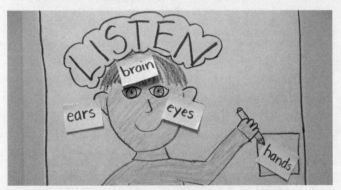

This anchor chart promotes listening closely to read-alouds and media.

This anchor chart focuses on listening to directions.

Literacy Work Stations for Listening

Students listen to recorded directions to make something, such as a Valentine's Day project.

Two kids share a portable listening station by using a splitter for the headsets. They talk about the information after listening, using the prompts at this station.

Kids at this listening station use a listening guide as they listen to informational text. They talk and/or write together after listening.

This listening station takes minimal classroom space. Headphones hang on Command-brand hooks on the wall under a dry erase board. Kids sit on the floor to listen here.

Using Correct Grammar and Parts of Speech

When I visit primary classrooms, I am delighted to see students reading and writing independently. As mentioned in the above sections, I think it's also important to have students engaged in speaking and listening (as well as reading and writing) at work stations, especially children who are second language learners or those who have low oral language skills. But what about grammar? Where does it fit in?

In examining kindergarten through grade two state standards closely, I've noticed that the verb in most of the grammar-related standards is *use*. In third grade, I notice the words *explain the function* added. For example, the Common Core State Standards for first grade say that children should *use* common, proper, and possessive nouns *when writing or speaking*. They should *use* verbs to convey a sense of past, present, and future. Likewise, the Texas Essential Knowledge and Skills (TEKS) standards say that second graders should *use* and *understand* the function of verbs, nouns, and adjectives *in the context of reading, writing, and speaking*. The Virginia Standards of Learning (SOL) for kindergarten say that the student will *use* words to describe/name people, places, and *use* words to describe/name actions. However, I often see kids doing worksheets

and activities where they are *identifying*, not really *using* parts of speech. It's important to focus on teaching ideas that truly help youngsters *use* nouns, verbs, adjectives, and pronouns while speaking and writing.

Grammar begins with oral language. Again, speaking is foundational. How do young children learn Standard English grammar and usage? By listening to others who *use* Standard English and grammar as they speak. Over time, children who *speak* with Standard English grammar are more likely to *write* using the same. Begin by listening carefully to how your students speak in everyday situations at school, and scaffold them in using standard grammar in their speech.

You don't have to correct or embarrass the child, but kindly restate using Standard English what the child has said. For example, when children say things like, "They is going to lunch" or "She done good on that," you'd simply repeat, "Yes. *They are* going to lunch" or "I agree. She *did well* on that." Have children repeat the way you said it and remind them that that's how we say it at school (or in Standard English). Oral language is the foundation. We can't just teach grammar in isolation.

When teaching about parts of speech more formally, introduce students to the idea that we can give names to different types of words to help us *use words* when we're writing. Make anchor charts with your class over time that focus on nouns or verbs or adjectives. Then display the charts side by side on a classroom wall with the label of "Writers Use Different Parts of Speech." (See photos on page 265 in this section.) Refer to the charts while teaching children how to use these special types of words.

We can also look at how authors use different kinds of words to make their writing clear to us as readers. Help children understand why we learn the names of these different kinds of words. Specifically, when we have *language* to name the parts of speech, it's easier to discuss how to improve our writing. For example, you might tell students, "Using a *proper noun* to name your character makes him come to life and helps the reader/listener know exactly whom you're describing." Or "It's important to include a *noun* in every sentence; it helps the listener/reader know *who* or *what* you're talking about."

Likewise, when revising writing, verbs make a piece more vivid. Tell kids, "A stronger *verb* will help the reader visualize the action here. Did the character *say, shout, whisper, or screech* those words?" Or "You've used the same *verb* in every sentence in this section. Let's try another *verb* to show the action. Instead of saying a bee *goes,* we can say a bee *flies, travels,* or *zooms.*"

And "*Adjectives* add details. You can use them to paint a clear picture. Tell about that boy using *adjectives.* Is he *tall, cheerful, silly, athletic,* and/or *shy?* To make this work on parts of speech meaningful, use familiar favorite books that you've read aloud to your class many times. The teaching example below uses nouns, one of the first parts of speech with which we acquaint our students. It's important for them to understand nouns well, since they are foundational to speaking, reading, and writing (because they name people, places, objects, and events).

Here's how I used literature to help students *use* nouns. One of my favorite authors is Kevin Henkes. His books are written with clear language and tell stories kids love. After reading aloud *Old Bear* (2008) to a first-grade class, we returned to it at a later date as a mentor text to examine how writers use different kinds of words. I began by placing the book under a document camera, so kids could see the words and pictures while I reread it. I began the lesson by telling the class (and pointing to our anchor chart on nouns), "Today let's look at how Kevin Henkes uses nouns to write his story. He uses many interesting nouns to name things.

Let's read the title. Whom did he name? Who's the main character? Please use a sentence. Yes, the main character is Old Bear. See how Kevin Henkes names the bear. He doesn't just call the main character *bear.* Why do you think he did that?"

I began reading the book but didn't pause at every noun. (That would destroy the story!) Instead, I selectively asked kids to think about nouns, or people, places, or things that Kevin Henkes included in the illustrations *and* the words. For example, on the first page, this author writes, "By the time Old Bear fell asleep for the winter, it was snowing hard." I had children turn and talk and name any nouns that the author used in the picture and the words. Their responses were, "Kevin Henkes drew Old Bear in the middle of the page and used the words *Old Bear.*" I then asked if they noticed anything about those words, and they said the words had capital letters. We talked about how names of characters are nouns and are capitalized. We added that information to the anchor chart. I told them these are special nouns called *proper nouns.* I simply exposed them to this academic vocabulary. My goal wasn't for them to identify *proper nouns,* but instead was to let them know that these kinds of words are special nouns that should have capital letters.

I continued to read several pages and stopped on the page that said, "He dreamed that spring had come and he was a cub again." Again kids looked at the illustration and the words and noticed that the bear was in the middle of the page again, but this time he wasn't old. He was little. "That's because the bear is the main character, so he's in the middle," one child told the class about the illustration. Another noticed the word *cub.* "Kevin Henkes didn't call the bear a bear this time. Now he used the word *cub.*" This gave us the opportunity to see how the author uses different nouns to tell about the bear—he calls this character *Old Bear* and then refers to him as *cub.* I was able to help children see that the author deliberately uses different names to show how the character changes throughout the story.

On the next page (with prompting), children noticed that the words *flower* and *crocus* name the same thing, too. We figured out that Kevin Henkes sometimes uses two different nouns to name the same thing on one page to make his story more interesting. Kids noticed that the only noun with capital letters is *Old*

Bear, which is used several times in the story. We also talked about how the author doesn't call Old Bear by his name on every page. Many times Kevin Henkes uses the words *he* or *him* instead of *Old Bear.* I showed them how boring it would sound if the author kept saying *Old Bear* on every page. For example, "How would it sound if Kevin had written, 'And when Old Bear walked out into the beautiful spring day, it took Old Bear a minute to realize that Old Bear wasn't dreaming'?"

In subsequent lessons on how authors use nouns, I included a simple conversation card that read, "The author uses the *noun* _____ to _____" to help students incorporate this academic vocabulary. As we studied verbs or adjectives, we used similar conversation cards for those parts of speech. We used the cards often as we examined how authors crafted stories and informational texts. This work takes kids beyond just identifying parts of speech into understanding why and how these parts of speech are useful to writers and readers.

Over time, these conversation cards and the books we'd been reading were placed in a grammar station, and I was delighted to hear partners talking about parts of speech and how authors use them in their writing. We also added conversation cards to the writing station as children examined their own writing and talked about how a *strong verb* would show more action or a different *noun* would make their writing sound more interesting.

These conversation cards for parts of speech were used during whole-group discussions. They were then used by kids at a grammar station as well as the writing station (*below*) to discuss how authors used specific words in their writing.

Sifting Through the Standard: Using Correct Grammar and Parts of Speech

What It Is	Grammar is a set of rules that explains how words are used in a language.
	• Grammar includes labels for different kinds of words, or parts of speech (for example, nouns, verbs, adjectives, pronouns, determiners/articles, adverbs, prepositions, and conjunctions), why we use different parts of speech, and how they all work together.
	• Grammar also refers to different kinds of sentences, such as simple, compound, declarative, interrogative, imperative, and exclamatory.
Why It's Important	• Learning all the grammar rules and labels for parts of speech and kinds of sentences should not be our goal with primary students.
	• It's important to know what a noun, verb, or adjective is so that you can use that vocabulary when talking about student writing and how to improve it. For example, "Using stronger verbs will help the reader visualize the action in your story." Or "Let's look at describing words. Adjectives help readers paint a picture."
	• I recommend that you not talk about parts of speech as you are reading a book, unless you're using that book to show how an author uses different kinds of words.
	• Teach about grammar when kids are speaking and writing.

	Sifting Through the Standard: Using Correct Grammar and Parts of Speech (continued)
Student Prerequisites	It's important to begin teaching grammar in the context of oral language. If kids can't speak with Standard English grammar, they will have difficulty writing with standard grammar. (If a child says, "That boy like to mess with other kids," he or she will write it the same way.)
Academic Vocabulary	Kindergarten: • *nouns* • *words to describe/name people, places, and things* • *verbs* • *words to describe/name actions* • *descriptive words/words to describe* • *complete sentences* • *question words* First grade: • *different kinds of nouns* (common, proper, singular, plural) • *past, present, and future verbs* • *adjectives* • *pronouns* • *prepositions* Second grade: • *adverbs* • *declarative and interrogative sentences* Third grade: • *grammar* • *subject* • *verb* • *conjunctions* • *simple sentence* • *compound sentence* • *complex sentence*
Real-World Connections	• Most children don't truly understand grammar to any depth and complexity until about middle school. That's when I could remember the rules of grammar and learn about things like direct objects, dependent and independent clauses, and the like. • Primary children should learn to speak using standard subject-verb agreement, not just learn to identify it. • The emphasis should be on helping children use labels for different kinds of words (parts of speech) when talking about writing.

Example Test Questions	• "Read this dictionary entry. In the sentence above, the word _____ is
	    a. a noun
	    b. a verb
	    c. an adjective
	    d. an adverb"
	• "What is the correct way to write sentences 6 and 7?"
	• "How should sentence 12 be changed?"
	• "What change, if any, needs to be made to sentence 15?"
	• "Use correct grammar when writing." (This is often part of the directions for writing compositions on state tests.)

Team Planning Tool: Using Correct Grammar and Parts of Speech—First Grade

Note: The following lesson focuses on verbs, but it could be varied to focus on nouns or adjectives or a different part of speech. Teach similar lessons to help kids look at how authors use particular parts of speech. Start with just one part of speech at a time.

Standard We're Teaching	**First grade:** Students are expected to understand and use the following parts of speech in the context of reading, writing, and speaking: verbs (past, present, and future).
Academic Vocabulary We'll Use and Expect to Hear	• *verbs* • *words that express actions* • *illustrations* • *author*
Whole-Group Ideas	• Read aloud and return to mentor texts (fiction and nonfiction) with well-chosen verbs to build vocabulary as well as guide students to look at how authors use verbs in books. • Provide highlighter tape for kids to mark some of the verbs and talk about why the author chose those words.
Partner Practice at Literacy Work Stations	**Author study (or topic) station:** Partners read and examine familiar books written by an author whose work you've been studying, such as Kevin Henkes, or about a topic of study (like animals and how they live). Provide highlighter tape and conversation cards, so they can look at the books and find different kinds of words (for example, verbs) and talk about why the author chose those words. Include a community journal or a display board where students can record and share what they learned. They might use an iPad to record their conversation. **Writing station:** Students work together on their own writing to look for verbs and how they've used them. They look at one piece of writing together and talk about how to use verbs to express action. They also add action to their illustrations, using mentor texts as models.

Lessons That Last: Whole-Group Mini-Lesson Plan for Using Correct Grammar and Parts of Speech—First Grade

Looking for Verbs

Focus: how authors use different kinds of words (specifically, verbs to make their writing interesting)

Method to Maximize Student Engagement: engaging text with a variety of verbs and high-quality illustrations; highlighter tape (for marking verbs); anchor chart

Model: how to think about author's word choice; how to look at words and pictures and how the verbs and illustrations match; thinking about how the author's choice of verbs expresses action

Prompting for Independence:

• "Let's look for some words that express action on this page. What do you picture happening? Why do you think the author used that verb?"

• "What do you notice about how the author used verbs on this page?"

• "What actions are shown in the illustration and the words on this page?"

• "Do any of the verbs on this page relate to the same thing? The author did that to make the writing interesting."

**Lessons That Last: Whole-Group Mini-Lesson Plan for
Using Correct Grammar and Parts of Speech—First Grade** (continued)

Mini-Lesson Procedure:

1. Choose a high-quality read-aloud with illustrations that match the pictures well, such as *Feeding Time* (a DK Level 1 Reader) by Lee Davis (2001). Be sure to have read it aloud previously when looking at word choice or grammar, as in this lesson. (When teaching about grammar, I find it helpful to pick books with complete sentences written in Standard English to start. I also look for books that have sentences that begin and end on one page. I chose to use an informational text in this lesson, but plan to teach similar lessons with fiction.)

2. Make an anchor chart about verbs with the students. Keep it simple. (See samples in this section.) Don't put too many words on it. Display it nearby, so you can refer to it during the mini-lesson.

3. Look at the cover with the class and read the title together. Briefly show a few pages from the book. Ask kids about the actions that might take place in this book. What will the *topic* be? (African animals eating.) What are some of the verbs they might find? Tell them we'll pay attention to the verbs the author uses to tell how these animals eat.

4. Read the book together, one page at a time, having students think about the words the author uses to express action. Ask kids to take turns marking the verbs with highlighter tape.

5. Then have them turn and talk about what they notice about the verbs. "How do the verbs express action? What do the verbs help us learn about these animals?" (For example, elephants *wrap* and *curl* their trunks around their food. They *snap* branches from a tree and *chew* the bark.) "How did the verbs make the writing more interesting?"

6. Repeat this work with several pages. Have kids find interesting verbs; don't worry about them identifying every verb. Instead, focus on how the author *uses verbs* to paint a picture.

7. During writing workshop, have students look at a piece of writing with a partner to look at how they've used verbs to express action. Have them highlight some of their verbs. Ask them to help each other use verbs to add interest to their writing. Be sure to have some students share how they changed their writing to improve it.

On-the-Spot Assessment: Were the children able to find verbs that expressed action? What kind of thinking were they able to do about how the author used verbs in the text? Are they learning to think more deeply about author's word choice and the text's meaning? Does their oral language reflect standard usage of verbs as they talk about the book?

Connections to Whole-Group Mini-Lesson

Independent Reading Connection: During independent reading time, ask students if they noticed anything about how the authors of their books used verbs today. Have them share with a partner or the class.

Small-Group Connection: As you talk with students about what they read in small group, you might talk with them about how an author uses verbs in a piece of writing. Don't dwell on parts of speech, but occasionally use a discussion of these kinds of words to help deepen the meaning of a story.

Writing Connection: This is the most important connection to whole group when it comes to grammar. Be sure to give students opportunities to peer conference and look at how they're using verbs in their own writing. They can highlight verbs, evaluate their use of verbs, and strive to add a few more interesting verbs on a page of writing.

Evaluation: Are students using correct forms of verbs in their speaking and writing? Are they able to vary the verbs they use as they speak and write? Are they starting to understand how authors use verbs in their writing?

Mentor Texts for Modeling:
Using Correct Grammar and Parts of Speech

- *Old Bear* by Kevin Henkes
- *Feeding Time* by Lee Davis
- *Nouns and Verbs Have a Field Day* by Robin Pulver
- If You Were a Noun . . . series by Michael Dahl

- A Mink a Fink a Skating Rink . . . series by Brian Cleary
- *Things That Are Most in the World* by Judi Barrett
- Merry-Go-Round: A Book About Nouns series by Ruth Heller
- *A Is for Angry: An Animal Adjective Alphabet* by Sandra Boynton

Teaching Tips for Using Correct Grammar and Parts of Speech Across the Grades	
In Pre-K and Kindergarten	• Lay the foundation for grammar by paying attention to kids' oral language. Insist that they speak in sentences. Scaffold their language to help them use correct subject-verb agreement. If children use non–Standard English, have them repeat the "school way" of talking after you. • The emphasis should be on *using* parts of speech, not simply identifying nouns and verbs. • Note that in kindergarten children should learn how to *orally* form regular plural nouns by adding /s/ or /es/. (This is not a spelling skill at these grade levels.) Have students also pay attention to the *s* sound at the end of words when they are reading to "make it sound right."
In Grades One–Two	• The most important thing is not that young children can identify personal, possessive, and indefinite pronouns. (Yikes!) It's critical that they begin *using* pronouns correctly in both their speech and their writing. For example, if a child says, "Him go to the store," restate it as "He goes to the store. That's how we say it in English [or at school]." If children can't say it, they won't write it correctly. This will take lots of practice for some students, especially English language learners. The practice is best done orally, not on worksheets. • At these grade levels, help children *expand* sentences to include more complex structures orally. If a child says, "The girl is happy," ask "Why is she happy?" Then help the student repeat the whole thing: "The girl is happy because she is going to a birthday party after school." When children learn to talk this way, it will be reflected in their writing (with prompting).
In Grades Three and Up	• This is the age range at which children can think more abstractly and probably better grasp the idea of what nouns, verbs, and adjectives actually are. (Remember that these labels for words are rather abstract.) If the foundation has been laid well in pre-K through grade two, children will be familiar with the idea that there are different kinds of words that can be labeled. We use those labels (*pronoun, conjunction, preposition*) to help us talk about our writing. • It's still important to help kids develop correct English usage in their speaking first. If you see issues with usage in children's writing, listen to how they talk. Scaffold their oral language, much as we did in pre-K and kindergarten. • Again, the expectation isn't that students can diagram sentences and name every part of speech. Rather, they are gaining understanding that different kinds of words are used in language for different purposes and that they can use those terms (especially *nouns, verbs, adjectives, pronouns* in third grade) when talking about writing.

Sample Anchor Charts for Using Correct Grammar and Parts of Speech

This anchor chart for verbs was developed over several lessons. Kids thought of actions and dramatized them; then the teacher added their photos and corresponding verbs to the chart, a few at a time.

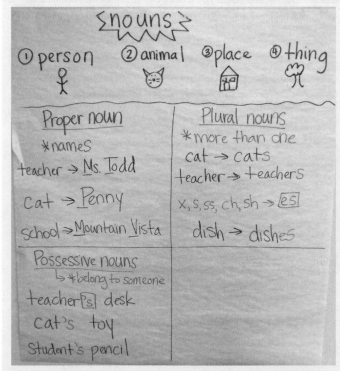

Another class made this anchor chart for nouns. Kids added sticky notes of nouns found in books read aloud or at stations.

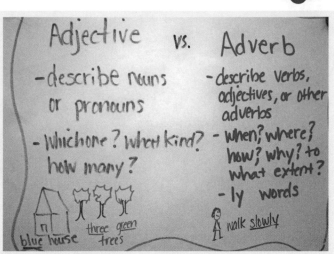

Adjectives and adverbs are the subject of this anchor chart made over time with intermediate students.

Literacy Work Stations for Using Correct Grammar and Parts of Speech

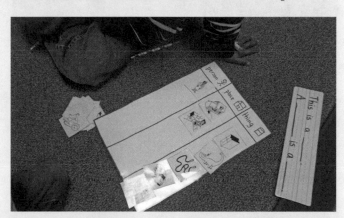

Kindergartners sort pictures of people, places, and things. Then they use a conversation card to name the picture. They can tell sentences using the picture and record it using technology. They can also write about the pictures, using nouns.

Pairs of students highlight nouns in one color and verbs in another at this poetry station. Vary the work by having kids identify and discuss how the poet used *singular nouns, possessive nouns,* or *pronouns.* Conversation cards can support their talk.

Kids choose several adjective cards and make a circle map by writing a noun in the middle that goes with them. They can also make circle maps with nouns and adjectives from books they're reading. The same work can be done by intermediate readers with verbs and adverbs.

Students draw pictures of themselves or others and write adjectives to describe that person. These are displayed with the heading "Who Am I?" Kids could also write riddles about people, places, things, or events (nouns) on paper folded in half like a card. They write the clues (verbs, adjectives) on the front of the card and draw a picture with a noun label on the inside. Others can read the riddles.

Here's one of the riddle cards made by second graders.

Students highlight interesting verbs in news articles. (Laminate articles so they can be reused.) Then they talk about the author's choice of verbs. Add conversation cards here. Also have kids write their own news items and consider verb choice.

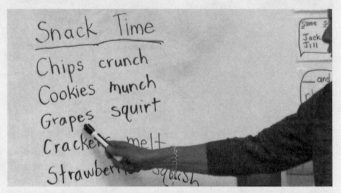

In whole group, we did shared writing of a very simple poem using a noun-verb pattern. I didn't call these words *nouns* and *verbs*. We just named familiar snacks and then told the action that would take place when each was chewed. For example, *chips crunch* and *grapes squirt* (in your mouth).

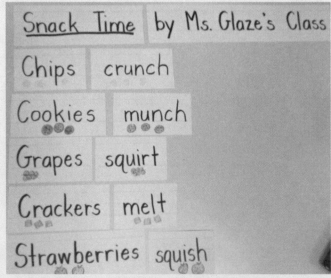

I copied our poem onto sentence strips, added illustrations, and had kids put the poem back together at the poetry station. They also wrote their own poems at the writing station. Similar poems could be written with adjective-noun-verb patterns.

Expanding Vocabulary

Vocabulary begins with—you guessed it—oral language once again! Children use words in their speech that they have heard modeled by adults at home, in school, or in the media. Students who speak with more advanced language are most likely to use more sophisticated vocabulary in their writing, too.

Using advanced vocabulary as we talk with our students is an important way to expose kids to these bigger, more complex words. Reading aloud carefully selected text with rich vocabulary, helping students pay attention to the new words, and then scaffolding them to use those same words is one of the best approaches to helping kids develop vocabulary at school and at home. Couching new words in meaningful context is the way to help children remember vocabulary.

Bringing Words to Life (Beck, McKeown, and Kucan 2002) details how to choose vocabulary words from rich texts and introduce the words in kid-friendly ways so that students will own them and use them correctly. A key to helping students deeply understand and use rich vocabulary in their speaking, reading, and writing is to provide multiple exposures to those new words, often in rapid-fire ways. When kids can see the words, hear the words, say the words, act out the words, and use the words orally in multiple contexts, they will know those words at deep levels and enrich their vocabularies.

For example, before reading aloud *Scaredy Squirrel Makes a Friend* by Melanie Watt (2011) in whole group, I displayed the words *encountering, risk, impression, potential,* and *realizes* and told students to pay attention to those new words in the text. We decided to touch our ears if we heard one of those words in the story. When children heard two new words in the sentence "He'd rather be alone than *risk encountering* someone dangerous," we took a minute to talk about what it meant. Students were able to substitute the synonym *try* for *risk* and *meeting* for *encountering,* which helped them begin to understand what these words meant. Instead of moving on, I had students work briefly with these words in the context of the story right then and there. "Pretend you're Scaredy Squirrel. How does he feel about *encountering* a new person? Show how he might act if he did *encounter* someone new. Have you even *encountered* someone new or a new situation?

Tell how you felt when you *encountered* someone new. Did you take a *risk*? Use the words *encountered* or *risk* in your sentence."

Then I continued to read the book aloud. After reading (don't feel you have to complete the book in one sitting), we reviewed the new words, and I challenged children to summarize the story using the new vocabulary. Over the next few days, these vocabulary words were moved to independent practice. Students were encouraged to use them in their retellings and writing about *Scaredy Squirrel* during literacy work stations. It was exciting to hear kids using these words throughout the day, too. "Mrs. Diller, we took a *risk* when we were reading today. We chose a book that was a little harder. We *encountered* some new words and figured them out." Likewise, I made sure to integrate these new words in other contexts, too. During social studies, we talked about how explorers took *risks* as they were traveling to new lands long ago. They *encountered* difficulties and challenges along the way.

Dale and O'Rourke (1986) described four levels of knowing words:

1. I never saw the word before.
2. I've heard of it, but I don't know what it means.
3. I recognize it in context, and I can tell you what it's related to.
4. I know the word well.

I'd take it one step further: along with knowing words well, it's important for students to *use* the words. My goal is for children to move to the deepest level of understanding vocabulary and use words well. For instance, Marzano (2009) recommends the following steps for children to learn vocabulary:

1. Teacher provides a description, explanation, or example of the new word.
2. Kids restate this description or explanation in their own words. Or they give an example of their own.
3. Students make a picture or visual representation of the new term.
4. Engage students periodically in activities that help them deepen their understanding of the word.
5. Periodically have kids discuss these words with each other.
6. Have kids play games with the new vocabulary words periodically for review. (83)

Building on the work of vocabulary research by those mentioned earlier, I've included ideas in this section to help you think about instruction and connected literacy work stations that help students learn words deeply and use them in a variety of meaningful contexts. Read on to learn how to help your children move beyond just looking up dictionary definitions or memorizing meanings and matching them to words.

Sifting Through the Standard: Expanding Vocabulary	
What It Is	Vocabulary refers to the words (and phrases) we know and use to communicate with others. It includes the words we understand and have meanings for (Diller 2007). There are four kinds of vocabulary: 1. speaking (words we use in conversation) 2. listening (words we understand through hearing) 3. reading (words we decode and comprehend) 4. writing (words we can write to convey messages)
Why It's Important	• English language learners (ELLs) who experience slow vocabulary development are less able to comprehend text at grade level than their English-only peers (August et al. 2005). • There is a strong relationship between vocabulary development and reading comprehension in monolingual students, too (Lonigan and Shanahan 2009). • In today's schools, students need *academic vocabulary* to be successful on tests. But more importantly, vocabulary development is especially important for understanding content-area materials and higher-level text.
Student Prerequisites	• Children need to interact with each new word multiple times with periodic practice to retain those words. There is not a "magic number" of exposures to a word, so think "multiple times." • Background knowledge helps kids learn new words. Seeing photos, examining real objects, and having kids act out new words can build their schema for new vocabulary.
Academic Vocabulary	Kindergarten: • *meanings* • *word* • *unknown word* • *clues* • *picture dictionary* First grade: • *vocabulary* • *phrase* • *sentence* • *root word* • *category* • *compound word* • *alphabetize* Second grade: • *prefix* • *suffix* • *glossary* • *multiple-meaning words* • *synonym/similar* • *antonym/opposite*

Sifting Through the Standard: Expanding Vocabulary *(continued)*

Academic Vocabulary	Third grade: • *affixes* • *homographs* • *homonyms* • *thesaurus* • *figurative language*
Real-World Connections	• Learning new words improves comprehension, not just of what's being read but of everyday life. • People with more developed vocabularies are often viewed as being more intelligent and more capable than those with limited vocabularies. • Every career field has its own special set of vocabulary to learn, so having a system by which to take on new words and their meanings is important throughout life.
Example Test Questions	• "Which words from paragraph 4 help you understand the meaning of _____?" • "In paragraph 2, _____ means _____." • "Read this dictionary entry. Which meaning most clearly matches the word _____ as it is used in paragraph 11?" • "Which word is a synonym for _____ in paragraph 8?" • "What is the meaning of the word _____ as used by the narrator in paragraph 2?" • "Which detail from the text uses a word or phrase that also means _____?" • "Which phrase helps the reader understand the meaning of _____?" Note: Besides the fact that there are many questions specific to determining the meanings of words in context on a test, students need a solid grasp of *academic vocabulary* to understand what the test is asking.

Team Planning Tool: Expanding Vocabulary—Second Grade

Standards We're Teaching	**Second grade:** Use sentence-level context as a clue to the meaning of a word or phrase; identify the real-life connections between words and their use (for example, describe foods that are *spicy* or *juicy*); distinguish between shades of meaning among closely related verbs (for example, *toss, throw, hurl*) and closely related adjectives (such as *thin, slender, skinny, scrawny*).
Academic Vocabulary We'll Use and Expect to Hear	• *unknown* word (or phrase) • *clues*
Whole-Group Ideas	• Read aloud a story with Tier II vocabulary (words used by people with mature speech), such as *Tacky the Penguin* by Helen Lester (1998). • Choose five to seven Tier II words and copy each one onto a plain index card. Later have kids illustrate and use them to retell the story. (I used *companions, clasped, in the distance, puzzled, chanting, graceful, hearty*.) • Act out words with kids and connect them to real life (for example, *bracelet clasp; puzzled looks; graceful dancers*).
Partner Practice at Literacy Work Stations	**Retelling station:** Students work with a partner to retell a familiar story, using retelling pieces and vocabulary cards. They might also use a graphic organizer for beginning, middle, and end. **Listening station:** Listen to a familiar recorded story and locate vocabulary words on cards. Act out those words when they are heard. After listening, use those words to discuss the story.

Lessons That Last: Whole-Group Mini-Lesson Plan for Expanding Vocabulary—Second Grade

Note: Also use informational text for the following type of lesson.

Vocabulary Card Retelling

Focus: to learn new vocabulary in the context of an engaging story; to also use vocabulary in retelling the story

Method to Maximize Student Engagement: read-aloud of an interesting story that contains rich vocabulary; students use body movement when they hear selected words read aloud; children act out new words in the context of the story; students create retelling pieces and use them to retell the story collectively

Model: how to think about new words and figure out their meanings from the context of the sentences in the story; how to connect new words to real life; how to determine shades of meaning (compare chanting to talking or singing or humming)

Prompting for Independence:

- "Who is your *companion*? Could a dog be a *companion*? Why? Could an apple be a *companion*? Why not?"

- "Listen to the sentence: _____. What do you think the word _____ means in this sentence? What's another word, a synonym, we could try in its place?"

- "Think of a time you were *puzzled*. What made you feel *puzzled*? Show me a *puzzled* look. What does *puzzled* mean? Let's try that word in the sentence instead of *puzzled*."

Mini-Lesson Procedure:

1. Choose a book to read aloud that has rich vocabulary. Then pick five to seven words that you want your students to learn and use. Choose words that can be used in a variety of contexts or those with multiple meanings, if possible. The words should also be related to the big idea of the text.

2. Write each word on a 4-by-6-inch plain white index card in large black letters.

3. Gather students near you on the carpet. Show them the book you'll read aloud, such as *Tacky the Penguin.* Tell them that you picked this book because it's a great story and the author has used some amazing words you'd like them to learn, too.

4. Show the class the word cards, one at a time, and ask children to read the words with you. Help students look at parts of a word, if needed, to decode it. For example, if students have trouble decoding *companions,* cover up the rest of the word, showing just one syllable at a time, and then read the parts in order—*com/pan/ions.* Tell them to pay attention for that word in the book to figure out what it means.

5. Take a minute to give them some background knowledge on a few of the words. First, ask children if they know anything about this word and what it means. Then use the word multiple times. For example, *"This word is* clasped. *Say* clasped *with me. My bracelet has a clasp. A clasp is the part that holds my bracelet together. A clasp lets me take my jewelry off and on. Do any of you have a clasp on a bracelet or necklace? You can clasp your hands, like this. Everyone clasp your hands. What are you doing? Yes, we're clasping our hands, or joining them together tightly."* In less than a minute, you'll find you can use the new word about ten times!

6. After you've briefly introduced each word, attach its word card to the board with magnets or tape, so the class can see it. Then come up with a signal, such as a thumbs-up, that you can all use if they hear one of the words read aloud.

7. Begin to read the book aloud, asking students to listen for the new words and think about what they mean. When you come to a new vocabulary word, pause and see whether students noticed it was one of the words. Then have them help figure out the word's meaning from the context of the sentence and story. Talk about what would make sense. Is there another word, a synonym, that could be used in place of this word? For example, read, "There once lived a penguin. His home was a nice icy land he shared with his *companions.*" Stop and ask what *companions* might mean. Help students substitute the word *friends* in this sentence to figure out the word's meaning. Have children act out a word (for example, *clasped, in the distance, puzzled*) if this will help them understand its meaning.

**Lessons That Last: Whole-Group Mini-Lesson Plan
for Expanding Vocabulary—Second Grade** (continued)

8. After reading the book, ask children to take turns using one of the words to tell something about the story. For example, a student might say, "Graceful." Ask her to tell you about a place in the story where a character is graceful. She might reply, "The penguins were graceful at diving." Then have everyone show what it means to be a graceful diver. Ask, "Was Tacky a graceful diver?" A student might reply, "No. He did cannonballs." Use the word several times to help the meaning sink in more deeply.

9. At another time, have students help prepare materials for retelling. Assign a job to pairs or groups of three: have some use pencil and crayons to illustrate the meaning of each word on the word cards; have others create stick puppets of the characters for retelling; still others can create a backdrop showing the story's setting.

10. On another day, reread the book, starting with a quick review of the words. Post the now-illustrated word cards on the board, so students continue to pay attention to them. Tell children to listen carefully, because today they will use the new words to retell the story. As you read, invite students to dramatize or give a synonym for each of the new words.

11. After reading, invite students to take turns using the retelling pieces to retell a bit of the story. Have them take turns adding on to the story. Challenge them to use the new vocabulary words as they retell. Then tell them you'll put these materials in the drama station for them to continue using.

On-the-Spot Assessment: Do the students use the new words appropriately? Are they able to determine shades of meaning between similar words? Do their dramatizations accurately depict a word's meaning? Are they also using the new vocabulary in their speaking and/or writing?

Vocabulary words are written on cards, displayed on the board with magnets, and used during a read-aloud of *Tacky the Penguin*. We'd pause when we heard one of the words and think aloud and act out its meaning.

Kids illustrated vocabulary cards to make characters and setting pieces for retelling. Then students took turns retelling bits of *Tacky the Penguin* in front of the class, using the cards and retelling pieces. Later, these materials were placed at a retelling station.

Mentor Texts for Modeling:
Expanding Vocabulary

- *Scaredy Squirrel* by Melanie Watt
- *Tacky the Penguin* by Helen Lester
- *All the World* by Liz Garton Scanlon

- Fancy Nancy series by Jane O'Connor
- *The Junkyard Wonders* by Patricia Polacco
- *Miss Alaineus* by Debra Frasier
- *Glamourpuss* by Sarah Weeks
- *Chrysanthemum* by Kevin Henkes
- *A Sick Day for Amos McGee* by Philip Stead

Connections to Whole-Group Mini-Lesson

Independent Reading Connection: Encourage students to pay attention to new words as they read independently. Then invite them to tell something about their books using at least one of the new words they found. Many times, they'll start noticing the same words from read-aloud that are in their just-right books.

Small-Group Connection: Bring attention to several new words (no more than seven) you want children to pay attention to *before* they read by writing the words on cards. Choose words that are essential to the comprehension of the text. After reading, have students use these words to tell about what they read. You might have each student illustrate a word card to help deepen the meaning. These words could be placed with a copy of the guided-reading book to be used for retelling at a differentiated buddy-reading station for this group.

Writing Connection: Help students be thoughtful about their word choices as they write. Challenge them to use higher-level vocabulary like the authors of read-aloud books. Talk about how Helen Lester uses the word *companions* instead of *friends* and *chanted* rather than *said*. Discuss the shades of meaning.

Evaluation: Listen to students' retellings. Are they using the new vocabulary with greater ease and deeper understanding? Are children also using these new words beyond retelling—during class discussions or in their writing? It is only when we see evidence of students using new vocabulary that we know they truly own these words.

Teaching Tips for Expanding Vocabulary Across the Grades	
In Pre-K and Kindergarten	• Expose young children to higher-level vocabulary through read-aloud and other meaningful contexts in the classroom. Then scaffold them to use these words while speaking and retelling stories. • Encourage young children to ask about new words to expand their understanding of vocabulary. Then help them *use* these words, too. • Use picture sorts to help students develop vocabulary. Have children sort photos by meaning, not just by beginning sounds. For example, sort pictures of ways people move and then use words to describe those movements—*running, jumping, skipping, hopping, throwing,* and so on.
In Grades One–Two	• Teach children about shades of meaning of words by having them explore synonyms or related words in the context of reading and speaking about texts. For example, while reading the nonfiction book *Gravity* by Suzanne Lyons (2010), explore the following words related to motion: *force, push, bend, sway, presses, pull, tugs, orbits, travels.* Have kids act them out, illustrate them, and use them while speaking about what they are learning. • Engage students in word sorts where they categorize words by *meaning* and not just spelling patterns. They can search for words while reading familiar text that can be added to categories to expand their vocabulary.
In Grades Three and Up	• Regardless of which standards your state has adopted, there should be a huge emphasis on helping students identify real-life connections between words and their use. For example, when learning about weather *conditions* in science, relate them to local weather *hazards* and *impacts.* (For example, "The recent blizzard *conditions impacted* our community by shutting down public transportation like buses and trains. There were *hazards,* such as icy roads and power outages, that affected many of us.") • Don't just do isolated work with prefixes and suffixes. Put the emphasis on learning what these affixes mean by creating simple anchor charts. Then have students find examples of words with these affixes in their reading and use them in their writing of "authentic" texts.

Sample Anchor Charts for Expanding Vocabulary

To accompany a read-aloud to develop high-level (or Tier II) vocabulary, the teacher creates an anchor chart with the class of five to seven new words from a book. Picture support helps kids remember the meanings of the new words. The teacher then encourages students to use the words in their speaking, reading, and writing. This example is from a kindergarten class, using the book *Max Takes the Train* by Rosemary Wells. Repeat this activity with a new book every week and display the charts to remind students to use some of these words in their retellings of these books.

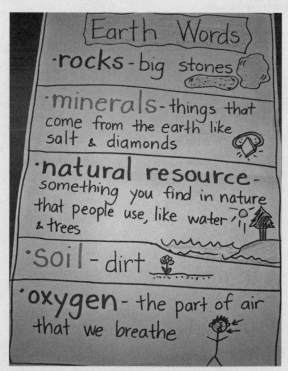

Anchor charts might also be made for content-area vocabulary. Instead of placing these words in alphabetical order on the word wall, create a chart with essential vocabulary that corresponds with a science or social studies topic. Kids can help illustrate the words. Display on a content area wall.

Literacy Work Stations for Expanding Vocabulary

Three students work together to retell *Tacky the Penguin* with student-made characters and settings at this retelling station. They use the vocabulary cards as they retell the story with the book as support.

The retelling materials are stored in an inexpensive basket and are used as a portable station. Students can make retelling pieces and illustrate vocabulary cards for stories and informational texts across the year.

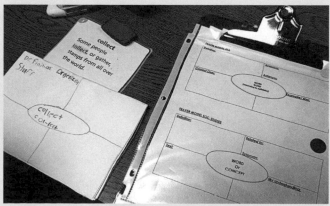

Third graders use the Frayer model to define new words from their core reading program (word cards come with the curriculum). There are two forms of the Frayer model for kids to choose from, depending on their reading group. Colored dots help kids pick the correct level to work on.

Chicken Words

egg

chicken
hen

chicks

hatch

incubator

Students match words with definitions. Then they ask each other questions about the text (from a core reading program); the questions use the week's vocabulary from the selection they've been reading. For example, "Where might you find *fossils* in your state?" or "What is your favorite *location* to play and why?" The questions (from the teachers' edition) were typed on green paper and placed in a clear plastic sleeve. This is an oral language activity.

During whole group, the teacher makes word lists related to content-area topics of study with students. Children are encouraged to use these words when they speak in class. The word lists are then placed at the writing station for reference. The list above is from a kindergarten class that was watching chicks hatch from eggs. The list below is from a third-grade class studying earthquakes.

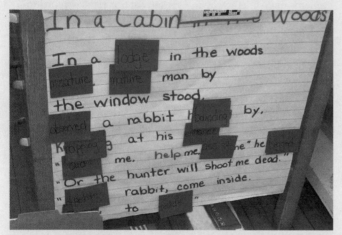

Partners read familiar poems and songs and substitute higher-level vocabulary on sticky notes on some of the words. Here they sing their own rendition of "Little Cabin in the Woods," using words such as *lodge*, *bounding*, and *miniature*. Kids brainstormed these new words in whole group.

In whole group, first graders read a Big Book about jobs. We made sticky-note labels of the names of the careers in the book. We also added a conversation card that said, "I infer that . . ." Kids later work at the Big Book station using these materials, talking together using the new vocabulary, and saying things like, "I infer that the chef is making a pizza, because he's throwing a big piece of dough into the air."

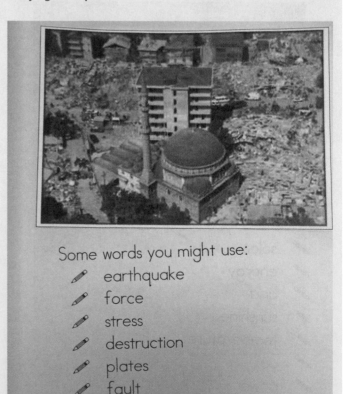

Some words you might use:

✎ earthquake
✎ force
✎ stress
✎ destruction
✎ plates
✎ fault
✎ seismic

Digging Deeper

I hope this chapter has you thinking about the foundation that oral language plays in all the reading and writing your students do. I've included the questions that follow to help you delve more deeply into considering how to integrate listening, speaking, and language throughout the school day. Remember that whenever we can help students make connections between what they are learning and how they can use this in their everyday lives, they will own the learning and show progress.

1. Do your students speak in complete sentences? How adamant are you that they do so? Discuss the importance of oral language and what you can do to increase opportunities for your students to speak in sentences and use higher-level vocabulary as they engage in conversations with adults and one another all day long.

2. How much speaking do your students do throughout the day? (Not just your "talkative kids" . . . but *all* your students.) Are *all* students talking with one another about what they're reading, writing, and learning? If you haven't yet tried it, work on establishing partner practice for students to have this opportunity at literacy work stations. Set up a "Let's talk" station and share results with colleagues.

3. Think about ways to expand opportunities for the listening station beyond basic listening to a story. Discuss ideas with your grade-level team. Use your state standards to plan for instruction and connected practice using ideas from this chapter.

4. What do you notice about your kids and how well they follow spoken directions? What ideas from this chapter will you try for strengthening this skill?

5. How are you currently teaching grammar to your class? Are children *using* words representing different parts of speech or simply *identifying* nouns and verbs? Create meaningful grammar-related anchor charts that will help your students think about how authors use different kinds of words (such as nouns, verbs, and adjectives).

6. With your grade-level team, look for literature you can use to plan meaningful grammar lessons, using the examples from this chapter. Plan for related literacy stations where students can apply what they're learning as they practice with a partner.

7. What does vocabulary instruction look like in your classroom? Look at your state standards for teaching vocabulary. Which do you think your children are mastering? Which do your kids need more exposure to and experience with?

8. Examine your whole-group lesson plans for the past few weeks. What kinds of lessons have you taught that specifically teach children about vocabulary? Discuss how effective these lessons have been for expanding your students' vocabulary.

9. Work with colleagues to find high-quality picture books and poems you can use for building vocabulary. Plan and teach whole-group vocabulary lessons using ideas from this chapter. Move this work to literacy stations for children to continue working with these same words. Share what you notice about your students' vocabulary growth.

Appendix

An appendix of comparative standards charts and reproducible word lists is available online at www.stenhouse.com/gilappendix.

References

Professional Books and Articles

August, D., M. Carlo, S. Dressler, and C. Snow. 2005. "The Critical Role of Vocabulary Development for English Language Learners." *Learning Disabilities Research and Practice* 20 (1): 50–57.

August, D., L. Shanahan, and T. Shanahan. 2006. *Developing Literacy in Second Language Learners: Lessons from the Report of the National Literacy Panel on Language Minority Children and Youth.* New York: Routledge.

Bandura, A. 1997. *Social Efficacy: The Exercise of Control.* New York: W. H. Freeman.

Bandura, A., and R. Walters. 1977. *Social Learning Theory.* New York: General Learning.

Bear, D., M. Invernizzi, S. Templeton, and F. Johnston. 2011. *Words Their Way: Word Study for Phonics, Vocabulary, and Spelling Instruction.* Boston: Pearson.

Beck, I. 2010. *Making Sense of Phonics.* New York: Guilford.

Beck, I., M. McKeown, and L. Kucan. 2013. *Bringing Words to Life.* New York: Guilford.

Britton, J. 1970. *Language and Learning.* Coral Gables, FL: University of Miami Press.

Calkins, L. 2003. *Small Moments: Personal Narrative Writing.* Portsmouth, NH: Heinemann.

Carroll, J. B., P. Davies, and B. Richman. 1971. *The American Heritage Word Frequency Book.* Boston: Houghton Mifflin.

Clay, M. 1994. *Reading Recovery: A Guidebook for Teachers in Training.* Portsmouth, NH: Heinemann.

Clay, M. M. 2005. *An Observation Survey of Early Literacy Achievement.* 2nd ed. Portsmouth, NH: Heinemann.

Commission for Architecture and the Built Environment. 2002. "The Value of Good Design." Report available online at www.cabe.org.uk.

Covey, Steven. 1989. *7 Habits of Highly Effective People.* New York: Free Press.

Cunningham, P. 2012. *Phonics They Use.* Boston: Pearson.

Dale, E., and J. O'Rourke. 1986. *Vocabulary Building.* Columbus, OH: Zaner-Bloser.

Diller, D. 2007. *Making the Most of Small Groups.* Portland, ME: Stenhouse.

———. 2008. *Spaces & Places.* Portland, ME: Stenhouse.

———. 2011. *Math Work Stations.* Portland, ME: Stenhouse.

Dolch, E. W. 1936. "A Basic Sight Word Vocabulary." *The Elementary School Journal* 36 (6): 456–460.

Duke, N. 2014. *Inside Information: Developing Powerful Readers and Writers of Informational Text Through Project-Based Instruction.* New York: Scholastic.

Duke, N. K. 2000. "3.6 Minutes Per Day: The Scarcity of Informational Texts in First Grade." *Reading Research Quarterly* 35 (2): 202–224.

Duke, N., and V. S. Bennett-Armistead. 2003. *Reading and Writing Informational Text in the Primary Grades.* New York: Scholastic.

Dunst, C. J., A. Simkus, and D. W. Hamby. 2012. "Children's Story Retelling as a Literacy and Language Enhancement Strategy." *Center for Early Literacy Learning (CELL) Reviews* 5 (2): 1–14.

Farstrup, R. E., and S. J. Samuels. 2011. *What Research Has to Say About Reading Instruction.* Newark, DE: International Reading Association.

Fletcher, R. 2007. *Craft Lessons: Teaching Writing K–8.* 2nd ed. Portland, ME: Stenhouse.

Frayer, D., W. C. Frederick, and H. J. Klausmeier. 1969. *A Schema for Testing the Level of Cognitive Mastery.* Madison: Wisconsin Center for Education Research.

Freeman, M. 2013. *Teaching the Youngest Writers.* North Mankato, MN: Maupin House.

Fry, E. 1998. "The Most Common Phonograms." *The Reading Teacher* 51 (7): 620–622.

Fry, E., and J. Kress. 2006. *The Reading Teacher's Book of Lists.* San Francisco: Jossey-Bass.

Gentner, D., and A. B. Markman. 1994. "Structural Alignment in Comparison: No Difference Without Similarity." *Psychological Science* 5:152–158.

Gillanders, C., D. Castro, and X. Franco. 2014. "Learning Words for Life." *The Reading Teacher* 8 (3): 213–221.

Graves, D. 1989. *Investigate Nonfiction.* Portsmouth, NH: Heinemann.

Harvey, S., and A. Goudvis. 2007. *Strategies That Work.* Portland, ME: Stenhouse.

Hyerle, D. 2011. *Student Successes with Thinking Maps: School-Based Research, Results, and Models for Achievement Using Visual Tools.* Thousand Oaks, CA: Corwin Press.

Janusik, L. A., and A. D. Wolvin. 2006. "24 Hours in a Day: A Listening Update to the Time Studies." Paper presented at the meeting of the International Listening Association, Salem, Oregon, April.

Justice, L. M., A. Mashburn, and Y. Petscher. 2013. "Very Early Language Skills of Fifth-Grade Poor Comprehenders." *Journal of Research in Reading* 36 (2): 172–185.

Katz, L., S. Chard, and Y. Kogan. 2014. *Engaging Children's Minds: The Project Approach.* 3rd ed. Westport, CT: Praeger.

Kim, Y. S., V. Petscher, B. Foorman, and C. Zhou. 2010. "The Contributions of Phonological Awareness and Letter-Name Knowledge to Letter-Sound Acquisition—a Cross-Classified Multilevel Model Approach." *Journal of Educational Psychology* 102 (2): 313–326.

Lonigan, C. J., and T. Shanahan. 2009. Executive Summary. *Developing Early Literacy Report of the National Early Literacy Panel.* Washington, DC: National Institute for Literacy.

Lundsteen, S. W. 1979. *Listening: Its Impact on Reading and the Other Language Arts.* 2nd ed. Urbana, IL: NCTE/ERIC.

Marzano, R. 2009. "The Art and Science of Teaching/Six Steps to Better Vocabulary Instruction." *Educational Leadership* 67 (1): 83–84.

Marzano, R. J., D. Pickering, and J. E. Pollock. 2001. *Classroom Instruction That Works: Research-Based Strategies for Increasing Student Achievement.* Alexandria, VA: Association for Supervision and Curriculum Development.

McREL Foundation. 2010. "Classroom Instruction That Works." *Changing Schools* 61:9–10.

Michaels, S., M. C. O'Conner, and M. W. Hall, with L. B. Resnick. 2002. *Accountable Talk: Classroom Conversation That Works.* CD-ROM. Pittsburgh, PA: University of Pittsburgh.

Miller, D. 2008. *Teaching with Intention.* Portland, ME: Stenhouse.

———. 2012. *Reading with Meaning.* 2nd ed. Portland, ME: Stenhouse.

National Early Literacy Panel. 2009. *Developing Early Literacy: Report of the National Early Literacy Panel, Executive Summary.* Washington, DC: National Institute for Literacy.

National Institute of Child Health and Human Development. 2000. *Report of the National Reading Panel: Teaching Children to Read; An Evidence-Based Assessment of the Scientific Research Literature on Reading and Its Implications for Reading Instruction* (NIH Publication No. 00-4769). Washington, DC: U.S. Government Printing Office.

O'Flahavan, J. F., S. Grabowsky, and S. B. McCraw. 2012. "Exploring the Importance of Critiquing for Raising Self-Determining Readers and Writers Across the Grades." Pre-conference institute, 57th Annual Convention of the International Reading Association, Chicago, April.

Pink, D. 2006. *A Whole New Mind.* New York: Riverhead Books.

Rowe, M. B. 1972. "Wait-Time and Rewards as Instructional Variables, Their Influence in Language, Logic, and Fate Control." Paper presented at the Conference of the National Association for Research in Science Teaching. Chicago, April. ED 061.103.

Smith, M., and J. Wilhelm. *Reading Don't Fix No Chevys.* Portsmouth, NH: Heinemann. 2002.

Stahl, R. 1990. *Using "Think-Time" Behaviors to Promote Students' Information Processing, Learning, and On-Task Participation: An Instructional Module.* Tempe: Arizona State University.

Williams, R. 2008. *The Non-designer's Design Book.* San Francisco: Peachpit.

Wood Ray, K. 2003. *About the Authors: Writing Workshop with Our Youngest Writers.* Portsmouth, NH: Heinemann.

Yopp, R. H., and H. K. Yopp. 2012. "Young Children's Limited and Narrow Exposure to Informational Text." *The Reading Teacher* 65 (7): 480–490.

Children's Books and Poems

Bridwell, N. 2010. *Clifford, the Big Red Dog.* New York: Scholastic.

Bunting, E. 1992. *The Wall.* New York: Clarion.

———. 1991. *Night Tree.* Boston: Harcourt Children's Books.

———. 1997. *Ducky.* New York: Clarion.

Burke, M. 2009. *Monarchs Migrate South.* Science Reader from Scott Foresman Reading Street series.

Catling, P. S. 2006. *The Chocolate Touch.* New York: HarperCollins.

Chin, J. 2014. *Gravity.* New York: Roaring Brook.

DePaola, T. 2007. *Stagestruck.* New York: Puffin.

Dewdney, A. 2005. *Llama Llama Red Pajama.* New York: Viking.

Galdone, P. 1981. *The Three Billy Goats Gruff.* Boston: Houghton Mifflin.

Haydon, J. 2003. *Dangerous Professions of the Past.* Boston: Rigby.

Hughes, L. 1995. "April Rain Song." In *The Collected Poems of Langston Hughes,* ed. A. Rampersad. New York: Vintage.

I Wonder Why series. New York: Kingfisher.

Kalman, B. 2002. *The Life Cycle of a Frog*. New York: Crabtree.

Lester, H. 1988. *Tacky the Penguin*. Boston: Houghton Mifflin.

Lyons, S. 2010. *Gravity*. Pelham, NY: Benchmark Education.

Martin, J. M. 2002. *12 Fabulously Funny Fairy Tale Plays*. New York: Scholastic.

Pilkey, D. Captain Underpants series. New York: Scholastic.

Piper, W. 1954. *The Little Engine That Could*. New York: Platt & Munk.

Raczka, B. 2010. *Guyku: A Year of Haiku for Boys*. Boston: Houghton Mifflin Books for Children.

Rylant, C. 2006. *The Journey: Stories of Migration*. New York: Blue Sky.

Schachner, J. 2003. *Skippyjon Jones*. New York: Dutton.

Scieszka, J. 1996. *The True Story of the 3 Little Pigs!* New York: Puffin.

Silverstein, S. 1996. "Snowball." In *Falling Up*. New York: HarperCollins.

Vanada, L. S. 1986. "Fuzzy Wuzzy Creepy Crawly." In *Read-Aloud Rhymes for the Very Young*, ed. Jack Prelutsky. New York: Knopf.

Watt, M. 2011. *Scaredy Squirrel Makes a Friend*. Tonawanda, NY: Kids Can Press.

Index